ADAM NICOLSON is the author of many books on history and the countryside. He is the winner of the Royal Society of Literature's Ondaatje Prize, the Somerset Maugham and the W.H. Heinemann Award. One of his recent books, *Sissinghurst*, became a television series, presented by the author. He lives at Sissinghurst Castle, with his wife and daughters.

For more on GENTRY, go to www.thegentry.org.uk

From the reviews of Adam Nicolson's books:

WHEN GOD SPOKE ENGLISH:

'This fascinating story is told with brilliance by Adam Nicolson'
Glasgow Herald

'An engaging and moving account … marvellous'   *Economist*

'Pays that Bible eloquent tribute, not least in its passionate homage to the power of language as, and in, history. His own words give us not only the rich history but a moving commemoration of the Bible that has so much shaped our utterances and lives'   *Independent*

'Nicolson's portraits of Jacobean intellectuals, theologians, politicians and princes overlay the lasting achievement that underpins this book. His approach to personalities humanises the beauty and ceremony of the biblical prose that still transcends its makers'
The Times

Further reviews of Adam Nicolson's books are on pages 463–71.

By the same author

The Smell of Summer Grass
Sissinghurst
Arcadia
Men of Honour
When God Spoke English
Sea Room

ADAM NICOLSON

Gentry

Six Hundred Years of a
Peculiarly English Class

Harper
Press

A catalogue record for this book
is available from the British Library

ISBN 978-0-00-733550-3

Typeset in Minion by G&M Designs Limited,
Raunds, Northamptonshire
Printed and bound in Great Britain by
Clays Ltd, St Ives plc

MIX
Paper from
responsible sources
FSC® C007454

FSC™ is a non-profit international organisation established to promote
the responsible management of the world's forests. Products carrying the
FSC label are independently certified to assure consumers that they come
from forests that are managed to meet the social, economic and
ecological needs of present or future generations,
and other controlled sources.

Find out more about HarperCollins and the environment at
www.harpercollins.co.uk/green

For my daughters

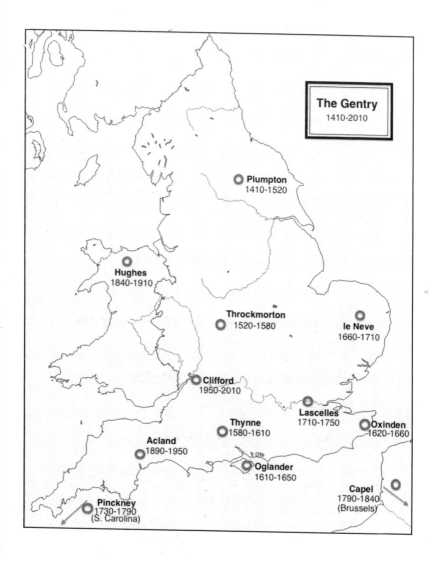

The Gentry
1410-2010

Plumpton
1410-1520

Hughes
1840-1910

Throckmorton
1520-1580

le Neve
1660-1710

Clifford
1950-2010

Lascelles
1710-1750

Thynne
1580-1610

Oxinden
1620-1660

Acland
1890-1950

Oglander
1610-1650

Capel
1790-1840
(Brussels)

Pinckney
1730-1790
(S. Carolina)

CONTENTS

INTRODUCTION

Ungentle Gentles

No country has described itself so intimately and for so long as this one. The English have been the great self-recorders and England has preserved more of what its people have written about themselves than anywhere else on earth.[1] Inevitably, millions of English men and women have lived with no record of their existence but the writings of the self-recordists – the literate, the scholarly and the litigious, lovers and haters, accountants, manipulators, the worried and the triumphant, the gossips, the distant friends, people separated by business or ambition – have often been kept by their descendants. That is why the English gentry are such an intriguing world to explore: they both wrote and kept, and because of what they kept they are the most knowable English there have ever been. They may well be the most knowable people that have ever lived. Only governments and navies have been so careful about their own past.

Over the six centuries this book covers, the gentry wrote their lives down. Most of their documents, it is true, have disappeared. Often only one side of a correspondence remains. Sometimes a sequence breaks off without explanation. Sometimes there is nothing but the recording, yet again, of the properties owned, the debts incurred, the credit given. Individual families take up tens of shelf-yards with their title deeds. But alongside that, quantities of letters and journals have also found their way to the great public repositories with which this country is blessed: not only the National Archives in Kew and the British Library in St Pancras, but the strings of County Record Offices, all of which are stuffed with heartstoppingly vivid and unregarded treasures.

The people who appear in this book wrote in private and the experience of their words on the written page remains mysteriously private. When you sit at a desk in Exeter or Newport, in Norwich or Bangor, with their words in front of you, there is no discreet mulberry-coloured rope holding you away from them. There is no glass over the pictures, no *Please Don't Touch*. The young men and women, the paterfamilias and the desperate nephew, the estate steward and the indigent younger brother, are all there with you in the room. Each letter or journal entry articulates its moment, not only in its words but in its physical form, the hurry or care with which it is written, the sense of politeness or intimacy, or rage. The unfolding of a letter from an envelope always seems to me like the opening of time itself. Nearly always they wrote on beautiful, handmade paper, in now fading brown ink, occasionally in blood, sometimes with a lock of hair folded up in a twist of the paper, once in these stories with the hair glued to the paper with a blob of sealing wax, sometimes in tears, when big blurring puddles have fallen on the ink. In one passage in this book, a grieving father wrote with his own tears, his silvery grey words now scarcely legible on the page.

In part, this book is a journey around that manuscript England, poking about in the national attic, but twinned to paper is another substance just as central to the life of the gentry and in constant dialogue with it: earth. This is a book about land, or at least about the meeting of land and paper. There is nothing mysterious or mystical about this. For most of English history, land was the principal means of production. Land was the national industry. Even as late as 1730,[2] three-quarters of the population derived their livelihood from it and half was directly engaged in farming. By 1800 that proportion had dropped to a third, by 1850 to a fifth, by 1900 a tenth, by 1970 a fortieth and by 2000 a hundredth. Our distance from the realities of land is the biggest obstacle we have in empathizing with the past. We no longer have an intuitive understanding of the centrality of the culti-vated earth to the life systems of England, land not only as a way of growing food but for the gentry a source of income, in the form of rent, or the sale of produce grown and sold; and as a supremely secure asset, safer than houses. For the seventeenth-century political theorist James Harrington, 'the Foundation of Property be in Land: but if in Money, *lightly come, lightly go*'.[3]

Land was also more than money. On the frontispiece of *The English Gentlewoman*, Richard Brathwait's 1631 etiquette book for ladies, his ideal pupil is depicted with a motto floating beside her, saying, 'Grace my guide, Glory my goale.' But in *The English Gentleman*, published the year before, his touchstones are '*Pes in terris, spes in caelis*' (Feet on the lands, hope in the heavens). Land was the foundation for this life and in some ways a foreshadowing of the life to come. It was the realm through which landowners could extend their presence into a seduc-tive display, a theatre in which they could perform, a playground on which they could take their exercise and a visible, tangible and mould-able anchor in the world of men. Much of this book describes the hyphenated reality of a family-in-a-place, a genetic enterprise based on land which over generations (if you were lucky) was owned, loved, used, made, re-made and, if need be, defended against others. Gentry priorities – for order, settlement and continuity, for visible wellbeing and a hierarchical community of which they were the local summit – could all be read in the landscape, in the field systems, manor houses, gardens, orchards, churches and villages of rural England. These settlements were not arranged on purely ergonomic or finan-cial grounds. They were self-portraits of the families that owned them. Gentry landscape was autobiography in earth.

England is covered with these deeply symbolic gentry places and they form the counterpart to the privacy of the manuscripts. Landscape was the gentry face; archives the gentry heart. Many houses do survive, often with the parish churches next to them, with the gentry tombs in their own chapels at the east end, often beautiful and highly articulate memorials to a forgotten ideology. But gentry exist-ence was less well funded and more vulnerable to change and failure than that of the great aristocrats and so their houses and the surrounding skirts of landscape do not always survive intact. I have walked the lands of all the families in this book[4] and it is a poignant pleasure to beat your way through an overgrown wood, or to walk across the stubble of a just-harvested wheatfield to find nothing but a soggy hollow, or a single ivy-bearded wall, while knowing in the most intimate detail from their papers the events that occurred there three, four or five centuries before. Whole destinies unfolded where now there are only a few crabbed trees or the lingering aftersmell of fox.

Reality is intimate and rather than attempt a heroic and Olympian survey of the whole gentry world, I have taken a sequence of twelve individual gentry families, each at a particular crisis in their lives. I have chosen them only if they were richly articulate about themselves, and if their archives have somehow survived. Although there are oceans of ordinariness here, each family is not quite ordinary; each throws a slightly different sidelight on to the gentry phenomenon. Their lives are highly individual but I have lined them up, like a series of organ pipes, to make a history of England over the last six hundred years, variations on the same tune played across six centuries.

Each family has fifty-odd years in the spotlight, usually an arc of three generations: parents, the protagonists and their children. Some of the histories overlap with others, some cover longer time-spans, but nearly all are lessons in survival: how to keep going when the world wants to do you down; how to make the best of the opportunities that are on offer; how to manipulate others; how to make government and the law work in your favour; how to resist or destroy your enemies. One or two are lessons in defeat: how to get it wrong, what happens when resolution fails, or more importantly, when a family loses its grip on the nature of reality. Together, they are, in effect, a self-portrait of England, or at least of its central and culture-forming class. The people in this book are neither the poor nor the great grandees of the country, but the responsive and continuous middle of Englishness.

I have often thought that the twelve leading gents described here could have sat down to dinner together and not felt they were in alien company. Some would have been charming or gawky, some a little graceless and domineering, one or two quite garrulous, but none would have felt that the other people around the table would not have understood them. The gentry as they first appear in their letters in the late Middle Ages are astonishingly like the gentry as they slide on into the twenty-first century. Each would have known the same places and have been able to discuss the ever-reliable standbys of hunting, shooting, fishing, farming, cattle, politics, money, God and dogs. All of these run through this book as the background music, the noise you hear in gentry life when nothing else is going on. And although I did not choose them for this reason, but gathered them as a set of emblematic figures, it turns out, needless to say, that through family connections they would all have known each other, even if a little remotely.

I have scattered them quite deliberately all over England and parts of the English-speaking world, and so this connectedness is not about a local cousinage or a county community. Every one of these families had important London – or usually Westminster – connections. And although their own local countries mattered to them, none from the very beginning was constrained by the boundaries of the places they owned. Even as they emerged in the late Middle Ages, this was a class with local roots but a national perspective. And if this all sounds like the introductory chat at an upper-middle-class dinner party – how did you get here, who do you know, how is Aletheia? – that is probably a true impression. At one level, this book is about networking.

But who were they? The gentry net spreads across space and time but what defined them as gentry? That is an unavoidable question but definition and the gentry have stalked each other a little warily for at least six hundred years. What was the frame in which these families were trying to make their way in the world? What was their role in the making of England? And what made them what they were?

Those questions interlock but at the core of the gentry story is a subtle and particular ripple in the status of the English nobility which from the fourteenth century onwards distinguished England from the rest of Europe. The idea of gentility, of a particular class of propertied and cultivated people, distinct from what the unashamed Richard Brathwait in the seventeenth century would call 'the bleere-ey'd Vulgar', was not exclusively English. It was common to most parts of western and southern Europe in the Middle Ages. France and Burgundy were the heart of it and the arbiters of its standards of behaviour. Elegance, courtliness, poetry and architecture all came from there.

Gentleness, in that sense, was French and England was part of this French culture-province, but an English difference emerged towards the end of the fourteenth century, when a powerful English crown established the ability to appoint peers by writ or summons to Parliament. The peers were part of the government of England not by right but by royal invitation or instruction. Those barons and other peers constituted the tiniest possible minority, about sixty men out of a total of about three million in the late fourteenth century. This crown-imposed distinction between the noble and non-noble had profound effects on those people whose social and economic standing came just below them. Those 'gentry' – the word is related to 'gene' and means essentially 'people of good breeding' – were not considered noble. They were gentlemen and gentlewomen, were often related to and intermarried with the nobility, but were not noble themselves. They were members of the Commons.

The House of Commons was where they gathered, openly distinct from their cousins, uncles and fathers who were in the House of Lords next door. And so the gentry occupied a richly ambivalent position, as members of the governing class but with no visible boundary between them and the people immediately below them, socially and economically. They were continuous with both the yeomen – independent, freeholding farmers – and the merchants and traders of the late medieval cities. Neither merchant nor yeoman had claim to much education, lineage, a coat of arms or a part in government, local or national, but they were not in any way distinct from the gentry in terms of the law.

This deep structure meant that the English gentry were open at both ends: sharing a French culture of courtesy, chivalry and knightliness with the nobility above them; entirely accessible to the English world of the yeomen and the growing urban middle class below them. Both the upper and lower boundaries of the gentry were, as the modern historians Felicity Heal and Clive Holmes have said, 'permeable membranes'.[5]

The openness was surprisingly radical. The English gentry did not, for example, need to own land. From the fourteenth century onwards, merchants from the City of London were given knighthoods, the ultimate signal of high gentry status. Medieval lawyers were considered gentry, as were the upper clergy. High royal officials were gentry by virtue of their office. You could marry into the gentry and become a member, become a city alderman and be considered gentry, thrive in the law, inherit money, become a university don or medical doctor: all qualified the individual to be considered a member of this class. In 1434, the military theorist Nicholas Upton calmly accepted that 'in thys days openly we se how many poor men by theyr grace, favour, labour or deserving' had become gentlemen.[6] Engaging in business or in entrepreneurial developments of docks, harbours, roads, canals and markets, opening mines and quarries, developing land, investing in overseas trade, becoming a partner in any kind of business from sheep transport to hansom cabs: none of this disqualified a man or woman from the gentry. Sir John Fastolf, the fifteenth-century Norfolk gentleman whose name Shakespeare borrowed for his fat, drunk, cowardly and mendacious knight, was in fact an ex-soldier who bought himself a pub in Southwark (the Boar's Head, which may be why Shakespeare chose him) and ran a shipping line taking Norfolk pork to European markets. As the central organ of the English body politic, the gentry from its origins was flexible, founded on the principle that its members were adapting and adjusting to changing circumstances. No revolution was required for this to happen. This flexible class lay at the foundations of English culture and its long history of liberty and independence.

Younger children of the nobility sank into the gentry and younger children of the gentry sank into the urban middle class. This threat of failure, of losing the status into which you had been born, recurs in this book as one of the central motivators of the gentry class. A gentleman whose status was not guaranteed was necessarily active, engaged with the world, adaptive and open to change. Any exaggerated respect for the past and your lineage was an inflexibility that would threaten your fortunes.[7]

This is the mirror image of the modern English idea of a gentleman as someone to whom dignity and a ramrod morality were the foundations of his life. But the long career of the English in the world is not explicable if stiffness was their governing characteristic. One member of the gentry after another in this book recognized that openness was the key and when travelling abroad they noticed the difference in social structure. The situation in France and Italy, Thomas Fuller, the church historian, wrote in the mid-seventeenth century, was 'like a die which hath no points between cinque and ace – nobility and peasantry'. In England, he went on, 'the temple of honour is bolted against none who have passed through the temple of virtue'.[8] England was a place which could congratulate itself on allowing high social standing to anyone who qualified for it through his achievements or education, and through his qualities as a person, not what his ancestry said he was.

This distinction became a cliché and by the nineteenth century antiquaries had begun to establish just how much better the English system was. Sir James Lawrence, writing his paper *On the Nobility of the British Gentry Compared with Those on the Continent* in 1824,[9] told his appreciative audience that in Germany, Hungary, Russia, Sweden and Denmark the children of all members of the nobility had titles. In France, Spain and Portugal only the eldest male heir was officially titled but all descendants were nevertheless considered noble. In England, the gentry were, as everyone knew, 'the nursery garden from which the peers are usually transplanted'[10] but they were not nobles themselves. Hence the nature of English society. Lawrence computed that in 1798 9,458 families in England were entitled to bear arms, adding the aristocracy and the gentry together, compared with Russia where there were 580,000 nobles, Austria 290,000 (men only), Spain 479,000 and France (in 1789) 365,000 noble families.

The English gentry, in this light, were the great exchange medium of the culture, where high ideals could interact with the harder and more demanding pressures of a fierce and competitive world. And this turns another easy assumption on its head. The gentry are largely associated with land and landed estates, which is where they invested most of their wealth. In fact, at the gentry's late medieval origins, it was the growing dominance of London that was the key engine in their creation. Between 1420 and 1470, it was a version of London English that became the language of cultivated people. The connectivity which London provided – a market in marriageable girls, among many other commodities – was the means of getting on. London and Westminster were the centres of power, the law and money, in whose combined gravitational fields all future wellbeing lay. Every family in this book gravitated there in the end and gentry that could not thrive in London were unlikely to thrive at all.

The American historian Ellis Wasson has analysed the source of wealth of new entrants to the English gentry, defining that elite as those families which had three members or more elected as MPs, or went on to gain a peerage.[11] The pattern he has uncovered reveals that those entering the governing class from a background of land represented about 50 per cent of the new entrants in the fifteenth and sixteenth centuries, but they were on a dropping trend, declining to less than a fifth in Georgian and Victorian England. Very few indeed at any time entered on the proceeds of office, on money picked up around the skirts of government. A steady supply of lawyers always fed the gentry, varying between about a fifth and a quarter. Business was there from the beginning, and remained on a nearly consistent upward trend, from a quarter of all new entrants in the late Middle Ages and rising to nearly 70 per cent in Victorian England. This was a confirmation of both the original and the growing openness of the English gentry. It was never a closed landowners' club. As Wasson says, 'founders of parliamentary families came from almost every conceivable type of background'.

Grocers, fishmongers, merchant tailors, privateers, shipbuilders, tanners, wine merchants, drapers, goldsmiths, coal fitters, ironmasters, army victuallers, mercers, silk merchants and gunpowder manufacturers all succeeded in entering the elite.[12]

But there are paradoxes, arguments and irresolutions here because, despite all this talk of openness, it was also a class obsessed with blood, honour and lineage. In large parts of its mind, but not consistently, the gentry was anxious about the respectability of trade. For the early eighteenth-century etiquette specialist Geoffrey Hickes, the key distinction gentry had to learn was the 'Difference between *Prudence* and *Trading*'.[13] One was all right – gentry should attend to the management of their estates – the other certainly was not. Three hundred years earlier, in July 1433, William Packington Esquire – esquire being a gentry title, the rank just below knight, significant at least until the end of the nineteenth century – who was then Controller of the English garrison at Bayeux, was having a drink in a Bayeux pub with another Englishman he knew called Thomas Souderne. After plenty of wine, and quite a lot of chat, Souderne told Packington that he 'was no sort of gentleman' but had been a haberdasher in England where he had '*porté le pennier*'. Packington murdered him on the spot, lunging across the pub table with his dagger and killing Souderne with '*un seul cop*' in the chest.[14] There were limits to what one could put up with.

So was gentrydom a question of blood or of qualities? There was an everlasting blurring of these categories and the anonymous author of *The Institucon of a Gentleman*, published in 1555, saw around him examples of both 'Ungentle Gentles' – people who had the qualifications to be gentry but did not come from a gentry background – and 'Gentle Ungentles', the bad sons of old families. How to categorize them? The ungentle gentle of 1555 was

he which is born of a low degree, [but] by his virtue, wyt, pollicie, industry, knowledge in lawes, valiancy in armes, or such like honest meanes becometh a welbeloved and high esteemed manne, preferred then to a great office … euersomuch as he becommeth a post or stay of the commune wealth and so growing rich, doth thereby auance the rest of his poore line of kindred: then are the children of suche one commonly called gentleman, of which sorts of gentlemen we have nowe in Inglande very many, wherby it should appeare that vertue florisheth among us. These gentlemen are now called upstarters, a term lately invented by such as pondered not the groundes of honest meanes of rising or coming to promocion.[15]

Acreages of the gentry story are contained within that paragraph. No one should deny a hardworking person of 'virtue and wit' the chance to rise in the esteem of the world. But plenty of people looked down on them and despised them for the poverty of their origins. Teams of novelists were still mining this theme in the twentieth century. But the sixteenth-century author was no democrat before his time. His understanding of the gentry world was fuelled by a powerful vision of it as a moral community. There were people who had risen into the gentry of whose means of ascent he did not approve:

The new sorte of menne which are runne oute of theyre order and from the sonnes of handycraftmen have obteigned the name of gentle-men, the degree of Esquiers, or title of Knightes, [who] get landes neyther by their lerning nor worthines achiued, but purchased by certeyn dark augmentacion practices, by menes whereof, they be called gentlemen … These be the right upstartes.[16]

Just as constantly, though, over the passing centuries, other warn-ings were doled out by the old to the young. Lineage was not enough: you had to earn your place in the class. The superbly obnoxious Lord Chesterfield, in his advice to his nephew, maintained that line. 'Never be proud of your rank or birth', he told Philip Stanhope, the nephew, 'but be as proud as you please of your character.'[17] Education was all, 'a smattering constitutes a coxcomb',[18] and 'A drayman is probably born with as good organs as Milton, Locke or Newton; but, by culture, they are much more above him than he is above his horse.'[19]

For Geoffrey Hickes in the early eighteenth century 'Peasantry [was] a Disease (like the Plague) easily caught by Conversation',[20] but he nevertheless thought it vulgar to talk of your family or to 'fling the Register of your Genealogy on the Table before all Company'.[21] 'Whoever rakes in the Ashes of the Dead, may fall upon the Stench instead of Perfumes.'[22]

This radical uncertainty at the core of English class consciousness was its principal virtue. As a result, this book is in part about money and struggle, and also about blood and family, but essentially about the fusion of those categories, the blood-and-money struggle for survival. The gentry depended above all on the coherence and efficiency of the family, the genetic corporation, as the most reliable form of keeping going in a rival-thick world. The varying power-relationships of father, mother, siblings, step and half siblings, stepmothers, mothers-in-law, brothers-in-law, uncles, nephews, cousins and nieces take up many of these chapters. This was where the questions of enterprise and lineage, inherited virtue and self-generated virtue all intersected. There is much more here than a simple picture of the patriarchal family, in which the father ordained and the family obeyed. Even at the medieval beginning, or at the height of Victorian patriarchalism, the children did not always do what they were told. In several of these families, the father failed and the mother sustained the business. Women are ever-present in the archives, as writers and recipients of the letters, as managers and entrepreneurs, plotters and shapers, signing themselves 'your bedfellow', 'your owne lover' and 'deare hart'. When looking at these connections between individuals, so alive in the manuscripts they left, and the subtle power-balances they represent, it is difficult to think that much has changed in 600 years. Family histories cannot be generalized but almost any one of them could be transferred without difficulty to another point in time. That is one of the purposes of this book: to make the experience of individual moments, with all their contingencies, the substance of the story.

PART I

The Inherited World
1410–1520

The high Middle Ages, from about 1100 until about 1300, had been blessed with golden summers and mild winters.[1] That beautiful warmth in the northern hemisphere had created both the great cathedrals of Europe and the contemporary surge far to the east in the population of the Mongol steppes. By the early fifteenth century, though, bleaker conditions prevailed, so that the growing season was at least three weeks shorter than it had been 150 years before. Winters were sharper and summers wretched. One winter in the 1430s a frost lay over London unbroken from the middle of November until the middle of February. The Thames froze solid and the French and Gascon wines usually delivered by ship to the Vintners' wharves in the centre of the city had to be brought in by wagon through Kent. Frost in May, when flowers on vines are at their most vulnerable, had been unheard of in England in the twelfth and thirteenth centuries. By 1400 it was common, even usual, and the vineyards disappeared from England. The Norwegians and Icelanders were finding ever more summer icebergs on their route to Vinland, while the English and other northern Europeans suffered from wetter summers, low productivity in their difficult and heavy lands, a shortage in seed corn, a deficit in calories, a dimming in the spark of life and a shrinkage in rents.

Walk over the Plumpton lands in Yorkshire and Nottinghamshire now in the early spring and the clay thickens around your boots:

3

England was never the easiest of land to work. Even though the fourteenth-century epidemics of plague had savagely reduced the number of Europeans, a century later villages, particularly those on north-facing slopes or at some altitude, were still being deserted. The continent was short of money and the general crisis of authority which spread across the whole of Europe, the bitter squabbling over lands and lordships which marked the end of Middle Ages, may have been simply the reaction of a human population to the most difficult of planetary changes: global cooling. The story of William Plumpton and his family may be a private reflection of a world in bio-climatic decline.

The governors were still for the time being the crown, the church and the great lords. Between them they owned over half the country. Gentry like the Plumptons were dependent on them, feudally attached, and owning no more than 20 per cent of the land themselves, the same as the yeomen farmers in the social stratum below.

It was a legalized and commercial world – lawyers appear at every turn – but at the same time one heavily dependent on personal prestige and power. Law, for all its complexity and expense, was chronically vulnerable to the corruptions and distortions of big men's threats. A glowing Arthurian vision of nobility and gentleness may have floated over these people but more as a longed-for world than a reflection of their own reality. Members of the medieval gentry can seem at times like little more than armed businessmen, gangsters on horseback, cannily in tune with the ways of the law but usually prepared to assert their will through their own and their gangs' physical violence.

Of all the great medieval letter collections that survive, those of the Plumptons reveal these desperate conditions, a frontier existence in which personal extinction and the possibility of an entire family being extinguished did not seem like a distant prospect. As the authority of the English crown, weakened by the personal unworldliness of Henry VI, collapsed around them, and the great magnates fought themselves to a standstill, gentry families were caught in the backwash of chaos. Different branches of the Plumptons ended up facing each other in a pair of long, growling and destructive court cases, which is why most of these documents survive, gathered in evidence by the teams of opposing lawyers. That is also why little of the sweetness and elegance of life is apparent here. Not all of England was like this – typicality cannot be read from any of these families – and there are alternative visions. Englishmen, according to the Tuscan historian Polydore Vergil, writing at the very beginning of the next century, were

> tall, with handsome open faces, grey-eyed for the most part. Their women are snow-white and handsome, and graced with the most decent apparel. And just as they are very similar to the Italians in the sound of their language, so the build of their bodies and their manners do not greatly differ from theirs. They have fine manners, they take counsel with deliberation (since they know that nothing is as inimical to counsel as haste), they are gentle and inclined by nature to every act of kindness.[2]

That is not what it seemed like in the world of the Plumptons.

Survival

The Plumptons

Plumpton, Yorkshire

In early May, under the narrow footbridge at Brafferton, a few miles north of York, the river Swale flows over the shallow bed of what was once Brafferton Ford. The water is dirty, a thick, chocolatey brown, its silty fertility drawn from the rich country of the Vale of York through which it has run. A giant fresh-leaved beech tree shades the church-yard of St Peter. Pollarded ashes and grey-green willows stand on the river banks. It doesn't take much to imagine these broad wet acres in the Middle Ages: the oxen from the plough teams grazing on the spring fallow, the boys with their goads, the open fields with the new wheat up and growing, the crows scattered across the ridge-and-furrow and beside the river the long meadows thick with the first of the summer grass, the corncrakes hidden there and the skylarks above them.

Here, just at this crossing, deep in the middle of comfortable, unre-markable England, one morning in May 1441, this first story of a gentry family and its own particular catastrophe begins.[1] Sir William Plumpton was thirty-seven years old. He was a strong man, a soldier, knighted in the French wars, energetic, violent and assertive but also canny, a manipulator and deceiver, endlessly weaving webs of connec-tion and influence, knowing how to court the great and suppress the weak, consciously looking to sustain the fortunes of his ancient and dignified name, happy to receive the hatred and contempt of those he had crossed or betrayed, confident that in the turmoil of this chaotic and desperate century he would emerge a winner.

He was approaching the peak of his powers and had come here this morning, Friday 5 May, with his tenants and followers, the twenty-four men of his own household and many others, perhaps a hundred or more, with the idea of having a fight. His men were armed with bows, swords and pole arms, the semi-agricultural instruments with which a man could slash at an enemy as he would at a hedge.[2]

Plumpton had seen chivalry and heroism in action and had heard of it from his father and grandfather. That grandfather, in defence of ancient honour, had rebelled against the usurper Henry IV and been executed, his boiled head displayed for months on York's Micklegate Bar.[3] His father, Sir Robert Plumpton, had been a knight at Agincourt, a retainer of Henry V's brother, the beautiful and cultivated 25-year-old Duke of Bedford. Robert went to France, with his squire, two valets and eight Yorkshire archers, each paid five shillings a month, horsed, clothed and fed by him on condition that they 'pay unto him halfe the gude that they win by war'.[4] Money was never far from these chivalric arrangements. But this Robert was to die in the war, at the mud-drenched siege of Meaux on 8 December 1421, at which an English army, debilitated and made squalid by dysentery, subsided in its flooded trenches outside that city on the banks of the Marne.[5]

William was eighteen when his father died. Within five years he too had gone to France, as a squire, also with the great Duke of Bedford, and William was knighted there as his father had been. But English fortunes were on the wane. The siege of Meaux had been an early portent of English failure abroad. Joan of Arc soon swept them out of the country and the Plantagenet empire was reduced to the stump of the Pas de Calais. The Hundred Years War ended in English failure, and as it ended the English turned their appetite and genius for violence on themselves. The English civil wars, known since the sixteenth century as the Wars of the Roses, were, at least in part, the behaviour of a military class with no one left to fight.

The plague had become endemic in England since its first devastating eruptions a century before, and it struck again in the West Riding of Yorkshire in 1438 and again in 1439.[6] Harvests had failed, people were starving, their immune systems weakened. By the spring of 1441, something desperate was in the air. Since 1438 William Plumpton had been steward of the big royal forest of Knaresborough, 4,500 acres, much of it the wild and moory waste stretching up into the Pennines to the west of where Harrogate now stands. This royal appointment made him lord over hundreds of tenants, who were under no obligation to pay tolls levied by other authorities – on bridges, fairs, roads, quays and markets. In 1440, William and 700 of these Knaresborough men had ridden over in a frightening posse 'arrayed in manner of war, and in ryotous wise assembled' to the market town at Otley, where the Cardinal Archbishop of York had been trying to enforce the payment of his market dues.[7]

He was no innocent in this and from the mid-1430s onwards had been aggressively attempting to widen his influence and enlarge his income.[8] He hired mercenaries from the Scottish border, battle-hardened and well-armed men from the valley of the Tyne and near Hexham on the Northumberland moors, and on Thursday 4 May, decided to send them on a raid out into the Knaresborough country, south-east of Ripon towards York. In the twin villages of Brafferton and Helperby, Plumpton's men put up a road block to meet them, 'with stoks, thorns, and otherwise, to thintent that when the said officers, tenants and servants came thither, they should be stopped their and incumbred'.[9]

The crisis came early on Friday 5 May and moved fast. Before sunrise, 'on the morne, by the spring of the day',[10] William and his gang came up the road 'with all the diligence that they could, makeing a great and horrible shoute upon the said officers, servants, and tenants.' The archbishop's men, attempting to get away, made for the ford over the Swale at Brafferton, crossed the river, where the footbridge now is, and rode up past the church into the main street of Brafferton-Helperby.

Here they met Plumpton's roadblock. Desperately the Archbishop's gang looked for ways of escape, some finding 'a long straite lane' along the back of the village; others got out 'by breaking of an hedge into a feild'.[11] But Plumpton and his men were not happy with frightening their enemies. They pursued them out of the village on to the dark wet boglands of Helperby Moor, riding after them for more than half a mile, shouting at them, as they had all morning: 'Sley the Archbishop's Carles' – an Old Norse word meaning 'men' – and 'Would God that we had the Archbishop here.'[12] The brutality was unforgiving. The Plumpton mob killed Thomas Hunter, a gentleman, and Thomas Hooper, a yeoman, even after they had given themselves up to their pursuers. They were killing prisoners in cold blood. A man called Christopher Bee, one of the Archbishop's affinity,

> was maymed, that is to say, smitten in the mouth and so through the mouth into the throat, by the which he hath lost his cheeke bone and three of his fore teeth, and his speech blemished and hurt, that it is not easy to understand what he speaks or saies, and may not use therefore the remnant of his teeth and jawes to th'use of eating, as he might before.[13]

Others were maimed and left for dead out on the moor.[14] Those not beaten, stabbed and cut by the Plumpton men were robbed and terrorized, their horses, harness, gold and silver all taken from them, gentlemen, yeomen, artisans and labourers alike. Plumpton was left in possession of the field, his war transferred from the wet fields of France to the springtime green of the Vale of York, his status enhanced and his future good.

When people think of the English gentry, this may not be the picture that comes to mind: the unforgiving assertion of violent authority in a disintegrating world; the application of the habits of war to a legalistic, economic and almost domestic dispute; the gathering of one's people, 'the affinity', as a form of self-promotion; the crude gang identity of those shouted taunts. But there can be little doubt that this triumph stood William Plumpton in good stead. Within two years his feudal superior, the young Harry Percy, Earl of Northumberland, had put him in charge of all the Percy estates and castles in Yorkshire. The crown had rewarded him with a gift of twenty mature oak trees, felled and trimmed, delivered to Plumpton Hall. He was now steward of the castle at Knaresborough and a Justice of the Peace, and was to become Sheriff or chief law officer of Yorkshire and a few years later of both Nottinghamshire and Derbyshire, each appointment for a separate year. The violence at Brafferton was a mark of Plumpton's willingness to impose his authority, even if it was at the cost of murdering gentleman and yeoman prisoners. That entrepreneurial virility, in the unravelling word of mid-fifteenth-century England, was the most valuable quality a man could have.[15]

The Plumptons were loyal followers and tenants of the Percy Earls of Northumberland. They had even imitated the Percy coat of arms (yellow lozenges on a blue background), merely differencing it, as the heralds said, with five red scallop shells. Visually and heraldically the Plumptons bound themselves to their feudal overlords. They were gentry; they had no claim on nobility, but were part of the same knightly world inhabited by the truly great.

But as gentry they were heavily involved in the dirty details of local government. They had held and ruled the manor at Plumpton since the twelfth century, and others higher in the Pennines, including the beautiful limestone woods and meadows at Grassington in Upper Wharfedale, and the Airedale manors of Steeton and Idle. William's father had married an heiress who brought still more and richer lands in Nottinghamshire, Derbyshire and Staffordshire. Like many of the medieval gentry families, the Plumptons had their place, their centre, but were attached to others across the country. They were lords in their own country but tied to their feudal superiors. They could be summoned at will by the earls or by the King. They travelled, as Justices of the Peace, and as Sheriffs of all the counties in which they held their lands and as Members of Parliament in Westminster. They were local grandees but with a national perspective. They pursued without hesitation their inferiors. And they were fuelled by ambition, a desire not only to preserve the name of Plumpton but to enhance it and enlarge it, to insulate it from the shocks of mortality and the failure to breed.[16]

The Brafferton affray was symptomatic of this gentry life: it borrowed from the world of martial glory; it asserted lay and royal authority in the face of the church; it required competence in command; it played fast and loose with legal niceties; it relied on a sense of local loyalty; and it did not hesitate to do dreadful deeds. It may also have looked at the time like the beginning of Plumpton's ascent to greatness.

From the 1440s onwards William's public career could not have been clearer. He stayed loyal to the Northumberlands and to the Lancastrian crown which he and his father had both served with such honour in France. He acquired local office and with it influence and riches. And at least to begin with, his policy for his family and its name followed the same well-defined path. He had been married when he was twelve in 1416 to a local gentry girl, Elizabeth Stapleton, and on his return from the French wars in 1430, a son, Robert, had been conceived, born the following year. A younger brother, William, was born four years later. With this male inheritance, the future of the Plumptons seemed secure and Sir William took a mistress to whom a further two sons were born. So powerful was the patriarchal mandate in this class that they too were called William and Robert.[17]

This phenomenon, which was common to the gentry throughout the centuries, was especially marked in the Plumptons: William Plumpton's father was called Robert, his grandfather William, his younger brother Robert and his eldest son William, his younger son Robert, his elder bastard son William, his younger bastard son Robert, yet another son Robert – of whom much more below – and his grandson William. It is as if these people's genes did not belong to them. They were no more individualized than pieces on a chess board, all Plumptons but there to play a role. In an age both obsessed with the transmission of value from one generation to the next and struggling with the erosion of knightly values, each successive Robert and William must have felt that burden more acutely than the last.

Elizabeth Stapleton, the boys' mother, died in the early 1440s and in 1446 Sir William embarked on elevating the prospects of the next generation. His eldest son, Robert, now fifteen, was married to

Elizabeth, the six-year-old daughter of a great Yorkshire and Westmorland magnate, Lord Clifford. They were 'wedded at the chappell within the castell at Skypton'.[18] The Cliffords' castle remains complete, a muscled, stony northern fortress at the head of Skipton market, but the chapel in which these children were married is now a bruised and broken wreck, the mouldings on its roof timbers still there but with later windows and doors crudely knocked through its walls. In the 1440s, it was glorious, a family shrine to northern warlords. Here, a Clifford retainer 'John Garthe bare [Elizabeth Clifford] in his armes to the said chappell', where her young Plumpton husband was standing waiting for her. It is the most poignant image in this story: a small girl carried into her marriage and her destiny, no choice, little understanding, the men of the cloth, a blessing, a party, smiles, drinks, toasts in the great hall of the castle, the stranger of a boy, a young man, her husband, smiling down at her. It was agreed, as usual, that they were not to 'ligg togedder till she came to the age of xvi yeres'.[19]

Sir William Plumpton settled wonderful lands on the pair: manors and estates in Yorkshire, Nottinghamshire and Derbyshire, including among many others Edensor, where Chatsworth now stands. For the privilege, he also paid Lord Clifford a fee of £40, two-thirds of a year's income from his manor at Plumpton.[20] For William, this was an elevation: the knight's dream of transition to the nobility was made more likely by such an alliance. The descendants of young Robert and Elizabeth might at least have the money to support the status and dignity of a barony. For old Lord Clifford, his daughter's marriage to such a boy was not only profitable but politically useful. The marriage of a peer's daughter to a knight's son required less of a dowry than would be asked for by a peer, as the increase in status made up for the lack of cash. And Plumpton, with his undoubted vigour, and a connection which Clifford valued with the Lancastrian Earls of Northumberland and the Percy family, was a form of mutual insurance, an element in the power grouping set against the other great northern family, the Yorkist Nevilles, with their power base in the north-west, hated by the Cliffords and with whom the Percys were on the point of a long and brutal feud. Political, martial, personal, dynastic, financial, status conscious, courtly, handsome and splendid: the Clifford marriage can only have warmed Sir William Plumpton's heart.

The bridegroom was dead within three years, aged eighteen, from an unknown illness, and the marriage of course was unconsummated. But too much was riding on the alliance with the Cliffords for the boy's death to alter the arrangements. The young Elizabeth Clifford, now aged twelve, was married again in 1453 to Robert's younger brother, William Plumpton, now aged seventeen, the same terms applying. That is how it had to be: girls did not walk to their weddings; boys stepped up when their brothers died; Williams followed Roberts; and girls complied.

All apparently remained well with the Plumpton enterprise. England was drifting into civil war, but civil war might be an opportunity for a man of his stamp. Sir William was pursuing his personal enemies through the courts both in Yorkshire and in Westminster with unparalleled toughness, crushing his victims with teams of expensive and effective lawyers. He took part in 1459 in the English battles on the Scottish border and emerged from them with martial credit. In the same year a granddaughter, Margaret, was born to Elizabeth and two years later another granddaughter, another Elizabeth, joined her. Daughters and granddaughters were poor currency compared with a male heir, but they were at least a sign of fertility. All might yet be well. There was no reason the Plumpton name would not continue happily into the future.

At Plumpton itself, the towered sandstone hall, with its own chapel of the Holy Trinity, was richly decorated and furnished.[21] Some twenty servants worked and lived there. Silver-chased hunting horns and salt cellars were part of the furnishings. The family chapel, where they worshopped with their own full-time priest, had rich silk dressings for the altar and for the priest himself. The Plumptons had beautiful clothes: cloaks 'furred with martyns',[22] a coverlet of red satin and a canopy of white silk. Men and women wore silvered belts and girdles, amber beads and gold, sapphire and emerald rings. They had books and psalters covered in red satin and red velvet. The little children learned French and could speak it by the time they were four.[23] In the great fishponds which are still at Plumpton, bream, tench and pike were raised for the table.[24] Rabbits, hares and pheasants came from the Plumptons' beautiful manor at Grassington in Upper Wharfedale. Game, including venison, came from the wide open stretches of Knaresborough forest. The house was well armed with stocks of bows, swords, shields, armour and the pole arms with which the retained men were fitted out. The hall itself, the heart of the manor, was decorated with those coats of arms which reflected the dynastic and land-gathering enterprise on which the family was embarked: Plumpton quartered with Foljambe (his mother's family from Nottinghamshire), Plumpton with Stapleton (his own wife's), Plumpton with Clifford (his son's).[25]

In the cold and frozen spring of 1461, catastrophe overtook them all. A letter from the Lancastrian king, Henry VI, on the run at York, was brought by messenger to Plumpton. Edward IV, known to Lancastrians as the Earl of March, had been declared King in London on 3 March and was now on his way north to destroy his rival. Henry and the whole Lancastrian affinity to which Plumpton had pinned his hopes and loyalty were now to fight for their lives. The letter was endorsed on its outer sheet: 'To our trusty and welbeloued knight, Sir William Plompton.' Unfolding it, he read:

By the King. R[ex]H[enricus]
   Trusty and webeloued, we greete you well, and for as much as we haue very knowledg that our great trator the late Earle of March hath made great assemblies of riotouse and mischeously disposed people; and to stirr and prouocke them to draw vnto him he hath cried in his proclamations hauok vpon all our trew liege people and subjects, thaire wiues, children, and goods, and is now coming towards vs, we therefore pray you and also straitely charge you that anon vpon sight herof, ye, with all such people as ye may make defensible arrayed, come to vs in all hast possible, wheresoeuer we shall bee within this our Realme, for to resist the malitious entent and purpose of our said

trator, and faile not herof as ye loue the seurity of our person, the weale of yourselfe, and of all our trew and faithfull subjects.

Geuen under our signet at our cyty of York, the thirteenth day of March.[26]

Another of the same kind required him to gather the royal tenants from Knaresborough forest. The world of a fifteenth-century court, even in terminal crisis, shines out of these urgent, affecting, courteous and explanatory letters: no fear of violence; an exquisite care in dealing with men of Plumpton's sort; an underlying brute reality; a dream of Arthurian perfection, already in its fading hours; the prospect of a final battle, a Camlann for real; reliance on the formal, feudal love of a king and dread of his kingdom disintegrating; recognition that 'the weale of yourselfe' relied on the bonds of loyalty which, in a kingdom now with two embattled kings, were already broken.

The letters mark the beginning of the crisis in William Plumpton's life. He gathered the men of his household and those of Knaresborough forest and armed them. The young Lord Clifford, Elizabeth's brother, and the Earl of Northumberland were doing the same across the whole of the north of England. Young William Plumpton joined his father, and the entire Lancastrian affinity marched south to meet the Yorkists. The huge armies, 40,000 on each side, met in the lanes, on the open fields and in the sharp stream valleys between the villages of Towton and Saxton just south-west of York. It was Palm Sunday, 29 March, and desperately cold. Heavy snow showers blustered between the armies all day. 'This deadlie conflict', according to Holinshed, 'continued ten houres in doubtfull state of victorie, uncertainlie heaving and setting on both sides'.[27] Heaving and setting: the seismic movements of a mass of armed men. The dead choked the streams, making dams and bridges in the water, and the river Wharfe ran red with their blood. Fighting men had to drag the bodies out of the way to clear a space so that others could be killed. About 28,000 men died, 'all Englishmen and of one nation',[28] as Holinshed wrote mournfully, more than the number of British dead on the first day of the Somme, the bloodiest day in English history.

Archaeologists have excavated a mass grave on the edge of the battlefield. It was hastily dug, only eighteen inches deep, and held 43 bodies tightly packed into a space six feet by twenty. In the words of the archaeological report, they were the 'casualties of an extremely violent encounter'.[29] Most of the Towton dead had been hit over and over again, suffering 'multiple injuries that are far in excess of those necessary to cause disability and death'. The cuts, chops, incisions and punctures all clustered around the men's heads and faces.

Ears had been sliced away, eye sockets enlarged and noses deliberately cut off. Very few of the wounds were below the neck, on parts of the body protected by armour. The archaeologists thought that the wounds had probably been delivered when the victims were already on the ground, helpless, dead or dying 'in a position that did not allow them to defend themselves'. It was savage and enraged mutilation. 'Many were left in a state that would have made identification difficult.'[30] Nor were these men – who as usual had been stripped of their armour after they were killed but before they were thrown in the grave – a crude peasant horde. Analysis of their skeletons has shown that they were stronger than the medieval norm, 'appearing similar to modern professional athletes'.[31] Many had clearly trained in lifting, thrusting and throwing. Several had old, healed wounds. Their upper bodies were developed symmetrically, the result of having been trained from childhood in the longbow, which requires strength in both the string-pulling and the bow-holding arms. The trace elements in their bones have also revealed that they had been fed on the best medieval diet: plenty of protein, much of it from fish. These were the best young men the country had. But there was nothing polite, graceful or chivalric about their dying. The Towton mass grave is a monument to brutality, terror and rage, a frenzy of killing and destruction, a dirty desecration of defenceless victims, among the elite warriors of late medieval England. It is a world in which Sir William Plumpton would have been entirely at home.

The Lancastrian cause was broken at Towton and Plumpton's world collapsed with it. Each side knew this was a fight whose victors would not spare the defeated – 'This battle was sore fought,' the chronicler Edward Hall wrote, 'for hope of life was set on side on every part'[32] – and that alone explains the scale of destruction. Plumpton's son William, aged twenty-four, was killed, lying anonymous among the thousands of Lancastrian dead, drowned or mutilated in his grave. The young Lord Clifford, his brother-in-law, aged twenty-six, a brutal warrior and murderer of prisoners, known as the Butcher, lay there with him, thrown like others into some anonymous body pit, stripped and unrecognized, after he had been killed by an arrow in the throat. The Earl of Northumberland, their feudal lord, mortally wounded, staggered off the field and made his way to York, where he died too. An affinity was destroyed that day, between sons and brothers, cousins and brothers-in-law, the whole spreading set of connections that made up a political-social-familial world. It was a community, as Gawain says in the *Morte Darthur*, which had 'gone full colde at the harte-roote'.[33] The Lancastrian peers were attainted, their heirs deprived of lands and titles. This was revolution by butchery, no less traumatic than the events of the 1640s and just as deep a cut into the body of England.

Sir William himself, who at fifty-seven was certainly too old to have been in the thick of battle, fled from Towton field, down the roads of the frozen north, escaping the frenzy of the Yorkist killing machine, and remained on the run for some weeks. But the levers of power were in other hands now. By the middle of May he was up before the new régime, being interrogated by a judge in York, who as a means of maintaining law and order demanded of him a bond guaranteeing his acceptable behaviour for £2,000, more than thirty years' income from his manor at Plumpton, equivalent perhaps to £5 million today. The bond was set at a level Plumpton could not meet and by July he was a prisoner in the Tower of London, held there as an enemy of the Yorkist state. His decade of suffering had begun.[34]

All offices were taken from him. The Cliffords and Northumberlands, in whom he had invested every penny of his political capital, were dead meat. A world that had been running in Plumpton's favour was now a bed of shards set against him and he had to wriggle for his life. He managed to get himself released from the Tower but was confined to London and prevented from returning to the north. Large pockets of Lancastrian resistance were still holding out against the Yorkists, even then being suppressed by Richard Neville, Earl of Warwick, the 'proud setter-up and puller-down of kings',[35] as Shakespeare called him. Warwick was at the height of his powers, in his mid-thirties, arrogant, ruthless, by far the richest member of the nobility England has ever seen, personally responsible for killing the old Lord Clifford in 1455 and so tied by blood-hatred to destruction of the Lancastrian cause. He mopped up all the rewards: Great Chamberlain of England, Master of the King's Horse, Warden of the Cinque Ports and Constable of Dover Castle. Government of the whole of the north of the country was given to him and his brother. Those great estates which had belonged to his enemies were now handed over, including most of the Percy lands in Yorkshire and the Clifford lordship of Skipton. Yorkshire became Warwick's fiefdom. A Frenchman joked about the country under Edward IV: 'They have but two rulers: M de Warwick and another whose name I have forgotten.'[36] Plumpton could have found no refuge in that unforgiving, Warwick-dominated world.

Deprived of his offices and their income, kept away from his own lands in the north, Plumpton found himself exposed to his enemies. Arms were stolen from his house at Plumpton, precious household goods and even a surplice from his chapel was taken. The monks of a monastery sieved his fishponds for bream, tench, roach, perch and 'dentrices'. His timber trees and underwoods were cut down and taken away. Oxen were stolen from his lands at Spofforth and stones already cut for houses were carted off. In his manors up in the limestone dales of the Pennines, his hay was mown and stolen in the early summer, and rabbits and hares were taken from his warren at Grassington.

From his lodgings near Hounslow outside London, he was conducting secret negotiations with his co-Lancastrians in the north but was caught by Yorkist informers and denounced to the authorities. They had been watching him, the way he 'had receyved, red, and understaud false, damnable, diffamatory, and slaunderous writing, traiterously by pen and other forged and ymagined against the honor and welfare of our said soveraigne, and the same sent to other suspicious persons to corage and comfort them by the same'.[37] There had been comings and goings, agents had arrived at his house and Plumpton had 'secretly cherished them, succored, forbored, and their secrets concealed'.[38] Foolishly, he had not concealed his true feelings. 'When any turble or enterprise was leke to fall hurt or scaythe to the Kings people, the said Sir William Plumpton, with oder suspected, rejoyced, and were glad in chere and countenance.'[39]

The pressure did not let up. In a world where legal standing was so dependent on personal strength and status, everything in William Plumpton's life in the early 1460s was vulnerable. His property was being continually raided. Money to fight for legal redress was desperately short. The letters preserved by the Plumptons describe a world in dissolution, full of the difficulties of dealing with people who were 'right hard and strange' and shot through with murderous arguments. His men were being 'dayly threatened'[40] with beatings or worse. All involved had to navigate the tangled and expensive jungle of late medieval law. Those with something to get out of Plumpton addressed him with imploring and self-abasing humility. Others wanted only 'a remedy as shall accord with reason'.[41] His lawyers prayed that God would give him 'good speed against all your enemies'.[42] He seems to have been surrounded by them. His tenants asked him to show 'good lordshipp and mastership',[43] their only hope in a world where their own newly increased vulnerability was exposed to the competitiveness and thieving of those in power.

On top of all this, with his status crumbling, Plumpton was faced with the most intractable of gentry problems: daughters. He had seven of them, most of them coming into marriageable age in the 1460s. To maintain the dignity of the family, daughters had to be provided with dowries. The class average was something near £100 per girl and the deal was usually quite straightforward. The girl's father would provide the lump of cash (usually payable in instalments over five years or so) and the boy's father would settle lands on the young couple that would provide an annual income of about 10 per cent of that sum, called a jointure. If the husband died first, his widow enjoyed the jointure for the rest of her life. After her death, the lands would descend to her and her husband's heirs. It was a civilized and humane arrangement, the equivalent signal in law to the co-presence in every parish church of the knight and his lady laid out side by side in equal honour and with equal dignity. Women were important: they ran estates, they mothered the all-important heirs, they stood as trustees in legal agreements and as widows they became powers in the land. Their arms were quartered equally with their husband's. It was a given that every father would provide every daughter with an old age that fitted her 'worship', her honour. A proper dowry would get a proper husband. The Plumpton coat of arms would continue to be associated with others of equal or better standing. The family corporation would be allied in blood with those who could support it.

But seven daughters! Figures for the dowries provided by Plumpton have survived for three of his girls: £123 for Elizabeth at some time before 1460, £146 for Agnes in 1463 and £100 for Jane in 1468.[44] Catherine, Alice, Isabel and Margaret Plumpton were all married in the 1460s, and all to equally distinguished members of the gentry, most of them knights, who would certainly not have accepted girls with less to offer. Somewhere or other William had to find some £900 to give away with his daughters. It was a necessary investment in new plant. The poor man was caught between his catastrophic political circumstances and the demands which the family business required.

He was no lamb. Beneath the surface, he had plans. Among the many lawyers he was using to fight his legal battles, he employed two from Yorkshire: Brian Rocliffe and Henry Sotehill. Both were rising and brilliant men, making their names and fortunes in the Westminster courts. Both, significantly, were supporters of the great Earl of Warwick. They were Yorkists, Plumpton's natural enemies, and to each of them, plotting carefully, he sold a granddaughter.

Lying in bed in Plumpton Hall in 1463, William considers the situation. Daughters need dowries, a drain on resources. Both sons are dead, but William, the younger, slaughtered at Towton, has left Margaret (born in 1459) and Elizabeth (born in 1460). Two tiny girls, the joint co-heirs of the entire Plumpton inheritance. On them would descend all the beautiful manors in the Vale of York and up in the Pennine dales, in the Vale of Belvoir and the limestone uplands of the Derbyshire Peak District. Their hands in marriage are worth money. The two Yorkist lawyers Rocliffe and Sotehill would glow at the prospect of their heirs acquiring the Plumpton riches. And more than that, their connections to the great Earl of Warwick might surely ease some of William's other pressures. And so in November 1463, Margaret, aged four, was sold to Rocliffe for his son John to marry. The tiny bride went to live with the Rocliffes, where she embarked on her education. 'Your daughter & myn', Brian Rocliffe wrote about her to Plumpton that December, 'desireth your blessing and speaketh prattely and French, and hath near hand learned her sawter.'[45] Her sister Elizabeth, aged three, was consigned to Sotehill's son John the following February and went to live with them in Leicestershire. Elizabeth, the poor young widowed mother of these tiny girls, can have had no say in their fate. Too much hinged on it.

Brian Rocliffe was to pay for Margaret's wedding and the young Rocliffes were, to start with, to get the poor little hillside manor of Nesfield in Wharfedale, a beautiful place but scarcely of any value. Rocliffe was to give Plumpton £313, more than the annual income from all of his lands. It was agreed 'that all these couenants are to be performed without fraud or bad faith'.[46] At the same time Plumpton made a deal for almost £350 with Henry Sotehill for the other granddaughter 'the which Elizabeth the said Sir William hath deliuered to the said Henry'.[47] The price for Elizabeth was a little higher because Plumpton also agreed with Sotehill that if, by any chance, Plumpton should have another son by another wife, he would also deliver this son to Sotehill so that he could be married to one of Sotehill's daughters.

Hanging behind all this was the knowledge that these little girls would one day each inherit land worth at least £150 a year. Measuring past worth is not easy, but it is relevant to these figures that in fifteenth-century England you could get a spade and shovel for 3*d*., a spinning wheel for 10*d*., a sword for 3*s*. 6*d*., a bow for the same, a draught horse, an ox or a good linen surplice for £1, a knight's war horse for £6 and twenty acres of grass, on which twenty cows and their calves could graze for the year, for £10. Land of that kind might cost £80,000 today. The girls were worth over £1 million each in today's terms.

Everything was tied up. The little girls were securely established as the Plumpton heirs. Sotehill got William to promise he wasn't lying or committing fraud. He required him to agree in writing not to persuade the tiny Elizabeth or her mother that this marriage was a bad idea. And to pay everything back if it went wrong. Here were the Sotehills, lawyers, small fry, riding high on the Yorkist wave, making their claim on gentry wellbeing. None of it would have been possible unless every single person involved accepted the power of the patriarch to dictate and deal in his family's lives.

But there was a problem. Plumpton had sold his granddaughters to two up-and-coming lawyers on the understanding that the girls were the joint heirs of all his property. He had taken large amounts of money from those lawyers on the basis of that promise. If those two girls became his heiresses, the name of Plumpton and the great Plumpton inheritance would disappear into other families' maws. But Sir William wanted to keep his own name and line going and so had embarked on a grand deceit. Since 1452 he had been secretly married to another woman. Very early one summer morning that year, before sunrise, between Easter and Whitsun, a Friday, Sir William and a gentlewoman of Knaresborough called Joan Wintringham came to the parish church of Knaresborough and stood at the door of the chancel. William was wearing 'a garment of green checkery', Joan was in a red dress with a grey hood.[48] The parish priest came in his vestments and solemnized the marriage between them in the presence of witnesses,

the said Sir William taking the said Joan with his right hand and repeating after the vicar, Here I take thee Jhennett to my wedded wife to hold and to have, att bed and att bord, for farer or lather, for better for warse, in sicknesse and in hele, to dede us depart, and thereto I plight thee my trouth, and the said Joan, making like response incessantly to the said Sir William that the vicar, having concluded the

25

ceremony in the usual form, said the mass of the Holy Trinity in a low voice.[49]

Immediately afterwards Sir William 'earnestly entreated those present to keep the matter secret, until he chose to have it made known'.[50] The reasons were of vital importance. It is likely that Joan was pregnant at the Maytime wedding because the next year, 1453, she bore a son, Robert Plumpton; and after the death of young William at the battle of Towton in 1461, it was this Robert Plumpton, as the court official in York pronounced in 1472, who 'was taught to consider himself as the heir apparent of his father's house, and the future owner of his property'.[51]

This was the heart of Sir William Plumpton's deceit: he had been secretly nurturing his own son in the idea that everything the name of Plumpton stood for was to be his. After 1452, every minute of his negotiations with the Cliffords, the Rocliffes and the Sotehills had been a lie. His wife he had forced to live in what the orthodoxy would have viewed as whoredom, their son a bastard. And worse than any of that he left as a legacy to the next generation the prospect of rage and destruction. Everything he had was now to be left, in its entirety, to two separate, competing families.

He seems to have entered his last decade preparing bullishly for death. With legal instruments, he disinherited his granddaughters, leaving the way clear, as he intended, for young Robert to inherit everything. Against the law and without permission, he crenellated Plumpton Hall, perhaps to make it more defensible in the battles to come, perhaps as an assertion of a status that seemed under threat.[52] He stole timbers from the royal forest with which to beautify and strengthen the family house and the great barn that stood outside its gates. Illegally he made a private park around the house from the forest grounds. Rich textiles were bought in London to adorn the family chapel and tens of law cases were pursued against his enemies. When William Plumpton finally died in October 1480, it was at the end of a rampaging, brutal and desperate career. A man who had begun his life in the afterglow of Henry V's triumph at Agincourt ended it with his inheritance mired in the prospect of a long and bitter legal dispute entirely of his own making. His two sets of heirs each felt obliged to defend their name and lands against their own family. Their cousins were their enemies.

Sir William might have hoped that his gamble would pay off. From his own archive he stripped out any evidence that he had once left his patrimony to his two granddaughters. He had lined up a string of gentry connections across the county on which his son and heir could rely. He had strengthened and fortified Plumpton Hall itself. He had loyal retainers supervising his tenants and business arrangements in Nottingham, Staffordshire and Derbyshire. And he had given enough to the church to consider that Providence might be on his side.

But his son Robert, now about twenty-seven, was a softer, gentler man, a recipient of his fate not a maker of it, and perhaps not up to the challenge his father had left him. Gradually over the next thirty-five years, for the whole of his adult life, the effects of Sir William's machinations slowly and inexorably destroyed the fortunes of that son and his family.

On Sir William's death, the legal wheels were already turning but Robert's tenure began well enough. His mother, Joan, had been maltreated by his father, kept as a secret wife for sixteen years while the old man pursued his schemes. Robert did better, immediately giving her the proceeds of the manor of Idle in Airedale, on top of those from Grassington and Steeton, which his father had left her in his will.[53] But this sense of ownership was not to last. In 1483, after a dogged pursuit by the two granddaughters and their lawyers, a decision and a division were made. Margaret and Elizabeth were to get Nesfield, Grassington and Steeton and everything in Derbyshire. Robert was to get only Plumpton, Idle and the Nottinghamshire manors. They were the best lands but out of them he was to pay £40 a year to old Elizabeth Clifford, the granddaughter's mother. His own mother was deprived of those very lands which Robert had designated for her maintenance.[54]

This might have been the final arrangement. Even as the Wars of the Roses came to an end, and Henry Tudor claimed the throne as

Henry VII, this distribution of lands amongst the Plumptons lasted for the next fourteen years, relatively untroubled. Robert, half the man his father was, both in property and resolution, nevertheless pursued the ideal of the knightly squire. He was short of money but he did his best to look after his people. He took on the local government of Knaresborough and its forest. He was a little dilatory, but he kept his correspondence carefully (which is how we know any of this), he served the new Percy Earls of Northumberland in battle against the Scots and was knighted. Tenants and land agents wrote to him, thanking him for the 'tender mastership shewed me in all causes'.[55] He did his best to address his declining financial position, claiming the fees due from the release of bondmen – there were still bound serfs in late fifteenth-century England and their release provided a steady income for landlords feeling short.[56] Like his father, Robert was embroiled in long, expensive cases in Chancery, but going to the courts was not cheap and the threat of impoverishment was never far away.

Then, in February 1497, a letter arrived at Plumpton Hall which must have hollowed out a cavity in Robert Plumpton's heart. It was from his lawyer and cousin Edward Plumpton, writing from the Inns of Court in London.

> To my singuler good master, Sir Robart Plompton, kt.
>
> In my right humble wyse I recomend me unto your good mastership, acertaynyng you that ther is in thes partes a great talking of those that belong & medle with Mr Hemson, that he intendeth to attempte matters agaynst you …[57]

By 'Mr Hemson', the lawyer meant Sir Richard Empson, 'the great man E.',[58] as others referred to him, the most dangerous predator in the tangled wood of late fifteenth-century England. Empson, a lawyer, sophisticated, as slick as a slug, and his colleague Edmund Dudley were employed as debt-collectors-in-chief for the new Tudor crown. As Francis Bacon wrote a century later, they were Henry VII's 'horse-leeches and shearers: bold men and careless of fame'. Money was all, for them or their master, and to gain their ends, as Bacon went on, 'they would also ruffle with jurors and inforce them to find as they would direct, and (if they did not) convent them, imprison them, and fine them … [Empson and Dudley] preyed upon the people; both like tame hawks for their master, and like wild hawks for themselves; insomuch as they grew to great riches and substance'.[59] This was the enemy to whom Sir William Plumpton had exposed his son.

Empson, whose method was the detailed acquisition, by any means he could manage, of one property after another, however slight, sniffed an opportunity. He allied himself with the interests of the two granddaughters, Margaret Rocliffe and Elizabeth Sotehill, eventually marrying his own daughter to Elizabeth's son Henry. The ways of the law moved slowly and it wasn't until May 1501 that Empson began to close in on Robert. The predatory minister began first in Nottinghamshire, where he bought, packed and threatened the juries, and then went on to Derbyshire to do the same. Efficient, connected and businesslike, he took all the best rooms in Derby to house the jury members. Plumpton failed and probably could not afford to match this smooth manipulation of justice, despite the urgings of his lawyers. The result was inevitable. On behalf of his party, Empson got hold of Kinoulton and Mansfield Woodhouse in Nottinghamshire and the Staffordshire manors. Robert was now left with nothing but Plumpton and Idle in Airedale. 'Thus', as a Plumpton lawyer wrote of Empson's methods, 'he under myneth you.'[60]

The Plumptons' world was dissolving; a queasy dread begins to fill the letters they preserved. The following year, in September 1502, Empson moved on to their heartland:

The procuringe & stirrings of Sir Richard Empson, Kt, by corrupt & vnlawful meanes obteyned the fauour & goodwills of the Sheriffe of the said county of York by giuinge of fes & rewards vnto him, & soe caused the panels to bee made after his owne mynd.[61]

After 'diverse great gentlemen of the country' had letters from the King himself, asking them to look kindly on his minister's plans, Empson came to York. He brought a cavalcade with him of knights and squires, with two hundred of the King's Yeomen 'arayed in the most honnorable liverie of his said garde'.[62] Empson himself rode through the streets of York with 'his footemen wayteing on his stirreps, more liker the degree of a duke then a batchelor knight'.[63] This was justice entirely subservient to the facts and display of power. He was accompanied among all the others by Sir William Pierpoint, Plumpton's old Nottinghamshire enemy, relishing 'the vtter confusion & destruction'[64] of his family's ancient rivals. The Plumptons were trapped in a web not of kinship but of loathing.

Robert was lucky in the woman he married. Agnes Gascoigne was an educated and powerful Yorkshire gentrywoman. There can be no doubt he loved her, addressing her in his letters as 'my entirely and most hartily beloued wife Agnes Plumpton' and signing them 'By your owne louer Rob:'.[65] He was to need her in the years to come.

For the hearings at York that September, Robert had left Agnes and their son William, who was about seventeen, at home in Plumpton. Waiting for the court process to begin, with his retainers, the men of the forest and his cousinage around him, sixty-three men in all, he wrote to her:

To my entyrely and right hartily beloved wife, Dame Agnes Plumpton, be this Letter delivered.

My deare hart, in my most hartily wyse, I recommend mee unto you, hartily prayinge you, all things laid apart, that you see that the manor and the place of Plumpton bee surely and stedfastly kept;

and alsoe that I have this Tuesday at even 6 muttons slene, to bee ordained for the supper the said Tuesday at night: and alsoe that yee cause this said Tuesday a beast to be killed, that if neede bee, that I may have it right shortly.

And thus I betake you to the keepinge of the Holy Trinity, who preserve you evermore to his pleasure. From Yorke

By your owne lover Robert Plompton Kt.[66]

In court, Empson produced a document showing that old Sir William had left the manors of Plumpton and Idle to his granddaughters. Given the confusion of Sir William's affairs, it is perfectly possible that the document was real but Robert refused to accept it as anything but a forgery. His advisers urged him to make a compromise – there were negotiations with Empson's lawyers held in St William's Chapel on the bridge over the Ouse[67] – but Plumpton would not move 'and said that he would not departe with noo party of his land'.[68] The negotiations were broken off and the bought and frightened jury awarded everything Plumpton owned to his cousin-enemies. It was then that open war began.

Agnes and her son William had fortified the house and its yards 'with guns, bowes, crossebowes, bills, speares and other weapons &c. as if it were in of warr'.[69] The Plumpton men squeezed in there, taking in beasts and other supplies, bolting the gates, storing the water.

The attack on the hall occurred at some time that October, a ferocious fight in which at least one man of Plumpton's, Geffrey Towneley, who was probably a cousin, was killed, but the assailants were beaten off and the Plumptons remained in physical possession of the place.[70] The bravest of their cousins, Sir John Townley, offered to support them, assuring them that 'if ther be any thinge that I may doe for you, yt shalbe redy to you, as ever was any of my ansistors to yours, which, I enderstand, they wold have bene glad to do any pleasure to'.[71]

Other cousins and sons-in-law, scattered across the northern counties, found themselves besieged by the Empson gangs, writing anxious letters to Robert Plumpton, asking for 'knowledg by the bringer herof how that ye do in your great matters',[72] fending off threats and visits from men demanding money, their goods and lands.

Robert, as a last hope, rode to Westminster to implore protection from the King. Agnes and her son William were left anxiously at Plumpton: not exactly under siege but expecting at any moment a renewed attack. Money was short and, as they had all agreed before Robert rode south, William went out with his men, armed, to collect the rents from their tenants due at Martinmas, 11 November. Some paid up, some refused, ordered by the Rocliffes to do so as the

Plumptons were no longer their legal landlords. Those who wouldn't pay William evicted from their houses and lands, seizing their cattle and goods. The Empsons, Rocliffes and Sotehills hovered, waiting to pick up the pieces. Desperate letters from Agnes went south, looking for an answer to their predicament.[73]

In the middle of that winter, she went down to join him, perhaps to urge him on, perhaps to comfort him. The seventeen-year-old William was left alone in Plumpton. The forces of the establishment, including the Archbishop of York, currying favour with Empson, threatened William but he stood firm, upholding what was left of his family's honour and summoning 'divers other husbands, labourers, yeomen, shermen, a webster, and a smith'[74] to court for trespass on land where they did not acknowledge him as landlord. If they attempted to plough the strips in Plumpton's open fields to the east of the hall, he said he would attack them.

That winter, probably to raise some money when the sap was down, he had timber trees felled in the Plumpton woods, ashes and others, valuable property which Sir John Rocliffe claimed was his. The Archbishop wrote again, warning William of the consequences of this 'senestor' behaviour. The Archbishop was prepared to let him take boughs for fuel but not the whole tree. 'Sir, I wold advise you to doo otherwise. If ye will not be reformed, I acertaine you that the said Sir John shall be for me at liberty to take his most avantage.'[75]

In these circumstances, threat and legality become indistinguishable. In March 1503, William finally wrote to his parents in London, from where for weeks they had not bothered to tell him their news. Spring was around the corner and William was faced with the prospect of his Rocliffe enemies ploughing up the land they claimed they owned for spring wheat. 'Sir, I marvell greatly that I haue no word from you vnder what condition I shalld behaue me & my servants. Sir, it is sayd that Sir John Roclife will ploue, but we are not certayne.'[76]

With help from his Gascoyne cousins, William was re-arming. Ten longbows were delivered to the hall. He was ready for the next stage of the battle and suspected that his father might be guilty of wishful thinking or a lack of resolution. Any talk of royal protection, he told his father, seemed like little more than 'fayr words'.[77] His mother had returned to Plumpton and just before Valentine's day Robert for once wrote to her from London. Cash was short again:

To my right hartily and mine entyrely beloved wife, Dame Agnes Plompton, bee this delivered.

Best beloved, in my most harty wyse I recommend mee unto you. Soe it is, I mervaile greatly, that yee send mee not the money that yee promised mee to send with John Waukar within 8 dayes after you and I departed, for I am put to a great lacke for it. Therefore, I hartily pray you, as my especiall trust is in you, to send me the said money in all hast possible, and alsoe to send me money, for my cost is very sore and chargeable at this tyme: for I have spent of the money that I brought from you.

Therefore, deare hart, I pray you to remember mee. And as for my matter, there is noe mooveinge of it as yet. And for diverse consideracions and great hurts might falle to you and mee and our children hereafter, I heartily pray you to remember to hast the money unto mee, as my especiall trust and love is in you,

From London in hast, the Tuesday next afore St. Valentines day, by your lovinge husband, Robert Plompton, kt.[78]

Hurried, repetitive and emotional as this was, less coherent than she was to him, Agnes can have been left in no doubt.

Through the spring of 1504, the sense of an impending disaster grew more insistent, as did Agnes's realization that Robert was incapable of saving them. In mid-March she sent him the money he needed, which she had somehow scraped together, and asked him that he 'be not miscontent that I sent it no sooner, for I have made the hast that I could that was possible for me to do'.[79] She was managing the tricky situation with the tenants, evicting some, squeezing money out of others. In mid-April, her patience was breaking. He hadn't written; he had let the whole business go on too long. Word had reached her of his hopelessness and their adversaries' persistence and ingenuity: 'Sir, I marvell greatly that ye let the matter rest so long, and labors no better for your selfe, and ye wold labor it deligently. But it is sayd that ye be lesse forward, and they underworketh falsly and it is sene and known by them.'[80]

The rent that was due at Whitsun in early May would be a valuable prize for whoever gained the right to the manor by then. There was talk all over the county that Robert was allowing his enemies to win. 'Sir, I besech you to remember your great cost and charges, and myne, and labor the matter that it myght have anend.'[81] The Rocliffes had taken to arresting select individuals. They had got the machinery of the law on their side. And what was he doing? 'Ye dow none to them, but lett them haue there mynd fullfilled in every case.'[82]

The Rocliffes and Sotehills were tightening their grip on the county, by threat and persuasion excluding the Plumptons from the world they had once called their own. Plumpton loyalists were being charged and held. No one would buy the wood the family had felled over the winter, or anything else they were trying to sell. Robert needed to bring the whole question to an end, and soon.

> For without ye get some comaundement, I wott not how your house shalbe kept, for I know not wherof to levy one peny worth. No more at this tyme, but the Trenietie keepe you. From Plompton in hast, the xij day of Aprill.
> By your wyfe, Dame AGNES PLOMPTON[83]

Two weeks later she was writing again. She was holding the fort, telling him their news. They were all well, the children, their servants, herself. He had been anxious to know if the Rocliffes had received any of the rents ('the farm') from the Yorkshire manors, but as far as she knew all they had done was sell some of the timber trees, at way below the market price: ashes and oaks worth 40 pence had been sold for 12 pence, and some holly wood sold at Idle. But that was all, 'Scrybled in hast, the fryday next after St. Marke day. By your wyffe, Dame AGNES PLOMPTON.'[84]

Then at last a piece of good news. Against all expectations, Henry VII made Robert a 'Knight of the Body', an honorary member of the royal bodyguard, and as such screened him and his servants from all arrest. It was the trump card in any court. The Plumptons could keep hold of the manors at Plumpton and Idle, where they had been for 300 years, with impunity. The Rocliffes, at least legally, could do nothing.

A success but no victory. That summer Agnes Plumpton died, perhaps exhausted by the strain of maintaining the dignity of this ragged and tattered family. And despite the legal protection conveyed by Robert's new status, the facts on the ground, the fear cast into gentry and yeoman alike by the power nexus of Richard Empson and his lawyer friends the Rocliffes and Sotehills, were enough to keep the country almost entirely shut against them.

Symptomatic is an angry letter to Robert Plumpton, from a Yorkshire lawyer, delivered to Plumpton Hall by the lawyer's man, in November 1506. It was the second time of asking and a promise had been broken:

> I pray you that I may have my money now at this tyme, for I must occupy much money within thes iiij dayes, as this bearer can shew you.
>
> If ye will not delyver it at this tyme, I will send no more to you for it, but the berer shall goe to the Shereff and have from him a warrant to leve the sayd money, or els to take your body, the which I wold be as sory for, as any man in Yorkshire, if I myght other wayes doe, as knowes Our Lord, who keepe you in worship. At Staynley, this St. Martyn even. Yours to his litle power,
>
> ROBART CHALONER.[85]

Chaloner was in fact Rocliffe's man, helping him to increase the pressure on Robert Plumpton. Friends who had stood surety for Plumpton on loans of up to £100 found bailiffs at their doors, seizing their lands and goods, with Plumpton unable to pay or do anything about this spreading disaster. Month after month, Plumpton can have been aware only of the closing of doors. He had married again, Isabel, the daughter of a peer, Lord Neville. She too was soon at her wits' end.

No one would pay him what they owed him. No one would buy what the Plumptons could offer in the way of either underwood or timber trees.

No one would buy any land from the Plumptons as their title to it was so insecure. The Rocliffe-Empson band had shut them out of any timber or wood market. Isabel was reduced to sending Plumpton a few shillings through the post. Her mother, Lady Nevill, sent her £4 13*s*. 4*d*. in a letter, saying it was all she could afford and advising her that 'God is where he was, and his grace can and will poorley euery thing for the best, & help his servant at their most needes, and so I trust his Hynes, he wil do you.'[86]

At the death of Henry VII in 1509, Robert ceased to be a Knight of the Body, as the office died with the King. Both Plumpton and Isabel his wife, still guilty of occupying Plumpton Hall illegally and owing money at all points, were thrown into the Counter, the debtors' gaol in London. The Rocliffe and Sotehill cousins took possession of the manors of Idle and Plumpton itself. But the same turn of the wheel brought Plumpton release. Richard Empson and Edmund Dudey, the saw and razor of Henry VII's oppression, were also arrested on the old king's death and after conviction on false charges of treason were executed on Tower Hill to general delight, a sop to the masses from the new young King. Empson's death released the Yorkshire gentry from a reign of terror and the way was opened for yet another attempt at arbitration between the Plumptons on the one side and the Rocliffes and Sotehills on the other.

The final award was made in March 1515. Plumpton was indeed to have Plumpton. The others were to have everything else. If the Rocliffes and Sotehills didn't let the Plumptons back into Plumpton, they were to give them £40 a year, which was in effect Plumpton's net worth. Seventy years before, the family had been en route to glory; now they had sunk to this, an annual income below which almost no family could call itself gentry.[87]

Robert was broken. In 1516, he was sixty-three, his 'grand clima-teric', the moment at which, according to classical medical theory, a man's life turned down towards death. In that year he made a deal with his son William, by which, in a sad and haunted act of resignation, a Lear-like transition from this world to the next, the father surrendered all say over his own life and lands and allowed William to dictate the conditions in which he and Isabel would now live. Will was to 'have ordering and charge of all the household and goods therto longing'. Robert and Isabel were 'to take their ease and reast, and to be at board with the said William at the proper costs and charges of the said Will'. Will was to have all the income from the lands and rents and was to pay all the costs, 'that is to say, meate, drinke, and wages'. He was also to pay for his brothers and sisters and to be in charge of employing the servants, except that 'the said Sir Robert his fader shal have thre at his owne pleasure, such as he will apointe'. Robert was to have an allowance of £10 a year and Will was to listen to his advice on farms, woods and debts.[88]

It is a broken conclusion. Robert's legacies at death were a few shillings to a church here and there, a pound or two to his younger sons and daughters 'which sums William Plompton his son and heir was to pay'.[89] To Isabel Plumpton, his wife, all the goods in his chamber after his death, and the half of all his other goods. Witnesses to his will were his chaplain, a Plumpton cousin, and his servants Ralph Knowle and Oliver Dickenson, who had been with him at the siege of the hall and in prison in London.

The lands Robert had lost slid on in the hands of the Cliffords, soon to be the high-glamour Earls of Cumberland. None of those old Plumpton lands is more beautiful than Grassington in upper Wharfedale, none more unrecognizable than Idle, now buried in Bradford, none more poignant than Plumpton, where moss grows on the abandoned road and the stone walls on the edge of the wood have been allowed to collapse and crumble.

Is there a moral to this story? Perhaps only that there is no safety. The world of the gentry, even in its medieval beginnings, was not only endlessly negotiable but constantly in need of negotiation. If you happened to get caught in a tough political struggle or a tangle of deceit, it was perfectly likely for the entire family enterprise to be fatally damaged.

The Plumptons remained Roman Catholic at the Reformation, fell increasingly into debt and ended up on the wrong side in the Civil War. John, the last Plumpton of any substance, was wounded at Marston Moor and died after languishing for several days in Knaresborough, where he is buried, owing £6,393. The last of the line was another Robert Plumpton, who died at Cambrai in France unmarried in 1749. He had gone there to confer with his aunt Anne, a Benedictine nun. After his death, the manor of Plumpton was sold to Daniel Lascelles, the son and part-heir of one of the great and most brutal slave-financiers of the eighteenth century. Daniel intended to make it his seat. He pulled down Plumpton Hall and, as Thomas Stapleton, the nineteenth-century editor of the Plumpton letters, described, 'formed about its site extensive pleasure-grounds; but, after having begun the erection of a new building, he desisted and went to live at Goldsborough Hall, another of his purchases and which, like Plumpton, had once been the residence of a knightly family'.[90]

Everything medieval at Plumpton has gone, erased in the eighteenth century, no more than one or two bits of broken sandstone now surviving among the brambles and the bracken.

PART II

In the Renaissance State
1520–1610

The Tudors were the most successful gentry family in English history. Owen Tudor, an obscure and impoverished North Wales squire, working as a servant in the royal household, managed in about 1428 to catch the eye of Henry V's widow, Catherine of Valois, a few years after her warrior husband had died. It is not quite certain how he did it but Owen either fell into her lap when dancing drunk or went swimming in front of her and her ladies. It was a Mr Darcy moment. One chronicler, who knew Catherine well, said she was 'unable fully to curb her carnal passions'[1] when confronted with the magnificent sight of Tudor in the water – she was about twenty-five, he a year to two older – and English history changed. Their sons became power-players in the Wars of the Roses and from that long violent crisis their grandson Henry Tudor emerged the victor at Bosworth Field in 1485. On 30 October that year he was crowned King of England as Henry VII. In this way, the smallest of vicissitudes can change whole worlds.

The civil wars of the fifteenth century which had brought the Tudors to power had destroyed the world of the great medieval magnates. Under the Tudors, overwhelmingly aware of the vulnerability of a crown weaker than its greatest subjects, the great magnates were excluded from influence. After the 1530s, and Henry VIII's raid on church property and independent power, the church went too. That should have left the crown itself dominating the field, buttressed by the imposing and often terrifying authority of the Tudor state, but in an era before comprehensive taxation, the crown was chronically underfunded, inherently extravagant and forced to spend capital as income. Between the 1530s and the 1630s, it lost what it should have gained.

Statistics can only be the roughest of informed guesses. Nevertheless, through the sixteenth and seventeenth centuries there is no doubt that the economic and social structures of England underwent the deepest of transformations and the great beneficiaries of this double revolution – the failure of the magnates and then the failure of the crown – were the gentry. Their landholding rose from 20 per cent in the Middle Ages to something like half the country by the middle of the seventeenth century. The result was that where the crown, the church and the great lords had ruled medieval England, the great lords and the gentry came to rule early modern England.

This is the fluid and difficult environment in which the Throckmortons found themselves in the 1530s and where the Thynnes rode to riches and significance. Any number of sixteenth-century 'new men' understood the lesson promulgated by the old and cynical Tudor statesman William Paulet, Marquess of Winchester. When asked at the end of his career how he had managed to survive for thirty years at the centre of power, through so many reigns and changes, he said, '*Ortus sum ex salice, non ex quercu*, I was made of the plyable Willow, not of the stubborn Oak.'[2] The heart of survival: pliancy.

It would be a mistake to make the focus of this history only the pain and struggle of survival in a challenging world. Tudor England was beautiful. Nowhere else in Europe was as green as England and every foreign visitor remarked on it – the thickness of the overhanging trees, the day-long spread of pasture as you rode across country. It was a world of beef and sheep. To keep the fertility up, advisers on Tudor agriculture recommended sowing the meadows with a mixture of clovers, yarrow, tormentil and English plantain. The 'whole country is well wooded and shady', a Frenchman, Estienne Perlin, wrote in 1558, 'for the fields are all enclosed with hedges, oak trees and several other sorts of trees, to such an extent that in travelling you think you are in a continuous wood'.[3] English pigs amazed strangers with their size and fatness. The best chickens Polydore Vergil ever ate came from Kent. The horses were strong and handsome and were exported abroad. It was a thickened country, dense with locality. This was the wild thyme, oxlip and honeysuckle landscape that would form the remembered and dreamed-of background to a century of violent political and religious change. That is the definition of sixteenth-century England: government bordering on tyranny in a country filled with sweet musk roses and eglantine.

The sixteenth century was a time to be in land. The weather was improving and more children were surviving into adulthood. The number of people in England was rising faster than the amount of food that could be grown for them. With a mismatch of supply and demand, food prices rose, tripling between 1508 and 1551, and rents rose with them. Agricultural land in the sixteenth century was the most reliable source of cash there was. But the ability to deliver the increased yields depended on returning fertility to the ground. A mixed country, in which there was plenty of grazing, much of it already enclosed, was a recipe for financial success. Meadows were money in Tudor England and both these families were blessed with them. Much of the story that follows here – of ideological courage and daring in the face of power; of families squabbling to get their hands on an inheritance – would not have been possible without that pasture-rich background. Tudor gentry floated on grass.

Discretion

The Throckmortons

Coughton, Warwickshire

The Throckmortons' story is the life-track of a family attempting to ride the traumatic cultural uproar of the Reformation. Over four generations spanning the sixteenth century, they played in and out of honesty and duplicity, loyalty and betrayal, integrity and opportunism. They were both a barometer of their time and the clearest possible demonstration that to be a member of the gentry was no feather bed to lie on. Thomas Fuller, the seventeenth-century church historian, would describe yeomen, the farmers who had no claim to gentility or any part in the government of the country, as 'living in the temperate zone between greatness and want, an estate of people almost peculiar to England'.[1] That shady, calm country between significance and poverty was a kind of Arcadia that was unavailable to the gentry. Their duty, broadly expressed, was to govern, and in doing so to run the risk of want, or worse.

For at least three hundred years, the Throckmortons had been a Worcestershire family, who in the fifteenth century, partly by marriage, partly by purchase, had acquired lovely Warwickshire estates around Coughton in the damp grassy valley of the river Arrow, as well as others in Buckinghamshire and Gloucestershire. The Throckmortons had been astute managers of land for generations, enclosing pastures and woods, running a Worcestershire salt pit in the fifteenth century and heavily involved in both sheep and cattle, consolidating holdings, looking to maximize revenues from their farms. They had navigated the chaos and challenges of the Wars of the Roses, shifting from one aristocratic patron and protector to the next, deploying the key tactic of gentry survival: the hedging of bets.

Coughton, as suited the Throckmortons' nature, is just on the border of two different worlds: to the north, the small fields and dispersed farms and hamlets of the forest of Arden, 'much enclosyd, plentifull of gres, but no great plenty of corne';[2] to the south, beyond the river Avon, the wide open ploughlands of 'fielden' Warwickshire. Neither was entirely specialized – there were corn fields in Arden and animals were bred and fattened on the barley and peas grown in the fielden country – but Coughton lay happily in the hazy boundary between them and as a result was a good and rich place to be.

Within yards of the part-timber, part-stone buildings of Coughton Court, so close that the modern garden of the house completely encircles it, Sir Robert Throckmorton rebuilt St Peter's Church in the first years of the sixteenth century. Everything there was mutually confirming. The Throckmortons' house, the beginnings of its new freestone, battlemented gateway, the dignified church, their tombs within it, the productive lands surrounding them, their own piety, their charitable gifts to local monasteries, their place as the local enforcers of royal justice, as magistrates and sheriffs of the county: this was an entirely continuous vision. Everything connected, from cows to God, from periphery to centre, from the poor to the King, from the Throckmortons' own self-conception and self-display to the nature of the universe. Go to Coughton today, and very faintly, beyond the ruptures of the intervening centuries, the notes of that harmonic integrity can still be heard.

They were a pious family.[3] Sir Robert's sister Elizabeth was an abbess, and two of his daughters were nuns. In 1491, his eldest son, the infant George, had been admitted to the abbey at Evesham, as a kind of amateur member, for whose soul the monks would pray. The family was chief benefactor of the guild of the Holy Cross at Stratford. In 1518 Sir Robert Throckmorton, now in his late sixties, decided to make a pilgrimage to the Holy Land. He wrote a will before leaving, which is thick with late medieval piety. Masses were to be sung for his soul at Evesham to the south and by the Augustinian canons at Studley to the north. Dominicans in Oxford and Cambridge and the poor in the almshouse he had set up in Worcester were all to receive money to pray for his soul in purgatory. A priest in the chantry at Coughton was 'to teache grammer freely to all my tenantes children'.[4] The church itself was to be glorified with beautiful stained glass and gilded and painted saints. There was to be no shortage of Throckmorton heraldry. An altar tomb made of Purbeck marble was built in the nave for Robert's own body to lie in one day, surrounded by this evidence of his piety and works. He had rebuilt the church as a reliquary for Throckmortonism. The whole building was a Throckmorton shrine. There was no gap between social standing and goodness or between the metaphysical and the physical. It was all part of a single fabric, like Christ's coat at the crucifixion, 'without seame, woven from the top thorowout'. If the Plumpton story was about disjunction and failure, this Throckmorton vision was of integration and wholeness.

Robert was never to occupy the tomb he built for himself. When in Rome, en route to the Holy Land, he died and was buried there, and his son George, born in 1489, came into the inheritance.

George had been married since he was twelve to Kathryn Vaux, and from about 1510 they began producing an extraordinary number of children, 19 in 23 years, most of whom lived until adulthood. Lands, localism, children, a household, local politics and the law: all of that was a dominant reality in George's life. But the Throckmortons were far from parochial. Both George's and Kathryn's fathers had been close allies and courtiers to Henry VII. George would have considered Westminster and Whitehall his own to conquer. After some years learning the law in Middle Temple, he had entered the court of Henry VIII in 1511, fought alongside the King in France and was knighted in 1516. Royal favours began to trickle down: he became steward of royal estates and keeper of royal parks in Warwickshire and Worcestershire.

There is one minor incident which stands out from this steady progress. In the winter of 1517–18, he killed a mugger called William

Porter who had come at him 'maliciously' in Foster Lane, the Bond Street of its day, off Cheapside, full of goldsmiths' shops. It is possible George had been buying jewellery and his attacker was trying to rob him. George had slashed out at the man 'for fear of death and for the salvation of his own life' and killed him. A royal pardon followed.[5]

This was all entirely conventional: it was what people like George Throckmorton did with their lives. Legal competence, marriage and children, effective violence at home and abroad, minor functions at court and in Warwickshire, the management of the lands: this was the gentry in action, as it had been throughout the Middle Ages, the central, universal joint of English culture.

George Throckmorton could look forward to a life of unremitting and blissful normality. He was his father's son, pious, efficient, forthright, courteous, sociable, capable both of performing duties for his social and political superiors and of attending to Throckmorton wellbeing.

The 1530s ensured that would not happen. For two or three years, Henry VIII had come to think that his marriage to his brother's widow, Catherine of Aragon, was cursed. Leviticus said as much. The King had offended God by marrying her and God had ensured she would bring him no son. Catherine was now too old to bear children and, anyway, since the spring of 1526 the King had been entranced by one of Catherine's ladies in waiting, the young Kentish gentlewoman Anne Boleyn, with whose family Henry had long been familiar. He thirsted for divorce, to bed Anne Boleyn and to continue his dynasty. But a divorce was impossible. When his chief minister, the brilliant and deeply loathed Cardinal Wolsey, proved himself incapable of bringing it about, Henry's desire for Anne, for freedom of action and for legitimacy all fused into one, overlapping, multi-headed crisis.

George Throckmorton, who was forty in 1529, found himself embroiled in every part of this crisis. Before Wolsey's disgrace he had been working for him at Hampton Court, acting as the Cardinal's agent in confiscating the monastic lands Wolsey needed at this stage to endow his new college at Oxford (which later would become Christ Church). When the King dismissed Wolsey for his inadequacies over the divorce in November 1529, tides of loathing swept over the fallen man. All the arrogance, regal style, vaingloriousness and independence of mind that he had shown in office were thrown back at him. Throckmorton might have been tainted with these connections but he managed to slip out from under them. At Hampton Court he had made friends with Wolsey's rising assistant, the brewer's son Thomas Cromwell, sending him gifts of £20 and a greyhound, asking for some sturgeon and quails in return, with the assurance that he was his friend and 'hoping you wyll see me no loser'.[6] Now, as Cromwell moved towards the centre of power, that connection came good. George's son Kenelm went into service as a member of Cromwell's household and George himself was made a member of the commission looking into the possessions Wolsey had claimed in Warwickshire.

It looked as if Throckmorton was calmly doing what his forefathers had done, easily sliding from one power-allegiance to the next, the traditional method by which successful gentry families survived from generation to generation. But the Reformation was more than just another power shift. As liberating juices ran into the crannies of English minds, the bound-together world of inheritance, piety and service, which his father, dead in Rome, had left to him twelve years before, came under threat. Lutheran ideas; Thomas Cromwell's ambitions for a new and reformed relationship of church and state; the King's desire for a new and possibly unholy divorce and marriage: this was not only a crisis for England. It was a life crisis for George Throckmorton himself.

In 1529 he had been elected to the Reformation Parliament, which met from time to time, without re-election, until 1536. That parliament was the instrument, deftly steered by Thomas Cromwell, through which the Reformation was brought to England. In one Act after another, church independence was eroded and the authority of the crown enhanced. Cromwell made the English state watertight: church money and lands were channelled towards the crown; no appeals were allowed to any authority outside England, especially not to the Pope; and increasingly repressive laws were passed against anyone who disagreed with royal policy, culminating in the 1534 Act of Supremacy and the Treasons Act, by which the King was acknowledged as supreme in church and state. Any disagreement was punishable by death. The cumulative effect of the parliament was to destroy the role of the Pope, the inheritance of St Peter, and put secular terror in its place.

From his actions and words, it is clear that George Throckmorton was agonized by the conflict of allegiances. Crown or family, his past or his future? His father's church or the King's? To which should he be more loyal? Half secretly, he began to oppose Henry's reformation of church and state. But the whisper system of Thomas Cromwell's listening network heard much of it, and although the chronology is often confused, in Cromwell's papers you can hear and see this Warwickshire gentleman a little clumsily and a little foolishly navigating the shoals and tides of the Tudor seas.

A mass of business passed through the 1530s House of Commons, the regulation of towns, the tanning of leather and the dyeing of wool, the sowing of flax and hemp, the duties on wines, laws against eating veal (to preserve the stock of cattle) and for the destruction of choughs, crows and rooks (to preserve corn crops), for paving the Strand and 'for the saving of young spring of woods', against 'excess in apparel', and, amidst all this ordinary business, the cataclysmic 'Appeals to Rome forbidden'.[7]

All England was talking of the changes confronting them. Throckmorton liked to meet a group of Parliament friends for dinner or supper in an inn called the Queen's Head in Fleet Street. Others met and talked to him in private places around the City: the garden of the Hospital of St John, just north of the walls; or in a private room in the Serjeants' Inn near the Temple; or at other inns in Cheapside, the shopping hub of the City where he had been mugged years before. London was full of these evening conversations between like-minded conservative gentry. 'Every man showed his mynde and divers others of the parliament house wolde come thither to dyner & soup and comun with us.' Usually, 'we wolde bidde the servaunts of the house go out and in lik maner our owne servaunts because we thought it not convenient that they shulde here us speke of such mattiers'.[8] But conversations were reported and to Cromwell this joint and repeated privacy looked conspiratorial.

George's distinguished cousin and priest William Peto, a Franciscan friar and Catherine of Aragon's confessor, summoned him for a private and urgent conversation. He told George it was his duty to defend the old church in Parliament, and 'advised me if I were in the parliament house to stick to that matter as I would have my soul saved'.[9] Death, and with it a sense of martyrdom, was in the air. But Peto also had some more intriguing information. He had just preached a sermon to the king at Placentia, the Tudor pleasure palace in Greenwich, violently denouncing anyone who repudiated his wife, lambasting the courtly flatterers in the stalls beneath him and warning Henry that Anne Boleyn was a Jezebel, the harlot-queen who had worshipped Baal, and that one day, dogs would be licking Henry's blood, as they had her husband Ahab's.

A tumultuously angry king left the chapel and summoned the friar to come out into the palace garden. In this atmosphere of alarm and terror, Peto took his life in his hands and addressed the King directly. Henry could have no other wife while Catherine of Aragon was alive; and he could never marry Queen Anne 'for that it was said he had medled with the mother and the daughter'.[10] To have slept with one Boleyn, let alone two, would in the eyes of the church make marriage to any other Boleyn girl illegal.

Peto fled for the Continent but left Throckmorton in London with his injunctions to martyrdom. How far was this from the comforts of Coughton, fishing in the Arrow or improving his house, completing his father's new gateway! Throckmorton was swimming beyond his ken. Sir Thomas More, probably just on the point of resigning as Lord Chancellor,

then sent saye [word] for me to come speke with hym in the parliament chamber. And when I cam to hym he was in a little chamber within the parliament chamber, where as I do remember me, stode an aulter or a thing like unto an aulter, wherupon he did leane. And than he said this to me, I am viry gladde to here the good reporte that goeth of you and that ye be so a good a catholique man as ye be; and if ye doo continue in the same weye that ye begynne and be not afrayed to seye yor conscience, ye shall deserve greate reward of god and thanks of the kings grace at lingth and moche woorship to yourself: or woordes moche lik to thies.[11]

Throckmorton was flattered that these great men should be considering him as their advocate in Parliament. He was as vulnerable as anyone to the vanity of the martyr and prided himself on his courage and forthrightness as a man who was not frightened by princes or power. He wanted to be known, he wrote, as 'a man that durst speake for the comen wilth'.[12] He was not only a Catholic; he was a Warwickshire knight, whose tradition was to speak for the Commons of England. Peto had told Henry himself that his policies would lose him his kingdom, precisely because the commonwealth could not follow them. But for Throckmorton how could that position play out in the high-talent bear garden of the Tudor court? How could he survive if he were to defend the ancient Catholic truths?

In search of guidance, Throckmorton visited John Fisher, the Bishop of Rochester, soon like More to be martyred (when his headless body was left, as a lesson to others, stripped and naked on the scaffold all day until evening came), as well as the monk Richard Reynolds at Syon in Middlesex. He too would soon be dragged on a hurdle from the Tower to Tyburn, where with four others he would be hanged in his habit for resistance to Henry's supremacy laws. Everyone Throckmorton consulted, to various degrees, advised him 'to stick to the same to the death'. And everyone knew that word was no figure of speech. 'And if I did not, I shulde surely be damned. And also if I did speke or doo any thing in the parliament house contrarie to my conscience for feare of any erthly power or punyshment, I shulde stande in a very havie case at the daye of Judgement.'[13]

The choice they put to him was to suffer now or suffer in eternity, suicide or spiritual suicide. This advice 'entered so in my heart' that it set George Throckmorton on a path of courage. God had to come before man, whatever the consequence for him or his family. He was remaining loyal to the inheritance his father had left him and in doing so was endangering his children's future.

Then, quite suddenly, he was sent for by the King. When they met, Cromwell was standing at the King's shoulder. Confronted with this, Throckmorton bore himself with a directness and integrity of which his mentors would have been proud. He repeated to the King what his cousin Peto had told him:

> I feared if ye did marye quene Anne yor conscience wolde be more troubled at length, for that it is thoughte ye have meddled bothe with the mother and the sister. And his grace said never with the mother and my lorde privey seale [Cromwell] standing by said nor never with the sister nethir, and therfor putt that out of yor mynde.[14]

It must have been one of the most terrifying tellings of truth to power in English history. Henry had admitted his affair with Anne Boleyn's elder sister but this candour and apparent intimacy did Throckmorton little good. He appeared in Cromwell's papers as one of those Members of Parliament to be watched and not to be trusted. Cromwell was not replying to letters from George himself but instead wrote to him, advising him 'to lyve at home, serve God, and medyll little'.[15] Sewn in amongst Tudor tyranny and threat were these repeated moments of forgiveness and advice, like sequins of grace, anti-sweets, sugar coated in bile.

But 'meddle little'? Cromwell's language might have been tolerant; it was scarcely forgiving. There is a plaintive recognition of that in Throckmorton's letter to him: 'Ye shall see I wyll performe all promesys made with you.'

From other places around the country, off-colour notes arrived on Cromwell's desk. From Anthony Cope, a Protestant Oxfordshire squire and Cromwell loyalist: 'It grieves me to find [the King] has so fewe frendes in either Warwick or Northamptonshire. Mr. Throkmerton promised he would assist me to the best he cold. Nevertheless, secretly he workith the contrary.' From Sir Thomas Audley, one of Henry's hatchet men, who presided over a sequence of show trials and executions in the mid-1530s: 'Mr. Throgmorton is not so hearty in Warwickshire as he might be.'[16]

Not to be hearty in mid-1530s England, at least after the passing of the Treasons Act in 1534, one of the 'sanguinolent thirstie Lawes' by which men and women 'for Wordes only'[17] were condemned to death, was a dangerous position to be in. Thomas More and John Fisher would both be executed the following year on the basis of words alone. Anne Boleyn and her so-called lovers (which included her brother) were beheaded on the same grounds. Many monks were executed in the 1530s for doing no more. And George had been firmly identified with them as part of this verbal opposition. In January 1535, he wrote from Coughton to the worldly diplomat and trimmer Sir Francis Bryan: 'I hear that the kynges grace shuld be in displeasure wythe me. And that I shuld be greatly hyndred to hym, by whom I know not.'[18]

Throckmorton was a marked man, if not yet a condemned one, and as an escape from that predicament, he attended to his lands in Warwickshire and Worcestershire, retreating to the comforts of Coughton, consolidating estates, negotiating with his neighbours and with Cromwell for advantages and openings for himself and his children. Life had to go on. Acting as the King's servant, Throckmorton continued with his normalities, sending in accounts of the royal woods at Haseley, where he was the bailiff, and serving as a commissioner in collecting tax from clergy in Warwickshire, guiding church money towards the royal coffers. On his new gateway at Coughton, he put up two coats of arms: his own and Henry Tudor's.

But in October 1536, as the first of the monasteries was being dissolved, his life deepened into something much more dangerous. Large-scale rebellions, which broke out first in Lincolnshire and then in Yorkshire and the north-west, turned those months into the most threatening of Henry's reign. Known to history as the Pilgrimage of Grace, they were deeply conservative uprisings, driven partly by poor harvests, partly by anger and despair at the first suppressions of the smaller monasteries, partly by the sense that Cromwell's new religious and political policies were betraying old England and partly by the fear that the old aristocratic leaders of the country were no longer in charge. Wolsey had been a butcher's son, Cromwell a brewer's, and even Thomas More was the grandson of a baker. That was not how conservative England liked the world to work.

A longing for past certainty hung over the Pilgrimage of Grace as it did over everything George and his allies had been talking about for years. The rebels demanded that the Catholic princess, Mary Tudor, the daughter of Catherine of Aragon, should be reinstated as the heir to the throne. Cromwell's centralizing state was eroding the localities: 'And the profites of thies abbeys yerley goith out of the contrey to the Kinges highness.' This was the cause shared between the rebels in the north and the group of Catholic gentlemen around Throckmorton: protest and despair against the dismantling of the past.

To demonstrate his loyalty at this most fearsome test, Throckmorton raised 300 men from his Midlands estates for the royal army gathered to suppress the rebels. They marched down to Bedfordshire, with Throckmorton's sons appointed captains of the different bands. But his own soldiers let him down, claiming that if the great Catholic lords joined the rebellion, Throckmorton would turn rebel too.

This was dangerous talk – it is impossible to tell if it was true – and Cromwell got to hear of it. He also heard that two of Throckmortons' soldiers 'were with the rebels' – again probably untrue, but in the age of 'Wordes only', adding yet more dissonant notes to what was already a frightening reputation.

George came down to London, met his friends again in the Queen's Head and the perilous chat started up:

I do well remember sitting at a supper but I do not so well remember where, won at the boorde did axe what were the demawnds that ye rebels of the northe requirid, and everi man lokkid upon other & no man wolde make awnser. & then I said that it no matter for yt was in every man's mouth, and we were all true men there, so we mai talke of yt; and said the false knave Aske would rule the King and all his realms. & so rehearsid his demawnds, as far as I remembered them ... amongst others that to have my ladie Mary made legittymate, not approving that more than other. Who were at the boorde I do not well remember.[19]

It was convenient not to remember much. Fear was in the air. When the Duke of Norfolk had warned Thomas More that the wrath of the King meant death, More replied, 'Is that all, my Lord? Then in good faith is there no more differens betweene your grace and me, but that I shall dye today and yow tomorowe.'[20] Few could manage that level of calm. Thomas Wyatt's poem, written in May 1536, when imprisoned in the Bell Tower of the Tower of London, expresses what no one else dared say. From his barred window he witnessed the executions of Anne Boleyn's brother and the other four young men accused of sleeping with her. 'These blodye dayes haue brokyn my hart,' Wyatt wrote, as if he were the only voice of conscience in this terrible decade. 'The bell towre showed me such syght/That in my hed stekys day and nyght.'[21] *That in my head sticks day and night*: it is a literal truth that these people were living with their nightmares.

On Sunday 19 November, when the first Lincolnshire phase of the Pilgrimage of Grace was over and the trouble had spread north into Yorkshire, Throckmorton heard the sermon preached in St Paul's in London. After it he went with an old friend, Sir John Clarke, 'to dine att ye Horse Hedde, yn Chepe, ... with the goodman off ye howse yn a littill lowe parler',[22] another of those small dark London rooms in which the key conversations of the age occurred.

After we had dinid & ye goodman & his goodwife had left the boorde he & I fell yn to comunion of the rebellions off ye Northe, & he axid of me what I hard of yem yn ye cuntre as I came upp. He said it a saying yn London that thei be upp in Holderness [in Yorkshire]. I axid him, 'I prai yow, do yow know what be their demawnds & he said, Have yow not sene them I awnserid no but I said I had sene the bokke yn printe, the awnser to the Lincolneshere men's demawnds. He said so fairly I will send them yow them sone to lokke upon.[23]

Nothing too suspect there, the natural conversation of two men engaged with politics. They hadn't spoken in front of the proprietor of the Horse's Head nor his wife, but that was only necessary caution. Clarke's servant delivered the printed papers to Throckmorton that evening 'and after I had read them I threw them yn mi chamber window'.[24] The papers were explosive material: they described Cromwell as a 'simple and evil disposed person', who had 'spoiled and robbed, and further intending utterly to spoil and rob the whole body of this realm'. His policies were 'contrary [to] the faith of God and honour to the king's majesty and the commonwealth of this realm'. The oath the rebels took in Yorkshire swore 'to expulse all villain blood and evil councilors against the commonwealth from his grace and his privy council of the same'.[25]

Anyone who could be suspected of disseminating these words would clearly die. Throckmorton kept them in his room, lying in the window, until another old friend, Sir William Essex, came to London.

> the same nyght he and I mette met att supper at the queins hedde betwixte the tempull gates. And afterwards, when we two remained alone, we fell in communion of the rebells off the northe and then he axid me if their demawnds and those of the Lincolne shere men were all won. & I said they were much the same, as yt apperith bi the bokke yn printe, which he had seen. Then I sent mi servant to my chamber for them, and lent them to Sir William, who put them yn his purse and so departid.[26]

Sir George had said, 'Your servant may copy it if you will': now the seditious words were out and spreading in London and beyond, with Throckmorton and Essex perceived as the source. Essex's clearly literate chamber boy, Geoffrey Gunter, made another, secret copy for himself. When he accompanied Sir William down to his house at Lambourn in the Berkshire Downs, he gave it to a friend of his en route at Reading, where it rapidly travelled around the community of priests, innkeepers and no doubt their customers, copied at every turn. This was viral rebellion, first in print, then word of mouth, then by manuscript.

Essex discovered what had happened, knew how catastrophic it was and 'had but little rest all night'. Throckmorton made his way down to Berkshire, ignorant of what was happening, only to find a posse of Berkshire officials riding to court, with copies of the papers Throckmorton had shown to Essex only days before. When Throckmorton reached Essex's house the next day, he found Sir William in bed, having not been able to sleep the night before, but he got up and first in the parlour and then in the privacy of the garden, the repeated setting for secret and intimate Tudor conversations, they discussed the crisis.

They decided, quickly enough, to tell everything and to hurry to London, where they could divest themselves of the truth. Essex was to send his servant first and then to follow himself, and Throckmorton to follow only 'if the matter were not well taken. He should send me word, and I would come up myself.' No word came and Throckmorton, in early December, returned to London. On the road, his own servant met him and told him that Sir William Essex had been put in the Tower. When Throckmorton arrived in London, he too was arrested and by 11 December had joined him there, in the place of torture, terror and death.

We only know these intimate and concrete details of George Throckmorton's movements in the autumn of 1536 – his toings and froings, his dinners and suppers – because the interrogation in the Tower dragged it out of him. His confession is still in Cromwell's papers. No fact was too small to convince the Lord Privy Seal that the truth was being told: the papers lying in the window, the dinner with the landlord of the Horse's Head in Cheapside, the chamber boy, the rebellious servants, Sir William's exhaustion after his night of worry.

Yet Throckmorton was not entirely open in this confession. He said he couldn't quite remember where or with whom he had been sitting at supper when he talked the dangerous rebel talk. It was only six or eight weeks earlier; he must have been lying. To lie to the King and Cromwell in the Tower in the murderous police state of mid-1530s

England showed some mettle. He signed his confession with 'the heaviest heart that ever had living man' and he told the King that 'yt makith mi harte blede withyn mi bodie'[27] to imagine that he thought him disloyal, but there is no doubt that, to some extent, he was. It seems clear that at Christmas 1536, Throckmorton thought he could get away with his double game a little longer. He and Essex were held in confinement on into January 1537. Those in the know at court 'doubted of their lives' but they were wrong. Before the end of the month both men were released and Throckmorton was restored as a Justice in Warwickshire.

It was, as Peter Marshall has said, 'a close shave',[28] but far more desperate events were to unfold the following September. A high-glamour Knight of St John, Sir Thomas Dingley, an international warrior on behalf of all the deep-rooted, crusading and Turk-fighting traditions of the Catholic church, had been heard abusing the King and talking about rebellion. He was betrayed, arrested and sent to the Tower, where among much else he described to Cromwell's interrogators all the subversive remarks George Throckmorton had made to him in the early 1530s: how Throckmorton had talked so loosely in St John's Hospital in Clerkenwell, in the garden there, about the King's dabbling with all three Boleyn women, the frighteners which Cromwell put on Members of Parliament, all this in front of 'light' people, people of no substance, people who were bound to spread the rumours.

Dingley would be axed on Tower Hill in July 1539. For now, his garrulous confessions put George Throckmorton in the most dangerous place he had ever been. Kathryn Throckmorton, his wife and the mother of his many children, now wrote from Coughton in desperation to her half-brother William Parr. Parr was a ferocious Protestant ideologue, Cromwell's eyes and ears in Northamptonshire, with all the right connections to the new regime. Kathryn could be sure that her blood relationship – they had the same mother – even with a man who espoused everything her husband most loathed, would trump any difference in religion. Sixteenth-century blood, as Patrick Collinson has said, was thicker than bile. 'Good brother', she wrote on

20 October 1537, 'Mr. Throkmerton ys yn trobull, as I thinke yow knowe.' She begged him to come to her 'incontinent', without delay, 'upon the cuming off mi son's to yow'.

> Not that I will desire yow to speke to mi lorde prive Seale [Cromwell] for him, but that yow will come to giffe me yor best cownsill and advice … for the helpe off him and myselfe ~~and mi childerns~~. I dowghte not but for all his trobull & bissines the King will[29]

The letter is torn off there – it certainly went on, as the tops of the letters in the next line can be seen – but there is no doubting these are the hurried words of a desperate woman.

In the Tower, Throckmorton himself knew how serious this was. He abandoned the lack of candour from January and now poured out everything he had held back then: the meetings with Dingley, his boastfulness as someone who 'durst speak for the common wealth', his suppers at the Queen's Head, his friends there, their real names, their secrecy in front of the servants, the encounters with More, Fisher and Reynolds, the challenges thrown to him by those ideologues of the Catholic church, his own agonized conscience, his wavering between the idealism of the martyr and the need to survive, not only as an individual but as the person who held the future of the Throckmortons in his hand.

George said he intended no harm to the King. He had behaved 'lewdly and noughtly'.[30] He begged the King to 'have pitie on me, my wife and poore children for the service that I and all my blood hath doon to you and yor progenitors in tyme past'.[31] Now he could only ask pardon, having perceived his error by reading the New Testament and *The Institution of a Christian Man*, the bishops' guidebook to an acceptable form of religion.[32]

George Throckmorton was abasing himself before power. This was the moment in which he broke, when his allegiance to his inheritance could no longer survive the assault of modernity. He was no Thomas More. John Guy has said of More that 'his morality was his executioner'.[33] Throckmorton's frailty was his saviour.

He gave in. By agreeing not to oppose the King and the reformation of the church, he ensured that his family would survive. He had chosen to suffer in eternity. His wife's half-brother William Parr, who may have intervened with Cromwell, probably put the deal to him. Throckmorton was released in April 1538. For the remaining fourteen years of his life, he became the conformist squire and the family thrived. Like most of the gentry, Catholic or not, he did well out of the Dissolution of the Monasteries. He had developed a close relationship with the poisonous Richard Rich, whose lying evidence had condemned both Thomas More and John Fisher at their treason trials, but who was Throckmorton's second cousin. It was another blood-trump. Rich was in charge of the court that dealt in confiscated monastic property and he ensured that quantities of it came Throckmorton's way. This was a bitter place for Throckmorton's career to have reached – plotting with the mortal enemy of his Catholic mentors – but he would have calculated profit and loss. Better to gain monastic property than not to engage at all; and the only potent form of engagement was with those who had access to power. Throckmorton already had since Wolsey's day a lease on the former priory at Ravenstone in Buckinghamshire. Now, from Bordesley Abbey in Worcestershire he received a load of stone, glass and iron. Leases on previously monastic manors in Gloucestershire, Worcestershire and Warwickshire all steered towards the Throckmorton estates. In the fluid mid-sixteenth-century land market, everyone, of all religious persuasions, was trying to bolster his land holdings from the flood of ex-monastic property.

The situation of the Throckmortons in the 1540s and in the following decades became an extraordinary diagram of what happened to a family when faced with the questions posed by the Reformation. First, there was the problem of George's aunt Elizabeth. She was abbess of the small and ancient community of holy sisters at Denny, north of Cambridge, a beautiful, richly endowed place, on a gravelly island in the fens, with the lantern of Ely Cathedral presiding over the marshes to the north of it. Denny was finally surrendered to the crown at some time before October 1539 and Elizabeth came to live with her nephew at Coughton. She brought with her two or three of her nuns, who may have been George's two sisters Margaret and Joyce, and his cousin, Joanna Peto, the niece of the William Peto who at the beginning of the decade had urged him to stick with his faith to the death.

According to eighteenth-century antiquary William Cole, who heard the story at Coughton, these Catholic ladies lived in an upper room, wearing their proper habits, their days devoted to 'attendance in the oratory and work at their needle'.[34] Their room was connected to the rest of the house by a passage which opened into the hall. With them they had also brought the dole-gate from the abbey, a door in which there was a pair of small hatches, through which the nuns had spoken to strangers and given bread or money to the poor. This dole-gate is still at Coughton, with Elizabeth's name carved on it, and it may be that it was fixed on the door to that upper, private corridor, so that in effect the abbess continued to preside over a tiny, shrunken, secret nunnery concealed inside Coughton itself.

This little capsule of an earlier treasured world operating hidden in the middle of a post-Reformation house might be thought of as a model of George Thockmorton's heart: a private, buried Catholicism, still complete, encased in a conforming, outwardly proper, worldly shell, the only possible means of survival. If you had walked down the inner corridors of George Throckmorton in the 1540s, perhaps you would have found his Catholic inheritance sheltering there concealed but unchanged.

But the geometry of Throckmorton belief and behaviour was more complex than a simple division between inner Catholicism and outer Protestant conformity. The whole family came to embody the conflict and crisis of the Reformation. George and Kathryn had seven sons who lived to adulthood. Three of them became fiercely committed Roman Catholics, the other four equally committed Protestants. In his will George remembered them all equally well, instructing his son and heir Robert 'to permytt and suffer every of my younger sonnes quyetlie and without vexacion, trouble or interruption'[35] to have all the properties he had already given them. He would not betray a son on the basis of ideas he had been unable to reconcile himself.

There was nothing middle-of-the-road about any of the Throckmortons. The Protestant side, most of whom had come under the wing of their mother's relations the Parrs, were relatively straightforward. Once they had survived the suspicions of the Catholic regime under Mary Tudor (when Nicholas Throckmorton was imprisoned and tried for treason but was acquitted), they led, on the whole, good serviceable lives as loyal gentry to the Elizabethan state. Only Job, the author of the vituperative anti-bishop Puritan pamphlets called the Marprelate Tracts, embraced some of the ferocious religious fervour of his Catholic cousins.

It was on the Catholic side that the extraordinary inheritance of suffering and rage emerged in generation after generation of the family. Two of George's sons were imprisoned by the state for their Catholicism, as were a grandson and a granddaughter's husband, repeatedly, over many years, while subject to huge, repetitive fines of £20 a month for non-attendance at church.

Three of his grandsons lived and died in exile, plotting for the restoration of a Catholic England. One of his grandsons and the husband of a granddaughter, as well as four of his great-grandsons and two husbands of his great-granddaughters, were involved in murderous Catholic plots against Queen Elizabeth and her cousin James. All of them died in the course of their desperate rebellions, most of them a violent and humiliating traitor's death. Five of those descendants were central figures in the Gunpowder Treason of 1605. This inheritance flowed on through the generations at least as much in the female as the male line. Francis Throckmorton was executed for his part in the plot that bore his name in 1583, but it was his aunt Catherine and his cousins Mary, Anne and Muriel who mothered traitor after traitor, martyr after martyr, in the Catholic cause.

This division of a family is what Peter Marshall has called 'a crisp microcosm'[36] of the religious divide of Reformation Europe. But that is not the whole story. Loyalty and a sense of shared family enterprise lived alongside the deepest possible divisions of the age. Religious and ideological differences, which in the country at large were leading men and women to their deaths, were accommodated within the corporate body of the Throckmortons as less important than family love. As the structures of the outer world lost coherence, as loyalty to state, loyalty to God and loyalty to the past came into conflict with each other, it was the family identity which remained whole. Despite the ferocity of the positions they adopted, and the uncompromising attitudes of government to religious dissent, these cousins, uncles, nephews and friends remained, on the whole, on wonderfully good terms with each other.

Privately, Catholic John gave Protestant Arthur legal advice. Protestant Nicholas asked Catholic John if he could get hold of a rare Anglo-Saxon New Testament for an archbishop who was a client. Catholic Antony went on hunting expeditions with Protestant Arthur. Both of them stayed the night with Catholic Thomas and with rabidly Protestant Job. Catholic Robert left Protestant Kenelm his best clothes in his will, as did Protestant Nicholas to Catholic Antony. Protestant Arthur wrote friendly letters to his fiercely Catholic cousin and plotter Francis, even on the same day that he wrote to his fiercely Protestant cousin Job. They witnessed each other's wills and stayed in each other's houses if they happened to be near by.

In the cool dark church at Coughton, there is one poignant memorial to this ambivalent Throckmorton legacy. In the chancel, right up at the east end, as near to salvation as they could possibly be, George Throckmorton's son John and his wife Margery Puttenham lie side by side under a marble canopy. John's moustache droops across a solid, Noah-like beard. She holds up her left hand, whose fingers are broken, as if in wary salutation. In his right, he has a staff of office but in the other, his fingers and hers (also now broken) just touch, her sleeve ruckled as she moves it towards him. It is no full-blooded grasping of the hand, just the lightest of signals, a private demonstration, unnoticed by others.

The gesture is invisible from the body of the church. You have to lean into the shelter of their tomb to see it. But what does it mean? There are clues. Under Queen Mary, John had been a distinguished and important judge. He had witnessed the Queen's will in 1558, and was clearly identifiable as a Catholic. But under Elizabeth he had, outwardly at least, conformed to the new religion and the new Queen knighted him, appointing him Vice President of the Council in Wales. He remained a loyal and outward Protestant until he died in 1580, when he was about fifty-six. Margery died about eleven years later.

All that time, in private, hidden from the world, his household and his wife remained as deeply Catholic as any in the kingdom. Margery brought up four fiercely Catholic sons. Francis plotted to murder the Queen and was horribly executed as a Catholic martyr in 1583. Their three other sons became Catholic exiles abroad, one, Edward, dying as a twenty-year-old Jesuit in Rome. A memoir of the boy was written by the English Jesuit Robert Southwell, praising his saintliness and attributing to his mother 'an invincible constancy to the Catholic faith, whence she never swerved in the least from the moment that heresy invaded the kingdom'.

John Throckmorton, for all his outward conformity, never abandoned the Catholicism of the heart, and in that deceitful devotion was sustained by Margery's private and invincible constancy. That is what her touch on his hand surely means: she was his guide, leading him towards a shared salvation.

Their wide-open eyes now stare at the marble ceiling above them and they have become their attributes: the gravity-defying pleats of her dress and cowl, his buttoned doublet and chain of office, her twisted girdle, the knightly helm beneath his head, the cushion under hers, travelling together into eternity. Only that secret and everlasting meeting of their fingers indicates the agony which, even then, their family was passing through.

The Throckmortons had a long and eventful history after the sixteenth century and are still living at Coughton today, proudly nurturing the Catholic inheritance for which their Tudor forebears suffered so much. It was only their attachment to their lands in the English Midlands that meant they stayed and dissembled until England turned more liberal and tolerant. If the Throckmortons had been equally committed Separatists or radical Protestants, they might well have gone to America to re-establish their family culture there. In that way, the inner corridors at Coughton, with their priest's holes and their secret vestments and altars, might also be seen as that most modern of things: a private settlement, away from the world, where conscience could be free, hidden from the prying and violence of the all-intervening state.

Control

The Thynnes

Oxford, Beaconsfield, Wiltshire, Shropshire and London

One morning in May 1594, three years after the death of Margaret Puttenham, Thomas Thynne was in his rooms in the quiet, pale-cider-yellow quad of Corpus Christi College, Oxford.[1] He was handsome, rich, dark haired, witty, a flirtatious sixteen-year-old undergraduate, no great scholar,[2] but a man of his moment. He owned copies of Sidney's *Arcadia*, perhaps the version published by Sidney's sister the Countess of Pembroke the year before, and a new English translation of *Orlando Furioso*, the great romance of the Italian Renaissance.[3] They were the two dream books of the age, designed to fill the minds of young men with erotic and heroic adventures in which their fantasy selves could star. Thomas was a musician, with a pair of citterns in his rooms, like flat-backed mandolins, and a big-bellied lute,[4] an emblem for the Elizabethans of the melancholy music that lived, as Sidney had written, in 'the mute timber when it hath the life lost.'[5]

A visitor called on him that morning, a man called Edward Tennant. He was the servant of one of the Thynnes' Wiltshire neighbours, Sir James Mervyn. Thomas would have known that all Mervyns hated all Thynnes. But Tennant brought a letter from John Mervyn, the forty-year-old nephew of Sir James and the great exception to that enmity. Unlike every other Mervyn in England, John Mervyn could be trusted. He was an old friend of Thomas's own father, John. But even here, at the very beginning of the story, there is treachery and deceit, because Tennant's mission, under John Mervyn's instructions, was to entrap young Thynne into the greatest mistake of his life.

Over the previous twenty years the two families had been conducting a vicious and at times murderous feud, a power struggle to control the county of Wiltshire in which they were both rich and powerful landowners.[6] There was nothing aberrational about this: all over Elizabethan England, particularly in those counties where there was no single great, controlling aristocratic or courtly family, the gentry battled for reputation, influence and office. Bribery, deceit, slander, threats, street fights, woundings and murders: all were part of the struggle between leading English families in the sixteenth century. Friends were appointed to juries and to the magistrates' bench; enemies had their reputations destroyed by whispers at court and in the local gentry community. Marriage alliances were made in the old way between families whose interests seemed aligned; provocations, insults and violence were thrown at rivals. The world of the Montagues and Capulets would have been entirely familiar to its audience.[7]

The hostility between the Thynnes and the Mervyns had first come to a head in the 1570s.[8] Each family was almost but not quite alike in dignity. Both were new gentry, on the up, emerging in the early sixteenth century from medieval obscurity into the vicious Tudor world of opportunity and riches. But they were far from satisfied and by the 1570s both still wanted more in the way of land, money and power. The Thynnes were originally modest Shropshire people.[9] The founder of their family greatness, John Thynne, born in about 1513, had become steward to Edward Seymour, the great servant of Henry VIII. Seymour had risen as high as a commoner ever could, eventually becoming Duke of Somerset and effective ruler of England as the Lord Protector of Edward VI. John Thynne, a man of purpose, culture and discernment, a loyal servant, had risen on Seymour's tails, acquiring large amounts of land in Wiltshire, including the old Priory at Longleat, where between 1540 and 1580 he built and then rebuilt the

most perfect Renaissance house in England.[10] He was a deeply cultivated man, urging his sons to learn Greek, sending from London
remedies for his children's afflictions in cold weather.[11] Much of his
expensive life was paid for with the money that came flowing into the
Thynne coffers from his marriage to Christian Gresham, the daughter
and heiress of Sir Richard, one of the wealthiest men in England, an
import–export merchant in the City, dealing in grain and fine textiles,
supplying Henry VIII with the tapestries, satins and velvets that
embellished his palaces.[12] Thynne had made use of the two key sources
of modern gentry wellbeing – office and trade – and was busy pouring
them into a provincial power base.

The story of the Mervyns – or Marvins, as their name was also
spelled – had begun slightly earlier and a little more murkily.[13] In the
1470s, in ways that are not entirely clear, they somehow acquired the
manor of Fonthill Gifford, the far side of a beautiful high chalk ridge
from Longleat. By the 1560s, successive Mervyns had built up their
landholdings enough to put them among the leading Wiltshire gentry.
They lived in style: a stone house with the usual ranks of big glazed
windows on three floors, surrounded by a large park containing a
newly enlarged lake, with a turreted gatehouse, woods, a heronry, a
hop yard, a dairy and pasture for herds of sheep and cattle. There was
a vineyard here in 1633, which may well have been planted a century
before. It sounds like a gentleman's paradise, but as so often in these
stories, the physical description, the view you would get if you turned
up at sixteenth-century Fonthill Gifford as a tourist, belied the realities of tension and struggle behind it.[14]

They were approaching from slightly different places in the gentry
universe: both knightly families but the Mervyns three or four generations deep as Wiltshire gentlemen; the Thynnes richer, more explicitly
Protestant, less provincial, sharper, riskier, with the currents of court
politics, noble service and City money all running through them.
Each family had something to offer the other. But one further status-
colouring element may have been in play: in 1549 and again in 1551,
as the rivalries surrounding the Tudor crown reached their mid-
century crisis, Edward Seymour, Duke of Somerset, was arrested and

sent to the Tower.[15] His loyal servant John Thynne was sent there with him. The Privy Council's warrant to conduct Thynne to the Tower was addressed to 'Mr Mervyn, sheriff of Wiltshire'.[16] It was a moment of humiliation: Thynne, the parvenu steward, being conducted to prison by Mervyn, the ancient county gentleman. Status, to say the least, was nuanced here.

By the 1570s, the head of the Mervyn family was Sir James, a wily practitioner of gentry arts, and in 1574, the memory of the arrest a quarter of a century earlier was set aside. Negotiations were opened between him and Sir John Thynne for a marriage between Mervyn's daughter Lucy and Thynne's son, also called John. Lucy Mervyn and young John Thynne were betrothed and it seems as if John fell in love with the girl.[17] Family agents discussed terms and, as usual, Sir James Mervyn offered his daughter along with a set of Wiltshire manors as her dowry, land that by convention would then descend to the heirs of the marriage. But Sir James was cheating: the manors he was offering were entailed, designated by law to be heritable only by male members of the Mervyn family. Sir John Thynne was in danger of making a contract with his neighbour (Fonthill is about fourteen miles from Longleat) which would fail to enrich his own family at all. His son's hand in marriage, the most valuable property a member of the gentry possessed, would have been sold for a pup.

Enraged at this insult, perhaps at the assumption of his gullibility, perhaps at the lack of respect it implied, Sir John broke off the negotiations.[18] But love is a smoke raised with the fume of sighs and young John was so in love with Lucy that he would not give her up. Only the threat of disinheritance from his father persuaded him that Longleat was preferable to Lucy and instead he was married to Joan Hayward, the daughter of another wonderfully rich City merchant and Lord Mayor of London.[19] It was no brutal marrying of money to power. A letter to Sir John survives from his agent and fixer Richard Young, written halfway through the negotiations. It was important to all parties that the bride and groom to be should approve of each other. Richard Young had agreed with Joan's father that 'Unless the two parties could the one so like of the other and they themeselves to be as joyful as the father, there should be no displeasure but to part in great friendship on both sides.'[20] Young asked Joan, who was not quite seventeen, what she thought of John.

> She said she would not nor could say nothing, for she had not spoken with him and at our speaking, she said, it is possible he shall not like me, and in the other side I may say the same of him, but I do put my trust in God and in my good father that God will put into my father's heart to choose me such a one as God will direct my heart not to dislike.[21]

Lucy Mervyn was consigned to an impoverished military lord, the 11th Baron Audley, an ally of the Mervyns in their great feud, his immensely ancient Wiltshire family larded with a history of lunacy and incompetence. One of their daughters, Eleanour, would eventually claim she was the Bishop of Lichfield, sprinkling tar, which she called holy water, on the hangings in the cathedral there, after which she was committed to Bedlam.[22] Their son and heir was beheaded for sodomizing his servants and holding down his wife while their servants raped her.[23] The benefits of an Audley marriage were not entirely unequivocal.

Here is one way of understanding the Thynne–Mervyn difficulty: relatively small-time gentry family (the Mervyns) aim to hitch their star to high-rolling, ambitious professionals (the Thynnes) but imagine that their higher county status can allow them to cheat. It doesn't and so each party in the encounter withdraws to a safer place – the Mervyns to old hopeless aristocracy, for status enhancement, the Thynnes to City money, for further enrichment.

Thynnes allied to Mervyns would have been an entirely satisfactory marriage of money with status. As it was, the marriage of Thynnes with Haywards was money allying itself to money. Mervyns joining with Audleys was status joining with status. For each family the second marriage left them lacking something: the Mervyns wanted cash and the Thynnes wanted rooted county standing. Sir James Mervyn's greed, and his inability to play by the rules, had wrecked the deal and he had made the wrong choice. The Thynnes had done better: alliance to money would guarantee their future.

Ever since that moment of betrayal, the Thynnes and the Mervyns had been at each other's throats. A more general struggle for control of the Wiltshire courts and political structures lay behind it and there had been bloody street fighting between followers of the two parties at the Marlborough quarter sessions and the Salisbury Assizes in 1589, endless status struggles and mutual humiliations, sending each others' servants to jail at successive court hearings, raids on stock, destruction of hedges, the killing of deer in parks, a self-sustaining mutual antipathy.[24]

Teenagers do not always know their family histories but a miasma of half-remembered enmities and loyalties must have hung over the May morning encounter in Thomas Thynne's set of rooms in Oxford. Thomas was the son and heir of the marriage between John Thynne and Joan Hayward, the London merchant's daughter. Edward Tennant brought him a letter from John Mervyn, nephew of the hated and duplicitous Sir James.

But here there is a complexity: John Mervyn, despite the history and although he was of an older generation, was Thomas's 'very familiar friend'.[25] It is not known how the friendship had evolved or what it consisted of, but it was real enough because Thomas responded instantly to John's invitation to ride thirty miles or so down the London road to High Wycombe, where, John Mervyn said, they would 'make merry'.[26] Thynne, bored with his work – it was a Monday – and 'desirous of some Liberty and recreacon from his booke and study',[27] set off with Edward Tennant, taking about three hours to reach High Wycombe. Thomas Mosely, another Mervyn servant, met them there, with the message that they should ride on another six miles to Beaconsfield, where at the Bell Inn they would find John Mervyn waiting. There is no telling if this part of the plan was deliberate – John Thynne might have thought Wycombe easily reached from Oxford, Beaconsfield perhaps a little too far – but in retrospect, we can see the hand of Sir James Mervyn slowly and gently closing in on his intended victim.

At the Bell, Sir James himself was not there, but his nephew John was and so was Sir James's favourite daughter, Lucy, Lady Audley, with her two daughters, Amy Touchet and the brilliantly red-haired sixteen-year-old Maria Touchet, a superbly well-educated and fiery girl, one of the Queen's four or five maids of honour. With their mother, Maria and Amy had travelled the twenty-five miles or so from Westminster in a coach that afternoon. There were numerous other Mervyns there, and their retainers: it was to be a party.[28]

The Mervyns ordered sweetmeats and 'a great store of wine'.[29] Everyone sat and drank, toasted and talked, laughing and joking around a table. The evening ran on and at some time, as the wine flowed, and as the Mervyns intended, the young, handsome, adventurous, romantic Thomas Thynne found himself sitting next to the beautiful Maria Touchet. They had 'frendly and familiar speache' together.[30] Then, unlikely as this sounds, unless the teenagers were very drunk, as they probably were, or Maria's mother had a supremely tight control over the unfolding of events, as she probably did, the two of them, at least according to the deposition of one Edmund Mervyn at the later court case, 'grew into such good liking of each other as that they seemed desirous to be married presently',[31] meaning, in sixteenth-century English, 'straight away'.

Lucy Audley, according to her own testimony, then displayed the wares and

> caused her said daughter to be turned about, to the end the same Mr Thyn might see that she was no way deformed, but that if he liked her outwardly she wowld assure him that for the disposicon of her minde it showld appeare to him to be much more perfecte.[32]

Thynne liked what he saw, and imagined the higher, hidden qualities as even better. An old man called Welles, whose eyesight was failing but who was said to be an ordained minister, was then spirited into position and a Book of Common Prayer was found. The party migrated to a candlelit upper room in the inn and there Edward Tennant, the man who had inveigled Thomas Thynne that morning to leave Oxford for a party, read out the words of the service because the Reverend Welles could not see properly in the flickering candlelight. Welles repeated Tennant's words and Thomas and Maria made the solemn vows. According to sixteenth-century law, these vows spoken voluntarily in front of a minister constituted a valid and legal marriage.[33]

The Mervyns, in a spectacular coup, had captured the heir of the Thynnes. No dowry had been promised with Maria's hand and so the deceitful deal which Sir James had tried to make with Thomas's father twenty years earlier had now come good for him the next generation down. All that humiliation, Sir John Thynne's rejection of Lucy in favour of a London merchant's daughter, all those years of whispered contempt in the gentry houses, parks and hunting fields of Wiltshire, all had now been revenged.

A bed was made up in the inn and, as usual in Elizabethan marriages, the newly-weds went to bed together in front of the company. Edward Tennant was later clear that neither of them took their clothes off. They certainly didn't have sex but the Mervyn witnesses were adamant that the two did 'imbrace and kisse each other being in bed very lovingly'.[34] Maria gave Thomas a beautiful pair of gloves. Eventually, as dawn approached, everyone else went to bed too, happy at the triumphant outcome of the evening.

Even when the newly married Thomas Thynne woke the next morning, he was said to be 'joyful'.[35] His beautiful bride, the daughter of a peer, whose godmother was the Queen, was surely the most wonderful catch. He wanted to go back with her to the court at Westminster, but the canny seriousness of the Mervyn clan intervened. Everyone who had witnessed the events of the last twelve hours was sworn to secrecy. Maria gave Thomas a needleworked waistcoat with which he was to return to Oxford.[36] She went back to court, from which the Mervyns had arranged no more than two days' leave, and where the Queen was to hear nothing of the marriage. The Thynne parents were to be kept in the dark, as were any Thynne retainers.

It was a dream of Elizabethan teenage happiness. The word 'secret' appears forty-eight times in *Orlando Furioso*[37] and here now, for real, Romeo had at least kissed and slept in the same bed as his Juliet.

One can only imagine Thynne's levels of anxiety that autumn when the feud between the two families turned bloody. Two allies of the Mervyns, the Danvers brothers, both distinguished and powerful soldiers, burst into a house at Corsham in Wiltshire, accompanied by seventeen or eighteen armed men, all carrying swords and pistols. Henry Long, John Thynne's brother-in-law and Thomas's uncle, was dining there with his fellow JPs. Between the Danvers and the Long families, there was a long-running subset of the Thynne–Mervyn feud. Charles Danvers began insulting and then cudgelling Henry Long but he was caught in a corner and injured. His brother Henry then took out his pistol and shot Long dead with a single bullet in the chest. It was murder. The Danverses fled abroad to France and renewed bitterness spread through the feuding Wiltshire families.[38]

In this heightened and dangerous atmosphere, Thomas Thynne managed to keep his marriage secret until the following spring. In April 1595 it somehow erupted into the public world of court and gentry gossip – perhaps at the hands of the Mervyns, who would have wanted to regularize the situation – and the Thynne parents exploded in grief and rage. Thomas's mother, Joan, was in the Thynnes' castle at Caus in deepest Shropshire, his father, John, in their house in Cannon Row in Westminster. Both were hard at work, Joan defending their castle and Shropshire lands from another family who claimed it, John attempting at court to promote his family interests and get himself a knighthood. The kidnapping of their son and heir was one disaster too many, one that combined treachery, humiliation, disobedience and financial disaster.

On 15 April 1595 Joan wrote to a cousin:

How hard is my hap to see my chiefest hope and joy my greatest grief and sorrow, for you know how much I have always disliked my son to match in this sort, but alas I fear it is too late. Alas the boy was betrayed by the Mervyns which I have often told Mr Thynne what they would do, and now it is too sure. But I trust they may be divorced for it is no good marriage in law for that he is under age.[39]

She was wrong. Properly witnessed marriages, as this had been, were binding contracts, even if the partners were under age. John Thynne was enraged and refused to see and talk to his son. Joan attempted to find intermediaries who might excuse 'the deceits that hath been used to deceive a silly child'.[40] But John Thynne was suffering more than humiliation. The essential calculations, the necessary money flows for a continuing gentry existence, had been disrupted by Thomas's precipitate behaviour. Because there was nothing coming into the family account from Thomas's wife, there would be no money for the Thynne daughters' own dowries. No one would touch them without a dowry. The system was interlocked and if one part failed, all was in danger. The disobedience of one, as Joan wrote, would be the overthrow of the others. In the light of this, the dowry was the most important of social bonds. As a shared practice, dowries constituted the exchange medium of gentry life. A dowry allowed one family to accept a new member without any diminution of its own estate; and allowed that family to pass assets on to others. If the flow was dammed, the network dried up. Gentry society was tied to itself through the dowry system.

Letters ran between them. John wrote to say that Sir James Mervyn had approached him, attempting a negotiation. Joan was furious and could not 'but marvel to hear with what face Sir James Marven can come to you, considering what traitorous abuses he and his have offered unto you and me'.[41] The code had been broken and, as she wrote, 'I will never think well of him nor any of his.'[42] The Thynnes could not quite believe how carefully the Mervyns and Lucy Audley had arranged their deceit.

> They have used all the policy and cunning to make it so sure that you nor I shall not break it. For after the contract she caused a pair of sheets to be laid on a bed and her daughter to lie down in her clothes and the boy by her side booted and spurred[43] for a little while that it might be said they were abed together, herself and Edmund Mervyn in the chamber a pretty way off, and hath caused her daughter to write divers letters unto him, in the last naming herself Maria Thynne which name I trust she shall not long enjoy.[44]

Thomas Thynne was made to beg for forgiveness from his enraged father.[45] His mother stood up for him, reporting Thomas's account that he had asked whether his father approved of the marriage and the Mervyns had all assured him they did. He was 'heartily sorry, and hath vowed to me to be ruled by us hereafter'. Discipline and obedience were the essential companions of inheritance and the future welfare of the family business. As John Thynne had in his time been threatened by his father, Thomas was threatened with disinheritance. 'I have told him', Joan told his father, 'what your determination is if he will not be ruled. Otherwise let him never [have] you for his father nor me for his mother if he consent to them.'[46]

But the boy was under siege. He was buttonholed by Sir James Mervyn in the gossip shop of St Paul's in London.[47] He was promised letters from Maria, who had been hidden from him since that first Beaconsfield night. He was threatened by his own father and clucked over by his mother, who longed to protect him. The correspondence is almost entirely warm and loving. This was a family disaster but the love between man and wife, mother and son, boy and girl are all palpable on the page. Joan Thynne in particular knew that love and family welfare were not separable. She wrote to her husband at court that he was to look after himself, not only for his sake but for hers. 'I trust your troubles will turn all for best,' she wrote to him in May 1595, 'and to both our comforts, although the strain be great for the present.'[48] Of the erring Thomas, she begged his father 'to accept of his true repentances which I hope you will receive him into your favour again, and to have that fatherly care which heretofore you have had of him, although he hath justly deserved your displeasure'.[49]

She followed those phrases with a sentence of great psychological acuity and a sense of moral equality with her husband. 'Yet consider of him by yourself when time was.' Judge your son, in other words, by the man you were when you were his age. John Thynne at that age had been in love with Lucy Mervyn, the very woman who had now hijacked the Thynne family enterprise. He had probably remained in love with her even as his parents introduced him to Joan Hayward, the young merchant's daughter from London. A touching letter from her survives at Longleat from that early period in their lives, soon after their first meeting in 1575. 'Good Mr Thynne,' Joan wrote to him,

> I give you most humble thanks for your letter, but that will not suffice me from letting you to understand of my heavy heart and my pensive [i.e. sorrowful] mind, hoping that when you understand the cause you will do your endeavour to release me of some part of it, which if I could speak with you it should not be long unknown to you. For as the distance is short, so I think your absence long.
>
> By your pensive friend in heart and mind
> J.H.[50]

The subject of this letter is not clear, but could it be that she was urging him to relinquish his love for Lucy Mervyn, to obey his own father and turn to loving the twice-pensive Joan herself? Perhaps. And this favouring of love over obedience was perhaps what Joan was reminding him of twenty years later.

But their son Thomas wasn't playing entirely straight. He had lied to his parents, by saying that he thought his father had given permission for the marriage, and even while submitting to his mother's pleadings and father's ferocity, he was sending letters to the ever-more desirable Maria, one including a gold ring, another signed 'your loving husband'.[51] Lies were the only way Thomas could find to creep through the labyrinth of fear, love and guilt in which he found himself.

The patriarchs of the two families now took their battle to the courts, first to the Star Chamber, where Mervyn had Thynne demoted from the most prominent magistrate in Wiltshire to the bottom of the list; then to the great church court held in St Mary-le-Bow in Cheapside, where Thynne wanted to prove the illegality of the marriage. There, in the Court of Arches (named after the huge arches of the Norman church), all the principal players were summoned and asked to give witness statements. Those long hearings, which dragged on for four years, are the reason we know so much about this story.

Everybody lied in court. Witnesses were suborned and patience-sapping speeches by lawyers explored the precedents. Aspersions were cast on the character and validity of the man called Welles who had appeared in the pub that evening as an ordained minister. Slurs were laid on the character of the Mervyn witnesses as adulterers and fornicators. Threats of violence were made or alleged. Both sides lobbied the Queen herself. John Thynne attempted to exhaust the Mervyns' money and courage with expensive and vastly irrelevant legal delaying tactics.[52]

Not until the early spring of 1601 was there any sign of an end to the fight. Maria Touchet had consistently appeared in the various courts defending the propriety and reality of her marriage. Thomas Thynne had been kept by his parents in hiding somewhere in England, although it seems he may from time to time have managed to see his wife. But then, perhaps at the moment everyone was bored and frustrated by the long legal struggle, the Thynnes seem to have given in. John Thynne's sister-in-law, Elizabeth Knyvett, wrote to him to say that he and Joan in their anger should not forget to love their son. He had made a mistake, as sixteen-year-olds do, and they should forgive him, and take it as a mistake rather than 'bitterly in displeasure condemne [it] as an unpardonable offence'. She was a wise woman. Thomas and Maria were now twenty-three. 'It resteth nowe seeing it is fallen out thus that it be followed advisedly for a fynall end thereof.'[53]

Only then, extraordinarily, as all appeared to be moving to a kind of resolution and the Knyvetts looked as if they might be organizing some kind of agreement between the parties, did Thomas finally appear in court. It seemed as if he had finally submitted to his father's will. First, he told the court everything his parents would like to have heard. When Edward Tennant came to his Oxford rooms, Thomas said, he had no idea that the man worked for Sir James Mervyn. He thought this was just an invitation to a party from John Mervyn, his father's old friend. Nor did he have any idea that John Mervyn had 'turned Judas', betraying the Thynnes to the Mervyns. That he should have done so is not in itself surprising: Mervyn family loyalty out-trumped mere friendship. At Beaconsfield, Thomas went on, Lucy Audley and her daughters and all the other Mervyns had plied him with drink and he was 'so much distempered therewith that he did not, neither doth, knowe or remember in any particular what was further said, done, or practized by him nor them that night'. Crucially, then, he had not been conscious of getting married to Maria and if that was true the marriage was invalid and the Thynnes were free.[54]

How could the dignity of a man be preserved in this world so dense with manipulation if he did not manipulate things himself? And Thomas, it seems, had learned the arts of survival. Maria, his wife, had with immense self-possession declared the reality of the marriage in hearing after hearing and deposition after deposition. Thomas had been tucked away in the country, effectively imprisoned by his father. Now, it seems, he had got himself to court by agreeing to say what his father wanted him to say. But once that was said, he could then declare his love for Maria. Now at last evidence was produced in the Court of Arches which showed that the marriage was real. When back at Oxford Thomas had written to Maria, signed the letter 'your loving husband', sent her a pair of gloves, instructing they should be delivered 'to his wife' and another letter with a gold ring in it, on which he had the words 'a frendes guifte' engraved.[55]

This was evidence that Thomas had not been quite so much of a drunken victim on the evening in Beaconsfield. The letters had been asked for earlier in court proceedings but had never appeared. The Oxford historian Dr Alison Wall, who has studied this case in great depth over many years, thinks they may not have existed before 1601 'and Thomas may have written them now [in 1601] to prove a marriage his father had forced him to deny'.[56] Certainly the judge was impressed by Maria's lawyers' claim that 'the letters this day exhibited in the Court are wholly written with the hand of the said Thomas, and the said letters and ring this day exhibited are the same Thomas sent'.[57]

Having heard his son's new evidence, John Thynne's rage returned at full force. The escape that seemed to be within his grasp had been snatched away. He wrote to Joan, still in Shropshire, from London, where he had been enmeshed in dealings over property disputes. Now he was confronted again with the everlasting crisis over Thomas, his proud undutiful son … [who] hath to me most undutifully demeaned himself to my no small grief, and for which cause I will also especially stay to see the same either settled or no longer dissembled, and you and myself no more abused, for to my face he used me undutifully, and is such cause of contempt of me as I neither can nor will endure, but will put him to the point either of having of her or utterly leaving of her, to the end I may no more spend in that suit my time and charges in vain.[58]

This was a gentry cry from the heart: the most important family asset, the son and heir, was not conforming to the managing director's vision but instead was asserting his own short-term interests over those of the family corporation. These financial-cum-strategic problems were emerging in terms of private family emotions. Thomas was failing to tell the truth, was proud, knew nothing of duty and was abusive and inconsistent in his actions. He could have been sacked (or disinherited) but that in itself would have been shameful. The paterfamilias, so often portrayed by modern historians as a source of grief for his imposed-on children, had in reality few places to turn. No one was more vulnerable than a father to his children.

The great contrast between this overburdening sense of frustration in his relations with Thomas was John's real love and affection for his wife, Joan, still struggling with their affairs in the wilds of Shropshire. 'I have sent you a keg of sturgeon and vinegar and Rhenish wine', he wrote to her on 26 July 1601

And ever live to love thee more and more, I protest I now only desire to live and be with thee. And so good Pug farewell and God bless you and all my children, and send me peace, with all the world
    Your ever loving husband during life
    John Thynne.[59]

Soon after this, perhaps in early August, the judge examined Thomas Thynne on oath again and in private, when he 'confessed the marriage'. The judge then pronounced it valid, the Mervyns the victors and John Thynne defeated. Sir James Mervyn, meeting the judge at a court gathering a little later, 'told him that in regard of his kind and judicial dealing in that cause, that if he could find any reason to go from the Court, that he should come to me [at Fonthill] and kill a buck, and that from henceforth I would be his guide to Longleat'.[60] That was the victorious fixer talking, the courteous and high-status reward – only grandees with parks could offer the killing of a deer as an entertainment – to a public servant who had done the right thing by them.

Usually in this sort of story, that is where it ends: the court case is over and the documentation disappears. Not here, though, because in September 1601 a correspondence opened between Thomas Thynne's newly acknowledged wife, Maria, and his mother, Joan. These are letters between Romeo's mother and an unwelcome Juliet. Both sides of the correspondence are preserved in the archives at Longleat and almost nothing in sixteenth-century letters reveals quite so clearly the multiple tensions between generations, between women of subtly different classes, between conformity and individuality, and between the dignity of the self and the requirements of family order.

The first letter that survives from Maria to her mother-in-law is in convoluted and Latinate sentences which read as if they were being spoken from the lowest possible of ground-scraping bows. Maria had written to Joan before (in a letter that has not survived) but had received no answer. Why was that? Was she suspected of duplicity, of not telling her mother-in-law the truth of what she felt? Her manner now was pure obeisance, but the bow was somehow complicated. Her tone implied both family inferiority – a daughter to a mother – and moral equality. She felt no grounds for shame. In fact, she felt so little shame that a sense of irony hangs in curtains around her words. Could the proud, court-holding, seductive and beautiful Maria, maid of honour to the Queen herself, have meant to abase herself quite so much to the daughter of a City merchant, whose title to her lands in Shropshire was suspect, who may have been her mother-in-law but had little else in her favour?

If I dyd knowe that my thoughtes had ever intertayned any unreuerent conseyte of you (my (good mother) I shoulde be much ashamed so Impudintlye to Importune yr good oppinion as I haue done by manye intreatinge lynes, but haveinge binne euer Imboldened wth the knowledg of my unspotted Innocencye, I coulde not be so great an enimye to my owne hapynes, as to wante [i.e. lack] yr fauor for wante of desyeringe ytt.[61]

Thick with educated paradoxes, this is a form of supplication which is more than halfway to an insult. Its tone might have been calculated to receive no answer. It was Mervyn-speak, driven by rivalry and ambition, and in signing and sealing it, Maria slapped down another pair of challenges. She ended the letter with the phrase 'Yr *very* loueng and obedyent daughter Marya Thine'. That encapsulated the whole point: the fact that she had plotted to call herself 'Maria Thynne' was the essence of her disobedience. Then, as a final flourish, she enclosed what is either a lock of her red hair, or a now frayed silk ribbon, fixed to the paper with sealing wax, into which she pressed the ancient and noble cross-hatching of the Audley coat of arms. Every one of these signals was made to have its effect: Maria had stolen the son; she had little interest in obeying Joan Thynne; she was glamorous and sexy as Joan could no longer hope to be; and she was the daughter of a peer – one of only sixty titled men in England, a social universe away from the grubby deal-making and warehouses of Joan's own commercial family.

No answer was forthcoming from the older Mrs Thynne, even though further letters were sent to her at Caus in Shropshire. Maria was living with her own mother Lucy at the Audley manor of Stalbridge in Dorset. The following summer in June 1602, Maria asked her mother to write imploringly to Joan Thynne. All kinds of hazards hung around this letter too: not only had Lucy Audley arranged the kidnapping of Joan's treasured son; she was the first deep love of Joan's husband, John, who had given her up only when threatened with disinheritance. Lucy Audley met all of this face on: 'Notwithstanding the doubt long since conceived how any letters of mine might find a grateful acceptation of yourself (many reasons inducing a distrust) …'[62] She spared no eloquence and even through the fog of complexity and Latinity, the idea emerges that Lucy Audley wanted in her heart to see these families united.

> Good Mrs Thynne, let me not be wronged in these lines by a hard construction, for I protest that servile fear and base flattery my heart is not acquainted withal. If I desire your love or seek to embrace your friendship (as unfeignedly in all truth I do and wished it long since) believe it to proceed from such a mind as willingly makes offer of the owner for performance of the friendliest effect that her kindness and ability may discharge.[63]

This was stiff and awkward, a halting statement of love and warmth, which scarcely survives the frost of formality and distance. But the reason is not far to seek: Lucy Audley was trying proclaim her affection and honesty from a history which spoke only of deceit and exploitation.

> Lastly since your son is mine, and so beloved as my dearest own, let me obtain this request, my daughter may be yours, but accordingly as to her merits.[64]

Could you believe her? Perhaps you could, if you read only her imploring words. Maybe not, if you knew both what had come before and where her interests lay. It was entirely within the Thynnes' power either to acknowledge the validity of the Thomas–Maria marriage or to disinherit him. There were plenty of other sons. Only if Joan and John Thynne accepted Maria as a full member of their family could Lucy Audley and Sir James Mervyn be sure that their plot had worked and that the Mervyns had established their beachhead in Thynne territory. All kinds of access to power would stem from that connection and in pre-modern societies access to power meant access to wealth and wellbeing. No one had any conception of what a gene was in 1602, but here these people were acting to genetic dictates. The individuals writing these letters would scarcely benefit or suffer from these arrangements, however they turned out. Even if the language they used was of honour and honesty, of proclaimed integrity and persistent doubt, it was the genes themselves that were struggling for victory.

Still nothing from Joan. Thomas went to visit her and still she resisted. Maria wrote again into the silence: 'All that I desire is but to be blessed with your better conceit'[65] – a better conception of who she was as a person. But then, at the end of July 1602, Maria tired of her wooing of the mother.

I am determined henceforth to cease troubling you, believing that my letters do but urge the memory of one who is nothing pleasing unto you, but yet not despairing in God's goodness, I will betake me to my prayers to Him, with this hope, that He who hath wrought some as great miracles as this, will in time incline your heart to pity and pardon your son, and me for his sake.[66]

Still nothing, but then, months later, out of the blue, Joan wrote to Lucy Audley, Maria's mother. Her letter is the central document in this story, fusing a powerful consciousness of rank with 'discomforting grief'[67] at her betrayal, all the while taking refuge in her own individual pride. 'I confess your daughter's birth far above my son's deserts or degree,' she began, 'but since you were pleased not to scorn my son to be yours, methinks you should not have scorned to have acknowledged me to be his mother.' There was a dignity that went beyond rank. The rights and privileges of rank did not allow the mistreatment of an individual. This was a question not of the law but of the honourable regard for the humanity of others. Lucy Audley had accused her of feeding her husband's mind with slanderous tales about the Audleys and Joan replied to that accusation with the same mixture of acute social consciousness and an irreducible sense of her own moral position.

Now for Mr Thynne's calling of your honour in question, I cannot deny but I have heard it, but that myself was either author or demonstrator of any such reports I utterly deny. I am not so ready to wrong inferior persons, much less an honourable Lady of your place and reputation, and so conceive of me for so you shall ever find me.[68]

Joan Thynne placed these two codes – social hierarchy and the rules of dealing well with other individuals – face to face. She believed in both but recognized that they did not always acknowledge the value in the other. Thomas had broken one code in favour of the other: 'He hath hazarded for your love, and yours, the loss of theirs that he was born to honour perpetually.' It was a gamble he had lost. 'But this I confess,' she went on, 'I have more reason to respect your honour than your friendship towards me.' Lady Audley was her acknowledged social superior but there was no trusting her goodness.

For two years the situation remained unchanged. Joan repeatedly refused to engage with Maria or Thomas. Maria repeatedly wrote asking her for love. Joan was confined to her remote and difficult, windy and leaky castle at Caus in Shropshire; Maria was pining away either at Fonthill or in the beautiful timber-framed Mervyn manor house at Compton Bassett in the thick-cream-and-butter country of north Wiltshire.

Something of these geographical differences emerged in the letters. Maria, the daughter of a baron, was, despite her proclaimed grief over Joan's indifference, luxuriating in the lap of her father's and grandfather's various manors, distributed across England's richest and most luxurious county. Joan Thynne meanwhile was a little desperately defending and maintaining her remote property against rival claimants to it.[69] Her husband was busy in London; these Shropshire lands were part of the dowry she had brought to the marriage, and so it fell to her to defend and maintain them. Not that he was indifferent to their wellbeing. Joan was struggling to get the farm accounts in good order for her husband's approval; she found that no one in Shropshire would sell beef or sheep to her at reasonable prices and so asked for some 'very forward in fat'[70] to be sent over from Wiltshire; corn and malt were equally pricy; malt and hops had to come from Wiltshire;[71] she asked for salad oil and sturgeon from London;[72] lute strings and copper wires for the virginals were posted to her along with 'cambric thread, silver and spangles' or sequins.[73]

She worried from her distance that her husband, whom she scarcely ever saw from one month to the next, was not well. His eyes were troubling him. She sent him 'physic' for them along with her letters.

> I hope you will have more care of yourself for the good of me and your poor children, humbly desiring you above all things to have respect unto your health, and not to defer the time of taking physic, and let your greatest care be for the preservation of your health, in whose welldoing consist my only joy and comfort. And therefore sweet Mr Thynne, if you love or make account of me have a special regard of it.[74]

Nearly every other letter in this correspondence, or at least those that have been preserved, was to some extent in public. But Joan's letters to her husband had the affection and directness of intimate conversation. She hardly ever heard from him, let alone saw him, but struggled to maintain her world alone. The woman Maria imagined her to be was scarcely connected with the woman these loving, careful, generous-hearted letters revealed.

Then came the catastrophe which Maria, Thomas, Lucy Audley and the Mervyns had all been waiting for and which Joan Thynne had been dreading: on 21 November 1604, John Thynne died. Thomas had not been disinherited and so he and Maria took possession of Longleat, the heart of the Thynne estates. Thomas himself seems to have remained in London, leaving Maria in Wiltshire but not apparently trusting her to run his affairs at Longleat. This lack of respect for a woman's ability to run an estate, as his mother was doing so competently in the wilds of Shropshire, produced an excoriating letter from Maria. She was still at one of her father's houses, not allowed yet to be mistress of the Thynne properties: 'Well Mr Thynne, believe I am both sorry and ashamed that any creature should see that you hold such a contempt of my poor wits, that being your wife, you should not think me of discretion to order your affairs in your absence.'[75] It was, she said, her right to 'be mistress there' – at Longleat – but if he wanted to leave her 'like an innocent fool here [in her father's house], I will the more contentedly bear the disgrace.' It is the angriest letter in the collection, which she signed, furiously, 'Your loving wife howsoever, Maria Thynne'.[76]

He soft-soaped her (but his letters don't survive) and allowed her to take charge at Longleat. Mervyn servants were brought in and old Thynne servants sidelined. She became as she told him 'a careful officer' in his absence. His letters from London flirted with her and 'made her modest blood flush up into [her] bashful cheek'[77] so that she wrote back to him as her 'best and sweetest Thomken, and many thousand times more than these 1000 000 000 000 000 000 000 000 000 for thy kind and wanton letters Thine and only thine Maria'.[78] She managed all the men and the complexities of rent and tenancies at Longleat with aplomb. They were happy, in possession of his inheritance, with her now settled in the chatelaine's saddle.

From that position Maria could abandon the mask of deference. Her mother-in-law, silently or not, had abused her for so long. Now, as the next generation in possession, her loathing and contempt could be allowed to emerge. In a letter that is undated but was probably written not long after Maria's and Thomas's arrival at Longleat, the young woman in the comfort of Wiltshire wrote to the old woman in despair and isolation in Shropshire. They were openly at war, engaged on a bitter lawsuit over the Thynne estates and possessions. 'yf you or yr heyers haue an exspectation in revertion of Longleate howse or garden,' Maria told Joan, she might as well give up. 'The case beinge as ytt ys, meethinkes you Should not vnkindlye intermedle, more then mr Thynne doth wth all yr lande of inherytance' – a phrase meaning those lands Shropshire which Joan had brought to her marriage as a dowry and now formed her own sustenance or jointure.[79]

As she went on, Maria warmed to her task:

I confes (w*th*owt Sham) ytt ys true my garden ys to ruinous, & yett to make you more merrye ~~I wyll make~~ you shall be of my Cowncell, that my intente ys before ytt be better, to make ytt worse; for findinge that greate exspence Coulde never alter ytt from being lyke a poridg pote, nor never by reporte was lyke other I intend to plowe ytt up & Sowe all varitye of frute att a fytt Seazon, I beseech you laughe, & So wyll I att y*r* Captiousnes.[80]

Joan may have been captious and intent on finding fault but this is as bitter as a perry pear. For a class whose identity was bound so closely to the nature of land and to the shaping and moulding of that land, it would be difficult to find a more explicit form of hate. It is the voice of victory. The previous generation may have done its best to make the land around the house at Longleat into an elegant garden but it had failed and Maria now was planning to erase everything Joan and John had done. Often enough you see in old English houses a new wing added, a garden transformed or an old one demolished; how rarely, though, can you see through a window like this to the vengeance and rage which lay behind the change.

In her anger, and not immediately intelligibly, Maria went on at Joan in language deliberately vile:

now wheras you wryghte y*r* grownd putt to Bassest vses ys better ~~then~~ manurde then my garden, Surelye yf ytt wer a gandmoother [*sic*] of my owne ~~Should~~ & equall to my Selfe by bearth, I Should answare that oddious Comparison w*th* tellinge you I beleeve So Corpulent a La: Can*n*ot butt doo much y*r* selfe towards the Soyllinge of lande, & I thinke that hath binn, & wyll be all the good you intend to leaue behinde you att Corslye.[81]

What does this clotted set of insults actually mean? Joan had clearly said in a letter now lost that she was managing her lands in Shropshire better than Maria was capable of doing at Longleat. Even Joan's roughest ground was more richly fertilized, she had said, than Maria's best garden. Maria turned dirty in response: first reminding Joan quite how old she was, 'a grandmother', when in fact she was in her mid-forties and only twenty years older than Maria; then emphasizing her own noble and Joan's mercantile origins ('equal to myself in birth'); then telling her how fat she was ('so corpulent a Lady') and then implying, in a brutal and brilliant image of scatological contempt, that, given her size, Joan would clearly be effective at manuring the land herself ('cannot but do much towards the soiling of land').[82]

The site chosen by Maria for this performance was the beautiful stone manor house at Corsley, three miles from Longleat. It and the lands around it formed the Thynnes' dower manor, set aside for the use of the widow of the previous head of the family. Maria was imagining a future in which her vulgar, old, fat, widowed mother-in-law was ensconced at Corsley, squatting on the pastures for the good of the ground. It is as cruel an image as anything in these gentry stories, of a broken woman whose life was good for nothing but some droppings on her dead husband's ancestral lands.

That takes some coming back from, but as time went by, Joan attempted to mend the breach. She arranged for a marriage of one of Thomas's sisters to a Mr Whitney, who was remotely connected with the Audleys, 'a gentleman of a very ancient and worshipful house, and an aliesman [a relative, allied by kinship] to your Lady'.[83] If the marriage came off, she told Thomas, 'it might renew a mutual love in every side to the comfort of many and besides his estate so great and his proffers so reasonable and well.'[84] The old sense of class anxiety is never absent:

I credibly understand that all the lands whereof Mr Whitney is now seised was Whitney's lands before the conquest of England; and that ever sithence it hath and doth continue in the name and blood of the Whitneys, but although himself be but an esquire, yet there were eighteen knights of his name before the Conquest which were lords and owners of the same lands which are now his.[85]

That can only have been received at Longleat with derision. Quite consistently Thomas Thynne refused to release lands or money for his sisters' dowries, even though he had previously agreed to give them £1,000 each, engaging in endless correspondence with his mother on the subject and no doubt encouraged in his meanness towards them by his wife. Although Thomas was a Member of Parliament and had been knighted in 1603 in the great rush of honours that accompanied James I's arrival on the throne, the romantic young man had by now turned into a slightly weak thirty-year-old. Maria's family had him where they wanted him, telling him how to manage his timber in the park at Longleat[86] and selling him their neighbouring manor of Warminster for a sum (£3,650) and on terms – the full amount payable within the year – which as Thynne said was 'so unreasonably high a rate as no man would come near it'.[87] The Mervyn–Audley gang were cashing in on the trick they had played so many years before at the Bell in Beaconsfield.

Maria's mother, Lucy Audley, wrote her a letter about the deal in phrases which stink even 400 years later: 'Well Mall', she began, using the family nickname for her daughter,

> I am exceeding glad that the iron is stricken being hot, for there is a time for all things, and sorry should I have been in both your behalfs, if it had now been omitted; and truth is I know it so great a grace to Longleat as if another had enjoyed it I should have rained tears upon Warminster whenever I had looked upon it. I was more confident that you would have dealt in it, as supposing that you know me a loving mother, and not a cunning shifter, to put a trick upon my son Thynne and yourself for serving any turn, and the truth is enough on that.[88]

The precise meaning of that last sentence may be a little clouded, but the intended import and the subtext are both radiantly clear: Would I ever cheat you, my darling girl, or your lovely husband? I only have your and Longleat's best interests at heart. And underneath that, the inadvertently conveyed message: I am indeed a cunning shifter, which is why you are where you are, and I am now squeezing money out of you and Thomas in the way that I have always done to others.

And the fate of these families?

The Mervyns soon disappeared from history entirely. It was important to Sir James, the architect of much of the grief in this story, as to many gentry families, that his land and name should remain attached. He had no sons but he got round that by ensuring that his granddaughter Christine, Maria's younger sister, was married to her cousin Sir Henry Mervyn. Connected to her by both genes and name, Sir James could leave her his beautiful Fonthill estate and other manors elsewhere in Wiltshire. But he was thwarted. As soon as Sir James died, Sir Henry starting selling off the inheritance, a large chunk of it including Fonthill to Christine's brother Mervyn Touchet, Lord Audley and Earl of Castlehaven. In him the lunacy of the Touchets flowered expansively and he was beheaded in 1631 for sodomizing his servants and participating in the rape by those servants of both his wife and his twelve-year-old stepdaughter.[89] After this hiccup, things were soon restored to something approaching normality and that family also persisted, if on a declining path, selling off Compton Bassett in the 1660s, until the last and 25th Lord Audley died in 1997. Fonthill ended up in the hands of the Beckfords and became the site of the eighteenth century's most extravagant folly. In none of the Audleys did any attachment to Wiltshire land remain.

The Thynnes are one of the great success stories of the English gentry. Like the Cavendishes, the Spencers and the Cecils, the family escaped the vulnerabilities of a gentry existence and entered the realms of the higher – and richer – aristocracy. Longleat became the headquarters of an enormous and ever-growing estate, comprising thousands of acres in addition to the Shropshire lands brought to them by Joan Hayward and the Wiltshire manors they had bought from the Audleys. As Barons, Viscounts and finally Marquesses of Bath they persisted across the centuries in a way that few gentry families have ever managed.[90]

One of the ironies of this encounter between Mervyn greed and Thynne gullibility is that the Thynnes were the victors. But that is not the salient point: the key aspect of this story is the way in which its women – Lucy Audley, Joan Thynne and Maria Touchet – are its principal players. The entire dynamic of the three families is inexplicable without their sense of honour, ambition, propriety and threat. They are not merely – as women at this stage are so often portrayed – the default administrators of estates when their men are away. They are the setters, creators and maintainers of the family cultures which governed the internal relationships of the class. They are subtle and powerful, passionate and impassioned. No child could have been uninfluenced by these women, their mothers and their wives, and no history of the gentry can make sense without them.

PART III

The Great Century
1610–1710

The seventeenth century was the heartland of gentry culture. The sense of looming threat from grandees or the crown, or from people not admitted to the gentry's own charmed circle, was – at least outside the great crisis of the 1640s and '50s – surprisingly and wonderfully absent from their lives. England was constitutional and their own place in that constitution as Members of Parliament, Justices of the Peace and sheriffs of their counties, upholders of what seemed like an ancient tradition, was deeply self-confirming. Their letters and journals, the houses they built, the landscapes they created and the portraits they had painted all exude an atmosphere of arrival, of this being the great century in which to have been alive.

Many of the gentry were obsessively retrospective and this was one of the glory periods for false genealogies. The Cecils at Hatfield (Welsh sheep men in 1500) had a beautiful, illustrated pedigree drawn up that traced them back to Jesus and from there to Noah and Adam. But the time glittered with the kaleidoscope of modernity, a world we would all begin to recognize: fast food in London streets; shopping centres; newspapers; town squares; terraced houses; suburban villas; experimental science; botany; archaeology; the Stock Exchange; commercially available finance; mortgages; wood screws; microscopes and telescopes; the country house as a centre of culture and art; a professional navy; a private but coherent postal system; most of the hedged landscape; floated meadows; estate maps; landscape paintings; a national market in agricultural products and the end of self-sufficiency; a consciousness of England as the emporium of the world; the pervasive presence, at least in gentry houses, of global commodities, especially sugar; garden exotics (tulips, Persian fritillaries); the empire – Ireland as a trial run, the West Indies, Virginia, the Carolinas; eventually a constitutional monarchy; political parties; and liberty as the essence of Englishness.

'Felicity' was the word Edward Hyde, Lord Clarendon, the great Royalist politician-historian, used to describe this moment, when

> this Kingdom, and all his Majesty's Dominions enjoy'd the greatest Calm, and the fullest measure of Felicity, that any People in any Age, for so long time together, have been bless'd with; to the wonder and envy of all the other parts *of Christendom.*[1]

But this was no effortless glide into a pre-chewed future. It was not as if the usual constraints on existence were somehow suspended: the demands of family life, the inadequacy of pre-modern medicine, the unkindness of others. These, needless to say, impinged on all lives. Added to them was the larger context of ferocious political and religious argument, which coloured the entire century. England underwent two revolutions, two civil wars, and had two kings deposed. Right in the middle of the century it became a republic for the only time in its history, run by a politburo of military-religious men, with an all-pervasive informer network. Individuals lived in fear and private diaries from the time were slashed and razored by their authors to cut out any incriminating passages. That experience explains much of the following century, characterized by a hunger not for the fierce statement of metaphysical truths but for a kind of easy civility in which order and freedom could sit side by side.

The Civil War of the seventeenth century was fought by the gentry against the gentry. On one side were those who felt a conservative if at times reluctant loyalty to the king; on the other those who felt that the autocratic manner of the King's government and its quasi-Catholic beliefs had betrayed them and the country which they owned and of which they were the bedrock. It was a war between the gentry's belief in inherited order and its belief in its own significance as a governing class.

That war and its causes have loomed large in all modern discussions of the gentry. The brilliant and vituperative academic debate between a group of largely Oxford historians in the mid-twentieth century left the gentry itself a bruised battlefield, littered with the corpses of competing theories. Every one of those theories was hamstrung by the difficulty of identifying watertight socioeconomic groups which could be seen to be acting in singular and coherent ways. Any examined group tended to fragment into its individuals and to blur all possible definitions. In the aftermath of 'The Storm over the Gentry', historians have retreated from large-scale theorizing towards closer descriptions of individual families, the net of allegiances in the gentry world, the county communities, and the non-ideological and self-protective nature of much of gentry life. That is certainly the picture that emerges from the families which carry the seventeenth-century story here: one family, the Oxindens, spread across many social layers; another, the Oglanders, strongly constitutionalist but reluctantly needing to support the King; another, the le Neves, divided between its urban-mercantile connections and its rural-Tory inclinations; some, the Hobarts, Puritan-Parliamentary, in pursuit of power; others, the Gawdys, disengaged from the questions of politics, pursuing bluntly conservative lives.

It is certainly possible to be sidetracked by the glamour and tragedy of that war. Much of gentry life continued past and through it largely as if it had not happened. At the end of it, and at the Restoration of the crown in 1660, the gentry as a group were in pretty much the same economic and political position as they had been before, owning the same proportion of the country and as deeply engaged in parliamentary government as they had been a hundred years earlier. The revolution of 1688, when they expelled the last Stuart, a despised Roman Catholic, and brought in a satisfactorily Protestant Dutchman,

William III, seemed like the apogee of their power. Government would be constitutional and the landowning class would control it.

But this triumph contained the seeds of its own decline. The end of the seventeenth century was difficult. The weather, which had also been atrocious in the 1640s, entered a bleak spell in the 1690s with a series of pitiably poor, starvation harvests. Revenues and rents from land began to be depressed. The growth in population slowed. On top of that, the new government that had come in with the Dutch William III was now militarizing fast. Between 1689 and 1714, the Royal Navy became the biggest in Europe. In 1692 a land tax was imposed at four shillings in the pound, a 20 per cent tax on gentry incomes. A government which had looked as if would be the embodiment of landholding England became instead the government of a combination of the Whig aristocrats, the commercial interests of the City of London and its growing Atlantic empire.

In the century to come, which would belong to the merchants and the great Whig oligarchs, the nature of the gentry began to divide into an old Tory world view and a new Whig one. If there is a hinge in gentry history, this is it. The Tory squires of the 1690s belonged to a world that was palpably continuous with the thought patterns of Sir William Plumpton and the old Throckmortons. After them, gentry culture conceived of itself, at least in part, as something that was out of kilter with modernity. That was one of the things the duel between Oliver le Neve and Sir Henry Hobart on Cawston Heath was about.

The squire was starting to become yesterday's story. His belief in inherited virtue, in the whole idea of transmission from a semi-feudal past, was looking fragile in the face of the new ideas of educated virtue, of virtue to be acquired not by inheritance but by learning and good behaviour. 'A man of polite imagination', Joseph Addison wrote in the *Spectator*, enjoyed 'a kind of property in everything he sees.'[2] That is not what the landowners of Norfolk would have thought. They knew all about property but, for these voluble and scarcely polished squires, learning was something of a foreign country. It is true that Oliver le Neve owned a copy of John Locke's *Essay Concerning Human Understanding*, but it was a rare flower amidst a bookshelf filled with *Peppa – A Novel, Muse's Farewell to Popery, Britain's Glory, Ladies' Travels into Spain* and *The New Art of Brewing.*

The squire was becoming a slightly laughable figure. The man of honour was slipping into the lovable, old-fashioned, uneducated Tory, who could not quite keep up with the badinage of the coffee house or the London club and who remained happily unaware that everyone around him was laughing at his accent, his clothes, his wig, his ideas, his whole marinaded, antiquated roast-beef self and his obsession with hunting and shooting.

Why so much about hunting? In part, it was inherited behaviour. The hunt was gentry communality, jointness, what they did, who they were, the sort of thing they had always been. As that, it was also an act of dominance, of lordliness, ownership, nostalgia, control and removal from the world of an earned living. It was a form of play-warfare in which the enemy was absent. It was also a stimulus to the blood, a source of adrenaline, the seventeenth-century substitute for a skiing holiday, an escape from the house, from the wifely 'bridle' – a term le Neve's friends use – and the stir-craziness of being too long at home. 'I am longing much for a little libberty,' Sir Bassingbourne Gawdy confided to his brother-in-law le Neve in February 1698, when his father had been ill, 'for I have bin A Prisoner this thre weeks or more.'[3]

I wonder if there wasn't something else in play here too. These Tory squires, knowingly or not, were on a downward trend. The focus of value in England was moving away from land and land ownership towards an increasingly dynamic and urban market. The last decade in which any part of England remained self-sufficient and did not grow crops for sale, or derive its food from elsewhere, was the 1680s. The medieval vision of integrated, rural communities, each a 'little commonwealth' as the great Jacobean surveyor John Norden had called a manor, was now over.[4] Throughout the seventeenth century rural rents had been dropping; London property was increasingly valuable.

But the world of hunting was the squire's province. You could dragoon and whip a pack of beagles in a way that the electors of

Norfolk would never allow. You could live a fantasy life when out with your friends all day on horseback in a kind of toy theatre and as a nostalgic dream of significance. When your credit (financial or otherwise) was looking thin or your tenants found it difficult to pay their rents, it may have been the only consolation there was.

Steadiness

The Oglanders

Nunwell, Isle of Wight

Sir John Oglander was in love with his own life: with his vision of the past and his long line of ancestors stretching back into it; with his own role as the guardian of his family's wellbeing in the troubled seventeenth century and on into 'futor Adges'; and with Nunwell, the Oglander house and lands at the eastern end of the Isle of Wight, the matrix of his being, to whose health and happiness he dedicated year after year.

His deep attachment to Nunwell and the Isle of Wight is intriguing because although he was born here in 1585, the family left in 1588, after his mother had been frightened by the sight of the Spanish Armada sailing up the Channel.[1] They kept the property but went to live on the mainland, settling on land they owned in Sussex. Only in 1609, when his father died and John was twenty-four, did he return to the Isle of Wight. This late return to a place John Oglander thought of as home may be at the root of his passionate attachment to Nunwell.

He is more knowable than anyone in these stories, largely because of his extraordinary notebooks, his 'Bookes of Accoumpts', the surviving leather-bound volumes written between 1620 and 1648, which have been treasured by the Oglander family ever since.[2]

At heart they are no more than a steady calculation, quarter by quarter, of what he spent and what he owed, what he lent and what was owed to him, what income he could expect and what, in total, he was worth. But he was too active and too curious to stick merely to figures and over the years the notebooks gradually filled with all the multifarious contents of his mind. The result was a real-time depiction of a man's life and priorities, a portrait of a member of the seventeenth-century gentry alive in that moment, jumping from one subject to another, from one pre-occupation to the next, from memories to plans, regrets to delights, enemies to friends, events to principles.

Page after page reveals him as a man buoyed up with love for his wife, Frances, always called Franck, the daughter of a Surrey gent, and their children. He was a deep conservative with a powerful sense of duty, a man who loved the gentry (or at least the idea of them more than the individuals he knew) and loathed the aristocracy for their self-indulgence, a near-Puritan Royalist with a flickering, scatterbox, magpie-ish way of thinking, entranced by the past (he was an amateur archaeologist), loving continuity but dreading mutability, fascinated by himself, and all this sewn in among his calculations of profit and loss.

It was, at its simplest level, a world held to account.[3] To take one year at random, before Christmas, John Curtis, Oglander's butler, was paid fifteen shillings and sixpence for goods he had bought on his master's behalf. Labourers, carpenters and sawyers all received their wages. Oglander had bought ten pounds of 'Malligoe raisins' for Christmas, the fruit perhaps shipped in from Malaga, a sign of the Isle of Wight's multiple connections to the wider world. His hop garden at Sandham, now Sandown, on the east coast of the island, was dug and his ancestors' tombs in the church at Brading, just the other side of his park, were mended. His son Richard, who was a mercer in Pater Noster Row next to St Paul's in London, had sent him some paper, some medicine and 'this Booke' in which the accounts were being written, for all of which John had paid him twelve shillings.

The getting and spending carries on, into January, with presents at New Year for his wife, daughters and nieces and charity for the poor, dinners in Newport, some new locks and the staves and hoops with which his men could make some barrels. There were repairs to his horse harness, and he dispersed money for French wine (although he did not like it very much), for a barrel of butter to be sent to Richard in London, for a messenger to take £5 to his son John who was a don in Oxford, and for quite a lot of cheese, meat and fish.

There was a large staff at Nunwell (their attic bedrooms are still there, good, well-lit, habitable rooms, looking out on the chalk downs to the south or the ancient, warty oaks on the other side). As well as John Curtis, the butler (his wages were £4 a year), there was a coach-man called William (paid the same), a bailiff called Baby, the shep-herd Henry Reade (£5, the same as the cost of a coach to London[4]), three other men, called John Deal, Thomas and Ralfe, two chamber-maids, a 'cook maid' and an undercook maid, and a 'milke mayde and wash mayd', called in the accounts 'the 2 Janes', who were paid £2 10s. each for their year's work.

In all, the Nunwell wage bill for these thirteen people came to £40 a year, an amount of money vertiginously smaller than what Oglander gave his eldest son, William, who received an annual allowance of £160. Every year Sir John also gave his beloved wife, Franck, £40 and his unmarried daughter, Bridget, £30. Each year the Oglanders spent nearly £700 on themselves, or about £180 for each dependent member of the family, something approaching sixty times the average annual income of their servants and employees. There can be no doubt that Nunwell was a kind of community but one in which the social differ-ence between members was extreme.

The Oglanders did not want for anything. 'Suckinge pigges', a pound or two lost at cards, prawns and lobsters, herrings, bass and soles, salmon and mullet, 'a Hollan chese', 'tulip roots', 'ffrench wyne', 'Pamflett bookes of newes', payments to a man called Crocker for 'the Image' and 'ye making of ye statue'[5] – for about £11 he was designing and then carving the wooden effigies of Oglander, his father and his son George for their chapel in Brading church: the expenses were unending. For the whole year, Oglander spent £668 5s. 11d.

Looking at the total, he reflected as usual on just how much the gentry life was costing him: 'I confes I must Come to a Lower rate or else my smale ffortunes will not holde owt.'[6] The income to pay for it all – despite his anxieties, revenues usually hovered around £800 a year – came largely from the rents of farms which the Oglanders owned, many of them recently bought. Sir John worked 120 acres directly with his own employed labour but about 2,000 acres were let out, including valuable grazing land on the marsh beyond Brading and land in Hampshire. Those farm rents were topped up with the rent from a windmill and a watermill, with the rents from houses and cottages, the death duty or 'heriot' – usually the value of their best beast – payable on the death of a customary tenant, the sale of timber (mostly oak at £2 a tree, but some elm), spiles and faggots from the coppice wood (at £4 15s. the acre) and 'wyndfalls' from other trees, the wheat, barley, peas and oats he had grown and stored himself, the fat lambs from his flock of some five hundred ewes, the herd of 'ffattinge Cattell' he bought in as heifers and steers to grow on, as well as small quantities of his own hops, butter, cream, straw, hay and geese.[7]

It was a variegated system. 'Keep howsbandri and grownde enough to finde thy house,'[8] he told his descendants, using 'finde' to mean 'provision'. The household at Nunwell produced its own beer, bread, beef, mutton, butter, cheese, bacon, pork, rabbits and pigeons,[9] as well as veals, wheat, wood and 'rent capons', chickens which formed part of the rent on some of his leases. He kept 'all sorts of powltery with Convenient howses for them' as well as bees, from whose honey they made mead, 'which with a Hogshed of strong beare or 2 and a Runlett of Sacke will serve the without ffrench wyne'. Every year the Nunwell staff made 'a Hogshead or 2 of sydor and a barrel of verges', a bitter, vinegary juice made with crab apples. Partly for this reason, Oglander advised planting apples and crabs in every new hedge they made, mixed in with the quickthorn. The Nunwell girls made their own candles with 'cottonweeke' – wicks bought in London. If a new plough was required, the timber was cut, seasoned and 'hewed' at Nunwell. Most of the hauling and the ploughing on the lighter land were done by oxen which Oglander bred himself.

At the centre of this complex, interlocking mechanism, tucked under the downs and sheltered by them from the raw south-westerlies coming in off the Channel, was the house at Nunwell itself.

Before 1609, the family had been living away on their lands in Sussex. On his father's death the young John Oglander returned to the family's ancient estate at Nunwell to find it in a decrepit condition. He kept hold of the Sussex land but rebuilt much of Nunwell in brick and the local Bembridge limestone, with a handsome hall and parlour, with plastered ceilings and chambers over them, heated by simple, efficient stone fireplaces, the rooms lined in oak wainscot, and with a beautiful oak staircase, its treads now a pale, worn, long-washed grey.

It was not the richest of houses – several tons of wheat, peas or barley were habitually stored in the dry of the dining room,[10] the tobacco in the damp of the cellar beneath[11] – but far from the meanest. John Oglander had two wainscoted studies, one on the ground floor, one above the dining room, and his beloved wife, Franck, had her own closet or study which was plastered and hung with tapestries.[12] It was a profoundly loved place, furnished with heavy, oak, melon-legged tables and tall-backed chairs, where Oglander could entertain his neighbours and accommodate his friends, nothing showy but comfortable and graceful. The house was a vessel for hospitality. 'I always kept a good house, not much inferior to any in the Island', he consoled himself in the misery of his old age. 'I could never have donn itt without a most carefull thrivinge wyfe, whoe was upp before mee every daye and … woold not trust her mayd with directions, but woold wett her shooe to see itt all her selfe acted.'[13]

Around the house he had stables, a brewhouse, a malthouse and a bakehouse (with warm rooms above), fishponds, a twelve-acre rabbit warren[14] and a vegetable garden, a bowling green and several barns, a chalk pit from which the chalk was spread on the arable fields (to no great effect) and a marl pit (which did more good.) He bred pheasants and partridges in an area that was fenced off with 'pales'. He was not such a keen shot as his father, who had liked wildfowling on the marsh, but he enjoyed hawking with a goshawk or lanard in the summer. 'I have been so foolisch as to bestowe more monyes then a wyse man woold have done', he told his notebook, 'in fflowers for ye Garden. It wase my Content, wearyed with studdye, to solace my selve in ye Garden and to see the spoourtes of natur how in every Several species she sheweth her workemanshipp.'[15]

Above all he loved his orchards, which he planted and replanted himself, adding as a side note at the corner of one page: 'When my successors hereaftor reape ye ffrwyte of my labours, remember the ffounder.'[16]

In his own mind, he was never absent from his descendants' thoughts, just as his own ancestors, who as minor gentry had certainly been at Nunwell since the twelfth century, were never absent from his.

This near self-sufficiency gave Oglander the independence he valued but it was also more than that. The interfolding of people, land, animals, food, housing and hospitality was in itself a model of the gentry's idea of goodness. It was the oldest of systems, civilization attached to a particular place, a form of organizing the land which was also a way of organizing society, an interlocked complexity, which was intended to be both stable and long lived and to lie at the root of the honourable, just and hospitable life.

This unabashed continuousness coloured every aspect of his mind. There is no higher praise in his lexicon than the word 'husband', not in its narrowed modern sense of a man married to a woman, but in the larger sense of a man who knows how to tend, over time and cumulatively, to the wellbeing of those people, creatures and things which are in his care. 'Ye family of ye Oglanders hath always bene good howsbandes', he wrote in May 1620[17] and in his evaluation of his neighbours their ability to husband their resources was always the touchstone by which he judged their worth. His account books themselves are dedicated to that end: they are evidence of the careful monitoring of household, land, stock, money, possessions, family and above all self which lies at the heart of husbandry.

When, near the end of his life, Oglander addressed his descendants, his 'Good rules in husbandri'[18] began by plunging into the realities of Nunwell life: 'If ever you have a horse sicke and swell in his Bodie, presently [i.e. immediately] gett one to Rake him by thrustinge his arme unto his fundament and by giving him soomwhat to make him Purge.'[19] He was deep down in the belly of the country – 'hate London as to live there',[20] he told his ghostly audience, not as an opinion but an instruction – and in the way he wrote you can hear his Isle of Wight accent and manner. Barns, fields and trees were all 'him' and 'he', 'fallow' fields were 'vallow' and ferny grounds 'vearnie growndes'. He was a gentleman, educated on the mainland, but there is no doubting he came from here, his whole existence endlessly attentive to just what Nunwell needed:

> Sett young oakes and asches about thie growndes neare thie hedges and stake them that ye wind may have no force of them and bucsh them that the Cattell may not rubb agaynst them.
>
> All foursye [furzy] boomie [?broomy] vearnie [ferny] growndes [grounds] your Cley maulme [marl] will also doo very well on them: for your cold cley grownd, Lime, Seasand taken at low water marke, piginsdounge [pigeons' dung], pottsoyle [from the house], or ye fowld [the dung of the flock of sheep shut up on the arable ground].

Nitrogen-fixing vetches, used as a kind of green manure and called 'phatches' by Oglander, were to be grown and turned into the ground to improve it. Ferns ('verons') were to be cut in June, still green, and laid as a mulch on the garden. A hop garden could give you £50 an acre if 'in good grownd, well-ordered and Dounged' but it had to be carefully looked after: 'You must digge him in October, … you must Cutt him in ye beginninge of March. Pole him and hill him in Aprill.'[21] Nutrients needed to be recycled to keep the system healthy and new resources carefully taken: 'Cutt for thy Brewinge and Baking Bush faggots but preserve those Bushes in whome thou findest younge trees to growe or lyke to growe.'[22] Goats were a mistake 'for it is ye harmfullest beast that is, he spoyleth all wood and younge trees, and quicksett hedges.'[23] (He wrote that, but it was the voice of experience, as the account books show that he bought and sold them.) Rooks were to be killed and hung up and 'skarekrowes' made to keep them away.[24]

Land for Oglander was not just an inheritance, a money-making machine or a financial asset. It was, at root, a living organism, a system of life, over which he presided and to which the existence of his family and name was indissolubly wedded. 'Be sure whatsoever misfortune befalls thee', he told those listening descendants, 'sell not thie land which wase with mutch Care and paynes provided and kept for thee and have continued so many adges in thie name. Rather ffeede on bredd and water then to be the confusion of thie howse.'[25]

This intensely personal understanding of his family's history is allied to a demotion of the individual's role within it. The lands might have been kept for the Oglanders, one by one in succession across time, but it was not for any of them to interrupt the stream. The river mattered more than the people floating on it. Benefit and service, personal gain and loyal behaviour were, in this world, indistinguishable. 'Erect som tenementes in Great Whitefield for to place there Labourers for to do the Servyce that thou must have of Necessitie as Mowers, Hedgers, Threshers and the lyke. So shalt thou have thie turne served and improve the Lande.'[26] Do the right thing and you would gain from it. Nowhere was that more important than within the walls of Nunwell itself: 'Above all thinges love thie Wyfe and Children otherwyse thou canst nevor love thie home and then all thinges will be distastfull unto thee, but if thou lovest them thou wilt love thie home and not mutch respect other companie.'[27]

None of this was sentimental. There was an entirely canny understanding of the need for self-interest, and for a sane evaluation of other people's motives. 'Lend monyes to thie frynde: but be Bownde [stand surety] for none. It is ye best poynt of Good husbandrie; observe itt.'[28]

That was also why children needed educating properly. It was no good to your children to send them out ill equipped into a difficult world. He employed private tutors for them at home, including one called Mr Adams who taught them dancing[29] and another astronomy (part of the Virgilian syllabus: the turning of the year could not be understood without a knowledge of the stars), and set up a grammar school in Newport in the Isle of Wight, to which they were sent. He knew that each needed educating in his own way: one to be his heir, another into holy orders and an intellectual life at Oxford, a third into business in London. His eldest son, George, was 'well red in Common and Statute Lawes, Logike, History, Philoshye, the mathematickes, and all other good partes'.[30] Sir John would help his children on their way but it was no good them imagining they could ride in on their inheritance:

Above all poyntes of good howsbandri be sure (if God bless yee with Children) to bringe them all up in vocations make none of them Bird-catchers or doggdrivors. Settle them in a coorse of life and then lett them shift, alwayes provided that thou assist them as farr as thy estate will permit.[31]

He was a type who has almost entirely disappeared: utterly embedded in the details of his land and place, at home negotiating with mowers or threshers, with paying a man '1 shilling for cutting ye Bull, 4 shillings for killing seven porkers and a Beef'[32] for 'grubbinge the grove' or 'drayninge the Cuttes',[33] but for whom those were the foundations not the limits of his life.

He was a highly political man, a deep conservative if no adulator of cavalier grandeur or any kind of mystical, royal absolutism. When, in January 1642, the King made an armed raid on the House of Commons in an attempt to arrest his five leading opponents, Parliament sent round a 'Protestation' for signatures in their support. Oglander's name was at the head of that list.[34] He was in that way a deep constitutionalist. Since his father's death in 1609, he had been part of the government of the Isle of Wight, a Justice of the Peace and then Deputy Lieutenant, the man in charge of the military forces on the island. He had spent three years as the Deputy Governor of Portsmouth and personal authority was as natural a part of his idea of himself as any orchard, dairy herd or poultry pen. The island was his parish and he felt towards it something of what he felt towards Nunwell: a place in which he was the natural-born governor. 'If thou hast not Somm Commande in thy cowntery, thou will not be estemed of ye Common Sort of people, whoe hath more of feare, then love in them.'[35]

He was certain of this: only gentlemen of his kind were capable of command and knew the meaning of honour. No Oglander should ever court the people who were dependent on them

> or thinke to tye them to thee eyther by favours or ye belly. I knowe, and have seene them, that have bene hyghly obleyged to somm Gentlemen, yet to gayne 5 s[hillings] they woold Cutt there throates. Never thinke to binde them to thee by benefites. Gratitude and they (I mean ye Common Sort) are as farr asounder as Virtue and Vice.[36]

It was an unsentimental view. Many of his tenants held their land from him by copyhold, a form of tenure which often involved paying rent in the form of work on the landlord's fields, usually at harvest time, when many hands were needed to get the crop in. In return, the landlord was bound to provide them with food and drink. Oglander didn't think the deal worth it and recommended to his descendants that they ignore the copyhold provisions and hire people in the open market to do the work. It was much better to pay people 3s. 9d. the acre to reap a crop than to compel them to do it in return for the breakfast and drink it was customary to provide, 'for they will both scamble thie wheate and eate up more then the other will cost thee'.[37]

This commercial, rational, sceptical, loving, traditional, attentive and proud set of attitudes could all be bound up in the one word husbandry. In Oglander's spelling of it – variations on 'howsbandry' – it embeds the idea that the *house*, conceived of as a family in a building with its attendant lands and people, was the defining focus of gentry life. Everything was part of one world. 'If thou wouldst have good and handsome children,' he wrote to his descendants, making the connections plain, 'have as much Care of thy wife, as of thy Mares. Breed not on a Crooked Deformed stocke.'[38] If a man thought only of the money which a rich ugly wife would him bring as a dowry, he was depriving his children and grandchildren of the happiness and beauty it was his duty to give them.

That sustained connectedness across categories is the lasting quality of Oglander's account books. His own idea of himself is indistinguishable from the idea of his family-in-its-place, conceived of as a single hyphenated reality. He was his ancestry and his posterity. 'Reade all thie Awncestors bookes of accoumptes,' he told his descendants. 'It may be thou mayst find soomwhat owt of them that will be worth thie labour. I have fownd it so.'[39] But he was also his relationships with his neighbours. He was the just government of the island. He was the view from his windows. His love for his wife, children, uncles and cousins was a form of self-love, as if his entire being was distributed among the structures that framed and supported him. He thought of himself as a figure in a landscape. 'Wouldest thou feign see me, being dead so many years since?' he asked his descendants from beyond the grave.

I will give thee my owne Carracter. Conceive thou sawest an Aged, somwhat Corpulent Man of middle stature, with a white Beard and somwhat big Muchatoes, riding in Blacke or some sad coullored clothes from Westnunwell up to ye West Downe and so over all the Downes to take the Ayre, Morning and Eveninge, and to see there his ffattinge Cattell, on a handsome midlinge blacke stone-horse [a stallion], his hayre graye and his complexion very Sangwine, and, as Tully sayde, *Nunquam Minus Solus, quam Cum Solus.*[40]

Never less alone than when alone. Sir John Oglander lived in a crowd of others, dead and alive, present and yet to be born, sustained by a blithe sense of that continuity across space and time. The soil in which he grew was the community of gentility but it was no bowl of sugar babies. The Isle of Wight, like any gentry community, was full of mutual supervision and judgement and Oglander made a list of verdicts on his fellow 'gents of Owre countrey'. Here, in the privacy of his own book, very few of them came up to the mark.

Woorsely of Aschey his many vayne tryckes argued an unsettled
   brayne
Mr Rychards lived and dyed a dissembler
Sir John Meux was of a homely behaviour, as nevor havinge any
   breedinge or good naturals

Sir John Leygh was an honest gentilman, active and handsome, but no artist, nor overmutch beholdinge to Nature.

Dennis and Lislie ... drowned by overmutch drynckinge.

Woorseley of Aschey, Cheeke of Motson, sold theyre patrimonie, and left ye Island.

Thomas Cheeke, a lewde sonn of a discreete fathor, solde Motson to Mr Dillington 1623

Sir John Meux wase the veryest clown (of a gentleman) that evor the Isle of Wight bredd. As he was destitute of learninge, soe of humanitie and civillitie;

Sir William Meux wase as well a quallified gentleman as anie owre countery bredd; but of no sprite, for in my presence Sir Edward Dennis too mutch braved him.[41]

The other gentry families on the Isle of Wight provided a set of educative tales. Not steady ('stout' is one of Oglander's favourite praise words), not brave, not educated, not generous, not prudent, not honest and not naturally gifted: the life of a gentleman was surrounded by tiger traps. Fall into any one and you fell below the approval horizon. But the really loathsome outsiders were those who were systematically ungentlemanly, above all courtiers who 'promise mutch and p'forme nothinge, and for that hated of all'. The lawyers came a near second, who 'with theyre stirringe up of swytes [suits] betwene ye ffermors and Yeomandrie, they [have] utterlye undon ye whole communalitie'.[42]

Communality comes near the heart of Oglander's understanding of where value lay. By the 1630s, he was already nostalgic for a past in which no one ever moved:

Owre ancestors lived here soe quietly and securelie, beinge neythor troubled to London nor Winchester, soe they seldome or nevor went owt of ye island, insomutchas when they went to London (thynkynge itt a East India voyage) they always made theyre willes.[43]

When Oglander was writing that, the age of rooted innocence was long gone. '*Mutamur*', he wrote in the margin next to it, 'We are changed.'

'Ye whole gentry of ye countrey' – that was the idea Oglander loved, a community which stretched not only to his own neighbours and friends but across the generations, both those that came before and those still to come. But he was no stick-in-the-mud. He understood and accepted the realities of social change. 'There are people between fermor and gentleman on the iland,' he wrote. This was no caste system and social mobility was an accepted reality. His best friend, Mr Emanuell Badd, 'wase a very poor mans Sonn'. As a boy he had been apprenticed to a shoemaker 'but by god's blessinge and ye losse of 5 wyfes', he became rich and bought lands throughout the island. 'He wase a very honest man, and a very good ffrynd of myne.'[44] The accumulation of wealth and the acquisition of land could provide a route into gentility.

But there were others in this tight, mutually supervising world whom Oglander was more reluctant to admit to the charmed circle. The ironically named knights 'weare nevor accoumpted any Gentlemen', Oglander told his descendants in case there was any uncertainty later on. 'I knewe well Michaell Knyght, the fathor of this Thos. now livinge, who woold nevor be called other then Goodman Knyght.' 'Goodman' was a yeoman farmer's title. It was his son, 'this Thomas, now livinge,' who had the pretensions, married 'one of ye dawghtors of Page, of Sevington, a rytch ffermor, and in tyme he (gettinge wealth) may tourne Gentleman.'[45]

There were also the 'Gardes', whom Oglander spotted as being on the rise: 'Becawse ye Gardes nowe begin to growe rich in owre Island, I thought it fitt to sett here downe their Pedigree, that aftor adges maye know them bettor.'[46]

Of all his neighbours, only Sir John Leigh (even without much talent, let alone education) was without blame or blemish.

He wase a Gentleman of ye most temperatest diott that evor I knewe, contented and satisfied with a small mattor eythor of meate or drinke. At ye ordinarye with us, he woold not eate above 3 or 4 bittes of meate, and proportionabelie of dringe. I wase with him in ye Commission of ye Peace [as a Justice] 20 yeres, and most of that time noe other butt our selves in ye Island; he wolld nevor differ in opinion, butt of a milde and good Natur; no scholler, nor mutch redd, but verie paynefull [careful], and willinge to doo what good he Could, very pitifull and mercifull; in his lattor tyme weepinge at every disaster.[47]

Leigh was a man of honour and sensibility, of moderation and loving-kindness: the model on which Sir John Oglander at least in public aimed to follow.

If you walk today on the downs above Nunwell, taking the grassy path where the turf is no more than skinned over the chalk, the route Oglander and his handsome black horse would have taken day after day, on his way to Newport, or to visit the Worsleys at Appuldurcombe or the Leighs at North Court or the Chekes at Mottistone, you see a country below you which is not unlike the one he would have seen. To the south, beyond other distant downs and the wet valleys between them, are the grey waters of the Channel, the realm of opportunity and threat. Clifford Webster, the Isle of Wight archivist and historian of the Oglanders, reckons that in the late sixteenth and early seventeenth centuries the family was set on its way by William Oglander, Sir John's father, financing pirate ships in the English Channel and sharing in the profits. This semi-official privateering, encouraged by Elizabeth but later suppressed under James, preyed on the passing Spanish traffic, a kind of armed commerce in which most of the Isle of Wight gentry invested. That alone, as Webster has written, can explain the sudden wealth and spate of land acquisitions made by John Oglander and his father, William, in the 1590s and early 1600s. Little of the world portrayed in his notebooks would have been possible without it.

To the north, beyond the thorny combes and dark absorbent woods of the downland edge, is the world which that piracy made possible: a wide span of fields and hedgerows, nearly all of which, in this view, belonged to the Oglanders. Hedgerow oaks, some shattered by lightning, stand above the fields like pom-poms. At the very foot of the downs is the brick and pale Bembridge limestone of Nunwell itself, smoke curling up from its chimneys past the white-painted dormers and huge Cornish slates which John Oglander records in his notebook as having bought himself.

This Grand Circle prospect shaped Oglander's world view. It is a surveying platform. On almost every ride out from Nunwell he would have taken these high roads and drunk in a vision of the island, set in the waters of the Channel to one side, the milky Solent on the other. It is steep but elegant country, with an easy roll to it, knowable and lovable as one place. Buzzards cruise over the woods and ivy climbs the oaks in a way Oglander would not have admired. The fields are orderly. Cattle are grazing on the chalky turf. On the down tops, the plough-softened remnants of Bronze Age tumuli scarcely protrude above the sheep-nibbled grass, and in early summer the streamside woods are full of bluebells and woodspurge. At their feet, glossy blades of hart's tongue fern reach down to the waters of Nunbrooke, the stream from which Nunwell draws its supply. It is a world complete in itself. Who would not have dreamed of being king of it?

That vision of completeness, so richly addressed in the notebooks, broke down and shattered in the last two decades of Oglander's life.

By 1630, John had seven surviving children, four boys and three girls. George, the eldest, and the boy of whom he was proudest, was twenty-one. He had left Merton College in Oxford and gone to Middle Temple, as his father had done, to acquire the outlines of the law. The others were en route to productive lives, either at Winchester or at Oxford. Ann, his eldest daughter, was now sixteen, deeply loved by her father, who claimed she 'wase famous far and neere for her handsomnes, and was called Tre-bell-Anna'. She was 'as hansome a Gentilwoman as euor this Isle Bred, and the handsomest that evor came owt of the famely of ye Oglanders'.[48]

John himself had been a good husband and his financial situation was good:

When I went to the Parliament the 17th of March 1628 I left in the
    hole behind my bed's head in the parlour chamber, in a trunk, in
    gold – £2,400
In the white box in my study, in gold – £220
I carried up to London with me, in money – £60
    In my study I left my book of accounts, in which appear all my
money debts and estate whatsoever.[49]

In George, his heir, Sir John could look forward to a glorious
future for the family. He was not faultless, 'somewhat given to Choller
but of a manlicke disposition' and something of a dandy, in love with
fine clothes. He flirted with girls – his father tried to steer him
towards Elizabeth Hobart, the daughter of a distinguished Norfolk
judge, largely because her promised marriage portion of £4,000, all
of it 'in ready gold',[50] was so enormous, but nothing came of it.
George ran up debts, which his father paid off, and didn't always
attend to his work. 'Nothinge could Comfort mee more then to here
yt you had settled your Selve to ye studdye of ye Lawe', his father
urged him in March 1631. George was to 'catch time by ye fourlocke,
and make better Use of those pratious houres'.[51] But John loved him
immoderately and trusted him with the matchmaking for his
wonderful sister Ann, or Nan, with whom Oglander was offering a
dowry of £1,000.

In the summer of 1632, their cousin John Kempe suggested he and
George go abroad for an adventure. Franck and Nan Oglander were
set against it but John 'persuaded my unwillinge wyfe to lett him
spend one Summer in ffrance'.[52] On 11 June, with many tears from his
mother and sister, the boys set off, crossing the Channel from Ryde to
Barfleur in the Cotentin, twenty miles or so north of Orglandes from
where John thought his family had come to England in 1066, 566
years before. He would have loved the idea of his son adventuring in
the ancestral lands. George was going to be back in the island by
Michaelmas and John was hoping 'that he should succeede mee in ye
affayres of ye Countery and pourchase my ease by undertakinge ye
burden on his owne shoulders'.[53]

They landed on 12 June at Barfleur, where they stayed one night, and then rode down to Caen, from where 'a chain of happy letters'[54] began to arrive. George was staying with the Mayor, a perfumer, and was having his portrait painted, which he was going to give to Ann.

At home his father, who, when profound seriousness or emotion overcame him, had the habit of pricking his thumb and writing in his notebook in his own blood, the writing still iron-red on the page four centuries later, was not in quite such a cheerful mood:

> I must spend lesse otherwayes I shall be undone, and which waye to beginn I knowe not Sir John Oglander, with his owne Blood his Blood grieving at his greate expences.[55]

On the following page, after a note jotting down the number of faggots his woodmen had made (4,400), the number he had sold (1,700) and so the number he had left on his hands in the coppice (2,700), he wrote this:

> On the 21st July 1632, I beinge at Newport and ther busy in many thinges Concerning ye good of ower Island, in hearinge differences between partie and partie … I heard a murmuringe and Sadness amongst ye gentlemen and clergy and ye rest. Mr Price of Calbourne towld mee he hoped that ill news yt was come to towne was not truwe.

Oglander's natural sense of drama, of himself as a player in his own life, shapes his account of this moment of sudden uncertainty.

> I then, being more suspitious, demaunded wheather he had herde any ill newes of any of my famely. He, presently findinge my ignorance, converted it to a Losse of ye Kinge of Swedens army. Many moe Overtures I had, but knewe nothinge untell I wase puttinge my foote in ye stirrop. Then ye Mayor Sir Robert Dillington and Sir Edward Dennys came unto mee and tould mee of a flyinge reporte, yt should come by a Barke of Weymouth, lately Come from Cane, that my eldest sonn George wase very Sick – if not Dedd.

That final monosyllable clangs across the years:

> Let those judge yt have had a hopefull younge son 22 years aged, well brought up and learned in all ye Artes, dewtifull, wise, sober discrete, and geven to no vice; but talle, handsome, judicious and understandinge, yea far above ye Capacitie of his younge yeares, what a Case I wase in, and howe deepely strooken, insomutch as I had mutch adooe to gett home.[56]

'Deepely strooken', he had struggled back to Nunwell on his horse, filled with grief and guilt that he had ignored the worries of Franck and Ann. '*Sero sapiunt Phriges*', he wrote in his notebook once back at Nunwell, from the *Aeneid* (Late were the Trojans wise).

> With my tears in steed of incke I wryght thes last Lynes. O George, my beloved George is Dedd, and with him most of my terrestioll Comfortes, although I acknowledged I have good and dewtiful sons left. He dyed of ye Smale Poxe in Caen in Normandy ye 11th of July 1632.

Crammed into the margin besides these fading words he added, in that same colourless script:

> Only my Teares with a fowle pen wase this wryghtyn.[57]

And in his blood,

> Oh My Sonn George my son George, woold my Lyfe Could have excused thine, then hadst thou lived, the honnour of thie family and my selfe, being Owld, have gone but soom weekes before my time. [He was forty-eight][58]

On 20 July he bought mourning clothes, spending the enormous sum of £38 on them 'for my sonn George whome I Bred with all ye Care and Chardge that a lovinge ffather might bestowe on a Dewtifull Sonn'.[59]

Although, as George lay dying, he had asked his cousin Kempe to 'embalme my body and send it to my ffather and Mother (A dolefull present) to bee interred amongst my Awncestors', he could not be brought home 'for ye poxe had so putryfied his Bodye'[60] and the Oglanders sank into 'unutterable Gryfe'.

In September, John paid off George's debts of £28 17s. 6d.[61] and wrote a long account of how he had replanted his beloved orchard and garden, making it a place fit for a gentleman and somewhere George would have enjoyed.[62]

This was the perfecting of an estate as an act of courage but in the margin, beside this account, he added these verses:

> I goe, I goe, but to my Grave,
> To find owt him I Could no save.[63]

For years afterwards, when looking over his old notebooks or when filling new ones, he would find himself overcome with grief at this loss:

Oh George, my Sonn George, thou weart to good for mee: … hadest thou Lived thou hadst bene an honnour, to thy ffamely and Country. But thou art ded, and with thee all my hopes: *vale: vale: vale. tempore sequor* [Farewell: farewell: farewell: in time I shall follow][64]

Often writing in his own blood:

Melius est oblivisci: quod not potest recuparari [Better to forget what you cannot recover][65]

Then in marginal notes to George himself:

> Thy like I looke not for to see
> Till beinge Dedd I meete with thee

Or strangers:

Enquier no more wheather Sir John Oglander had an elder sonn or whoe or what he wase. If thou wilt be Curious thou wilt but Discover thye owne shame, for I must tell thee he wase sutch as thou wilt nevor bee. He wase the Phenix of Owr house, the Phillip of the Sydnyes. Sutch as owr ffamely neuor had before, And I ffeare neuor will have agayne.

And finally on that page to himself:

My sorrowe confowndes me and maketh my wryghtinge to bee non Sence.[66]

John Oglander never recovered from the death of this boy. His next son, William, became his heir, but the psychological burdens of not measuring up to the dead and increasingly sanctified hero can only have been intolerable.

With the coming of the Civil War, Oglander's world took a further step towards collapse.

He drew up a 'Declaration' as war approached in early 1642, agreed to and signed by most of the gentry on the island, that they would defend it 'with their lives and estates' against any 'ill affected persons' or 'new government.'[67] But this was whistling in the wind. For all his long experience and many administrative positions, Oglander was politically naïve and was outmanoeuvred by the Parliamentarian gentry on the island. Their supply ports of Portsmouth and Southampton were both soon in Parliamentarian hands and there was no way the island could stand out against them. Bands of Parliamentarian sailors were roaming the islands and gentry were having their houses 'rifled and robbed in their absence'.[68]

Although the times meant he could not write down everything he wanted to, Oglander filled his notebook with hints at his anxiety and dread: 'Lett me advise thee take a Nyghtes Deliberation Before thou Concludest on any greate action.'[69]

In August 1642, he was deprived of his offices.

O The Tirannicall Misery that the Gentlemen of England did Indure from July 1642 till Aprill 1643 and how much longer the Lord knowith, they Cowld Calle nothinge therowne, and lived in Slavery and Subiection to ye unruly base multitude. *O tempora O mores*[70]

The Virgilian system represented by everything at Nunwell was falling apart under threat from the people it had controlled for so many generations.

I beleive such tymes were never before sene in England, when the Gentry weare made Slaves to ye Comunalty, and in theyre Power not only to abuse but to Plunder any Gentleman. No lawe, and Government, but every mann to act his owne will without Controle, no Courtes at Westminster, no Assises, no Sessions, no Justices that woold be obeyed, no Spirituall Courtes. If any notorious Mallefactor weare sent to ye Goale, the next soldiers that came realeased them by breakinge up ye Goale. Wee expected better fruytes from those Parliaments but as yet wee test nothinge but Sower grapes. Our feares arr the worst is to Come.[71]

Close up against that, this bleak entry, in ragged handwriting, in his blood: 'Tuesday nyght the 13th Aprill had a most fearfull dreame of my Daughter Lennard.'[72] His beautiful and treasured daughter Ann – whom he called 'Nan' – had married Sir Stephen Lennard of West Wickham in Kent. For Oglander to dream of her in trouble was a sign of deep anguish. He had been ill himself all spring and the notebook, with its usual filterlessness, transcribed exactly what had been wrong with his body: a cold caught when riding across the Downs to Newport, a cough with it, but 'it lay most in my hedd ... Every day my nose fowled 2 handkerchiefs and glaunders [a streaming nasal discharge] Came from mee as from a horse.' He had suffered a 'Distemper' all over his body 'insomuch as I left of Tobacco, cowld neyther rellisch that or my beare'. Only after two months did it leave him.[73] This was part of the connectedness of the man: if the body politic was in turmoil, it was almost inevitable that Oglander's body would take on the pain.

Births and deaths were recorded, of neighbours, cousins, grand-children, employees and friends. Children dying young, mothers dying in childbirth, a man dying in the same week as his father: all were noted down as part of 'a miserable distracted time'.[74] As soon as the war had begun, Oglander found himself in a hostile universe and the notebook gathered the fragments of pain, loss, regret and indignation.

The world had turned against him and he was surrounded by enemies. But what had Oglander done to summon this hostility? Was the beautiful Virgilian system, in which he could pay £5 for a coach to London and pay two young women the same money for an entire year's work, in fact a mechanism for rage? His own voice of unques-tioning contempt for those who were not born into the governing class breaks through occasionally into the notebooks:

> We had here a thing called a Committee which overruled Deputy lieu-tenants and also Justices of Peace and of this we had brave men: first Ringwood of Newport, the pedlar, Maynard the apothecary, Matthews the baker, Wavell and Legge, farmers and poor Baxter of Hurst Castle. These men ruled the whole Island, and did whatsoever they thought good in their own eyes.[75]

Those sentences are very nearly an invitation to revolution. He was heard by his enemies to remark that he would willingly give £500 out of his own pocket to see the King's ships returned to 'their rightful owner', 'dangerous talk' that was reported to London.[76] Oglander's remorse went straight into the account book:

> It wase the greatest fawlt in Sir John Oglander, that he wase to precipi-tate in all his Action, not suffitiently Chawinge the Chidd [or cud] upon them. It was a wyse mans sayinge he woold sleepe before he woold doo any thinge.[77]

In May 1643, under the rubric 'What ffatting Cattell I have now to putt of', he listed his oxen, his bulls, his heifers and barren cows and then this:

I only knowe this, that I knowe nothinge I cannot read eythor my selve, or other men, this wordle is Changed, and our Antipodes possesseth owr places, althinges are tourned Tosi-tourvy *In nova fert animus, mutates dicere formas.*[78]

Oglander was quoting Ovid, the opening lines of the *Metamorphoses*: 'My spirit urges me to say that the shape of things has changed.' The world was neither what it had been nor what it should be. Oglander was told that he was considered the 'only Malignant in ye Isle of Wight'. 'I have not one of my Neyghbours that speakes well of me.' This was a moment of profound and disturbing isolation. 'I am hated of every man almost in the island, and live like the owl amongst birds.' Why should this charming, industrious, dutiful, affectionate and loving man feel so friendless at his time of need? Almost certainly the roots of his trouble were political: he was a (moderate) Royalist in an island full of natural Parliament men. And he was in the habit of taking bad news very hard, so that the political turn of events came to seem like a moment of personal and social failure.

A week later a body of horsemen rode up to Nunwell, banged on the door and presented him with a warrant for his arrest.[79] The Parliamentary Committee for the Safety of the Kingdom required him in London and the next day he was taken up there to hear the worst.

Franck was left at home at Nunwell.

June 27th 1643

    Dear Husband,

    I knoe you long to here from me as I doe from you how you did in your going and how you have your helth sence, I give God thankes we ar all well yet, the gratest Sicknes I have nowe is the grife for your absence.

Your newe Shepperd when he came sade you had made no bargin with him and if I would not let him have the keping of 6 yoes [ewes] for himself he would not com so I granted it him till you com home and for no longer. Our servants mete will last but on week longar right me word whether I shall kill or by sum. Your baby [the bailiff at Nunwell] seth you haue left no order what hay you would haue kepe for your Shepe, but I hope you will be at home before that time.

This with my love remembered to you praying to God to send you a happy end of all your troubells and to send us a happy being together agane

I ever remain your Loveing and sorofull wife

Francis Oglander[80]

In London, a river of information flowed up against him from the island and his prospects looked bleak. On 11 July he wrote to Franck, bemoaning the fact that 'now in owr owld adge we showld be fforced to live asounder, even when wee had most need one of ye others Company'.

I am glad Baby prooves so well. Pray Incourage him, and lett him followe ye hayinge when fayre weather comes, and to lett the wheat out by the acre to cuttinge, and ye Barley to Rakinge ... Lett the Coachman look to the hop gardens. If the butchers will Buy any of the Fattinge beasts, let my sonn, with Babys advise, sell them, but for ready Monyes.

My Black swyte [suit] begins to be torne Wherefore, pray, in the trounke in the seller, where ye tobaccoe is, send up my sattin doublet and Cloth hose, and Claoke lined with plusch, and som tabaccoe; and put the other tobaccoe in the Binn.

Good ffrancke, be Merry, and lett him have your prayers whoe louves you Dearer than his owne lyfe

Your louvinge howsband

John Oglander[81]

There is no suggestion that she was not his equal co-bearer of this misery:

> Only lett mee intreate you not to seme discontented, but beare itt owt with a Masculine Courrage, and to carry it patiently. I am much affrayd wee shalbe Plundered if I doo not comply with theyre demaundes. Woold your hanginges were well secured.[82]

Oglander sent his grandson 'little Jack' a coral to chew on and by late August was back at Nunwell, having paid a fine of £1,000. But he was too dangerous and inconvenient a figure to leave on the island and by early October he was back in custody in London, where he would stay for the next two and a half years, for much of the time held at 'the basest place in London, A messengers howse at ye farthest Ende of Cabidge Lane in Westminster',[83] a place of cramped sub-mondaine lodgings.[84] If geography had for most of his life been his glory and the theatre for his significance, this was geography as humiliation, degradation by address.

Franck went up to London to try to help, lobbying for him and arguing his case. At the end of May 1644, she at last met with success: John was released from his hovel in Cabbage Lane and allowed to move to his own rooms at the Seven Stars, a lawyers' inn in Carey Street off the Strand.[85]

Now, though, the terminal disaster of his life struck:

> June 12th 1644
> My poore wyfe overheatinge her bloode in procuringe my Liberty, gott ye smale poxe and died, and made me a worse Prisoner then before.[86] O my poor wyfe, with my bloud I wryght it thy death had made me most miserable. Indeede greater Gryfe and Sorrowe Could not have befallen any mann.[87]

She was fifty-four, five years younger than her husband. The parliamentary authorities had the grace to allow him to bury her on the Isle of Wight, but after the funeral he returned to London, where he was compelled to remain within the defences. Only in February 1646, on the payment of another fine, was he finally released to Nunwell.

His notebook for these years is a ragged thing, whole sections cut out of it, many parts of pages removed with a razor, all for fear that what he had written would incriminate him with the authorities. From being a man who was central to his own world he had become marginal to it. He had to pay off his coachman Henry, as he had been in arms against Parliament, and again and again he poured into his notebook a surging nostalgia for the past:

> This Island was beyond Compare Anno Domino 1630 So full of Knyghts and Gentry, ... It wase the Paradise of England, and nowe Anno 1647 itt is Just like the other partes of ye Kingdome A melancholy deiected Sadd place/no Company/no resort/no neyghbors seinge one of the other so you may truly say/tempora mutantur.[88] Would I could write or that I could be permitted to write, the history of these times.[89] I have lived so much too long as to se myself deprived of all the places and to be vilified and condemned to be imprisoned and to have all affronts and disgraces put on me.[90]

A moment of bittersweet delight came to Oglander when the King himself stayed the night at Nunwell in November 1647. He had arrived on the island two days before, imagining with faulty intelligence that it might be a refuge for him, but on landing found himself a prisoner. Oglander was appalled at the news and 'could doo nothinge but Sighe, and weepe, for 2 nyghtes and a Daye'. At Nunwell the King 'graciously accepted a purse of gold ... proffered on bended knee', and stayed in 'my wrought chamber, so called because it was hung with wrought stuffs'.[91] The tapestries have all gone now, destroyed by moth, but the elegant room and its accompanying cabinet is still pointed out to visitors. Oglander gave his guest oysters, prawns, shrimps, whiting, cod, woodcock, 'Sweetemeates' and wine, as well as his own provisions,[92] but their conversation, of necessity, went unrecorded. The sense of disorientated failure and self-pity must have hung heavily in the rooms at Nunwell.

Oglander eked out the remainder of his life, a terminally saddened man. In 1648 a Roundhead, 'Captayne Stratton', was billeted at Nunwell,[93] a horrible experience for a man who had once considered this house the centre of his own universe, but he could speak no truth to his notebooks:

There was a time in Rome, when it wase not (as Tacitus sayth) lawfull for a mann to thinke, by his Countenance, and Carriadge his very thoughtes weare scruted. Wonder not then that such times may Come wherein wee dare not wryght none dare wryght a Cornnicle duringe ye life of ye Prince exespt he bee very virtuous. *Mors in olla: nemo falix ante obitum.*[94]

'There is death in the pot' – the phrase referred to a famous story from Kings, but in the Latin of the Vulgate: 'There is no happiness this side of death.'

He read his copy of Sir Walter Raleigh's *History of the World*, which was scribbled in by his grandson, also called John Oglander, playing with pens in the library. And he longed for death:

O, that man had but that happines annexed to his nature that without any Offence to gods or mans lawes he myght departe this wordle when he is willinge, then showld I bee a happie mann.[95]

I am Confident that whenever it pleaseth God to Calle mee owt of this worldle (which havinge lost my poore wyfe, I infinitely desire) it will be with a Dropsy.

Owr ffamely weare never long-lived. About theyre Cleymiterricoll yeare 63, they most of them died, and I believe (and hope) that will bee the yere wherein it will please god to take me owt of this Earthly pilgramige. A good, and a short life is best.[96]

Oglander died in November 1655 in his seventy-first year and had the painted wooden effigies he had commissioned placed on his tomb and on his father's in the Oglander chapel in Brading.[97] His dear son George was commemorated by a miniature knight in a niche on the wall above him. All of this was antiquarian, his armour wildly out of date, his crossed legs an ancient signal which in the seventeenth century was thought to mean the knight portrayed had been a Crusader, the best and most honourable of men. There is no reason to think that his huge eyes, his florid complexion and his giant moustaches are not a depiction of the man as he was. He had, after all, approved and paid for a drawing before Crocker the sculptor got to work. Everything here depicts his idea of himself: a knight from the old days, full of vigour, entranced by antiquity, just raising himself from his bed for the resurrection to come, when he and George would meet each other again in an everlasting embrace.[98]

The Oglanders never wrote like this again but their achievement can be measured in a worldly way. A baronetcy was acquired by Sir John's son William and the family made a spankingly successful marriage in the eighteenth century, acquiring the 16,000 acres of Dorset and Somerset that came with the Parnham estate. Sir William Oglander, 6th Baronet, possessor by now of a house in Portman Square in London and 24,000 acres of prime English earth, married the Duke of Grafton's daughter in 1810. But he was 'lacking in many of the qualities which go to the making of a career', 'was never known to write an unnecessary letter'[99] and spent most of his life in the bosom of his family. The Oglanders continued rich; there were soldiers, scholars and imperialists among them. That tenor of life lasted until the 7th Baronet, Henry, died childless in 1874. In 1892, on the death of his widow, the Parnham estate was entailed elsewhere and the Oglander acreage shrank. Sir Henry's cousin assumed his name but the twentieth century was, eventually, not kind to the family. In 1982 the house at Nunwell was sold and although Oglanders still live near by and still own many of the lands Sir John had loved, as well as the precious notebooks and the paintings from his hall, the house itself is occupied by another family, with their coat of arms displayed on the ancient walls, and no more than the ghost of Sir John treading carefully up the grey oak stairs.

Withdrawal

The Oxindens

Denton, Kent

In 1632 Harry Oxinden, tall but 'over-slender', a scholar and poet, a reader and admirer of John Donne, was twenty-three. His portrait, painted in the late 1630s by the Fleming Cornelius Janssen, shows a slightly spaniel-eyed man, with a scratchy moustache and wearing the fine linen his correspondence often mentions or desires.[1] For the two years since his father's unexpected death he had been looking after his lands and living in the family's house at Maydekin, at the northern end of Denton, a small Kentish village a few miles south-east of Canterbury. The village's tiled and thatched roofs are pushed deep into the cleft of one of the many dry valleys of the North Downs. Bunches and drifts of woodland decorate the valley sides. Steep pastures separate them. Where the footpaths come to a narrow gateway, they wear down through the turf to the whiteness of the chalk. Hares bolt away across the grassland from under your feet and grey-legged partridges creep into the margins of the woods. Above those pastures, on the smoothed hillbacks, you can look out, across the eastern chin of Kent, to the North Sea.[2]

It is a mushroomy, private, creased country, where signs of the gentry are thick on the ground. No great houses dominate this strangely remote and unvisited province. The aristocracy was never important here. This is the gentry world above all else, every mile or two marked by another small manor house and its associated gardens

139

and closes, so that the country itself comes to seem like a kind of social network. Go for a walk along its lanes draped in old man's beard, between the orchards, the woods and the pastures, and you will find yourself buried in a world of small places, the threads and nodes of a gentry system, none of the significant houses more than a mile or two from its neighbour, twenty minutes' ride away. It is like walking through a map of localism, of places shaped by a deep, shared attachment to place. It becomes clear that civility here is not an urban quality. If there is such a thing as an urbane landscape, this is it.

East Kent was as alluring then as it is today. A seventeenth-century traveller, Thomas Baskerville, rode down the Dover road,

> a great part of my way that I went being through delicious orchards of cherries, pears and apples and great hop-gardens. In husbandry affairs they are very neat, binding up all sorts of grain in sheaves; they give the best wages to labourers of any in England, in harvest giving 4 and 5 shillings for an acre of wheat and 2 s. a day meat and drink, which doth invite many stout workmen hither from the neighbouring country to get in their harvest.[3]

This was as rich as England came, much of the wheat and most of the fruit and hops bought by London fruiterers and brewers and shipped to the capital from quays on the north Kent coast. Peas, onions, carrots, asparagus and artichokes were all grown in this market-gardening hotspot, where families of Flemings had been practising intensive vegetable and seed production since the middle of the sixteenth century.[4]

About six hundred acres of this perfect country belonged to the Oxindens of Maydekin. It was a little estate and they were the most minor of gentry. Harry Oxinden's father, Richard, who was a younger son, had been left this little subsidiary estate by his father when his elder brother inherited the main Oxinden property at Dene just to the north. The Maydekin acres consisted of a mixture of grassland, wood and some arable, on which they grew peas which they sold to London merchants. Maydekin is still a beautiful place, best seen from above now, clumped in its trees, a house in a sheltered hollow, with barns, cart sheds and stables gathered beside it. The raging Folkestone road now drives past but strip that away and you can imagine what the records describe: a history of attention and care. A ring of sixteenth-century ash trees and an orchard above the pigeon-house, persisting throughout the following century; perry pear trees, winter pear trees, and pearmains or warden trees, whose fruit were the longest keeping of all, planted here in the reign of Elizabeth, still fruiting in the 1660s. After he came to live here in 1610, Richard planted a new hedge between the Cowlease and the cherry garden and another between the two horse leases. When Harry's sister Elizabeth was born in January 1616, her father planted a cobnut to commemorate her coming.[5]

Richard had died young, when just forty-one, and Harry had returned early from Corpus Christi in Oxford, to take up the reins of his inheritance. He set about improving the house: he 'seeled the chamber over the little parlour' – it had been open to the rafters before and this was for comfort and warmth – 'and enlarged it from the chimney to the little closet', took down the old malthouse which had been outside the 'with-drawing roome' (the smell of the damp-ened grain had become intolerable), added a new staircase in the house and rebuilt several of the outbuildings, including the brew-house and the milkhouse.[6] All his life long he tucked and tended to his house and garden, putting in new floors, opening new windows, laying paved paths in Purbeck stone (delivered from Dorset by sea),[7] adding a porch, planting more cherry trees, putting in a hop garden, planting the yews with which the house is still surrounded, setting up oak gates in the garden wall, 'making and levelling my flower garden and artichoke garden, carrying out all the rubbage, and bringing in mould [rotted compost], levelling of it, quick-setting it [with hawthorn], planting it, making the summer houses, and setting up the frame for the vines, making the pear garden and the terrace walk in it'. Friends and relations would come for winter lunches and plant an oak tree or a damson. The landscape was the vehicle through which the gentry expressed its sense of order, sociability, mutuality and wellbeing.

For all this connectedness and rootedness, Harry was nevertheless a man slightly removed from the world around him. His letters show him to be a little aloof, both restless and filled with vague melancholy, at one crucial moment overwhelmed with passion for a young woman, at others withdrawn from the dramatic events of seventeenth-century England, perennially short of cash, warmly affectionate to those he loved, a deep thinker, self-consciously driven by his nobility of spirit and ragingly dismissive of those he considered treacherous to himself and their own duties.

Every house and place in Harry Oxinden's story can be visited on foot in a single long summer's day, about eighteen miles on the lanes and footpaths through these chalky valleys. Not quite uniquely, but with extraordinary richness, it is possible to look beyond the brick and timber façades and their fields and gardens and to re-construct the social landscape of Harry Oxinden's realm. It is a little world deeply connected by marriage and inheritance, but also tense with rivalry and distrust, usually mended by a kind of forgiveness, supremely aware of minor differences in status, touchy with hierarchy anxiety, if not always constrained by it, and sometimes surprisingly loose at its margins. These netted East Kent valleys were the scene for a kind of corporate gentry existence, and as in most corporations, that enterprise was both coloured by joint purpose and riddled with the discontent and strain that joint enterprise breeds.

The reason we know all this is that Harry Oxinden was both a fixer, communicator, plotter and planner and the most extraordinary hoarder, recorder and keeper, not only of any letter that he received but of letters to other members of his family and the network of friends and relations scattered across these valleys, as well as any draft of any letter he sent. The accumulated mounds of correspondence, a compost heap of seventeenth-century gentry consciousness, has ended up in the British Library, along with the assorted notebooks and journals which the squire of Maydekin kept through the vicissitudes of his life. He is, in his way, a minor, rural, slightly earlier Samuel Pepys.

After his father's death, Harry became the head of his own small family. He had three younger brothers. James was at Cambridge and destined for the church. Richard was apprenticed to a Mr Newman, a cloth merchant in Fish Street in London, but hated that life and went off instead to fight in the Netherlands with his uncle, a man blessed with the name of Colonel Prude. The youngest brother, Adam, was also in trade, apprenticed to a Mr Brooks, who dealt in merceryware – silk cloths, gold and silver ribbons and fringed gloves. Adam hated it too and went to sea instead. Harry's sister Kate was married to a high-class draper in London, Thomas Barrow, mercer of Cheapside. And there was the youngest sister, Bess, who lived with Harry at Maydekin. By his father's will, Harry owed each of these siblings a legacy of £300 (no distinction between girls and boys) which he had to pay them out of the rather slight income of the Maydekin estate.[8] Needless to say, he was slow in doing so and for year after year they pestered him for tiny instalments, a few pounds here and there, of the money that was rightly theirs.

These are the lower fringes of the gentry world: not quite adequately funded, sliding off into the riskier dimensions of war and London trade. But these Oxindens were also connected to the higher and more potent reaches of gentrydom. Harry was married on Christmas Eve 1632 to Anne Peyton, the sister of a great Kentish knight, Sir Thomas Peyton. On marrying her, Harry gave her a diamond ring, which cost him 'eighteen pound eleaven shilling'.[9] The Peytons came from Knowlton, a beautiful, many gabled brick house a few miles to the east of Maydekin, still in the middle of its own park, with its own church close next to it and its windows enriched with painted glass, its chancel decorated with the many banners and helmets of the Peyton knights and their predecessors, an interior dim with antiquity and provincial grandeur. (Not any more: the Victorians swept most of this away.)

A few miles to the north at Dene near Wingham was the elder branch of the Oxinden family itself, vastly richer, more powerful, more connected than their Maydekin cousins, presided over by Harry's uncle, Sir James. Harry's cousin Henry Oxinden, later Sir Henry, baronet, became one of his dearest friends, 'my second selfe' as he often called him,[10] a fellow huntsman but politically impassioned, a man with a sense of the gentry's political destiny. The children of this grand Oxinden branch, like the Peyton children, were all married into the great political gentry families of Kent. Their sons and daughters were carefully educated, unlike Harry's siblings, who apart from the vicar James were only marginally literate. None of those grander Peytons or Oxindens ever went into trade.

Harry's wife's sister Elizabeth was married to Robert Bargrave, another big Kentish squire, the descendant of a family of yeoman tanners, whose father John had been a mercenary and Virginia planter and whose mother had been the daughter and heiress of the wonderfully rich London haberdasher Giles Crouch. This joint inheritance (London trade + colonial land) had set the Bargraves up as powers in Kent, newly based on their wonderful house called Bifrons (it had two equal façades, perhaps to reflect the Crouch–Bargrave alliance) near Patrixbourne, just south of Canterbury.

A seventeenth-century painting of Bifrons is now in the Mellon collection at Yale and although it was painted at some time towards the end of the century – neither the artist nor the date is known[11] – and almost certainly the house had been extended after the Restoration, this is nevertheless a near-perfect representation of the subject of this book: gentry-in-the-landscape.

The group of horsemen cresting the rise in the foreground is something of a visual cliché, as is much of the *mise-en-scène*: the framing trees, the receding ridges, the sun falling carefully on the house and the Norman church at Patrixbourne. Command, ease, settlement, civility and the tidiness of the walled gardens and orchards, with the wall fruit trained against them, represent an order that extends to the fields in which the sheaves are gathered in stooks, and the distant roofs of Canterbury. There is newness and sharpness here but those new contributions take their place in a set of ancient patterns. The half-autumnal woods in which the oak standards stand high above the lower coppice; the sociability of the figures in the garden who are in conversation, gesturing to the worlds around them, past the little garden pavilion; the carefully distributed statuary; the new allées of trees and hedges, the elegant gates which are swept low to allow a view to the country beyond; the gilding evening light; the thatched cart sheds and the tiled barn with long outshots; the flocks of autumn starlings; the cattle; the near-elegiac lateness of the view: all contribute to a vision of beauty and settlement, of an ordered place in an ancient world.

No contemporary picture survives of Maydekin equivalent to the beautiful Bifrons scene, and that itself is a signal of the way in which the class diverged. The Bargraves, the greater Oxindens and the Peytons swam on into the assured riches of a landed future. The poorer Maydekin Oxindens, the children of a younger son, were mostly thrown on to the vagaries of the market, war and the beginnings of empire. Success in those risky fields might steer a family into the mainstream, as it had done with the Bargraves, but more often than not the poor relations sank from view, losing influence, political power, even literacy, depending as it did on expensive private education which even the relatively poor could not afford.

Nevertheless, even as the class divided, it remained in touch and Harry's vast letter compendium is witness to a continued vitality of family connection across social difference. This small slice of a gentry net extended across the whole spectrum:

from
a baronet (Sir Henry Oxinden, Harry's best friend and first cousin)
to
a knight (Sir Thomas Peyton, his wife's brother)
to
a rich squire (Robert Bargrave of Bifrons, his wife's sister's husband)
to
an impoverished squire (Harry himself)
to
a clergyman (his brother, James Oxinden)
to
an old military captain (his uncle by marriage, Colonel Prude)
to
a soldier of fortune (his brother, Richard Oxinden)

to

an apprentice in the Exchange, turned seaman (his younger brother,
    Adam)

to

a draper (Thomas Barrow, another sister's husband)

to

a London rake (John Hobart, his son-in-law)

and, eventually, as will emerge, to

a highwayman (Harry's wayward son Thomas)

It was a continuous and seamless web almost from the top of society
to the bottom. They borrowed money from each other, they stood
surety for each other, they went hunting and coursing with each
other, they became godfathers to each other's children, they offered
each other advice, the country squires bought goods from the city
merchants and they gave each other presents. They sent each other
medicines and cooking tips – 'the Sparagus must bee but a little more
then scalded' (it was ruined if boiled).[12] The lanes were alive with
family traffic. Footboys ('my little Mercurie') took notes from one
house to another,[13] even in the middle of the night. Sir James recommended a gardener and sent his 'cotch'[14] in the evening so that Harry
could visit him for lunch the following day. Harry's aunt, Mrs Prude,
asked him to inspect her woods at Woolage near Maydekin and
promised to inspect Harry's woods near her own house at
Garwinton.[15]

Harry sent some spaniels to a friend, who returned one of them
because it was 'prowde and deafe'.[16] With other neighbours he went
hunting hares on the high downs with his beagles.[17] The network
spread across genders and generations. So Robert Bargrave of Bifrons
wrote to Anne Oxinden, his sister-in-law, to thank her for her help
with an ailing child and asked her to prevail with the wet nurse 'to
bee with us then for a moneth or two'[18] as their baby was too weak to
be weaned. Harry wrote at length and with great eloquence to the
same brother-in-law, then acting as a magistrate, in defence of a
woman in his village, Goodwife Gilnot, who had been accused of

witchcraft. She was said to have 'a wart or Teat uppon her body wherewith shee giveth her familier sucke'. Harry had inspected her and found that she did indeed have 'a small wart upon her brest, which you may see an you please, and believe it there is none so familier with her as to receive any sustenance from thence'. Because 'the poore woman's cry, though it reach to heaven, is scarce heard here upon earth, I thought I was bound in conscience to speake in her behalfe; that noe hastie iudgment might passe upon her'. He signed this passionate plea to his brother-in-law the magistrate, as usual, 'Your very lo: Bro: H.O.'[19]

Everyone within the network acknowledged the subtle gradations of the hierarchy, but that did not diminish either the warmth or the sense of duty and shared honour between them. It was an open structure in which all members were deeply and personally connected to people whose social standing was unlike their own. That does not mean it was a recipe for contentment. Far from it. Harry Oxinden was aware that he was clinging a little anxiously to the bottom end of a charmed world and that anxiety emerged, at least when he was young, in an over-sensitive and rather pompous irritability. This was the tone in which he addressed his neighbour the knight and MP Sir Basil Dixwell, the latest and very rich representative of a Warwickshire family which had been in Kent for only a couple of generations.

The Oxindens, as part of the deeply interconnected and intermarried world of the Kentish gentry, had been there as an established and knightly family at least since the middle of the fourteenth century. Harry may have thought he should teach the vastly more important Dixwell a lesson in gentry behaviour. In this way, as so often, value systems and their associated hierarchies overlapped: Harry the ancient Kentish gentleman, the real thing, but poor and powerless; Basil Dixwell a parvenu, a Member of Parliament with superb connections at Westminster and money to match. Who, out of this pair, could think of patronizing whom?

In 1635, Dixwell was buying up land around his spanking new mansion at Broome Park, for which, as Harry noted a little sourly in his diary, 27,000 bricks were made 'besides thousands which he bought'.[20] Broome is a wonderful piece of 1630s, big-money, show-off, Lord Mayor classicism, its pink-plum brick façades framed in giant pilasters, with tottering mannerist accumulations, like a coiffured wig, of scrolls, broken pediments and windows mounting skywards above them. Harry Oxinden's own plantings and improvements must have seemed modest indeed.

Dixwell had bought some land next to Maydekin which Harry wanted himself, and for which he was prepared to swap some land of his own that was next to Broome. About fifteen acres were involved on each side but Harry, quoting scripture and the classics, weighed in with the false modesty of the truly touchy as if solving the problems of war-ravaged Europe:

> Far it is from mee to think that FAITH, IUSTICE, and HONESTY are ornaments only in fashion amongst private men, holding that the greater and richer a man is the more he is bound to excel in them.[21]

If Dixwell wouldn't do the swap as he had promised, Harry wrote,

> I must then rest myself contented with mine owne, upon which I shall receive one greater benefit then on any of the lands I should have of you, and that is the prospect of the superlative house of yours which is now a building, whose rare fabrick and unparalleled beauty cannot chuse but affourd an infinite delight unto mee, especially when I shall behold it without controlment at so neere a distance.[22]

Dixwell was too suave to be troubled by any of this, the land swap went ahead and in June 1638, when the wonderful new house was approaching completion, Dixwell invited his neighbour for a picnic:

> Mr Oxinden,
>   I request that you and your wife and the Capt that is with yow would be pleased to take the payne to walke downe on Thursday next about two of the clocke in the afternoone to Broome house wher yow

shall meete myself and the gentlemen and gentlewomen which are of my house, that are very desirous to see yow all there and to eate a cake and drinke a bottle of wine together and soe you are most friendly and respectively saluted by

Your affection. frend

Basil Dixwell.[23]

Amid all this toing and froing with the menfolk of gentry Kent, it is slightly difficult to make out the nature of Harry's marriage to Anne Peyton. Her near-absence from the letters might be seen as a witness to their companionship within the confines of home. When he did write to her, he called her 'Sweete Love' and she replied 'Deare Hartt'.[24] But he didn't write to her as often as she would have liked and she hoped that was a symptom of 'forgettfullness and no neglectt of me'.[25] On her part, when he was away, she dealt entirely practically with rabbits, partridges, silver plate, the barley and their children. In the eight years of their marriage, she bore him a son, Thomas, and two daughters, Margaret and Elizabeth. When he was in London, a place he hated, she asked him to remember to buy her a linen cap, 'a morning peake, which will cost 5s., and forgeat not a furnitur for my horse'.[26] Harry's cousin Henry Oxinden used to describe her as 'old oblivion', 'the greatest enimie to true frendshippe' who 'hath so stupifid your braines as to make you forget your best friends'.[27] This is how men joke with each other in private and it is probably a sign that Harry loved her.

Anne Oxinden fell seriously ill in the summer of 1640, this time – she had been dangerously ill before – with a nagging sore throat, for which Harry's 'afectionat Ant' Lady Oxinden at Dene sent her a cordial and a 'tisain to eas the paynfullnes of her coff'.[28] It did no good and on 28 August 1640, Anne died.

It is nowhere clear quite how Harry responded to her death but that December, as a gesture of warm, gentle, slightly teasing kindness, his Oxinden cousin Henry wrote to him from their house at Dene:

My father, my mother, my wife and myselfe doe earnestly and hartilie invite you to Dene to keepe your whole Christmas, and doe desire that you would neither denie nor delay your suddain coming, our request being so reasonable, you being neither tide to wife nor familie nor entertainement of neighbours.[29]

This was the larger Oxinden family gathering around a widowed relative but it wasn't the only reaction to her death. At the same time Anne's brother Sir Thomas Peyton, with scarcely a pause, applied himself to the question of Anne's children, his nephews and nieces, carriers of his own genes. Anne's death seems immediately to have severed the unity of interests between Oxindens and Peytons. Peyton wanted to know what exactly Harry was going to do financially for his half-Peyton children. Anne had died at the very end of August and in the first two or three days of September Peyton had already taken this up with Harry face to face. Peyton had got little satisfaction from that conversation and now he wrote intemperately from his gabled brick house at Knowlton, embowered in trees, almost a twin of the Oxindens' house at Dene. His ex-brother-in-law, with whom as recently as the beginning of August he had been happily coursing after hares on the downs above Barham, was to submit to his grandeur and authority. 'If writing have more poure [power] with you then speaking I should bee glad to have found this way to obtaine my request.'[30]

Sir Thomas Peyton, acting in effect as the trustee of the funds which his sister had brought to Harry's marriage, insisted that Harry was not to use those funds for his own purposes but to distribute them to the children of the marriage. Peyton required that Harry give his 'unblameable sone' Thomas £140 a year – the equivalent of a capital sum of £2,800 at 5 per cent interest – and his 'guiltlesse doughters' Margaret and Elizabeth £300 each 'presently' – that is, straight away.[31] This huge total of £3,400 claimed by Peyton on behalf of the children was unaffordable for Harry but Thomas was adamant.

Therefore by your presence I pray lett me receive some satisfaction without ambiguous termes, which are nott to be used in expressions of true and reall meanings. And this is the way nott to suspend that alliance and friendship which you have yet in good seisine and possession from

    Your very lo: brother

    THO: PEYTON[32]

In this way, which brought moral but not legal pressure to bear, the blood family of a wife could continue to make claims on the behaviour of her husband, even after her death. No nuclear family existed in isolation; each was only a small panel in the continuous quilt of gentrydom. Harry turned to his own blood family, in the form of his uncle Sir James, his virtual father, who advised him to go slow and be careful in anything he promised, 'to stand it out untille your time of mourninge be done. It will not be amiss for you to be very cautious what you write, for words written continue, sometimes, to stand as testimony against theire master.'[33] Peyton was asking for too much, Sir James said. Harry should do what he felt was right in terms of looking after his dead wife's children but he should also look after his own interests. It is not difficult to imagine the conversations at Dene that Christmas of 1640, as the Oxindens as a whole contemplated the shoals of the future, and their best means of negotiating them.

Something had come between him and Peyton. Their friendship had always had an element of sharpness in it. Tom Peyton had rejected a woman Harry suggested as his bride, as she was neither rich nor well connected enough. 'Me thinks the Diamond showes best when 'tis sett in gold and a comely face looks sweeter when it stands by the king's picture,' he told his brother-in-law. 'The other weaker vessel, woman,' he added, 'because of the generall depravity of that sexe' needed 'some good addition to sett her of and make her estimable in [a man's] eye, before hee will rest on her.'[34]

That was tough talk but now the great crisis of seventeenth-century England was stealing up on them and 'the rumors of warre'[35] were coming with every post down the London road. The world itself seemed to be in dissolution. Harry stayed at Maydekin but Henry Oxinden went up to London to be close to where the decisions were being made. Thomas Peyton was elected one of the Members of Parliament for the port of Sandwich and excitedly reported to Harry the speeches he heard in the chamber of the Commons. He had loved John Pym's great oration in April 1640 on the threatened liberties of Englishmen, lauding Pym as 'an ancient and stoute man of the Parliament'.[36] All three of these young gentry men, now in their early thirties, were, at this stage, resolved to see the ancient rights of the Commons defended against the ambitions and erosions of the crown.

But the world was shifting fast and by the summer of 1640, a change had come over Thomas Peyton. He sent Harry another vivid dispatch from the front line in Westminster in which his natural conservatism had started to swing over to the crown. All their youths, they had known England as 'soe flourishing a kingdom'.[37] They had ridden and hunted and played with each other as if this was the most blessed of countries. Now, to Peyton 'every houre seemed readie to bring forth some strange matter'. He had 'noe good newes to send' to Harry but had been swept away by the 'speech of a gratious and mild king'. Charles, to Peyton's eyes, had not responded to the taunts and provocations of the gentry in Parliament with anger and violence but 'as a true father of his subiects would rather choose to stroke them still, till he had overcome their natures and assimilated them to his owne goodness'. Peyton, under the influence of this gracious rhetoric, had become a Royalist. The Commons seemed to him full of 'tumultuous and popular spiritts'. The more zealous were disturbingly inspired. Moderation had gone and it was the King who 'suffers in the honor of his government' when everyone abroad heard 'at what disagreement hee is with his owne people'. Peyton now was sure of what side he was on. 'Since wee will nott give, the king must take … The king may use the goods of his subjects … for the conservation of the more universall and generall good.'[38]

Soldiers were in the streets of London and cannon drawn up outside the palace of the Archbishop in Lambeth. Crowds surged along the embankments and quays by the Thames. Troopers were committing outrages, thieving, setting fire to buildings, ravishing women. Everyone was in confusion and 'I cannot meete with any man butt knows what will become of these things.' 'Death's harbinger, the sword, famine and other plagues that hang over us are ready to swallow up the wicked age,' Peyton wrote to Harry. He looked with dread at what he and Knowlton were to suffer 'in this fiery declination of the world'.[39]

The sense of shared apprehension is palpable but to both Harry Oxinden and his Oxinden cousins, Peyton's turn to the crown was treachery. Peyton favoured what he called Duty (to the King) over what he called Virtue, the gentry values of self-sufficient honour. No Oxinden would ever agree with that and none would ever fight for the King. Peyton and the Oxindens now found themselves on opposite sides in the coming war.

But this was no clarified falling into camps. Gentry friendships and gentry tensions survived any ideological separation. And even between Henry Oxinden and his cousin Harry there was a division. What was Harry doing, Henry wrote to him from London, wasting his time in the country? 'Neither business, nor frends, nor rumors of warre, nor brother, nor sister, nor uncle, nor aunt, nor beautie, nor good companie can invite or draw you to this loathed of you place.'[40] 'The passages of the grand and weightie affaires now in agitation'[41] seemed to hold no interest for Harry Oxinden. He remained at Maydekin, even as the prospect of civil war grew darker. 'I am sadly much alone', he wrote to his aunt, 'and now much inclined to melancholy.' In a long and revealing letter to Tom Peyton he portrayed himself without irony as the Horatian gentleman, withdrawn from the hideousness of politics and business into the comforts of his own ancestral lands.[42]

The Horatian vision did not play well with Harry's friends and relations. In January 1642 an angry letter arrived at Maydekin from his cousin Henry Oxinden, then in Westminster, 'that great phsaere [sic] of Activitie, which now whirles about three whole Kingdomes Blisse or destruction'. Crisis was imminent: 'If division in a private house brings ruine, how more in a kingdome where itt is so great among the rulers of itt.'[43] It was now Henry's turn to be entranced by the vigour and power of John Pym, whose latest speech he had just heard. 'Never anything was delivered with that modest confidence and heroicke courage by any common of this kingdome.' Henry, have no doubt, was a Parliamentarian but his gentry world was in turmoil:

> I find all here full of feares and almost voyd of hopes. Parents and children, brothers, kindred, I and deere frends have the seed of difference and division abundantly sowed in them. Sometimes I meet with a Cluster of Gentlemen equally divided in opinion and resolution, sometimes 3 to 2, sometimes more ods, but never unanimous, nay more I have heard foule languig and disparat quarelings even between old and intire frends, and how wee can thus stand and nott fall, certainly God must needs worke a miracle paralelle to some of his great ones in the old time.[44]

For Harry to be dreaming of a Horatian heaven down in Kent at this time of crisis was a failure to do his duty:

> Were you butt heere to heare the drummes, see the warlike postures and the glittering armour up and down the towne, and behold our poore bleeding libertis att stake, itt would rouze your Sperits, if you have any left, socour that deepe drousie lethergie you are now orewhelm'd in; I could say much more, butt I feare I have gon alreadie too farre.[45]

What the politicized Henry did not know was the one very good reason that Harry was failing to engage with the great crisis of the kingdom: he was in love.

Sloping out from the mourning over the death of his first wife, he suddenly fell, uncontrollably, for a seventeen-year-old girl, Kate Culling, the daughter of a yeoman farmer, Goodman James Culling, whose house and land were a mile away from Maydekin on the other side of the chalk ridge at South Barham, and who, according to a poem the stricken Harry wrote for her, had bright brown hair, a 'faire' forehead and starlike eyes which had 'not their matches underneath the skies', damask cheeks, cherry lips and a smooth chin.[46] He was lost.

The thoroughly politicized Henry Oxinden had little patience with any of this:

> I am glad you have gott a horse; provide you of Armes; it is Mars, nott Venus, that now can help; shee is now so much outt of fashion that where she herselfe here present, in all her best fashines, she would be the gazeing stock of contempt to all but lashe and effaeminat mindes.[47]

But Harry, scholar, squire, father, widower, indebted defender of his own property against his siblings and relations ('I doe take my estate for my most assured friend in my necessities'), was now hopelessly smitten. Kate's father had died, she was the heiress and her father, who had known Harry all his life and was his friend, had appointed him her guardian. A crucial conversation had swept him away. An impoverished knightly family had whisked her off to London and tried to marry her off to one of their connections. Harry was keen that she should escape such traps:

> I advised her to beware how and to whom, she married, and told her that her fortune and selfe deserved a good match, five to one better then myselfe; to which (casting her eies upon mee and as soone them downe againe) shee replyed, I know noe man I can thinke a better match or [MS torn] so well as yourselfe; this amazed mee, insomuch that where [MS torn] before I loved her as my child and friend, I now was forced to consider of loveing her as a wife.[48]

Kate knew what she was doing: those up- and downward-sweeping eyes caught the lonely widower. Harry, now thirty-four years old, was adrift in the torrents of love, perhaps for the first time in his life. He knew he was 'talkinge at randome in moone shining nights' but what could he do?[49]

I have tryed to cure my selfe by labour, art and friendship, nay I have practised the heathen philosophers' rule, to drive out one love with another as they doe a fever. I have read over sundry authors uppon this subject ... and all to little purpose ... I have tried to cure myself by exercise and diet and fasting. I have endeavoured to hinder it in its first growing; in the bargaine I have kepte a whole quarter of a year out of her company. I have endeavoured to call to mind the weaknes of most women, their pride, their dissimulation, their uncertainty ... I have tried Philters, Chaceters and Chales and all to such purpose as if I had run my head agt a post.[50]

He had considered throwing himself headlong off a rock but was 'loath to go so far as to experience it'. None of it was any good: Kate Culling was his destiny.

Tides of anxiety quivered through the Oxinden network. Harry's ex-brother-in-law Sir Thomas Peyton wanted to know even more urgently that his dead sister's children would not be disinherited by the arrival of a new stepmother. Harry's uncle Sir James Oxinden wanted to know what the Culling estate looked like. The Oxinden cousins wrote anxiously to ask Harry if he knew what he was doing.

Harry's animosity to Peyton, already stoked by their political differences, looked as if it was deepening into real loathing. To his Oxinden cousins, particularly to the brilliant and educated Elizabeth Dallison, he embarked on a series of long and revelatory letters describing and justifying his love. There was, first of all, the question of money. Was Harry Oxinden going to burden himself with an impoverished wife? He laid it all out in detail to Elizabeth, giving a fascinating insight into the financial planning of mid-seventeenth-century gentry.[51]

The Culling farm at South Barham is still there, a small timbered farmhouse, with an eighteenth-century extension, and a rather larger, low-eaved barn next to it. The whole ancient ensemble is now half-submerged in the giant sheds of a modern dairy business based on a high-producing Holstein Friesian herd. But the atmosphere of a serious, working farming enterprise remains. This is not a place in which gentlemen have ever played with their Horatian visions. In the 1640s it sat at the middle of a small productive holding in the valley of the Nailbourne stretching up on to the wooded chalk hill above it. The coppice wood was worth about £17 a year, some used for fencing, but mostly as firewood. Between the coppice stools stood the much longer-lived timber trees, largely oak, with some ash. In all, the capital value of the woodland was worth £400. The rest of the farm was producing £109 12s. a year. Estates were valued in the seventeenth century at twenty times their annual income – a 5 per cent return on capital – and on that basis South Barham was worth about £2,192, to which Harry added the £400 value of the wood: a total of £2,592.[52]

That sounded good but Kate's father had left substantial legacies and debts: £100 at the next Lady Day to Mr Huffam, her brother-in-law; another £100 two years after that to the same man; £100 to Mr Denwood at that time and another £300 three years later; to James Fag, £200 eight years thence; and to Kate's younger sister Ellen Culling £600 when she was married or reached the age of twenty-one. When all that was taken into account, South Barham was worth £1,192 clear, which didn't sound so good at all, particularly as the value would not be realized for many years. 'But the house and seate [site] in this valuation', Harry told Elizabeth a little too insistently, 'is reckoned att nothing, which I esteeme at a considerable rate; for as concerning the seate, it is incompareably more pleasant than mine, and the house will not be builded for 4 or 500.'[53]

'None of the legacies can be expected faster than the revenewes will pay', Harry had written, but looked at rationally, this was clearly a plan driven more by love than by the financial interests of his family. Harry Oxinden was, in effect, slipping out of the gentry frame of mind.

There was another problem: class. Kate 'was a Yeoman's daughter; True itt is her father was a yeoman, but such a Yeoman as lived in his house, in his company, and in his sportes and pleasures like a gentleman, and followed the same with gentlemen'. She had been sent to school for four years 'amongst other gentlemen's daughters, att the same costs and charges they were at'. Besides, the Cullings were ancient

Kentish people, who had been at South Barham, Harry discovered, since 1280. 'If the definition which the heralds have given to Gentilitie be true (that is of antient rase) I see no reason why the possessors of so ancient an estate may not as well have the benefit of the foresaid definition as others.'[54]

A small revolution was going on in the heart of Harry Oxinden. Since the Middle Ages the discussion had flowed back and forth over the nature of gentility: did it rely on virtue or on blood? Was it dependent on your father's qualities or on yours? As the old definitions of a hierarchical society were for a moment dissolving around him, Harry now had no doubt: 'The wisest men have ever held vertue the best and truest nobilitie, and as sure as death it is soe, and for my owne part my former highlie esteeming of politicall nobilitie I now reckon amongst the follies of my youth.'[55]

The beauty of Kate's eyes had convinced him. There were some people in the world 'of soe stupid and grosse capacities, that conceive there is something extrordinarielie inherent in this politicall nobilitie'[56] but Harry had abandoned that idiocy now. Men were not born equal, but their virtues and nothing else was what distinguished the noble from the ordinary: 'If I see a man of what low degree or quality ever that is virtuous, rich, wise or powerful, him will I preferre beefore the greatest Lord in the kingdome that comes short of him in these.'[57] This line of thought, and the recognition that the young Kate Culling was as fine a person as he'd ever met, had changed his mind and his view of the world. Rather than being patronized and put upon by his Royalist brother-in-law Thomas Peyton, he was now engaged to a woman who loved him and looked up to him, as the rest of her family would. A new sense of liberty coursed through Harry, a sudden coalescence of public and private selves in this time of civil war. As he wrote to his cousin Henry

It shall ever be as far from my beleife as the East is from the West, that so many millions of men as are in the Christian world were created to bee slaves to about half a score mortall gods ... Put not your trust in princes for there is no healpe in them.[58]

The gentry value system fell away. It now seemed absurd to Harry Oxinden that one of his neighbours, Harry Palmer, had got himself knighted in service of the King. Why should Harry Palmer not 'continue in a degree with other men'?[59] On top of that, his own brother, the vicar James Oxinden, had now turned to the right and wanted 'to advance the pompe and libertie of the clergie over the Laytie'.[60] In Harry's view, all that the church needed was a true reformation.

The arguments and passions over which England divided in civil war had entered his life, even if it was sequestered in the depths of a chalky Kent valley. Now those passions were to come even closer to home. Early in 1643, Parliament had abolished all bishoprics and archbishoprics and the Puritan faction in the church had come to dominate the country. John Swan, the rector of Denton, took to his new significance with a passion, to Harry's contempt:

> Little did I once dreame that there would arise out of the ashes of the Bishops a precise offspring, outwardly pious and zealous, seemingly humble and lowly, but inwardly wicked and profane, secretly proud and ambitious, more medling, more temporalizing then those they condemned.[61]

Swan and his sort had decided 'to reigne like Lords and Kings themselves in their owne Circuits'. It was a system that would 'set up a teacher greater then a Bishop in everie parish, who, like Mr John Swan, will studie more to inslave his parishioners then to save their soules'.[62]

Late in October 1643, this clash between the newly enlightened squire and the newly empowered clergyman had come to a head at Maydekin itself. Two of Harry's tenants, Adam Jull and a man called Woollet, the assessors for the village, had levied a local tax on one of Swan's servants at double its usual rate. Swan maintained that this was because the servant had been chasing and killing Jull's hogs and Jull was getting his revenge. Harry Oxinden, clearly disgusted with the sanctimonious Swan, started shouting and swearing oaths at him, 'spoken in such passion as I scarce know I spake them'.[63]

Swan, whose father had also been the vicar here, was a malevolent presence in the village. 'I have greatly disliked many things in you since your father went from hence',[64] Oxinden told him. Swan wrote back to say that he would leave Harry to his 'owne wrath and to entangle yourself in your owne snares'.[65] Then on 31 October, Hallowe'en, a moment when by tradition the accepted order was turned upside down in rowdy village rituals – deeply disapproved of by the Puritans – Harry took part and Swan was furious.

Who would have dreamed that you would have so farre engaged your-selfe (in these sober times) in such a ridiculous sport as that was. Was it not folly for a gentleman of your quality to have a man dressed in women's apparel in your court and obseanely to hang up your serv-ant's smock on a pole and to follow that and an asse etc. accompanied with rude boyes up and doune the streete?[66]

Harry said it was just a 'harmelesse pastime, which to the opinion of honest divines is not only lawful but in some sort necessarie'.[67] Swan would not have that and summoned the trained band of the local militia captained by one of the leading Puritan gentry of Kent, Sir Edward Boys. For Harry, this was an 'uncivill odious and detestable affront',

(the verie thought whereof cannot chuse but put mee into an extreame passion) given mee and my dearest [wife crossed out] consort in my owne house, by being there, by men of meane qualitie, bid stand, stand; one of who charged the rest give fire upon us.[68]

It was obviously a tense moment. No one had the right to tell Mr and Mrs Oxinden to stand up in their own parlour. Kate had 'made a pish' of Mr Swan – teasing him in all his seriousness – and Harry had been in a red fog of rage.

There are layers of significance in this stand-off between the newly democratized squire and the intemperate Puritan minister. Harry's rage was both against a form of tyranny and against a lack of class respect; Swan's against a degenerate world, of which degenerate gentry were yet another symptom. Harry had not abandoned the idea of himself as a gentleman – 'all men that have the least sparke of gentillitie or breeding in them must equally resent with us who have suffered in such an intolerable and unexampled manner' – but he could not tolerate 'presbiteriall government'. He had acquired a form of wisdom. The Hallowe'en japes in the village street were to be defended against intolerant Puritan modernity because they were an integral part of the Maydekin world which Harry loved.

He turned to his uncle Sir James to make peace between him and Swan. The reconciliation was not immediate but in the following September Harry sent Swan a young swan as a peace offering. The vicar wrote a graceful reply: 'I returne you many thanks for your rara Avis in terris' – 'a rare bird in the lands', a phrase from Juvenal, and a joke here because Juvenal was referring to that impossibility, a black swan – 'and doe reckon it so much the greater Courtisy because your present is homogeniall to my name.' Swan added another elegant little witticism: 'You may assure yourselfe that with this Cygnett as with a Signett you have sealed your true affection to me.'[69]

For a few days Harry joined the Parliamentary army at the siege of Arundel Castle in Sussex, during the frozen first week of January 1644. He hated it, grieving 'to see men of the same Religion, and of the same Nation, so eagerly engaged one against the other'.[70] His friend and neighbour Mark Dixwell, nephew and heir to Sir Basil at Broome Park, was killed at the siege beside him. Harry never withdrew his allegiance from Parliament but he never fought again. Instead he continued to do what his situation in life led him to believe in: loving his neighbours and family, even when they were fighting on the other side. His Royalist brother-in-law Sir Thomas Peyton, who had treated him so condescendingly, was imprisoned by Parliament and heavily fined. Harry, though, did his best for him, writing to him in prison and making sure that his children were all right – they went to stay with the Bargraves at Bifrons. Peyton wrote a beautiful letter thanking him and telling Harry that he was 'a vertue betweene two extremes', a model of the true and evangelicall virtues of good neighbourhood. 'Tis nott the neerenesse of doores nor the confining of Inheritances makes us Neighbours; but the Acts of Love and Charitie which exercise their offices in all places and att all distances ... For myselfe, I must esteeme of your affectionate offers as enlargements of a liberal and kind heart; and lay them up in my owne breast for my study and observation.[71]

A kind of goodness had come to Harry Oxinden with his marriage to Kate Culling. Other neighbouring Royalists also benefited from his kindness and care. Sir Anthony Percivall, his Denton Royalist neighbour, was imprisoned and his property and rabbits came under attack from covetous Parliamentarians. In a letter to him in prison, Harry stated his credo: 'You shall suffer as little ecclipse as my small power will permitt, which shall extend to its utmost to doe you all the right and service I can, being none of those summer birds which take their leave before the winter and snows come.'[72]

On the other side, a deep friendship developed between Harry and a radical separatist preacher, Charles Nichols, who was on the run from the Parliamentary authorities.[73] Unlike many other Kentish gentlemen, who preyed as hard as they could on the property of their neighbouring enemies, Harry Oxinden was a neutralist, committed to no side, but positively engaged with all of them. 'I can assure you', Thomas Peyton wrote to 'his very loving bro Mr Hen Oxinden', 'more devoted affections have bin gotten you by the late reports of your non-confedircy than had you courted every man's particular humour for it'.[74] Quite distinctly, in his mid-thirties, Harry Oxinden had become a noble spirit.

But his goodness, and the sense of reliability which he embodied for his friends and some of his relations, became his downfall. He had long been in debt and any gust of difficulty was always in danger of capsizing the whole enterprise. His downfall came in the end from the most unlikely of sources.

When Harry's old friend Vincent Denne died in June 1642, his nephew and heir Tom Denne was not yet twenty-one and Vincent made Harry his executor until the boy came of age. There was a substantial inheritance: the manor house at Wenderton near Wingham, some surrounding farms and pieces of land further afield in Kent on the Isle of Thanet and on the rich summer grazing of Romney Marsh, worth in all some £8,000. Wenderton, as one seventeenth-century Kentishman described it, was 'eminent for its excellent air, situation, and prospect'.[75] It is still a beautiful and entrancing place, wisteria sprouting like a moustache from the plum-apricot brick, with pear orchards running down to the marshes by the river. Huge old chimneys give its date away as from the 1640s despite the big nineteenth-century windows. In its relationship to the lane – neither withdrawn behind a big wall nor hidden from view – it looks as calmly integrated with the wider world as Vincent Denne himself had been. As his will had instructed, he is buried under a slab of Purbeck in the church in Wingham, as near as he could be to the pew in which he had worshipped all his life.

Vincent had given legacies to his nieces but to his own older brother Thomas Denne of Denne Hill, young Tom's father, he left only a little land near Denton. Old Thomas was sixty-seven, an embittered, subtle and unscrupulous barrister in the Middle Temple. As soon as he heard that his younger brother had cut him out of the Wenderton inheritance, he resolved to sue both his son Tom and Harry Oxinden as the executor. He would go after them, as Harry wrote to Tom, 'till neither of us be worth a groat'.[76] Harry hoped that 'all these great words will vanish like smoake in the aire'[77] but they didn't. Thomas Denne subjected him to years of litigation, entangling him in multiple, overlapping cases, claiming that Tom's inheritance was in fact his own. When suddenly young Tom died in 1648 and left much of his property to Harry, old Denne turned his fire on him directly. Tom had left large legacies to his four sisters and for years they and their father pursued the executor, surrounded by an outer halo of dissatisfied creditors and legatees.

Months went by in which Harry was forced to be in London while Kate stayed at home attending to their lands. 'Pray put on the breeches until I come home'[78] he told her but being away from her was 'the greatest and longest purgatory I ever yet knew'.[79] 'Kate Dearest', he wrote in September 1651, 'I will not bee bound uppon any termes to live so long from thee againe, being contented to live uppon bread and waters rather with thy company then with any conveniences this Kingdom can afford without it.'[80]

In the end, but only after fifteen years' legal tussle, Harry won his case against Denne. But it was an empty victory. The webs of legal entanglement still meant that he could not get his hands on the money from the estate and he had been ruined by lawyers' fees. A little sickeningly, others seemed to be doing well. His brother-in-law Thomas Barrow had become draper to the aristocracy. His own younger brother Richard, known as 'Dicke Ox', who had gone off to fight as a soldier of fortune, returned dripping in loot, with

2 rings more then I saw beefore uppon each cuffe string, of the value of 50l. the piece, besids other rings uppon his fingers.[81]...

His cloath is of 35s the yard: his linen exceeding fine: he hath a chaine of gold goeth 7 times about his wrist and a Diamond ring upon his finger.[82]

Harry's neighbours the Dixwells at Broome Park were doing well out of the Commonwealth – one of them had signed Charles's death warrant – but only troubles clustered around Harry Oxinden. He married his daughter Margaret to John Hobart, a man who looked as if he had prospects – the Hobarts were an important Norfolk family – but who turned out to be a rake and ne'er-do-well. Margaret's uncle the Royalist Sir Thomas Peyton, still in prison, wrote upbraidingly to Harry in August 1653 when Margaret was six months pregnant:

There is a daughter of yours I heare towards lying in and her husband minds it as much as my Cowes calving. Shee is as unprovided for as one that walkes the highwaies and how to provide for all things I knowe not, nor will I have long to do with such incessant troubles.[83]

Peyton then wrote to Harry's uncle Sir James Oxinden at Dene, about 'my sister's children, whom [Harry] hath hitherto put to shift for themselves, and consumed all their patrimony in vaine imaginations'.[84]

This was humiliating, the unravelling of Harry's gentry world, the loss of honour, the loss of continuity, the loss of respect. His son Thomas was no better, falling in with a gang of highwaymen and turning to a life of violent crime on the highways of England and the continent. Harry Oxinden must have been holding his head in his hands. From the endless negotiations in London he wrote to Kate: 'I know not how I shall according to the saying keepe buckle and thong together.' And then he faced the ultimate solution: 'If I could have my price for land, I have a desire rather to convert itt into mony.'[85]

Harry's collapse is the rarest of glimpses into the ending of a gentry family, the final slither into insignificance. Harry asked Kate to find out how likely the Dixwells were to buy Maydekin if he offered it for sale.

Pray sift out to your utmost abilitie how they of Broome stand affected to the buying of what I have formerly acquainted you with; I do not value what was my forefathers if inconvenient to mee, as they would have altered their estates if for their conveniency; they have left me the same liberty and I may lawfully take it; and Posterity will take the same libertie should I do my utmost to prevent itt.[86]

This was whistling in dark. He had loved Maydekin all his life; everything about him was bound up with it. Now he had to claim otherwise. 'It is only that true love and a true lover's knot beetwene man and wife', he told his beloved Kate, 'continues indissoluble.'[87]

Harry drew up particulars for the sale and in July 1656 his cousin Henry Oxinden of Dene introduced him to Edward Ady, 'a Merchant that I found willing [to deale] with you for your house and Lands'.[88] But when things are on the slide, everything goes wrong. Harry was thought to have overvalued his land 'and your tres too, tops of ashes etc' and Ady was reluctant to close on the sale. Harry had borrowed money against it from several people, including one John Carpenter, 'of the City Stampe, hard and flinty, and very earnest for money, or for a very strict prosecution for the same'.[89]

When the sale was delayed, Carpenter wanted his money back and wrote insultingly to Harry: 'It is vayne for you to flatter yourselfe with the thought of obteyneing longer tyme, because my occasions are of that consequence which will admit of noe more delayes. Your answer (without a putt off) will oblige'.[90]

Harry's name, standing, financial position and ability to command any form of respect were now bankrupt. Only in 1663 was Maydekin and its lands finally sold, and then at a pitiably low price. Harry had wanted £1,500 but Ady paid no more than £800 for the main house and its premises. The orchards were to be valued by arbitration on top of that and there were some other cottages sold at fourteen times their annual rent, the bulk of the land at eighteen times, both well below the conventional twenty years' purchase. Maydekin was sold, in other words, at a buyer's price.[91]

In April 1663 Mr Ady gave Kate Oxinden leave to stay at the house until the middle of May. 'If you have any other goods that you cannot conveniently dispose of before our coming you may leave them in the garrette,' he wrote generously.[92] The Greenwich man bought quite a lot of the Oxindens' furniture, the brewing vessels and barrels, the table and benches in the hall, two beds, one better, another worse, and the things belonging to the dairy.

The world of Henry Oxinden, now aged fifty-five, was in collapse. 'Surely, surely, without considerable monie nothing can considerably be done'.[93] This was not how it was meant to end. Still writing from 'this stinking smoakie Cittie',[94] he tried to put the best possible gloss on it to his young wife, Kate. They had been deserted by their friends and by their class. The Peytons, the greater Oxindens, the Bargraves and the Dixwells had all abandoned them to their fate. A gentleman with no money was a gentleman no more. 'None of our real or pretended friends *would help us*' – Harry wrote those phrases which are printed here in italics in a simple code so that the courier could not read them – but he insisted that they had 'cause to bless God that *wee met with* such a one (*though a hard one*) as we have'. Edward Ady and his purse was a kind of ally when all help had deserted them. 'For *without mony nothing is to be had* of the best friendes, and that is a certaine Truth as anie I know.'[95]

He couldn't come down to Kent because if he did '*Those to whom I owe money to* will haunt mee *before I have it for them*.'[96] Kate was to take 'the hangings in the little parlour, the Long Chamber and the maids' chamber' as well as the diamond panes in his study windows on which a lion and fox were engraved.[97] Some furniture including the bedstead was to be taken to Kate's old house at South Barham, which they were going to rent out. Harry and Kate would themselves move to the small house across the road from Maydekin which they called the Red House or Little Maydekin, twenty yards away from the paternal house he had been forced to relinquish.

The Ady family arrived at Maydekin on Ascension Day 1663, coming from Greenwich in two coaches, full of excitement. Harry wrote to Kate at this most painful moment in his life:

My dere beyond all expression, this is to desire Thee not to be troubled in the least measure at that which joyes mee which is our removal to thy red house; before wee were sure of Nothing, now we are of some-what; for I have all ready setled it uppon Thee as it lyes not in my power to unsettle it.[98]

From his vantage point across the road, he watched carefully as Mr Ady made changes and adjustments to the old house, noting how 'in that yeare hee came, hee tooke part of the entry into the Kitchin, and removed the windore out of the little parlour to the south side of the Kitchin. He then paved the Kitchin with purbeck stone.'[99]

These were only the first of many such notes in his private journal, every one delineating the outlines of loss. He did come to some kind of necessary resolution about the disastrous turn his life had taken. His brother Richard, the now-wealthy soldier and adventurer, had spoken to Harry's son Thomas about the pain and hurt Harry must experience living opposite his old abandoned house. In October 1666, Harry wrote to Thomas:

As concerning my brother's wonder how I can endure the smoake of these chimnies which were my father's, I have only to say that if endeavours as much as in mee lay could have preserved what I was forced to sell I had not done it; and sure I am many have got estates with lesse care and trouble then I parted with mine.[100]

He had presided over the collapse of his family but he had done his best. Harry still felt he belonged in Kent, in the country of his own loss, because he saw himself not as the paterfamilias who had failed, but as the grandson who belonged. Richard had said that he hated that part of the country 'since his father's estate was gon'. Not Harry:

I must confess I know not how to understand that part of his letter; for though his Father's estate in Kent be gon, his grandfather's and great grandfather's family remaine in it, from whom he lineally descends; and can any man descended from a line expect the same respect in a strange country, where what hee is, and from whence hee comes, nobody knowes, as hee meets where he is known? True it is (as I find by experience) one's rich kindred will mightily disrespect such an one, and that upon proud and base principles, but others will have better respect of him where his extract is known then he will find where he is not known.[101]

These are the pitiable thoughts of a man near the end of his life. Those who had been his friends and allies when he was young and with property, including Henry Oxinden, Thomas Peyton and Robert Bargrave – his rich kindred – looked down on him now, but still he considered himself the 'extract' of the great Oxinden inheritance.

Harry spent the last few years of his life at Little Maydekin, ill, poor and weak, planting fruit trees and vines against any south-facing wall. His wicked son Tom was finally arrested for his various plottings, pickpocketings and thievings and died in a London prison in December 1668.[102] Harry lasted eighteen months more and died in June 1670. He had ordained that there should be two 'scutchions of Armes' painted for his funeral in Denton church, his own identity subsumed in the family which to the end he considered greater than his own self.[103]

Why did Harry Oxinden fail? Perhaps because he didn't fight the fight, didn't engage with business or London life, didn't marry a rich woman and didn't devote his life to furthering his own family's future. His failure was his own fault, the result of too much indulgence in an elegant, semi-philosophical detachment from the business of life. But that verdict may be too harsh. The resilience of a tiny 600-acre estate, particularly in the rough economic conditions of the mid-seventeenth century, was not enough to weather even one generation's failure to attend to the business of survival. Harry Oxinden's fate is a measure of the difference between gentry and aristocracy, or at least between lower and higher gentry. No cushion, nothing in reserve, meant time and trouble would soon enough cut into the bone. Harry's houses – Maydekin itself, Little Maydekin across the road, and Kate's farm-house at South Barham – all still exist; his branch of the Oxindens has not been heard of since the seventeenth century.

The richer branch of the family, the Oxindens of Dene, persisted until the early twentieth century. Then they too died out and at Dene today, the great house and its park have disappeared, leaving only a few barns, a coach house and a dovecote as a memory. In Wingham church, whose spire prods up across the fields from Dene, there is a wonderful Oxinden memorial, a model of its kind, erected in 1681[104] and testament to the intentions of the Oxindens who made it. Apart from Harry's correspondence, this remains their only record.

So alluring is it that a recent vicar tried to have it removed to the back of the church where it wouldn't distract the congregation during services. Conservationists saved it and the sunlight still falls on the helmeted cherubs, the huge black curly-headed marble oxen at each corner, the carved marble fruits, and the long lists of Oxinden knights, baronets and dames, the marble all paid for with money from the East India Company for which a late seventeenth-century Oxinden, Sir James's third son George, was for a while Governor of Bombay.

It is a monumentalization not of any great man, nor of his children, but of the Oxinden spirit itself, sturdy, armed, forthright, with an architectural vision of its place here in Kent as something that outlasted individual generations, a 'Family', as the inscription says, 'whose Ancesters have flourished in this County for severall Ages', a tribute to the corporate, trans-generational enterprise which lay at the heart of any gentry family.

Honour

The le Neves

Great Witchingham, Norfolk

In the early evening of Saturday, 20 August 1698, a small act of English class drama was played out on a patch of heathland at Cawston, twelve miles north of Norwich. It was a duel with swords, an honour-scuffle, which ended in one agonizing death and led to a murder hunt that stretched over the next two years. But this chapter is less about the after-effects of the fight than what led up to it. What brought two early-middle-aged Norfolk men to the point of death one warm August afternoon? Why were they there? What was at stake? What fuelled the loathing?[1]

Sir Henry Hobart (the name was pronounced and sometimes written Hubbard) was about forty that summer and for most of his life had lived with the idea of his own significance.[2] He was a member of a moral ruling class. England was his for the taking and the using. For two centuries Hobarts had been involved with power, as Tudor legal officials, Elizabethan lawyers and important Jacobean judges, as Members of Parliament for Norfolk throughout the Civil War years of the 1640s and as leading players in the English republic of the 1650s. They were highly cultivated Puritan gentry, readers of Milton, Spenser and Virgil, governors, agricultural improvers, committed Presbyterians and deniers of arbitrary royal authority. They had been happy to see Charles I deposed but, for all that, they were courteous men. One Hobart was described as blessed with 'an excellent eloquence, the éclat of ancestry [and] the most engaging sweetness animated with a singular gravity'.[3] It was not an unusual combination of qualities in the seventeenth century. Of the Hobarts' sense of their own importance there is no doubt.

After the Restoration, Charles II visited Norfolk in 1671, anxious to restore relations with his father's enemies. In the great galleries of the Hobarts' palace at Blickling, in the valley of the river Bure, the King knighted Henry, who was then fourteen. But the Hobarts did not love the Stuarts and when the choice came in 1688 to dismiss the Catholic James II and welcome in his son-in-law the Dutch Protestant Stadholder as William III, Sir Henry Hobart was in no doubt which side he was on. He became Norfolk's leading Whig, intimate with the Williamite crown and with power, his family en route to the aristocracy (his son would become the Earl of Buckinghamshire) and firmly committed to the Protestant religion.

It was a period of falling rents – the productivity of English land had dropped in the Little Ice Age of the seventeenth century – but, unlike many smaller men, Hobart was rich enough to be heavily indebted. On inheriting his father's seriously encumbered estates in 1683, he was forced to sell both lands and his father's large and cosmopolitan library.[4] The Hobart lands had shrunk by three-quarters since 1625 and what remained was mortgaged to a London merchant, John Pollexfen, who in 1683 was urging on Sir Henry 'a Lady … that had 5 or 6,000, and 700 per an'.[5] Hobart did better than that, in the following summer marrying Elizabeth Maynard, who brought him the £10,000 which allowed him at least to buy out the egregious Pollexfen.

For all these financial inconveniences, there is no doubting Hobart's grandeur. Money was poured into the furnishing and dignifying of Blickling and into paying the electors who would return him to Parliament. Men were sent out across the fens and marshes of Norfolk to find the young swans that would grace the expanses of water in the park.[6] An account of Sir Henry's wardrobe in the 1670s contains a great deal of sobriety ('a dark coloured druggat coat and breeches', 'a coate and a pair of sleeves of black cloath with black triming') but alongside that is the suppressed flamboyance of the powerful: 'a silk pink wastcoate', 'a light coloured branched silk wastcoate', 'a coate and a pair of breeches of a darke coloured searge lynd with flowrd silke and a wastcoate suitable to the lyning of ye coate and a pair of silke stockins suitable'.[7]

Amongst this well-equipped and manly elegance were some rather out-of-date armour and several pairs of pistols, as well as two rapiers with silver hilts, 'a short walking rapier', 'a scemytar hatcht with gold' and 'a walking sword with a damask'd hilt'.[8] Even at the end of the seventeenth century, gentlemanliness had not yet separated from expertise in martial violence. When, in 1690, William III was in Ireland, defeating his Catholic enemies there, Hobart was on his staff as a cavalry commander. As a reward, William made him one of the Commissioners of Customs, a post worth £1,000 a year.[9] Religious allegiance allied to military power and political influence meant, as ever, money in the pocket.

Sir Henry was at the summit of the gentry world, his eyes on the beautifully upholstered comforts of the aristocratic life for which he was aiming. Oliver le Neve was about thirty-six on the day of the duel. His own relatively small but beautiful house was about four miles south-west of Cawston Heath at Great Witchingham in the valley of the river Wensum, just along the valley from where a nineteenth-century mansion houses the modern headquarters of Bernard Matthews, the Norfolk turkey company.

When le Neve suggested to Hobart the place for their duel, many things were unequal between them, but the geographical symmetry was exact: both of them rode up from the lush, reedy, meadowy valleys of their two rivers, past the warm, cooked-tomato-red brick and pantiled farmhouses and cottages of their tenants, across the arable lands on the upper edge of the valleys, much of them still unenclosed and worked on the medieval strip pattern, and on to the sandy, sparsely occupied heath of the ridge which separated their two provinces. For each man, it would have been no more than an hour's ride.

The wonderful, landscape-defining presence of Blickling Hall, which sits in its slice of north Norfolk like an earl at ease in his portrait, has lasted in well-funded perfection until today. It is not like that in the Wensum valley, which is both emptier and a little rougher than in le Neve's time. The holdings and fortunes of the smaller gentry were far more vulnerable to loss and change, to disease, the death of heirs and mismanagement, than those of their greatest neighbours. And now at Great Witchingham the sheen of a loved place has largely gone. The ditches which once drained the riverside meadows are blocked and the grassland has become moory. Wide matted beds of Norfolk reed interrupt the fields. Willows and alders stand and collapse in sodden, owl-inhabited woods. Down here, in this damp and riverine world, Oliver le Neve had his house. It has almost entirely disappeared. The only remains are a beautiful brick barn and a length of ivy-bearded garden wall, twelve feet high but buried in a brambled wood, where nowadays gamekeepers raise partridges and pheasants. His stone coat of arms was dug out of the brambles here a few years ago and given to his distant descendants.

Le Neve and his friends and family always referred to Great Witchingham in their letters as 'Witch' or 'Witching',[10] the nickname for a place they loved, but you have to edit the modern landscape to recover the scene of his happiness. His wide-windowed, symmetrical brick house was surrounded by flower beds and fruit and vegetable gardens. Barns, kennels and stables were arranged in courts to one side. The river flowed past the south face of the house, beyond a lawn, from where a carriageway crossed it via a bridge to the Norwich road on the high ground.

It was the small gentry equivalent of the great riverside houses of England, Audley End, Wilton and Chatsworth, an image of well-watered contentment, and le Neve's correspondence brims over with the delights of his world. Peaches, nectarines, plums, cherries and dwarf pears were all trained up in the warmth of the walled garden, as well as bushes of black- and redcurrants and gooseberries.[11] May frosts and even snow in May both troubled the gardeners.[12] There was a bowling green.[13] His gardener grew yews from seed and grafted hollies for new hedges.[14] His carnations were well known to his neighbours, especially 'the white ones edged with red and purple',[15] and they wrote to him asking if he could send plants over for their gardens. Bay trees were imported from Holland in pots – and stolen on the Norfolk quayside before they were delivered to Witchingham.[16] In early summer he sent the asparagus he had grown to his friends, followed a few weeks later by prize artichokes ('heartychoaks').[17] Stone lions were ordered from London dealers.[18]

These were the immediate surroundings of the house, but le Neve lived in a richly layered world. Beyond the garden and the gardeners was the river, where le Neve, his employees and friends fished with nets, catching pike and bream which they transferred to the keep pond by the house, and for 'noble trout' with 'angles'.[19] One February the men at Witchingham caught seventeen pike with one drag of the net through the river 'which they were very brag on'.[20] Some live carp, packed in a tub between courses of rye straw mixed with grass, were sent to stock the Witchingham ponds but they died en route.[21]

Beyond these elegant playgrounds were the farmlands: meadow, pasture, arable and the woods of le Neve's estate. Some of it he farmed on his own account, alert to the newest European techniques, importing clover from Holland and sainfoin, the most nutritious forage crop for working animals, from London dealers.[22] Most of his land was let out to tenants, le Neve receiving their rents on Michaelmas Day in the autumn and Lady Day in early spring. That, anyway, was the theory but rents were almost always paid late, sometimes only a week or two, occasionally a couple of years, and le Neve in effect, by allowing these rents to come when they did, acted as a banker for his tenantry, tiding them over difficulties. At Christmastime he was charitable to the poor, slaughtering a beast and distributing the meat to them.[23] The people of Witchingham seem to have responded with affection, writing to him beforehand to say how 'we all long for your coming home'.[24] In July 1707 Will Looker, his steward at Witchingham, wrote to say that 'The tenants desire to know whether they may be permitted to meet you some part of the way when you come home'.[25]

At a time when you could buy a good cow for between £3 and £4, or employ a gardener for a year at £16, hire a man for the three weeks of the harvest for £1, or for the same amount buy three swans or get a good horse to take you the 130 miles from Great Witchingham to Westminster, le Neve's property gave him an income of about £1,500 a year – the basis for a comfortable life, if nothing like on the Hobart level. But Oliver le Neve was not the natural heir to all these comforts and delights. He could not look back, as the Hobarts could, to centuries and generations of squiredom. His father, Francis, had been a draper in London, to be found at the Crown near Pope's Alley, Cornhill, an upholsterer and retailer of chintzes, a poor cousin of a family which had been in Norfolk, if obscurely, for many years.[26] Oliver's mother, Avice, was the daughter of a City merchant. They had shops, warehouses and a little property in London. But his distant cousin, also called Oliver le Neve, a stationer, had accumulated lands in Norfolk, Surrey and Middlesex. This old Oliver had no children and in 1672 he decided that he would leave everything he had to his young, distantly related namesake, who was then ten years old, 'in consideration of the natural love and affection' he had for him. Money was following blood: young Oliver was old Oliver's great-uncle's great-grandson. But if anything can be judged by the verve and vitality of his later letters, young Oliver must have been a charming boy. He had a brother, Peter, who was two years older, but Peter was left nothing more than the 'remainder' to the property: he would inherit it only if young Oliver died heirless. This preferential treatment of the younger brother, rare enough in English history, would create its own difficulties later on. Peter le Neve was a herald, an expert in genealogies and coats of arms, a meticulous man and a distinguished antiquary, a great collector and preserver of documents. Every one of the stories in this book depends for its realities either on a court case, in which evidence had to be produced and preserved, or a scholarly hoarder in the family. It is through his brother's filing of correspondence that anything beyond the bare bones is known of Oliver le Neve.[27]

These, then, are the roots of the slightly amphibious position occupied by Oliver le Neve throughout his life: from an old but unimportant Norfolk family; with his own father in trade, and his mother from a trading background; with a large fortune settled on him and now substantially if not wonderfully rich; and with a love for the life of the Norfolk squire. He was both deeply attached to the hunting, hawking, fishing, farming, gardening, drinking, joking, racing, gambling existence summed up by the one word 'Witchingham' and a natural born Tory, suspicious of 'that glorious monarch king William',[28] as he and his friends habitually referred to him; both a local Justice and a captain in the local militia, who would look with suspicion on the court corruption and power-broking of the Whig grandees and their morally superior sense of authority; and for whom the phrase 'turn Whig' meant 'turn double rogue'.[29] At the same time he was a new man, a city boy, with important commercial links to London, the taint of commerce on him and a great deal of business to be done there.

The question of standing, of dignity and respect, of everything bundled into the word 'honour', would lead in the end to the crisis on Cawston Heath in 1698. It surfaced first fifteen years earlier in a letter which the 22-year-old Oliver wrote to Thomas Browne, in March 1683. Browne was his near-neighbour at Elsing Hall, a wonderful moated medieval house just the other side of the Wensum, an ex-Parliamentarian, his family part of the Norfolk gentry for more generations than anyone would care to hear about. Browne had dared to patronize le Neve among the local gentry and this letter was le Neve's flaring response, expressed in crazily overblown language (it was only a year or two after he had left Oxford). In a letter which has disappeared, le Neve had written to Browne and Browne had ridiculed his literary style in public, accusing him of writing in 'a bald, insipid (& as you are pleased to term it) mircatorian stile'.[30] Le Neve was being told by the old gent that he had the manner of a trader.

Now he went to town. Browne's own family, for all its grandeur, had also married beneath itself, le Neve wrote,

mingling your most generous, and ancient blood with Mircatorian blood ... I must boldly tell you that as I scorn to spiak ill of you behind your Back & flatter to your face (a gift most ripe in you) I am much of the opinion that it is beneath a Gentleman (as you pretend to be) to treat a neighbour's much less a friends name with that scorn, contempt and Reproach, of exposing his inferiority to common veiw.[31]

It was the rage that came from shame, from hurt and offended honour. Le Neve acknowledged that he had made the mistake of assuming, from their brief talk, too great an intimacy with this minor grandee. 'I reasonably concluded that our Conversation together had sufficiently entitled me to the same familiarity with you as you with me; and that I may as bluntly call you Tom as You me Oliver.'[32] As so often, the outcome of the argument is unknown, but the degree of social insecurity is unmistakable.

The following year, Oliver le Neve fell in love, and these same class and status anxieties and desires circle around his infatuation with the girl. Anne Gawdy had all the right attributes, came from the best sort of Norfolk family and had the right amount of money to her name. But there was a problem. A girl's parents, when she was to be married, expected the groom's family to provide her with a jointure, a quantity of land or investments that would be held back from the inheritance of the next generation and whose income would support her if her husband were to die before her. On her death, the jointure lands would return to the heir and so on into the future. But Oliver's own estate at Great Witchingham, for all its apparent ease and comfort, was heavily indebted and there was no way he could provide for her widowhood at the level which her family was demanding. Her father required that if Anne was to marry Oliver, he should guarantee to her a jointure of £250 a year. The rate of return on capital was dropping in the last years of the seventeenth century and so that figure represented a capital investment approaching £6,000. So Oliver wrote to his brother Peter in London.

I have a request which I hope you will not deny me, there is a woman in ye world yt I have a kindness for. Hr Fortune though itt is not grat but I think in ye circumstances of my estate itt is as much or more than I can challenge yt is £3000, if you will joyne with me to make a Joynture of £250 pr Ann, you will be instrumental to make me I hope ye Hapiest man breathing.[33]

It was both calculation and love, with no cynicism in that, but a worldly understanding that if he provided from his own resources such a large jointure for his wife, he would be depriving his heirs of a happy future. It had happened often enough in the past, that sons waited in relative poverty for years after their father had died until their mother died too and the unencumbered estate was released into their hands. But Oliver loved Anne. She may have had only £3,000 to her name as her dowry or 'portion' but her qualities as a person more than made up for that. She was 'the only women that I ever saw agreable to my temper which fortune of good temper and personal Perfections make up a very plentifull Portion, and indeed a woman I love and am certain will be acceptable and a Reputation to us both.'[34]

Oliver was not indifferent to preserving the family corporation in good shape; he was aware of the importance of love and personal happiness; but his third position was to see that these things could fuse, not least in the public mind: a marvellous woman would be 'a Reputation to us both'. If you remember that Sir Henry Hobart had pulled in a girl with £10,000, it is clear, in a perfectly straightforward sense, that Hobart, for all his debts, was three times the man le Neve could ever claim to be.

But Oliver's brother, who had married a shrew called Prudence Hughes, the daughter of a Bristol merchant, was feeling the pinch. He turned his brother down. Another flaring response came from Oliver. He had no more than £830 a year to live on. 'I must either live a Batchildor or marry a Biggar', he wrote to Peter.[35] It is not quite clear if Peter stuck to his ground or Anne's family changed theirs, but one way or another an agreement was reached and later that year Oliver and Anne were married.

Her family, the Gawdys, occupied yet another position in the subtly nuanced social ecology of late seventeenth-century Norfolk gentry life. Like the Hobarts, Gawdys had been lawyers and MPs in

Elizabethan and Jacobean England. Through judicious marriages to heiresses, they had accumulated land, with their headquarters in an old moated and fortified house at West Harling in the damp valley of the Thet on the Norfolk–Suffolk border. Anne's grandfather, Sir William Gawdy, had bought a baronetcy. They had been on the side of Parliament in the Civil War, but unlike for the Hobarts the ambition and power-seeking had drained from them. They were now an easy-going family, profoundly Norfolk based, with few London or Westminster connections, and not en route to aristocratic glory. Somehow but inexorably the Gawdys were going downhill.

The decline of the Gawdys can be put down to a sequence of disasters. First, deafness stalked the family through one generation after another. Of Sir William's four sons, two were stone deaf and completely dumb. Sir William, realizing that deaf sons could not operate in the world of politics or the law, had them trained up as painters. Both for a while became pupils in the studio of Sir Peter Lely,[36] whose fees were high but their father was doing his best for them. These deaf boys could not talk, but they could communicate by signs, among the first people in English history who are known to have done so. On 6 February 1665, George Freeman, their London tutor, wrote to their father:

> Mr Framlingham has been sick this ten days, and we thought he would have had the small-pox, but he is now pretty well. He was somewhat discontented that he had not black clothes for he made signs that the Court was in mourning, and that he was ashamed to go see his friends in his old ones.[37]

The other two sons, who could hear perfectly, were entered at the Inner Temple as law students. Then, in 1661, a terminal catastrophe: the two hearing sons, William and Bassingbourne, died within a week of each other of smallpox.[38] The family's future was removed at a stroke.

When Sir William died in 1669, it was John, the elder of his two deaf sons, who inherited his father's baronetcy and the creaking old house at West Harling. This Sir John Gawdy was Anne's father and became Oliver le Neve's father-in-law.

The tension between money and status was threaded into every corner of their lives. The Brownes could despise the le Neves for being too commercial; the Hobarts could enhance their standing by acquiring a royal sinecure on the customs; the Gawdys could dream of past significance and in effect sell some of that significance to the money-backed le Neves; and the le Neves could despise at least some of the Gawdys for their crusty old arrogance. When Oliver le Neve asked his brother Peter to pay a visit to old Framlingham Gawdy, his father-in-law's cousin, to arrange some business in London, he was frankly contemptuous:

> I ... have wrote to my Vncle ffranc: Gaudy whoe is now in London, and lodges at mr Squibs next Door to the Plough Stables in little Lincolns Inn feilds, where I told him you should waite on him, to know his resolution; you will finde him proude & ignorant. Tolerate him till ye affaire is over, then bid him kiss yr Ars if you pleese.[39]

That is the modern man knowing he could leave the old snobbery behind.

So bad was the Gawdys' financial situation that after his wife's death in the 1680s, Sir John Gawdy actually let his own house out to his neighbour, and drew up an elaborate document which would allow him and his family to remain in the house with the new tenants but as paying guests, paying for 'what soever wine beere or Ale' he drank and the pies he consumed.[40] Even later, when Oliver came to stay with his father-in-law or they with him, as they often did, they would all pay for their bed and breakfast, and negotiations would be had by letter over what might be 'resionable' as the fees due.[41]

Despite the financial worries, the relationship was warm between Oliver and his father-in-law, Sir John, and with his brother-in-law, the not over-brilliant Bassingbourne. Over many years, with one or two hiccups, their correspondence remained funny, jokey and deeply affectionate, fuelled by Oliver's own openness of character, Bass's unaffected love of him and Sir John's easy cultivated charm.

A sudden window opens up on to Sir John Gawdy's character when in September 1677 he attended a service of dedication and a lunch party at the Earl of Arlington's new house and church at Euston near Thetford. The diarist John Evelyn was there too:

> There dined this day at my Lord's one Sir John Gawdie, a very handsome person, but quite dumb, yet very intelligent by signs, and a very fine painter; he was so civil and well bred, as it was not possible to discern any imperfection in him. His lady and children were also there, and he was at church in the morning with us.[42]

This was the atmosphere of gentlemanly grace into which le Neve had successfully married. John Gawdy was clearly fond of him. He signed off his letters to Oliver 'with Blessing to your whole selfe'[43] or from 'yor very neare Relation by matrimony'.[44] He usually had either Bass or the vicar Mr Cressener write the letter for him, using sign language to communicate with his temporary secretary, and making jokes to Oliver at their expense: 'I was pleased last night to acquaint ye Lazy Scribe with my receiving a letter from you last Thursday.'[45] On other occasions he changed his mind in the course of dictating a letter: the wig Oliver had sent from London was too expensive; it had to go back; no, perhaps he should think again; he loved it; he would have to keep it; he would wear it only on 'hallowdays'; could Oliver send another, cheaper one from London?[46] Bassingbourne faithfully followed his father's wishes, occasionally adding his own note at the end. 'My fingers are now so cold', he wrote in November 1692, 'I can scherce feele them. I remain yr fridged Brother BG.'[47]

His friends and relations loved Oliver. When he was away, they longed for him to return. When he was at home, they clustered to his table and hearth at Witchingham. He was at the centre of a crowd of young Tory squires, whose fathers had been Cavaliers in the Civil War, who loathed and distrusted the court and the Whigs, who drank for England, and whose lives were embedded and enmeshed in those of their animals. They were 'the Rakes' of north Norfolk, their language full and florid, yet to be tempered by any whiff of Enlightenment *politesse*.[48] Men got in 'hufs', Oliver and his friends toasted each other in 'bowls of the old liquor',[49] siblings got in 'mifs',[50] fencing masters were to be distrusted, hangovers were an everyday reality: 'you may see by my scrawl I was at it last night, near a dozen knights and gentlemen here.' Hounds and horses, grooms and stable boys, partridges, pheasants and hares were the medium of friendship. 'Deare Brother', Bass Gawdy wrote adoringly to Oliver in April 1692, 'I have chose you a bitch whelpe & it will be fitt to take off within A fourtnight.'[51] It was his equivalent of sending a kiss.

Oliver asked his London agent if he could find him some imported hawks in the London docks, but Bass volunteered to find him a Norfolk sparrowhawk which would do just as well.[52] He was only sorry he couldn't 'plesure you with ferrits'.[53] One frozen January, over-anxious to please, Bass sent his man Bert the twenty-seven miles to Oliver at Great Witchingham with a young beagle but her walking in the frost 'rendered her unfit for anything'.[54]

Setters, spaniels, greyhounds, foxhounds, beagles: their entire correspondence smells of dog. Court, Seuky, Stately, Jollyboy, Smoaker – 'a very good character'[55] – Topper, Synger, Curious, Comely, Venus, Sempetris, Beauty, Jewell, Dido, Doxey, Little Lady, Duchess, Phillida, Pallace, Countess, Little Gypsy ('the finest beagle in England'[56]), Tinker, Tinkler, Ruler, Ringwood, Ranger, Daphne, Lovely, Flurry and a bitch called Virgin:[57] these were the beauties of his fleet, named from Tory hearts that were affectionate, admiring, classical, deep English, pretentious and unpretentious in turn. Sir Henry Hobart might be portrayed by the wonders of his wardrobe; Oliver le Neve's character appears in the names of his hounds.

The best of Oliver's hunting friends was John Millecent, always known as Jack, a rumbustious, wenching, gambling squire from Linton in Cambridgeshire, where he was in a multi-generational dispute with his local Whigs. His estate was worth no more than £700 a year, he tended to 'let my garden lie till I am ashamed of it'[58] and he was often strapped for money, but his letters exude all the fruitiness of this Tory culture. 'Ah! Noll!', he wrote to le Neve in August 1701, 'I want thy art for, next chamber to mine, has several nights lain a beautiful young lady, who, do what I can, is a *noli me tangere*.'[59] His resources were constantly depleted by 'all things chargeable, especially that of Petticoats.'[60]

Jack usually wrote to 'my dearest Noll' of little but 'dog-talk as we call it',[61] interspersed only with heavy doses of horse talk: Cockle, Cradle, Flint and 'Old Chuff, brother to the famous Why Not',[62] carried these gents over hedge and stream. Millecent suffered regularly from the gout, which made him 'fit only for Bedlam, raving and tearing my clothes'.[63] It was thought that turnips might be good for the affliction but not by Jack Millecent: 'I have such an aversion for eating turnips that I could [not] live upon them if I was to have the Indies.'[64] He often claimed other people's hounds in reality belonged to him and would travel across country with one hound to compare it to another so that he could prove that they were both from the same litter.[65] He recommended as a cure for any kind of melancholy or grief that 'innocent and wholesome recreation, hunting'.[66] When Oliver was in London, Millecent was usually stuck in Linton, unable to afford to visit the capital and forced to 'live in a vacuum, nothing but air, and that much rarefied by cold',[67] longing for le Neve to return so that they could get back out in the field.

In August 1700, Oliver sent him another dog present but it wasn't suitable. 'I recd the Bitch which I feare will not prove for my turn,' Millecent wrote, 'she having no promising 'fiz.'[68] Dog fizz was his principal joy in life and it was he who in 1694 had first urged Oliver to get his own pack of beagles – the whole pack could be bought for £15 or £20[69] – and although much more expensive than hawking, largely because a kennel boy needed to be housed and kept if the mange was to avoided, hunting with dogs was, in Millecent's view, quite clearly the better way. It was 'more pleasure to hunt with one's own pack', he told his friend, recommending 'a little short trussed, slow-running beagle, with a chumping tongue' as the style of hound le Neve should go for.[70] *A chumping tongue*: the whole Millecent-le Neve-Gawdy Norfolk world is in that phrase. Within a dozen years, Millecent would claim that le Neve was the owner of 'what was generally considered the finest pack of beagles in England'.[71]

They used to chase the hares near Reepham and net for partridges and quails.[72] If there were poachers, they used to carry small pocket pistols 'for the easyer disspatching of Pochers doggs or any other that offends me', as Bass Gawdy wrote to his brother-in-law.[73] They shot rooks, and occasionally pheasants, with spaniels to flush them and pick them up. A spaniel that would flush birds only within shootable range was among the most precious of all possessions. 'If you could help me to a dog that has been hawked you would do me knight's service,' John Rous, another neighbour squire, wrote to Oliver one August.[74] If someone shot a deer, joints and haunches were distributed around the net of friends.[75] They met occasionally in a pub for dinner, where a 'a good Dish of a Sea Fish for six or eight persons' would be ordered in advance.[76]

Not, of course, that Oliver le Neve himself conformed to the clichéd vision of the sequestered country squire. Much of his life remained attached to London, to his father's properties which he had inherited there and from which he received an important part of his income. He had twelve London houses and shops from which he received £480 in rent a year (a quarter of his total income) but he clearly did not see them as anything like an entrepreneurial possibility. Rather than investing in what might have been a developing portfolio, he simply milked them for their rents. In the 1690s, he even sold one London house and part of another for a capital boost of £1,500 to the Witchingham books.[77]

Le Neve employed London men to receive his rents and run the buildings, but it was incompetently done. None of the houses was kept in good condition. When Thomas Rose, his London agent, 'went with the carpenter' to view one of them in 1706, he 'never saw any house that was inhabited in worse condition, nor worse furniture, which makes it look worse'.[78]

Other tenants complained of his indifference and neglect:

August 12 1693

Mr Leneive Sr I very much admire that I cannot have the honner of a Line or two from you in answer to my last. I cannot imagine the meaning thereof without you think that I am soe sorry a tennant not worth takeing notice of

Yor humble servant and tennant

Eliza Millner[79]

Le Neve ignored his paperwork and tenants begged, up to a year after a deal was done, that 'the writings be completed'. In 1694, another tenant, Charles Fisher, complained of the rent which le Neve was requiring him to pay, a 'great extravagant price under which I have labored for these years past, only to work purely for you. The door pavement is out of order and the windows and bars are worn to pieces'.[80]

Here, for a moment, is a rare glimpse of the underside of gentry life, the exploitation of the weak on which the gaieties and pleasures of Tory squiredom relied. Mr Fisher's grievance is precisely to the point: it was his labouring in the London shop that sustained le Neve's delightful world of beagles, fishing and bumpers of strong-brewed Norfolk nog.

The le Neve files are also scattered here and there with begging letters from the truly poor. Again and again, from a sequence of mutely articulate addresses, a woman called Elizabeth Story wrote to him: first in February 1695, when she was living with 'Abratnats an oyle man next dore to the French arms in Drury lane over against Russill courte': 'knowing how kind yor family has bin to ours';[81] then in February 1696 from 'Next dore to the Sholder of mutton in Shew laine nere fletestrete':

Honoured Sir

I humbley bege your pardon for these presumeing lines, which is honoured Sir to humbly bege your charity for I had not presumed to truble you but yt my wants forces me almost beyond my common reason to aske ye charity of my frinds

Having not a farthing in ye world to help my self with nor sometimes bred to eate for three days together I humbly beg of you for god sake to send me something if never so smale to releave me in this my distressed condition & pray Sir be not angry with me for hunger and cold are perceing & j hope god will make it up to you againe[82]

Alongside this shiftless geography of despair was its opposite – shopping. Oliver was endlessly useful to his friend Jack Millecent, his father-in-law the deaf painter Sir John Gawdy and his adoring brother-in-law Bass Gawdy for the errands he could run for them when up in London. Their requests stretch unbroken from year to year.

A 'good tenor horn'[83] for Millecent; 'enough muslings for 12 neck-cloths, 2 of fine sort, & 4 of cours for hunting';[84] 'My father desires you wold buy him 100 of oringes, if they be anything resionable; and 30 lemonds,' Bass wrote helpfully.[85] 'I hope you will not forget some Beagles to add to your small number';[86] plus coach glasses and clothes for Bass: 'pray bye me a neat silk stitcht waste belt for my black belt is soe excessive Hott I am not able to endure itt this summer time.' He also wanted a more fashionable sword, 'either of Plate hilt or stele, which you se most worne'.[87] Anne Gawdy, Bass's sister and Oliver's wife, needed artist's materials for their father. She

desires you wold send down with the other things one grain of white marine [paint], & the same quantity of Carmine [ditto], with 8 fine pencills, with halfe a pounde of Trippelow [Tripoli, a sedimentary stone from North Africa used as an abrasive] to polish. You may have all of these at the Catt in Powle Church Yard [St Paul's]; with halfe a pound of the finest white fleke [white lead paint] & half as much Course [coarse Flake white paint][88]

Apple trees were sent for the walled garden at West Harling – 'Six Gouldin Russetings, four Deusans, foure Summer Paremains'[89] – as well as reams of paper, sugar, brandy, 'a dosen of whight hafted knifes & two Glass bottles with eares that will hold something more than a quart to rack liquer of into & 6 Glass salts, such as there are',[90] 'buck-hafted knives',[91] 'a payer of Brass candlesticks, I care not how playn they be, if strong,[92] 'a Copper Coffy pott like yours'[93] and wigs, the cause of much soul-searching, as Bass wrote to Oliver in London one day:

> The things cam all safe to my hand but ye Wigg is too shallow in ye head & I know not how to wear it I fear it cannot be altered for myself. Return it if ye person will take it again & make me another. I like ye coler & shape very well, it is wide enough but it does not cover my ears which will subject me to take cold.[94]

All of it came by sea, down the Thames from London and up the East Anglian coast to Yarmouth, from where a carrier would bring it to West Harling or Witchingham.[95] Mail order of this kind, with inadequate labelling, was never entirely satisfactory. Trees were delivered which would have been better if Oliver

> had Sene them, before they had bin sent. They are so small that they will not be out of the reach of Cattle, this thre or fore year if they live; the man has not sent me the names of any of them, onely tyed bits of sticks to them, with markes, which I cannot understand.[96]

They all missed Oliver when he was away in London and the correspondence oozes affection. 'My father sends his Blessing & I my Love to you,' Bass habitually wrote to him.[97] 'I wish you A merry Christmas', he wrote on 10 December 1695, 'tho I am sure of A very dull one in yr absence.'[98] The following September he was 'drinking yr helth with prosperity in A bumper of Nogg'.[99] 'I have often drank yr helth in yr absence & as oft wished for yr company.'[100] But for all this warmth between them, much was not entirely happy with this family. One of Oliver's sons had been deaf[101] and had died young and the other, Jacky, had also inherited the Gawdy deafness, had difficulty talking and was a sickly boy.[102] Oliver's wife, Anne, was not strong herself, weakened by repeated pregnancies and miscarriages, to the point where her father advised Oliver that she should 'ly fallow'[103] for a while. In February 1696 she died in childbirth.

Almost immediately the incorrigible Jack Millecent began urging new girls on his friend. 'A young, comely, good-humoured, ingenious widow', Millecent wrote to him the summer after Anne's death, 'aged between nineteen and twenty years, worth at least to our knowledge £15000, is stopping here, being Mrs Millecent's niece. You needs must come and court her before she gets snapped up at London.'[104]

That suggestion came to nothing but word of Oliver's flirtation so soon after the death of Anne upset his father-in-law. Bass wrote to Oliver in January 1697, mentioning a report they had heard of his being married to an unsuitable party, while saying reassuringly that they knew him 'to be a man of sence & so consequently one who will not act anything contrary to yr own reputation, nor the disadvantage of yrs'.[105]

In June the following year, le Neve married Jane Knyvet, a much-loved Suffolk girl whom Jack Millecent had found for him, and entered a happy and loving second marriage with her. Congratulations and presents arrived for the newly-weds at Witchingham. On 4 July, his steward reported, 'the sheep are clipped, the turnips sown, and the meadows will begin to be cut today'.[106] His friend Robert Monsey at Reepham sent over his congratulations with a few cherries 'which did outlive the severities of a May-winter morning'.[107] But the summer of 1698 was not to be happy for Oliver. It was election year and a moment of crisis for the Whig regime of which Sir Henry Hobart was a part and from which Oliver and his Tory friends felt bitterly excluded.

'Since they had been called to the direction of affairs,' Macaulay wrote of the Whigs in his matchless history of this period,

every thing had been changed, changed for the better. There was peace abroad and at home. The merchant ships went forth without fear from the Thames and the Avon. Soldiers had been disbanded by tens of thousands. Taxes had been remitted. The value of all public and private securities had risen. Trade had never been so brisk. Credit had never been so solid. All over the kingdom the shopkeepers and the farmers, the artisans and the ploughmen, relieved, beyond all hope, from the daily and hourly misery of the clipped silver, were blessing the broad faces of the new shillings and half crowns.[108]

But the country did not see it quite like that and 'the Tory gentry', as Macaulay described them,

> had special grievances. The whole patronage of the government, they said, was in Whig hands. The old landed interest, the old Cavalier interest, had now no share in the favours of the Crown. Every public office, every bench of justice, every commission of Lieutenancy, was filled with Roundheads. There were three war cries in which all the enemies of the government could join: No standing army; No grants of Crown property; and No Dutchmen.[109]

For the toasts made in the bumpers of nog by le Neve and his Norfolk Tory friends you could add a fourth: 'No Hobarts.'

Everything combined against Sir Henry Hobart in the election of 1698. He had been chairman of a club of influential Whigs who met in the Rose Tavern near Temple Bar. He had chaired committees of the House of Commons and acted as teller in crucial votes. But the mood of the country was impassioned, it wanted a change and suspected the Whigs of corruption. 'Nothing but their own tribe and gang will ever be employed in anything of profit', John Millicent would write later to le Neve, 'though never so prejudicial to the public.'[110] Sir Henry was closely identified with an administration which was thought to be lining its pockets and the result was a fiercely contested fight, involving huge numbers of people (maybe as much as 40 per cent of the adult male population could vote, according to the property they owned). In Norfolk over 10,000 votes were cast. If a candidate wanted a man's vote, he was expected to pay his travel, food and lodging on his visit to Norwich, the only place where a vote could be cast. With the need to secure at least 2,500 votes, these were vast expenses.

When the votes were counted after the election on 3 August 1698, Sir Henry had managed to gather 2,244, but Sir William Cooke, an old, rich and powerful Norfolk Tory, had received 3,107 and Sir Jacob

Astley, a Whig, 2,960. They became the Members of Parliament for the county and Sir Henry, despite massive expenditure, had lost his seat.[111] Given the wrecked state of his finances, he may have been outspent. A letter from Hobart written in April 1696 to Sir John Somers, one of the most powerful men around the King, reminded Somers that Hobart had formerly served the King as a 'gentleman of the horse' until he became ill. Now his 'circumstances are very uneasy' and he would like a further favour from the King.[112]

The man was sick and failing. Lack of cash may also have played its part in other ways. Two years previously, it was being said in Norfolk that he was treating his creditors disgracefully.

> Here is a lady of one of ye best families in ye countrey who hath all her fortune in his hands, and he hath not payd her any interest these several years, whereby she is put to great hardships for her subsistence. The case of severall others of ye like nature will come against him next sessions.[113]

The same gossiping clergyman reported the following year that 'an ejectment [a legal instrument for repossession of mortgaged property] hath been left at Sir H. Hobart's house for £8,000, which will reach a greater part of his estate'.[114]

The highly politicized and tense atmosphere of the election re-ran many of the animosities of the century – high church against low, court against country, Whig against Tory, the old world against the new. Fierce rumours were circulating and one reached the ears of Sir Henry Hobart. It was being said that Oliver le Neve was 'spreading a report that [Hobart] was a coward, and behaved himself so in Ireland' in 1689–90, when he had been a Gentleman of the Horse with William III.[115] Imputations of cowardice locked into other, larger and semi-subterranean questions – the legitimacy of the Whig government, its urban effeminacy, its self-seeking priorities – and the rumour spread. When Hobart lost the election, he blamed le Neve for destroying his name and sent a man to Oliver at Witchingham, challenging him to a duel.

Le Neve replied, denying that he had ever said such a thing and trying to find out who was accusing him of spreading the rumour. But Hobart, wounded by his humiliation and financial catastrophe at the election, was insistent. They must fight. On 19 August, he rode over to the small brick market square at Reepham near Witchingham, and repeated the accusations about le Neve, now adding that the only reason le Neve had denied he had been spreading the rumour was that he was too frightened to fight.

The next day Le Neve replied to the great Whig grandee:

Honored Sr,

I am very sorry I was not at Riefham yesterday, when you gave yor self the trouble of appearing there, that I might not only have further justified the Truth of my not saying what is reported I did, but that I might have told you that I wrote not that Letter to avoid fighting you; but that, if the credit of yor Author has confirm'd you in the belief of it, I am ready & desirous to meet you when & where you please to assign me; if otherwise, I expect yor Author's name, in return to this, that I may take my Satisfaction there, Or else conclude the Imputacon sprung from Blickling, & send you a time & place, for the matter shall not rest as it is, tho' it cost the life of

Yor Servt,
OLIVER NEVE
Aug. ye 20th: 98.[116]

There are many fascinating aspects to this letter. It draws itself up to its full height, in the same slightly opaque tone as le Neve had used to Thomas Browne fifteen years before. Oliver also dropped the 'le' from his surname at this critical moment, when his dignity was being questioned. Why? Because the 'le' was no more than affectation, introduced by a relative earlier in the century. His father had never used it and this was no moment for affectation. He was to play the true, solid and unquestionable man and he would do that as Oliver Neve. He saw himself as a coequal of Hobart's. There was no submission here to a man of wealth and power. He was courteous not curt in his response to the challenge, sorry not to have been at Reepham and aware of the trouble which this business had put Sir Henry to. He was portraying himself as a man committed as much to truth as to courage, ready to exact a price from the unworthy, or to pay it himself if required. Death was nothing in the face of shame. Captain Neve had become an Arthurian knight, acting to the principles Malory would have endorsed 200 years before.

The psychology of the duel was founded on the understanding that honour, if not revalidated in life, would rust.[117] Honour could not be drunk by babies from their mother's breast and then kept for ever. It could only be earned in conflict or when faced with shame. A man could claim to be from an honourable family, but honour was not heritable. Each generation had to earn it anew and this was, in effect, recognition that the gentry lived a life of struggle and competition. Their status was not fixed. It could only be claimed and reclaimed, shown and re-shown. A gentleman's ability to maintain his honour in an explicit and violent confrontation was a public declaration of who, as a gentleman, he was. The duel was a moment in which a private conception of the self and a membership of a class could be tested for their truth.[118]

Since the early 1600s, the government had repeatedly attempted to suppress duelling but this deeply absorbed code was indifferent to any sanction government could impose. The value of the duel was not in the destruction of an enemy but in the test it provided. Death or even pain was an irrelevance. There were plenty of guidebooks on how to do it and the repeated emphasis was on the gracefulness of your behaviour around the murderous act.[119] It was of course always triggered by an uncivil act – an insult, an accusation of lying or cowardice – but the duel itself was intended as a means of recovering the civility of the relationship. Once both men had stood up and faced each other, the community of honour was restored. It was a means by which jealousy, mutual loathing and suspicion could be accommodated within a single social fabric.

Samuel Butler, the author of *Hudibras*, claimed that duellists met with two weapons, 'a single rapier and civility … There is nothing of unkind in all the quarrel but only the beginning of it, and the rest of the proceedings are managed as civilly as any other treaty; and in the end when one falls, they part with extraordinary endearments.'[120] Civility and politeness were as essential parts of the duel as the test of honour it represented.

These conceptions would have been in the minds of Oliver le Neve and Sir Henry Hobart as they made their separate ways to the appointed site for the duel that Saturday evening. The legality of what they were doing was ambivalent. Charles II had sanctioned a duel between courtiers as recently as the 1680s but other duellists, when arrested and convicted, were burned on the hand as punishment. Several were transported to the colonies. The killing of a man in a duel might still be seen as murder and Scots duellists were still beheaded in the seventeenth century.[121] Perhaps as protection from prosecution, neither man this evening had any second with him. No witnesses meant no case to answer.

They rode up from their respective valleys through the corn fields yet to be harvested, along the net of curved medieval lanes, with medieval churches on the horizon and ivy clinging to the gnarly oak and ash pollards along the way. The sandy, brackeny ridge of Cawston Heath is still relatively unfrequented land now. There is the busy Norfolk–Holt road, with a petrol station and an old pub, the Woodrow Inn, now closed. The shooting range of a local gun club is buried in a modern stand of pines. Next to it is a patch of open heath where in summer, between the bracken and birch, the Silver Studded Blues and Small Skippers flit from the scabious to the thistles.

Somewhere here – the precise spot is not known – le Neve and Hobart met. There are two hints as to what happened. Narcissus Luttrell, the parliamentary diarist, heard that 'captain Le'neve was wounded in the arm' and Sir Henry 'run into the belly'.[122] The antiquarian John Nichols, in a book of anecdotes published in 1812, added that Oliver 'knew nothing of the sword, but had a great coat of coarse cloth; and his adversary's weapon being entangled in it, he easily stabbed him'.[123]

Whatever the truth of these accounts, they carry a metaphorical freight. Hobart was the grandee swordsman, with his exquisite blades, his familiarity with power, his overweening metropolitan contempt for the little Norfolk man who had dared to confront him and impugn his honour. Le Neve, in this account, was the man of the earth, no great expert in arms but equipped with something as rooted to the Tory soil as 'a great coat of coarse cloth'. Hobart managed to wound Oliver in the arm but that material thickness of English stuff clogged the rapier of the dandified Whig, made his slick weapon useless, disabled him and allowed le Neve to run him through. Can you not, even now, see the look of appalled astonishment on Sir Henry's face as the point of the Norfolk sword went through his guts, those beautiful eyebrows lifted into an arc of amazement, the elegant lips turned into an open O of surprise?

Can this picture be true? Surely not. For more than a decade le Neve had been captain of a foot company of the Eynsford militia and had regularly drilled and practised with them. As a hunting man, he was physically fit. There can be little doubt he would have known how to use a sword. Nor on this August evening, knowing that he had the fight of his life in front of him, would he have worn 'a great coat of coarse cloth'. It would have been too hot and hampered every movement.

These details have been gathered around the tale to turn it into an emblematic moment: this is the local defeating the metropolitan, the plain, upstanding country man trouncing the cynical power-broker, all that is good in the gentry world triumphing over its corrupt, deceiving, Westminster- and court-based culture-enemy. Any thought that Oliver le Neve was in fact involved in owning and running commercial property in London, or that the Hobarts were more deeply embedded in Norfolk than this minor branch of a London draper's family, has no part in this mythology.

The wounded Hobart dragged himself back to Blickling, bleeding and in pain, where he was met by his wife, Elizabeth, and their only son, John, then four years old. Henry died there the next day and the estate carpenter, Thomas Burrows, made him a coffin lined with six yards of white baize, in which Henry was laid in the Blickling vault.[124] A year or two later his widow had a simple stone urn put up for him near the site of the duel, bearing as an inscription nothing but the two letters 'H H'.

Le Neve was now on the run. Not only had he killed a man in a duel, but it would be difficult to think of anyone with more powerful connections. Lady Hobart was looking for revenge. Troops of the militia began to comb Norfolk for him. One body of men rode down to west Harling, where Bass Gawdy and old Sir John had heard nothing of the crisis. The soldiers turned over everything in the West Harling house, riding through the standing crops while the deaf and dumb Sir John stood on the steps of his house shouting huge wordless rage at the soldiers, several of whom raised their swords to him.[125]

Le Neve made for London and then for Holland, returning to England occasionally in secret, living under assumed names. His groom, Nat, and his much-loved wife, Jane, joined him in Rotterdam in April 1699. Bass Gawdy wrote lovingly to him in Holland:

> I am fearfully glad to heare you are safely arrived, after yr tedious & dangerous viyege, you cannot think how many hartakes I had for you, the time of yr being in England, fearing every post should have brought some ill news concerning you.[126]

His enemies – 'ravenous woolves' Bass calls them – were hoping to make £1,000 a year out of his estate while he was away. Lady Hobart offered £500 for his capture and Bass heard that he was 'very neare being surprized in town'.[127]

In Tory East Anglia, le Neve was a hero and a martyr. Jack Millecent told him his name was 'a general health to all honest gentlemen in two counties, being often drank when our greatest man's [the King's] is not'.[128] His friends warned him that informers and kidnappers were everywhere. He was not to go in private boats or stay out late at night. Attempts were made by the Hobart faction to have him outlawed if he did not return to stand trial. In response, his friends lobbied hard to have a sympathetic sheriff appointed and, as Bass wrote helpfully, to choose for the jury 'twelve honoust men … which I doubt not will be very serviceable to you, they being all verry responsable & men of sence'.[129]

For all the plotting and secrecy, the threat of punishment from a corrupt court and a packed jury, normal life went on. Oliver was missing all sorts of homely goods from Norfolk and they were dispatched across the sea: bottles of the strong Norfolk beer called nog, artichokes and flour from Witchingham all found their way to Rotterdam. In return, Oliver sent tubs of sturgeon and pieces of fine Holland and muslin, neckcloths and a well-made 'casting-net' for pike. His hunting friend Giles Bladwell ordered a dozen fine Holland shifts for Mrs Bladwell but Oliver was to 'remember she is one of the fat size'.[130]

At the end of April 1700, Oliver stood trial and the careful preparations paid off. He was acquitted of all charges, guilty neither of manslaughter nor of murder, and he could resume his life at Witchingham.

In 1704, his wife, Jane, died and as soon as she was safely interred in the beautiful church at Great Witchingham, the unstoppable Jack Millecent was again out on the trail looking for a marital deal for his friend. For several months Millecent nosed his way through the drawing rooms of Norwich and London until on 12 December 1706 he wrote excitedly to Oliver back in Witchingham. He was in Kensington (where he had also been negotiating to buy a new gout chair), in the house of Robert Sheffield, the grandson of the Earl of Mulgrave:

Through my cousin Biddy I have made enquiries about the Sheffields. £3000 ready money will be laid down, and if Mr. Sheffield likes, £4,000 and the estate, when he dies, between the two sisters, whose just characters are – the eldest, tall, well-shaped, mild-temper, extraordinary housewife, her father's commands a law, and not acquainted with any one young man, her face very agreeable, age 29. The youngest sister, a beautiful face, not tall, much inclined to fat, and in her temper a perfect stoic, not of so ready or pleasing conversation as the other, her age 26. If you find any suitable to your inclinations, I should be glad you'd begin whilst we are here, you might lodge near Dyett here, and set your horses at an excellent inn over the way.[131]

After protracted negotiations, Oliver chose Elizabeth, the elder, nicer, uglier, thinner, more easy-going and highly domesticated Sheffield girl, and married her in July 1707. The surviving correspondence doesn't record her thoughts on the matter, only that in November that year, without warning, three months after the wedding, she died too.

Oliver's enemies the Hobarts were pushing on to a grand aristocratic career as the Earls of Buckinghamshire – a title which still exists, but the present earl is no longer connected to Blickling – while the le Neves soon came to an end. Oliver died of a sudden apoplexy in November 1711. He was forty-nine. His sons had died before him and his estate at Great Witchingham went to his brother Peter, the herald, from whom it passed out of the family into the hands of a conniving Norwich lawyer. Oliver's three daughters inherited the Gawdy house and lands at West Harling (they soon sold them and moved away) and it was those three, Isabella, Anne and Henrietta, who put up a monument on the chancel wall of Great Witchingham church.

It is in white marble, with slightly wobbly lettering, and it describes without shame or cavilling the social framework in which their father had lived. He was a magistrate and a captain in the militia, a man of Mars, but his own father was a London draper and his mother the daughter of a London merchant, the deepest of mercantile origins. The girls' mother, Anne Gawdy ('who lyes by his side'), was the daughter of a baronet and Oliver's third wife was the great-granddaughter of an earl, described here a little distantly as 'longsince deceased', but the acknowledgement of trade comes before either of them. The Latin conclusion at the foot of the stone tells the story: '*Tam Marti quam Mercurio*' (As much a man of war as of commerce).

This was the mixed background which had been a cause of such shame and rage for Oliver in 1683. Was it now a source of pride for his daughters? Had his courage in 1698 somehow validated not only his honour but his family's 'Mircatorian' origins? Perhaps that is the ironic moral of his life. By the time this archetype of the Tory hunting squire died in 1711, many parts of the gentry had come to understand the value of business. If only he had recognized it, Oliver le Neve could have been a model for the future, a fusion of things that seems modern: a country-loving property developer.

Instead, the Witchingham world to which he was committed looked backwards. His friends lived on as relics of a previous age, widowed by modernity. Of all these Norfolk rakes, Sir Bassingbourne Gawdy Bt was the last. He survived, unmarried, until October 1723, when he died 'of a bruise in his privities, which he received by his horse's stumbling as he was hunting',[132] and both the baronetcy and the mental universe of which he was an ornament were extinguished.

PART IV

Atlantic Domains
1710–1790

Through the course of the eighteenth century, the gentry, crudely put, divided into rural, conservative, increasingly impoverished, ill-educated, backward-looking Tories and urban, progressive, commercially minded, government-controlling Whigs. From having been the unchallenged core of the political classes, at least part of the gentry started to look absurd. Geoffrey Hickes, the early eighteenth-century smart London salonnier, described one 'Deputy Lieutenant' who

> had confined his Knowledge within the Bounds of his own County; all the rest of the World was *Terra Incognita* to his *Worship*.
>
> Had this Lieutenant hunted less, and read more; had he cultivated his understanding, and let a Field or two lie fallow, he might have been Company for Men.[1]

But he wasn't and he stands at the head of the long sequence of out-of-it squires who began their unstoppable career in English fiction, from the bumbling Sir Roger de Coverley in the pages of Addison's *Spectator*, who insisted on walking through the streets of London, 'saluting everybody that passes by him with a good-morrow or a good-night',[2] like a country dog on a lead, and on through Squires Western and Allworthy in *Tom Jones* to the idiots of Thackeray and Surtees.

There is a social and economic background to that stereotype. At the end of the seventeenth century, the long ascent of the gentry stalled. The introduction of strict settlement of estates, by which individual heirs were prevented by their fathers from selling off bits of land and were compelled instead to leave them whole to their own heirs, meant that aristocratic landholdings were no longer divided up and the gentry was deprived of that drip feed from above of younger sons with small subsidiary estates. In the difficult conditions of 1660–1725, many small gentry and yeoman families failed, and the great landowners, benefiting from new commercially available mortgages and cheap finance, hoovered up the pickings. Those great landowners began to accumulate ever larger estates (one eighteenth-century Norfolk grandee liked to say that his nearest neighbour was in Denmark) while the yeoman farmers, whose entrepreneurial energies had traditionally fed the gentry from below, found themselves unable to survive in the more demanding commercial environment.

By the end of the eighteenth century, the crown and church still owned about 10 per cent of England and the great aristocrats about a quarter. The yeomen, who had been the owners of as much of a third of England in the seventeenth century, owned no more than 15 per cent of it by 1790. The residue – as much as half of the land surface of England – remained in the hands of the gentry, the rural squires who were becoming the laughing stock for the newspaper- and novel-reading public of the cities.[3]

Alongside all that, though, is another eighteenth-century gentry story, the one focused on here, of families striving to avoid the humiliations of the fading Tories and turning instead to the opportunities that a new imperial world was offering them. In these Whig families, the essence of the gentry spirit remained adaptability and responsiveness to change. For the less than great, the possibilities of the Atlantic began to look attractive. Both the eighteenth-century families here responded to that challenge, looking to create or re-create their destinies on the slave-powered plantations of the Caribbean and the seaboard of continental America.

It is the moment when the gentry step out on to a new global stage. The change in scale meant that the questions in play also evolved. What happened to inherited gentry ideas of gentlemanliness, neighbourliness, honour and 'worth' when exposed to the competitive, often corrupt and brutal conditions of Atlantic business networks? What became of honesty, directness and 'community' when business often required rather different qualities? Or of family relationships when they became the structure for a family business? How malleable were these gentry principles? Could the gentleman transform himself into the global citizen?

If you wanted to dip your ladle deep into the North Atlantic slave and sugar system, Barbados was the place. It was the easternmost of the Caribbean islands and so in the Trade Winds the furthest to windward, the first to be reached from either Britain or Africa. The British had been there for most of the seventeenth century. They had tried tobacco, cotton, indigo, ginger, aloes and dyewoods, but every one of those commodities was subject to boom-bust fluctuations in the English markets. Only the demand for sugar consistently outstripped supply and by the 1660s Barbados was a sugar island. It has been estimated that for every ton of sugar consumed in England in 1600, ten tons were eaten in 1700 and 150 in 1800. Money poured in, the income per head for plantation gentry by the end of the century a third to two-thirds higher than for their stay-at-home cousins in England. The island was a rough, frontier place, a 'Mighty Colossus of Vice',[4] thrusting, licentious, dishonest and drunk.

A generation later, as gentry like the Lascelles brothers set up as sugar merchants, those frontier days were over. Barbados had become a place of sophistication, run by 'men of highest Distinction ... of bright Characters and good figure',[5] or so they said themselves. It was the most densely populated and intensively cultivated area in the whole of the English-speaking world, with access to money less from the productivity of the plantations, whose soil was by now partly exhausted, than from the volume of trade passing across the island's quays. The Barbadians imported the luxury life from England. Canopied feather beds, leather chairs, silks, lace, pearls, silver candlesticks and sauce boats, oak and walnut furniture (mahogany was not yet fashionable), elegant chaises in which to drive along the dusty roads, tutors from Oxford and Cambridge for the children (£150 a year for a top-quality master, £60 for those fresh out of university; any with Glaswegian accents or 'mere scholars and not men of breeding'[6] need not apply), knives and forks from the best Sheffield makers: the whole gentry ensemble was shipped out to the Tropics.[7]

The houses they built on their plantations were reproductions of English manor houses, with heavy oak staircases and pointy gables, 'delightfully situated … with pleasant prospects to the sea and land'. 'No people in the world', it was said in 1695, 'have been more remarkable for a Luxuriant way of living.'[8] They had an assembly and assizes as they did at home, a militia as they did at home, and they cultivated 'hospitality' as they did at home. 'In point of numbers of people, cultivation of the soil, and those elegancies and conveniencies which result from both', Edmund Burke wrote in 1750, there 'was no place in the West-Indies comparable to *Barbadoes*.'[9]

Even the Horatian dream of rural, gentlemanly completeness made its way out to the Caribbean. 'There is something particularly picturesque and striking in a gang of negroes', one English planter would write some years later,

> when employed in cutting canes upon the swelling projections of a hill; when they take a long sweep, and observe a regular discipline in their work … The colour of the negroes, when bending beneath the verdant canopy of the canes, and these softened by the branching shadows of the majestic cotton-tree which rises in all the pride of vegetation and height, from the lowly glen in which its roots have taken earth … contribute to the moving landscape.[10]

That was written by an Englishman from Jamaica in 1790, when the Horatian vision had become deeply imbued with the picturesque, but everything about the way in which the Barbadians spoke of and developed their island – its giving soil, the warmth of the air, the constant twenty-five knots of clean, sweet wind off the Atlantic, the frequent showers of rain, even 'the high, large and lofty trees with their spreading branches and flourishing tops'[11] – was evidence that their vision of this place was not of somewhere that would give them untold amounts of money, but of acres that were continuous with their dreams of perfection at home. The heat might have meant that linen shirts, linen drawers and linen stockings replaced their English woollens but this was a place for delight where 'you shall find as cheerful a look, and as hearty a welcome as any man can give to his best friends'.[12] The fact that to make their plantations work they had to be 'stocked'[13] with African slaves, to use the word they consistently used, made no inroads into that vision. The great African fact behind the sugar riches was for all but a tiny, usually nonconformist minority no more than a technicality. It is the most extraordinary instance of the adaptability of the gentry frame of mind: to very nearly all of them, enslaving Africans seemed entirely acceptable. The world of the Lascelles was taut with anxiety but the unspeakable inhumanity of the slave trade and the chronic cruelties of the plantation system were not its source.

It was perfectly possible, in the midst of that essential and underlying barbarity, to cultivate a life that was courteous not abrupt, trustworthy, legal, co-operative and dignified. The two frames of mind, the dark and light of the cultural revolution of the eighteenth century, sat easily alongside each other.

As the century progressed, an element of femininity became increasingly important in the world of sensibility. In a pioneering 1740s essay, David Hume had identified the qualities of the 'true sage' as 'the softest benevolence, the most undaunted resolution, the tenderest sentiments, the most sublime love of virtue'.[14] That feminized vision of moral behaviour was also in play here, out in the Atlantic settlements of the English gentry, and the story of Eliza Pinckney, the astonishingly young woman from South Carolina who saved the fortunes of her family, is a long dialogue between David Hume's vision of goodness and the demands of her extraordinary situation.[15]

She was the heir to the great controlling and sustaining women who have preceded her in these stories – both Lady Plumptons, Mrs Throckmorton, the two Mrs Thynnes, Lady Oglander and Lady Hobart – but even so it seems as if there were qualities in her which had not appeared before: neither constrained by the public realm nor defensively self-assertive when confronted with it, confident, for all her self-deprecation, of the validity and interest of what she had to say, calmly fusing public and private, political and domestic, with an acute awareness of the role played in all of it by image and appearance.

As she grew older, the life of this Englishwoman became increasingly and emblematically American: self-reliant, brave and self-assertive, gathering an equally motivated family around her. The irony of their lives is that the more American they became, the more gentry-like they appeared. When the prospect of revolution finally raised its head, there was no question which side they would be on: they would fight for America against the British crown. But in doing so they were turning ancient gentry principles back on the British themselves. Perhaps like any revolution, it seemed to them a revolt of the honourable against the tyrannical, a defence of ancient freedoms rather than a new claiming of them, driven by the idea that America was the true heir to a tradition which an increasingly centralized British state was abandoning.

Dominance

The Lascelles

Yorkshire, Barbados, Richmond and London

At his horrible death in October 1753, Henry Lascelles was probably the richest man in England. The accounts are slightly difficult to disentangle but, including money he had already assigned to his sons, he was worth somewhere near £500,000.[1] In the 1750s that was enough to buy twenty-five good English estates of 4,000 acres each, with an excellent modern country house on every one;[2] or to buy your way, at the going price, into 100 seats in Parliament; or to acquire a fleet of several hundred well-laden, ocean-going merchant ships for the Atlantic business,[3] or 20,000 Africans on a Barbados quayside, or half as many again at one of the trading fort hells on the Guinea shore.[4] It was wealth of a kind few Englishmen had ever enjoyed and it came from the five key ingredients of the newly surging imperial British economy: sugar, shipping, finance, government office and African slaves. Lascelles was one of the gentry who had entered an ungentrified world.

Henry Lascelles was no *parvenu*, *nouveau riche* or *arriviste* – English terms thought to be unintelligible to those they described. The Lascelles were old, literate and educated if minor Yorkshire gentry. They – or at least people of that name; there is some question about whether the two families are connected – had owned land in Yorkshire at least since the late thirteenth century. They were based outside Northallerton, plumb in the middle of the Vale of Mowbray, grassy, rolling, comfortable country, where horses were bred for coach and saddle, and 'the old *common* stock of the Vale', according to William Marshall, the late eighteenth-century improver, was 'a thin-carcased, ill-formed, white-faced hornless breed' of cattle.[5]

Only part of the Lascelles's house survives at Stank Hall, a sheep farm now, perhaps named after the ponds or moat that once surrounded it. It seems to be a perfect monument to gentry decline. Large modern sheds cluster around the old stone building. There is a coat of arms above a blocked doorway, where the big, bobble-ended cross of the Lascelles arms is impaled with their neighbours and relations the St Quintins. You can still detect the faint turfy outlines of a Jacobean garden with its corner mounts.[6]

This might have been a picture of remembered glory and sunken destinies. It isn't. Stank Hall had been nothing but a stepping stone for the Lascelles. They had only bought it in 1608 on the proceeds of successful land management elsewhere in the Vale. They were on the up, 'rising gentry', Puritan and politically engaged. Henry Lascelles's grandfather Francis had become a Roundhead colonel in the Civil War.[7] He was a committed Parliamentarian but no rabid ideologue. When accepting the surrender of Scarborough Castle after a brutal siege in 1645, the conditions he and the other Parliamentary officers imposed on the surrendering Royalists were the model of gentry grace: the Governor and his 'Gentleman Soldiers' were allowed to leave for Holland, or to rejoin the Royal Army, taking their own belongings with them, on horseback and wearing their swords; the Governor's wife and the common soldiers were allowed to go home. These articles 'were much grumbled at by some of the Parliaments Party as too favourable',[8] but the incident is a window on to Lascelles's non-ideological nature. When as a Republican Member of Parliament for Northallerton he had sat in judgement on Charles I, he absented himself on the day the King's death warrant was signed.

This steering for the middle ground meant that although Colonel Lascelles remained an MP and was one of the Cromwellian Commissioners for Yorkshire, at the Restoration in 1660, unlike other regicides who were imprisoned, exiled or executed, he made his peace with the new regime and suffered no more than an enormous fine (a year's income) and a ban on ever occupying public office again.

It is tempting to see the passions of the Lascelles being steered into commerce by this political exclusion, but that is not quite true.[9] The family retained its Yorkshire lands but there were business interests already, at least from the mid-seventeenth century onwards, and commercial connections to Belfast and Scotland. The regicide's eldest son, also called Francis, became a nonconformist merchant, based in London, dealing with Virginia. His sister Lucy married a Virginia merchant (from another Yorkshire family). In 1648 an Edward Lascelles – probably a cousin, but the links are unclear – bought an estate in Barbados, where he also owned a warehouse and shipping. By the 1680s, four Lascelles brothers, including Edward, were in the Barbados trade together, one based in London as the anchor of the English end of the business, one a transatlantic ship's captain and the others out in the West Indies. With no excess of imagination they called their ships the *Frigate Lascelles*, 220 tons, its replacement, 300 tons, the *Lascelles*, and another the *Edward and Mary*, after the most successful of the brothers and his wife. This organization of a business and its ethos around family connections was an extension of the gentry understanding, of which this book is full, that siblings and children had an inherent unity of interest. In a world riddled with deceit and betrayal, the corporation of the family became the safest and most reasonable basis on which to arrange one's affairs.

By the beginning of the eighteenth century, the culture of the whole clan was a rich and potent mixture: gentry, Anglican but with nonconformist connections, anti-absolutist, anti-Catholic, contributing to local government in Yorkshire but entrepreneurial and ambitious. Gentry had fused with trader. They were Whigs, firmly opposed to the Stuarts. In December 1688, Henry's father, Daniel, had taken part in the Yorkshire rising which had helped eject the Catholic James II and replace him with the Protestant William III. Daniel became Sheriff of York, briefly a Whig Member of Parliament for Northallerton and a man of business himself.[10] The records for his life are patchy but he may have been out to Barbados himself. These people did not abandon their Yorkshire roots, but that was not where opportunity lay.

Trade for the Lascelles was not the dumping ground for junior brothers, nor the next best option after the church, but the highway which an entire family could take to money, significance and power. In the first decade of the eighteenth century, perhaps inspired by the success of their cousins, Henry Lascelles and his brothers began to establish their own family business on the booming Atlantic networks. Nothing is known of them or their upbringing before they emerged on to the commercial stage. The eldest brother, George, went out to Barbados in 1706. In 1712, when he was twenty-two, Henry joined him there. Three years later, their half-brother Edward came out too and George returned to manage the London office. The system that might in the past have run adjoining blocks of farmland in the Vale of Mowbray now had the magnifying lens of imperial riches applied to it. It was long-distance kinship capitalism.

Barbados, whose original Amerindian population was decimated by Spanish visitors in the sixteenth century, was first colonized by the English in 1625 and by the middle of that century was 85 per cent white. The land was largely worked by indentured servants, poor young English and Irish men and women who had (temporarily, for three, five or seven years) traded their freedom for the price of the voyage out to the West Indies.[11] But they had not coped well with the climate and had usually died young. By the time of the Lascelles, Barbados was worked by Africans, a slave to every two or three acres of sugar plantation. To stock a 500-acre plantation, about 130 slaves were required. The price varied between islands and from year to year but hovered around £20–25 for each slave, a capital cost in slave stock of £3,000. The blacker their skin and the curlier their hair, the more expensive they were, perhaps, ironically enough, on the grounds of Enlightenment taxonomies. Classifiers liked to think in terms of distinct species and varieties: a black person was regarded as distinct from a white person. Colours in between were a mixture of both and, so the theory went, less predictable and possibly less strong. Consistently, over many decades, merchants required their captains to seek out the blackest people they could find. Young men and women in their mid-teens were the most sought after.[12] The land they worked and the relatively high expense of equipping a plantation with wind-driven rolling mills to extract the juice from the cane, as well as the boiling, curing and distilling houses, the cisterns, stills, tubs and barrels, might well come to another £15,000 or £20,000. This high level of capital investment could easily produce an annual income of £9,000 on a 500-acre estate.[13]

The running costs were not minimal. Between 3 and 4 per cent of slaves would die each year. Clothing and feeding the slaves, servicing and repairing the equipment, the costs of transport and porterage, medical attendance, local taxes and payments to local managers, overseers and bookkeepers could all add up to between 25 per cent and 50 per cent of gross revenue. The cost of keeping the slaves alive was only part of this: the barrels for the sugar cost more than looking after the people who produced it. It was a place of torment. At the slave markets on the quaysides, the Africans were stood naked in front of the buyers and had their flesh squeezed to check their condition. Agents recommended that a man's penis should be handled to ensure it was good for breeding. Unbought slaves in unsatisfactory condition were left to die on their own. When slaves rebelled on the island, they were exposed in iron cages in which they were attached to the branch of a tree or left to die of hunger and thirst, a punishment known as 'hanging out to dry'.[14]

Conditions on plantations meant that life expectancy at birth was dismal: more than half of all slave babies would be dead before they were five. Another 10 per cent would die before they were ten. As the historian Simon Smith has said, many slave lives spanned less time than a butterfly's.[15] An unrelenting work regime, which began at the age of five, and exposure to the greed and cruelty of overseers meant that most adult slaves died before they were fifty.

Rainless years in which the cane did not grow could drastically reduce productivity, but you need look no further than the spectacular margins of the sugar business to understand the mechanisms at work. An investment of some £25,000 would be paid back in three good years, the profit a measure of the value created by an enslaved workforce which cost next to nothing to keep going. Demand was ever growing and that fat sweet river of slave-based money was the foundation of the Lascelles story. It was a long way from any beef or butter in the damp fields outside Northallerton.

Henry Lascelles did not go into West Indian land, beyond the ownership of a single plantation on Barbados, called Guinea. Increasing competition from other islands both raised the price of slaves and dropped the price of sugar. Trading in the key commodities, not producing the sugar itself, was where the future lay. Within months of his arrival, Henry Lascelles locked into the business community. He quickly married the daughter of Edward Carter, a leading planter and slave trader, who every decade was importing about £40,000 worth of slaves. Henry began trading slaves on his own account, on something like the same scale as his father-in-law. For those with entrepreneurial flair, the huge profits of the business meant that there was plenty of credit available. You didn't need to be rich to start as a slave-and-sugar man, only a modicum of courage and a grip on the figures. Victory went to those who had grasped the foundational fact, as one of Lascelles's business partners later expressed it, that 'The Larger the Concern ye better. We are now a tolerable Judge of our Expences, so that the more Cargoe Disposed of, the greater advantage the Concern will recieve.'[16]

Henry, still in his mid-twenties, was on a drive. 'Negros' and hogsheads of sugar were commodities to be shipped around the Atlantic. In 1712, there were 42,000 slaves in Barbados (against 12,500 white people) but as their life expectancy was short, constant re-supply was required from Africa. But that was only one aspect of what soon became a multi-headed business.

At the most basic level, there was money to be made out of victualling the Royal Navy ships which called at Bridgetown, for which Lascelles bought bread, biscuit flour and dried peas in Philadelphia[17] and New York, and shipped cheese, butter, beef and pork from Cork to the Caribbean.[18] He also courted the good offices of naval captains and made deals with them to ship goods as freight within Navy holds.[19]

He owned shares in ships, often an eighth or a quarter, never an entire ship, as risks in the Atlantic trade made it safer not to concentrate your assets, but it was agenting which fuelled his boom. Captured French indigo,[20] mahogany from Nicaragua,[21] tortoiseshell, cocoa and 'Jesuit's bark', from which a treatment for malaria could be extracted,[22] joined the rather weak Barbados rum,[23] the dark, sticky muscovados,[24] the molasses[25] and the more expensive part-refined or 'clayed' sugars[26] on the seas to London. There the Lascelles office sold the goods on and charged a commission on the sale. Storms in which ships would lose their masts, or even founder if deep laden,[27] and both French and Spanish privateers were a constant hazard.[28] Lascelles recommended 'a very stout ship well provided with men and guns',[29] but he could make money there too, taking commission both on the goods themselves and on their insurance.

Plenty of goods and men came back the other way. The London office arranged for plumbers,[30] brick-layers,[31] bakers and other tradesmen to be sent out from England, along with watches[32] (which had to be sent back to London from Barbados if they were to be mended), sugar-processing machinery manufactured in England on the basis of models sent to London from the Caribbean,[33] swords with scabbards (4 guineas),[34] cracked bells which had been re-cast, suits of night clothes for the planters' wives,[35] candles, claret, 'beef tongues'[36] and re-dyed gowns.[37] One planter had an organ sent from England, which the Lascelles office in London arranged to be tried and tuned by a musician before it was shipped on board in the Thames, along with a tea chest covered in shagreen, a form of elegantly worked sharkskin, 'with silver furniture & 3 chased canisters'.[38] 'Pipes of good wine' (600 bottles in each pipe)[39] loaded in Madeira joined medicines from London. Large quantities of metal hoops, for the West Indian coopers to make sugar barrels with, filled many of the outgoing holds.

Every transaction involved a commission; every aspect of life was networked. On reading the Lascelles business correspondence that has survived, the overwhelming sensation is of normality. From our perspective now, the trafficking of over fifteen million Africans from one side of the Atlantic to the other may rank as the greatest crime ever committed by this country. 'No nation in Europe ... has ... plunged so deeply into this guilt as Great Britain,' Pitt the Younger would say in the House of Commons in 1792,[40] but in the great growth years of the Lascelles business, there is no sense of aberration or wrongness. The tone of the correspondence is, on the whole, solicitous, civilized and Georgian, as if there were no crime to be recognized, let alone hidden. There was undoubted guilt here; there is not even a whisper of shame.

Lascelles certainly made a great deal of money out of these multifarious transactions, but none was as valuable as the government office he landed in 1714. The Whigs under Robert Walpole had just come to power in England and Henry's appointment as Collector of Customs at Bridgetown, Barbados, was a small outer ripple in the maze of interest and mutuality which was eighteenth-century politics. The family had long resisted the Stuarts and their Tory supporters; this was the reward.

A levy of 4½ per cent was raised on all sugar leaving Barbados for England. The Collector was meant to levy that tax in kind and then 'the Specifick Goods received for the Duties to be Shipt and sent home'[41] to an officer of the Customs Service in London known as the Husband of the Sugars. The Husband, based at Custom House Quay in the Pool of London, would then sell the sugar on to the grocers and the 'sugar-bakers'. Needless to say, Henry's standing at one of the key gateways of imperial finance was one of the most valuable posts in the whole of the British Customs Service. For the next three decades it remained in Lascelles hands, first Henry's and then those of Edward, his half-brother.

Both of them milked it for all it was worth, defrauding the British Treasury itself, and in several different ways and quite systematically tampering with the documents: erasing the quantity of goods landed; later inserting goods of lower value; pocketing the difference between the amount of tax they charged and the amount of tax which the amended documents showed; and straightforwardly selling blank documents to merchants so that they could enter what they liked on their customs returns. In this position of power, they were able to maximize all kinds of influence, extorting money from ships' masters, selling slaves from ships taken as prizes, the proceeds from which should have gone into official coffers.[42] No sense of any guilt over this behaviour is apparent anywhere in the Lascelles papers.

In 1720 Henry was summoned to London to answer charges, as was his half-brother Edward in 1744. And although the outlines of the long-running and bitter double case are far from clear, and political rivalry and faction fighting clouded both the issues and the outcomes, there seems too much smoke for there to have been no fire. The Treasury was aware that any Collector of Customs was chronically vulnerable to corruption of this kind and so they appointed an official known as the Comptroller, who 'ought to have been a Cheque on the Collector throughout his whole Management'.[43] Both Lascelles brothers bought the Comptroller off by promising him a cut and then embarked on their thieving spree.

The key change they made was to levy the sugar tax in cash not in kind. As the later government report expressed it, 'This practice of Commutation was the Foundation of the Frauds.'[44] It meant that the Lascelles had in hand large amounts of ready money, which they could lend out to planters and merchants, establishing credit networks on which they could keep the interest themselves. As interest rates in the Caribbean could rise as high as 10 per cent (against a 5 per cent legal maximum in London), this was valuable business. They also consistently estimated 'wastage' at 3 per cent of the sugars landed, when in other Caribbean islands it never ran at more than 1½ per cent. And they took to entering high-quality sugar in the books as if it were low-quality, pocketing the difference between the amount of tax that should have been raised and what was actually returned. When in the 1740s the government inspector Robert Dinwiddie came to see what was going on and asked for 'the Keys of the King's Warehouse to see the Duty Goods due to the Revenue, the Collector told him there were no Goods in the Warehouse, but a little Cotton and Alloes, and that he had Commuted the rest of the Goods for cash'.[45]

Overall, 'it was strongly suggested the Collectors had defrauded the Crown and made great Advantages to themselves.' It is thought that Henry pocketed between a half and a third of what should have gone to the Treasury. The London authorities accused him of cheating on the valuations of rum, sugars and lime juice 'and therefore they had directed him to be surcharged with the difference' – to the spectacular tune of £39,995 14s. 4d. in Barbados currency, or £30,000 sterling.

Lascelles, in his submission to the disciplinary hearing, 'absolutely denied' that he had anything to do with undercharging, or pocketing any difference that might have resulted, and in the first sign of a kind of bleakness that hangs around his character, blamed his underlings, the junior officials who actually supervised the landings on the quays: 'This charge is unjust to be made on the Collector who is an Indoor Officer, the Landwaiters & searchers only being answerable for an accusation of this sort, whose business is to attend the shipping, and compare the Quality of the Sugars.'[46]

Henry was let off, as was Edward in the 1740s, largely by politicking in London and by calling in political favours, but not before they had conducted a bitter correspondence with the government inspector, Robert Dinwiddie. The Lascelles's own letter does not survive but Dinwiddie's reply does. Edward and the Comptroller had been (temporarily) suspended from the job that had been bringing so much money into the Lascelles coffers and Henry, clearly in a rage, had asked Dinwiddie for the names of people who had betrayed them. Dinwiddie replied:

As you seem to write in a Passion, I shall not go thorow the whole Contents of your Letters.

I have passed my Word to the Persons that have furnished me with the Accts under your Hand, not to make use of their names here, but they will be Transmitted with my reports to the Commissioners.

I shall sacredly keep up to my Orders & shall endeavour to Act consistently and impartially in the whole transactions of my Duty.

I shall evade going into a Paper Warr on this Head … I think I have acted with friendship and Honour in giving you the Principles

on which I shall Surcharge your accompt & the reasons for
Suspending you

I wish you & yr Family well and am Sir

Your Humble Servant

Robt Dinwiddie[47]

Corruption, anger, passing the buck, greed, fearless hard-headedness, the alliance in crime with the younger brother: these were the foundations of Henry Lascelles's triumph.

After the death of his elder brother George in 1729, Henry returned to England to take control of the London office and became one of the big panjandrums of the City. Like many Barbados men, he was loathed by his fellow London merchants. Although, as they said, they had 'as good English Bloud in our Veins, as those that we have left behind us',[48] 'Phlegmatick Londoners' continued to treat them as colonial vulgarians. Barbados men were said to have 'fiery, restless tempers' and 'put no median between being great and being undone'. They were extremists with 'a more volatile and lively Disposition, and more irascible in general' than your average Londoner, with a penchant for 'Parade and Shew'.[49] They were 'foolish, ridiculous, inconsistent, scurrilous, absurd, malicious and impudent'.[50] They were also – which may explain some of these bitter and jealous adjectives – unconscionably rich.

Henry bought himself a mansion, Lichfield House, in Richmond-upon-Thames. The site is a block of 1930s Deco-ish flats now but his house survived until the age of photography and the old pictures reveal the building in which Henry Lascelles lived until his death on 6 October 1753: a pedimented façade from the early 1700s, a big, plain, masculine mass of brick, dedicated to commodity and firmness more than delight, nothing flirty or charming about it, not a rococo flounce to be seen, a house suited to the dignity, solidity and comfort of one of the great self-made men of the age. Its long garden stretched north to a glazed orangery, the whole ensemble a few minutes' walk from the river. London, with its 'smoke and dirt, sin and seacoal',[51] as Daniel Defoe had coolly described it in the 1720s, lay fourteen miles to the east, downstream and downwind.

There is no doubting the manliness of the Lascelles style: rugs on the finest clean deals or Dutch oak boards; the rooms all wainscoted or painted in 'a costly and handsome manner'; marble chimneypieces; the doors thick and substantial, with the best sort of brass locks on them; walnut-veneered chairs, with leather or damask seats; mahogany tables and chests of drawers, the timber from the West Indies, the silks inside them from Spittalfields; gilded mirrors above the chimneypieces and brass fenders around them, equipped with tongs, poker and shovel. Beds were made with beautiful linen, screens stood in front of the fires; silver candlesticks and sauce boats shone on the mahogany ground. The windows were fitted with wooden shutters; patterned chintz curtains were drawn across them. This was not about vainglorious display but undeniable substance, the irremovability of a man of worth.[52]

Richmond was London's most enviable suburb. Daniel Defoe called it a 'glorious Show of Wealth and Plenty, a view of the Luxuriant Age which we live in, and of the overflowing Riches of the Citizens'.[53] The suburb was a monument to the prodigious fortunes which England's first great commercial age had created, full of men 'whose Beginnings were small, or but small compar'd, and who have exceeded even the greatest Part of the Nobility of *England* in Wealth, at their Death, and all of their own getting'.[54] It was a commuter suburb and Defoe had to explain the new phenomenon that although these were enormous houses, they did not have 'any lands to a considerable value about them'.[55] Land and significance were for the first time pulling apart.

As a result, something else lay hidden in the great cellars of these modern, 'opulent Foundations':

It would take up a large chapter in this book, to but mention the overthrow, and catastrophe of innumerable wealthy city families, who after they have thought their houses establish'd, and have built their magnificent country seats, as well as others, have sunk under the misfortunes of business, and the disasters of trade, after the world has thought them pass'd all possibility of danger; such as Sir Joseph Hodges, Sir

224

Justus Beck, the widow Cock at Camberwell, and many others; besides all the late South-Sea directors, all which I chuse to have forgotten, as no doubt they desire to be, in recording the wealth and opulence of this part of England.[56]

This money was different from old landed money in one all-important quality: it was not safe.

The Lascelles business was based in the City of London. Their counting house and office was first in Mark Lane, then Mincing Lane and then in a court off Great Tower Street, all of them a few minutes' walk from the quays of the Pool of London, lining the Thames between London Bridge and the Tower. It was the greatest port in the world. In streets described by John Strype in 1720 as 'garnished with very good Houses, which for the generality are taken up by Merchants, and Persons of Repute',[57] the Lascelles office was a merchant's house, adapted for business. From here Lascelles ran his shipping network, extended credit, charged commission on other merchants' sales as well as trading on his own account, negotiated with office holders in the Customs and in the Treasury, berated his brother by letter in the Caribbean and maintained the giant invisible network he had created across the Atlantic ocean.

Windows on the ground floor were enlarged to bring as much light as possible into the counting house.[58] The central door, flanked by pilasters and with a moulded hood, was up a short flight of stone steps. A stone hallway, with a stair at its far end, greeted you as you came in. To one side was a waiting room, entirely panelled and painted, with window seats looking out on to the street and a fireplace, whose surround in the best offices would have been carved. On the other side of the hall was the counting house with its own fireplace, where goods were accounted for, bills paid, credit issued and custom dues reckoned. Wrought-iron railings and gates shut anyone unauthorized away from the money.

On the floor above would be the most important rooms in the house, facing on to the street, the panelling here richer, the mouldings bolder and more substantial, each of the two rooms up here with their own fireplaces, with fluted friezes and panelled pilasters, perhaps with some swags or carved eagles. Other members of the office had rooms on the floor above, where yet more coal-burning fireplaces kept them warm.

Everything about the set-up exuded gentlemanliness, a refuge of order and control away from the turbulence, hurry and incipient anarchy of the streets outside. It was a suddenly speeding city, an endless competition, as the journalist and dramatist Edward Moore described it in May 1755:

> If we observe the behaviour of the polite part of this nation (that is, of all the nation) we shall see that their whole lives are one continued race; in which every one is endeavouring to distance all behind him, and to overtake, or pass by, all who are before him; every one is Flying from his inferiors in pursuit of his superiors, who fly from him with equal alacrity.
>
> Every tradesman is a merchant, every merchant is a gentleman, and every gentleman one of the noblesse. We are a nation of gentry, *populus generosorum*: we have no such thing as common people among us: between vanity and gin, the species is utterly destroyed.[59]

Lascelles's London was a place in which all definitions were up for grabs. Mazy, cobbled streets ran downhill from Mincing Lane to the warehouses and quays on the scurfy tidal river, the money-conveyor to the Atlantic. The tide surged through the narrow gaps between the piers of London Bridge, a rushing passage which, as a visiting Frenchman had told Pepys, was terrifying in prospect but in fact 'le plus grand plaisir du monde'.[60] Offices were interspersed with the coffeehouses in which agents, merchants and investors met and did their business. Slave boys, spices, rare birds from the tropics, all were sold here. London was too busy to observe old customs: the rural and colonial habit of doffing your hat to a gentleman you met in the street had been abandoned. Slave boys in elegant coats wore silver collars like napkin rings around their necks on which the coat of arms and sometimes address of their owner were stamped. The City churches were crammed in between the offices, panelled with memorials to the successful City men, their achievements lauded in gold leaf (from Brazil) on mahogany (from Jamaica). The halls of the great City livery companies stood marooned in backstreets, the whiff of dinner never quite escapable in them.

All the ingredients of Lascelles's life were in play here: inherited courtesy; a straightforward commercial drive which allowed him and his colleagues to treat black people as just another commodity, not unadmired or unappreciated for what they were, but considered valuable only in commercial terms; a level of tension and anxiety at the degree of risk in the business; and at times a savage rage and severity in dealing with others. The atmosphere that survives in the letter-books of his business is a picture of gentry harshened in a commercial world.

On the day in the 1720s when Defoe 'had the curiosity to count the ships' either at anchor or tied up at the quays in the Pool of London, he 'found above two thousand sail of all sorts, not reckoning barges, lighters or pleasure-boats, and yachts'.[61] The volume of transactions, the sheer scurry of this world city dazzled contemporaries. At the Custom House, where 'in the Long Room it's a pretty pleasure to see the multitude of payments that are made', in the Excise Office, the Navy Office, the Bank, the offices of the South Sea Company ('South Sea' meaning at this time not the Pacific but the slave-worked Caribbean), the East India Company, the Royal African Company, in the insurance offices and in the Exchange, a 'prodigious conflux' of gentry were engaged in 'a negotiation, which is so vast in its extent, that almost all the men of substance in England are more or less concerned in it.' This frantic pace and scale of negotiation were transforming the geography and habits of the country.

Many thousands of families are so deeply concerned in those stocks, and find it so absolutely necessary to be at hand to take the advantage of buying and selling, as the sudden rise or fall of the price directs, and the loss they often sustain by their ignorance of things when absent, and the knavery of brokers and others, whom, in their absence, they are bound to trust, that they find themselves obliged to come up and live constantly here, or at least, most part of the year.[62]

Henry Lascelles cruised this brutal reef, his life in perpetual tension between gentry courtesy and commercial imperatives. He could be rudeness itself. His 'Daming, Villifying & abusing' was 'ye Public Taulk of ye Coast by all masters of ships out of London, Bristoll, or Leverpoole'.[63] But he was a man of power and his finance business became enormous: he had loans out on all sides of the Atlantic totaling some £200,000 in 1750, perhaps equivalent to £300 million today, delivering on average 7 per cent a year, a rate of return which English land could never hope to have matched. The other branches all boomed on the expansion and deepening of the Atlantic networks: the commission business selling sugar to London traders; the victualling and shipping businesses (his own son Henry was a ship's captain); and the Africa trade. In 1736 with seven other merchants he entered a joint enterprise which they called the Concern, committing £4,000 each, to establish a set of ships called the 'Floating Factory' and shore stations on the African slave coasts.[64] A permanent presence off Anamobu in modern Ghana would regularize the trade in Africans, gold, ivory, gum and pepper. It was an attempt to apply rational, Enlightenment methods to a previously ad hoc system. Supply ships from Europe made regular deliveries to the Concern's officers on the coast, shipping gold and ivory back to Europe, slaves to the Caribbean and Brazil. The money involved was enormous in this too. In December 1739, the Concern had £74,000 of assets afloat in Africa,[65] over £100 million in modern terms. A year later, one of the other partners reckoned that 'the Produce of the Gold & Teeth' alone was £37,000.[66]

The famous triangular trade – goods to Africa, slaves to the Caribbean, sugar to London – was only one configuration in a net of connections. The Concern stocked their ships with an enormous variety of goods: silk hats, shaving bowls, even horses (one horse could buy twenty-five slaves), beads, brass pots, silks, and sets of porcelain from the Far East which were loaded in Rotterdam, and a great deal of cloth: there was a steady market in the cold winds off the Atlantic for bolts of English serge.[67]

In return they bought gold, ivory, gum, wax and people. The Concern's captains kept the Africans in horrifying conditions either on shore in lightless cellars, or on board ship off the coast where high nets were rigged on deck to prevent the desperate men and women throwing themselves into the sea. Some were then shipped to Barbados and Jamaica in the Concern's own holds but they were mostly sold on to Portuguese slavers on the coast for gold or silver from South American slave-worked mines. The Concern was in effect running a slave shop for these Atlantic traders. The advantage for the Portuguese was that they did not need to spend any time on the disease-ridden coast. The advantage for the Concern was that they could charge a premium on such convenient delivery. Lascelles's profit was quite straightforwardly on the back of African slaves' and English sailors' lives.

The way in which the business was conducted was no stroll through life. Vigilance, arrogance, quickness, tension, exhaustion and worry hang over it all. 'Uneasy' is the eighteenth-century word. It occurs again and again in the correspondence of Lascelles's business partners. 'The Times makes him very Uneasie & it is a very large Concern … Mr Lascelles [is] most Uneasie for fear of either of your Deaths,' his partner wrote to George Hamilton, their leading sea captain in Africa in 1740. 'No Body will Insure on the Argyle or any of our Ships on the Coast.' Lascelles was 'tired of' his business, he was 'peevish', 'sick of it'.[68] Hamilton thought Lascelles had turned 'Threatening'[69] in his own letters. Treachery was in every corner. From the *Argyle* anchored at Anamobu, Captain Hamilton had written back to London about Edward Jasper, one of the partners in the Concern:

> The eyes of a hundred of people are on us, and I make no doubt Several that trade this way hartily wishes our overthrough whatever we ship home, the privater itt is Kept the better, Mr Edward Jasper, has that great failing, what ever Mr Lascelles & you acquaint him with, he will tell it to Every Body.[70]

Every last penny had to be squeezed from the business. Lascelles wrote to one of his captains, Richard Crookenden, in February 1741, that when taking on freight in the Caribbean, he 'must urge the extravagant charge of every kind & risques wch the ships now sail at wch is still much increased to what it was last voyage & that the shippers ought to consider it'.[71]

When in late 1740, his half-brother Edward allowed the captain of a ship to provide the casks in which the sugar was to shipped back to England, Henry could barely control himself.

> I desire you will let none of the captains for future have any hand in it, which will cut of the profit … Could handle [the captain] very severely but at this time of Day it may not be proper. Pray never suffer Casks to be furnished by any captain again.[72]

Edward was thirty-eight, Henry fifty-one when given this dressing down. The following year it happened again when Edward ordered flour and 'bisket' for the Navy from Philadelphia. He hadn't been dealing hard enough. Savage letters were sent from Henry to Edward when he failed to collect the debts that were due to the business or when Edward decided to sell slaves in Barbados and not in Jamaica, even though the price was 75 per cent higher there.

In the autumn of 1741 they had 237 'very choice' slaves which 'would have sold for any money [in Jamaica] the demand being so great for them.' But they had missed the opportunity.

> I see you were a fortnight getting off these, whereas at Ja[maica] the sale wd not have lasted a week & you've 1/3 of the slaves left on hand so I plainly see what'll be the consequence & the Gentlemen in the Concern wld rather have run the hazard of the ships going to the Bottom, they expect the difference will be at least £1,000.[73]

This was not the world in which a Harry Oxinden or an Oliver le Neve had ever lived. A certain modernity had entered the way the Lascelles spoke and wrote, a tautness, a rudeness, a shortness, a lack of gentility. Nonetheless, they had their gentry inheritance to consider and a man's word continued to be one of the key commodities. It was meant to be the basis on which gentlemen, so described, could do business with each other but the correspondence between Lascelles and his many trading partners is full of anxiety about just this. Could a man be trusted? When the gentry world revolved, in essence, around neighbourliness, a man's keeping his word would be in his own interest. When that culture found itself dispersed across the enormous widths of the Atlantic, where it took at least three months for a reply to come to a letter sent from London to the West Indies, any sense of neighbourliness, and of the principles of honour, worth and a man's word which relied on that mutual supervision, were stretched to the point of fragility. Something that might have been assumed before, in a pre-imperial gentry world, now required vigilance and policing. One of the investors in Lascelles's Africa concern, Charles Benyon, wrote to another, Thomas Hall, after a family dinner party:

> I trouble you with this to returne you and Mrs Hall many thanks for yor last kind entertainmt to me & mine, and to lett you know that Mr Pallett is not a man of his Word, for after he had ordered the Bill to be taken down on my Acco he has altered his mind & wants to lett it ready furnished, so that I am disappointed of the House.[74]

In October 1741 Thomas Hall had sent on his own behalf a valuable consignment of diamonds, 550 carats in 2,700 stones, worth £11,748 to an English dealer in Amsterdam. The dealer, George Clifford, had assured Hall of a sale.

> Sir
>
> We are sorry and ashamed to tell you that when we applied to ye person, who we advised you had made an offer for your Diamonds, he run back from his Word, and said that since that time so many Diamonds were come to Town that he absolutely could not afford to give so great a price for them which is mere trifling, but when we tell you it's a Jew, you'll wonder the less at such a Breach of his word,

they having few sentiments of honour, had it however happened to be a sworn broker, or more witnesses than one when the offer was made we could have forced him to take them, but as the word of a Broker who is not Sworn goes for nothing in these cases, we can do nothing herein but have patience, …

George Clifford and Sons
Amsterdam[75]

The ranking was clear: Africans were not entirely human; Jews were human but with no concept of honour; only gentlemen understood the workings of society. But for all this mutual assurance and assumption that a gentleman's word was his bond, it seems clear that Henry's practice of cheating, pursued so carefully as Collector of Customs in Barbados, never left him. Other partners in the Concern reckoned he was taking more than his fair share of the proceeds. George Hamilton didn't like the smell of the man Lascelles was employing to oversee their business.

Capt Tho Hill is a very capable man, but in my opinion not to be Intrusted in that affaire; for itt gives him an opportunity to know Every Thing we do, see most of ye letters we send home, and the Sortment of goods we write for att times. He is concerned in ships this way, which may be of greate prejudice to the concerned.[76]

It may be that the relative unprofitability of the Concern on the African coast – at least compared to the money Lascelles was making on his loans to planters and merchants and on the commission he was charging on the sugar landed at the London quays – led him to deceive his partners. The story is murky but the Concern came to a messy end in the early 1740s and a letter survives in the papers of Thomas Hall, one of the Concern's partners, from one of their aggrieved captains, John Dunning:

July 19 1747

The treatment you saw I suffered from Mr Lasselles last Evening, was so insulting, scurrilous, & unGentlemanlike that I am obligded to ask your pardon, for the Manner he obligded me to leave; I am determined never more to meet him, unless in Westminster Hall

I shall join my own demands, and the demands of all the Captains, and others whose hard-got wages Mr Lascelles detains.[77]

By Westminster Hall, Dunning meant the law courts, where the argument did indeed end up.[78] Another set of relationships had foundered on Lascelles's single-minded pursuit of his own ends and his breaking of the community of honour. The gentry inheritance had disappeared under the demands of the huge, new imperial market in which he was determined to prevail. There is no reason to generalize this, or to see Lascelles as symptomatic of a bad world. It was perfectly possible to be a courteous merchant in eighteenth-century London, but Henry Lascelles was a driven, greedy, hard-line individual who may well have recognized – none of this was committed to paper – that only a truly enormous fortune would lift his family into the un-assailable reaches of the aristocracy. Hard driving in one generation was the price of long-lasting significance.

In September 1743 he had acquired a new business partner, the cultivated Scotsman George Maxwell. Maxwell had been a customs searcher and slave owner in Barbados. He brought a new atmosphere to the Mincing Lane office and a change of the company's name: Lascelles & Maxwell was a new start.

An air of friendly, complicit, gentlemanly discussion, of ease and politeness spreads across the Atlantic in Maxwell's letters, an exten-sion of the familiar neighbourliness of the gentry world. Very much the junior partner, he seemed to be everything Henry Lascelles was not. On arrival from six weeks at sea, shivering in the London fogs, Maxwell wrote charming gossip to his friends and contacts still in the Caribbean: how much he missed the warmth and sunlight of the Caribbean; the smoky nastiness of coal fires; the efficacies of cold baths as a way of fending off the 'flu; how Sir Robert Walpole's new dog kennel at Houghton in Norfolk was bigger than most of their houses in Barbados; the spectacular way in which the Duke of Argyll had gone crazy; and how Dean Swift in his madness was being displayed by his family to passers-by in the street for money.[79]

The charm sashayed into marketing: 'If Mr Lascelles and I can be of any use to you here in any Shape we shall gladly serve you.' 'As it is my happiness to know I am of the number of your friends, I think it incumbent on me to embrace the first opportunity of writing to you after my arrival.' These were sentences written with a smile on the writer's face. And he could be more relaxed too, buying lottery tickets for his friends (£11 7s. 6d. each) '& we do wish you good success therein.'[80] If a ship was late reaching Bridgetown, he would write to apologize. If a ship's captain behaved boorishly, he would write to apologize for that too.

Partly this is the world of business, partly of mutual, gentlemanly obligation. When a Barbados planter, Nicholas Willcox, wanted to borrow money in November 1745, it was difficult because although Lascelles & Maxwell had already offered him a loan, Bonnie Prince Charlie's rebellion had disturbed the markets and as a result interest rates had gone up. Henry was forced to raise his price for the loan to 6 per cent.

> We mention these things Dr Sir, only to shew you how much times are changed. We have however so high an opinion of your worth and because we are much obliged to you that as we have said it shall be at your own pleasure to allow us 5 or 6 pr ct in case you should have occasion to draw on us for any considerable sum.[81]

This is fascinatingly transitional language, in some ways the forerunner of the obsequious Dickensian shopkeeper, in others the descendant of gentlemanly talk from the seventeenth century and beyond. The notions of 'worth' and 'honour' have started to slide away from general qualities of a man's character to calculable aspects of his bank balance. To 'honour' a debt, or the 'worth' of a man, was now half a moral and half a financial consideration, the sentences hovering between gentlemanly courtesy and the hand-wringing of the merchant. Was the whole idea of interest embarrassing to these people, an aspect of ungentlemanly usury? What did 'credit' mean in this world? When something was to a man's credit, was that a description of his soul or his wallet?

But there was more to Maxwell than this sophisticated, manly talk. His deep longing for release from the grinding world of businessmen ('the wiseacres of the City',[82] as he called them) emerged in a series of kind and melancholic letters written in 1744–6 to a young Barbadian planter called John Brathwaite.

20 October 1744

I hope this will find you sitting with great tranquility in your own Porch or under your delightful shady trees, after numberless Perils reflecting on the vicissitudes of humane life. If there is anything in this world that has any appearance of what is counted happiness, you must I think enjoy it where you are, and it is some kind of happiness to me to imagine that you are contented with your present situation, & while I have the pleasure of telling you so, and I would desire to do nothg else for one hour at least, I am called off by many impertinences, one comes with a Bill for payment, and another with one for acceptance, and a third to drag me away to Lloyd's, a place I hate as much as you do, to meet some people about business.[83]

London reeked of gloom for the lonely Barbadian, whose wife, Dorothy, had for some reason stayed in the Caribbean. The following January Maxwell had to write to Brathwaite again, as Lascelles had promised him a loan and had then withdrawn it, or so Brathwaite believed. 'That his first order was afterwards contradicted', Maxwell wrote, embarrassed, 'I was quite ignorant. He said you must have misunderstood him … I do not chuse to dwell any longer on this Subject.'[84]

Then in November 1745, Maxwell, who was now in his mid-forties, wrote movingly to the younger man.

I am extremely sorry, Dr Sir, at the many disappointments you found in Barbados, and that things appeared quite different from what you had been used to here and expected there. The treatment of the negroes I might have foreseen, had I considered, would ill Suit the Gentleness of your nature, but that I happened to overlook, after having lived many more years in that Island than you have done in the wourld. It was become familiar to me by use. But I must declare that I was once Owner of above 100, and perhaps was one of the mildest Masters. None clothed or fed better, yet they are by nature so Stupid that I found none so ill served as I was; and therefore some correction is necessary. I used to pity their abject state at first, but afterwards found they were just as happy as their nature was capable of being.[85]

Among the planter gentry, the humanity of that statement is exceptionally rare, and it is perhaps a measure of George Maxwell's civility that he could recognize the unsuitability of John Brathwaite to the world in which Henry Lascelles thrived.

There had been some kind of violent incident in Barbados in which Brathwaite had become involved and which had left him shaken. Maxwell continued to encourage him. 'I wish you would afterwards return to this place', he wrote from London,

as nothing here could give me greater pleasure than to see you well. You ask me, if I will not think my Self much happier than you are, by living free from such tumults. Did you know truly my Condition, you would not think it to be envied. My mind is in Continual agitation about business, and bating [i.e. leaving aside] my being in good health which I own is a great blessing, I have as little enjoyment of Life as anyone. Most people have real or imaginary Crosses, which are the same in effect. I confess I love Solitude, and hate to be in a Croud, but forever expect to have my choice. Some Friends I had in Barbados used to talk of our retiring Some where out of the busy world, and the most proper place to retire to was proposed to be Bermuda. When you have been there, pray inform me how you think it would do for 3 or 4 Select friends? I imagine you would incline to be of Such a Company.[86]

Here, ever green, the Horatian dream had re-surfaced – the loathed crowds, the continual agitation of business – with Arcadia now taking the form of a beautiful island in the Atlantic:

You give one great Pleasure, Dr Sir, in mentioning the affection that was between us while you was last in London. I am pleased as often as I reflect on the agreeable hours we passed together and I shall ever think it my happiness that I was acquainted with you.[87]

Amidst all his explanations of the way in which higher risk in war meant that money was more expensive and the apologies for the hard bargaining of Mr Lascelles – 'for I am sorry he once disappointed you' – these letters are an oasis of gentleness and longing.

'I should be glad to enjoy a Continuance of your Correspondence,' Maxwell had written to his young friend, but the Lascelles & Maxwell Letterbooks never come to this emotional level again. Between the two of them, loans are negotiated, problems with debts and overseers encountered, the spoiling of his sugars described, first in an Atlantic storm and then at the hands of some lightermen on the Thames who had failed to pull the tarpaulin over: all take their place alongside hundreds of equivalent pages. Only once, in April 1757, does an invoice appear in the accounts for '210 romalls [a kind of Indian silk check] handkerchiefs which Mr Brathwaite sends over as a present for his negroes'.[88] That last phrase is unique in this rich and deeply detailed archive. Perhaps Maxwell's example had carried with him and Brathwaite had joined the ranks of 'the mildest Masters'.

No doubt Henry Lascelles was one of the crosses which George Maxwell had to bear. His rages and intemperance, his going back on his word, the nifty increases in the interest rates he charged, his open contempt for his brother and other associates in their business dealings, his refusing to pay out to those officers who had worked for him on the African shore: all of that points to a man for whom contentment was no more than a distant dream.

One letter in particular reveals the man he thought he was. It was written in October 1741 to Thomas Stevenson, a Barbados official who not only had borrowed money from Lascelles but who also held the office of Marshal on the island. His job was to collect debts from non-payers. A quarter of the fees generated by Stevenson was paid to Henry Lascelles and his half-brother Edward. In 1741 Lascelles wrote to him to explain the principles on which debtors should or should not be forced to pay up:

> I am not urgent to have the Money for Debt, I only want to have it ascertained & fixed beyond contradiction to receive the interest of it annually but if this should not be instantly complied with, & secured to me, it is my positive order that the executions be forthwith levied without any pretense or evasion whatsoever.[89]

No verb to be without its intensifier, no instruction without its intolerant adjective: either people paid the interest they owed without delay or they should be pursued for the whole debt. Henry Lascelles was a man with no comprehension of the word 'latitude'. In that way, he had left the gentry world behind.

Next to nothing is known of Henry's wives, first Mary Carter, who died in 1721, and then Jennet Whetstone. Of his own son Daniel, a little more can be made out. He returned from Barbados aged about twenty-five in 1739 and joined the firm. But he must have been a Hogarthian ne'er-do-well, as in 1740 Daniel got married secretly to a beautiful and impoverished young woman called Elizabeth Southwick. Henry did not hesitate and cut Daniel out of the business. By June the following year, Daniel had left his wife and was looking for a reconciliation with his father. This was achieved first by Daniel going on a tour of Italy and France and then in 1742 being sent to the East Indies, where he remained until 1750.

The Act of Parliament granting Daniel's divorce came through in November 1751,[90] the grounds given that Elizabeth had been sleeping with a man called Henry Parminter of Lincoln's Inn Fields, a bankrupt,[91] which may or may not have been true. It was the sort of thing that was often concocted in the circumstances. She became a pauper, pawning all her possessions, including her portrait from the Lascelles moment in her life, 'set in gold & a fine India white satin Counterpane', pledged for £6.[92]

Henry was now one of the great men of England, sitting in Parliament for the family seat of Northallerton, commanding the sugar trade, one of the great financiers of the City, a voice in the ear of crown ministers and government officials, accumulating funds which after his death would be invested in Yorkshire estates for his sons Edwin and Daniel. Among Daniel's acquisitions was the ancient hall and lands of Plumpton near Knaresborough, where an earlier gentry family had flowered and died.

In 1750, Henry retired from the business to spend his time in Richmond with Jennet. He drew up his will, leaving most of his business interests to the rehabilitated Daniel, and an enormous fortune to his eldest son, Edwin, who had been cultivated at Cambridge, in the salons of Europe, on the battlefield (against the Jacobites in 1746), in Parliament for Scarborough and in his own newly acquired Yorkshire estates as a nascent grandee. It was Edwin who as Lord Harewood began the construction of Harewood House, its mahogany doors and its Arcadian landscape re-importing rich, exotic dreams into Yorkshire's damp, ancestral acres.[93]

If you expect Henry Lascelles to slide quietly towards oblivion and the grave, to retire as the childless George Maxwell did, leaving his estate to a grateful nephew, who would in time become a Hampshire squire, his grounds landscaped by Capability Brown, his children burbling around him, it wasn't like that.[94] On 6 October 1753, at Lichfield House in Richmond, Henry Lascelles 'killed himself, by opening the veins in his wrists'.[95] A Yorkshire diarist, Thomas Gyll, heard that he had 'cut his throat and arms and across his belly'.[96] He bled to death in a pool of his own blood.

Is there any explanation for such an end to such a life? He had been suffering for years from cataracts in both eyes, a horrible condition which in the eighteenth century could be remedied only with a pair of scissors and no anaesthetic.[97] But Henry Lascelles was too hard-boiled for a little blindness to drive him to suicide. Nor is it realistic to think that his life of slave dealing would have made him do it. He might have been one of the regents of hell, but he would not have known that. Up until the end he was pursuing those members of the government who wanted to give Jews the right to trade in the City of London. The threat which that represented to the Lascelles loan, mortgage and finance business meant neither he nor, it is fair to say, most of the English financier-merchants could tolerate the idea. There is no evidence of any final sweetening in the mind of Henry Lascelles.

There are perhaps two possibilities. The first is to do with the time of life at which he killed himself. It was an idea with deep classical roots that human existence naturally divided into phases of seven years each. Our celebrating twenty-first birthdays is a faint memory of that but in the eighteenth century these moments were seen more systematically. Each seven-year transition was known as a 'climacteric' and the sixty-third year, nine times seven, was the 'grand climacteric', described by the literary scholar Pat Rogers as 'a sort of autumn equinox in human existence, corresponding to the vernal marker of 21'.[98] The sixty-third year was the moment a man entered his terminal decline. Sir John Oglander (page 135) had realized that 'about theyre Cleymiterricoll yeare 63' most of the men of his own family died.[99]

As Henry Lascelles confronted the approach of his own grand climacteric, his sixty-third birthday on 20 December 1753, he may have looked on it with horror: the dissolution of his commanding self. Guilt may not be the appropriate word, but he must also have known what his life of corruption, domination and rage had done to his name. He was not loved. Not a single artefact among the huge, gathered riches at Harewood House records the founder of the Lascelles fortune. No portrait of him exists and his memory continued as a dark ghost over the name of the Lascelles well into the nineteenth century. He was buried in a lead-lined coffin in a vault in Northallerton church. In 1814, it was opened and Henry's memory was recorded then as 'one of those unprincipled men who were concerned in the shameful South Sea Bubble business, whereby he amassed great wealth to the ruin of many'.[100]

Lascelles had abandoned the way of the gentry, recognizing not only that greater rewards lay in the realms of the Atlantic, but that an uncompromising frame of mind, a readiness to gamble all, at least when combined with relentless and rigorous vigilance, would set his family on the road to impregnable riches. Perhaps he could be seen as a martyr to his own posterity?

Courage

The Pinckneys

Wappoo and Charleston, South Carolina, and Richmond, Surrey

If the story of Henry Lascelles was founded on a willing departure from gentry norms, the life history of Eliza Lucas Pinckney is its opposite: the emergence of gentry virtues in a world that might have been entirely hostile to them. Her father's family, the Lucases, had been in Antigua in the Caribbean since the 1660s. It was a harsh place, a small island twenty miles by seventeen, very dry and subject to both devastating fires and 'the terrible Hurry Caines that doeth everie year distroye their Houses & Crops'.[1] The French islands of Guadaloupe and Martinique and the Spanish bases in Cuba were just over the horizon and Antigua lived for year after year in a state of armed tension. Pirates cruised the intervening seas.

In many ways the strain of Antigua's exposed predicament seeped into the quality of life there. By 1729 the 3,700 whites on the island were living close alongside their 24,400 African slaves, in conditions which even for the eighteenth-century Caribbean were acknowledged as horrible. The English population lived in fear of a slave revolt. They had nowhere to run in a crisis and repressive measures were harsh. Any white man who killed a runaway slave was given £3 by the governor, £6 if he caught him alive. When runaway slaves were caught, they were prosecuted for theft and invariably found guilty of stealing themselves.[2]

The Lucases had about 700 acres in three sugar plantations, hundreds of slaves to work them and four windmills with which to process the cane, but it was no luxury life. Even the richest of contemporary planters in the Leeward Islands had houses of no more than five rooms, three on the ground floor, two above.[3] The island was hard driven, with more windmills per square mile than anywhere else in the Caribbean. It was a slave camp in the service of sugar and money.

The distance from the regulating Board of Trade and Plantations in England meant that a sequence of early eighteenth-century royal governors in Antigua ran corrupt and aggressive regimes. George's father, John Lucas, found himself on the wrong side of one of them, Christopher Codrington, who threatened him and his family, threw him in jail, demanded £5,000 bail, murdered one of his slaves and had 'his son [either Eliza's father or an uncle], a youth of tender years, hunted with dogs and heathen'.[4]

Eliza Lucas was born in 1722 into this jagged, frontier world, the daughter of her father's 'Curtizan' – his unmarried mistress.[5] A coat of gentry civilization was laid over the brutal slave-worked realities of their lives. John Lucas became Speaker of the Antigua Assembly and a Justice of the Peace. His son George followed him in both positions and in 1713 bought himself a commission in the army, providing access to government finance, a means of gentry survival when the sugar markets looked difficult.

In common with every planter family in Antigua, the Lucases were living on credit. Most of the land was mortgaged and the debts to London creditors went unpaid for decades. In about 1700 John Lucas had arranged with a consortium of London merchants to transport to Antigua a cargo of 'merchandizes, negro Slaves, goods and other valuable effects amounting to a very considerable value'. But he had failed to pay his co-investors their share of the profit. Not until thirty years later in 1729, after his father's death, did his son George finally pay the debt, then amounting to £1,080 plus £990 interest, by mortgaging to them a plantation on Antigua of 300 acres of land and its 200 slaves.[6]

By then, the sugar business was in steep decline and as Eliza grew up it sank further. Between 1729 and 1737, the Antigua sugar trade slumped by 83 per cent. Years of drought devastated the crops. In

1736 the island was 'almost burnt up' by a plague of insects called the 'blast'. In October 1736 a conspiracy to kill all the leading planter families was discovered, led by an African called Tackey at the head of 'a numerous and disaffected herd of African slaves'.[7] Early in the next year, 88 of the rebels were executed and 37 banished. Their owners were compensated for the destruction of their property but it marked the end of what contentment there had been here, the gentry of the island 'believing the Negroes will accomplish their Designs sooner or later'.[8] In what the Antiguans called 'the decade of misfortune', the island had become 'a meare grave'.[9]

A few years later, George wrote to his friend and new son-in-law Charles Pinckney explaining the chronic burden of

the Incumbrances on my Estate [which are] so large and heavy That I have no expectation of any thing from [the sale of it]. It will be sold for payments of debts due from it and that th[ere will be] no remains ... The estate left me by my father hath been sunk in his Debts, and such [debts] as [I was] obliged to create in improving a large Tract of Empty land, being over[come wi]th excessive low Marketts.[10]

It was a hard-bitten upbringing, in which, you might imagine, it must have been difficult to nurture many gentry virtues. Nevertheless, somehow, from the midst of this tension and trouble, came the remarkable sensibility of Eliza Lucas, undoubtedly fed by the love and trust of her father – he called her Betsey – and perhaps by his need to find in her an ally and joint sustainer of the family project.

'I was very early fond of the vegitable world,' she wrote at the end of her own life. 'My father was pleased with it and encouraged it, he told me the turn I had for those amusements might produce something of real and public utility.'[11] Even in the rough circumstances of 1720s Antigua, George mentored and tutored his daughter in botany and gardening, and perhaps in bookkeeping and estate management. In 1732, when she was ten, he sent her to London to be educated. She spent five years in England, staying with her father's commission agent, Richard Boddicott, in Savage Gardens, a few streets away from

247

the Lascelles office in Mincing Lane in the City, and receiving her education at Mrs Pearson's boarding school for young ladies, probably in the airy suburban village of Hackney.[12]

Fanny Fayweather and a Miss Parry, both cousins from Antigua, were there with her, as well as Catherine Martin, whose father, John, was one of the truly rich, inheritor of a fortune from the family bank, Martin's, to which he contributed nothing but 'appears to have chosen as a profession that of being his father's heir'.[13] There was some status gap here: Catherine was never referred to in Eliza's letters as anything but 'Miss Martin'.

At the school, as the South Carolina historian Harriet Simons Williams has described,

> The governess taught 'the acomplishments' with great emphasis on fine sewing. There would have been a dancing master, a French master, and a writing master who also taught reckoning and simple household bookkeeping, English literature, history, 'the globes', and a smattering of science, especially botany for girls.[14]

As Eliza's later letters show, she was at home with Plutarch and Virgil (in translation); she read John Locke, the governing mind of the eighteenth-century gentry; and studied music. Polish had been applied and in late 1737, shepherded by one of her father's fellow members of the Antigua Assembly, she sailed home to the Caribbean.

None of this was exceptional. The other girls at Mrs Pearson's were undergoing the same training. But what happened next, driven by a combination of her father's chronic indebtedness, her mother's lack of command, the developing military situation in the western Atlantic and George Lucas's deep trust of his teenage daughter, pushed Eliza Lucas's life far out of the ordinary.

In the summer of 1739, George Lucas took his whole family to South Carolina. The bleakness of Antigua had become too much, the simmering anger of the hard-driven slaves too threatening. His lands there were bowed down with debt. In South Carolina, which at that time had no designated western boundary but stretched theoretically on through the vast spaces of French Louisiana and Spanish New Mexico as far west as the Sea of Cortes, was the American sense of space and possibility. Perhaps there the Lucases would find the riches and contentment which Antigua had once promised.

They arrived in South Carolina in early August 1739 and settled at a plantation called Wappoo, which John Lucas had bought as long ago as 1714, a property to which George, his son, had added in the 1730s. It was a few miles west of Charles Town, the capital of the colony, on the north side of a salt creek, with many wonderful trees and wetlands in which rice could be grown. On the higher land were giant meadows, perfect for beef and pig pasture, none of which would thrive on Antigua. 'An ox is raised at almost as little expence in Carolina as a hen is in England,' the boosters had said, and Carolina farmers were known to feed their pigs on peaches.[15]

But the imperial rivalries with Spain in the Caribbean and on the northern coast of Venezuela were steepening fast. In November 1739, on pain of being cashiered if he did not comply, George Lucas, promoted Lieutenant-Colonel, returned to take command of his regiment in Antigua, and prepared to fight Spain in the War of Jenkins's Ear. At Wappoo he left Eliza in charge of her withdrawn and sickly mother, her sister Polly, her ill and depressed cousin Fanny Fayweather and twenty-odd slaves. George also put the two other plantations which he had acquired in his daughter's hands: 1,500 acres at Garden Hill, sixty miles away to the south-west on the Combahee River, and 1,650 acres in Craven County on the Waccamaw, the same distance to the north-west, both of them to be reached by sea. Both had their own resident overseers, but they were to report to her. When he left for the Caribbean, she was sixteen, six weeks short of her seventeenth birthday.

From the letters she immediately began to write and transcribe, she was clearly magnificently fearless. 'The part of the world I now inhabit,' as she wrote to her brother in England, was another version of the long-held dream – and the opposite of all the constraint and intensity of the Caribbean. South Carolina was a large country, wide in extent, with big navigable rivers and inexhaustible stands of timber. Fertility was in its soils and 'there is very few European or American fruits or grain but what grow here'. It looked like an edible paradise:

> The Country abounds with wild fowl. Venison and fish, Beef, veal and mutton, are here in much greater perfection than in the Islands, tho' not equal to that in England – but their pork exceeds any I ever tasted anywhere. The Turkeys extreamly fine, especially the wild, and indeed all their poultry is exceeding good, and peaches, Nectrins, and mellons of all sorts extreamly fine and in profusion, and their Oranges exceed any I ever tasted in the West Indies or from Spain or Portugal.[16]

If the frontier was no more than a day's ride away to the west, and the threat of Indian wars never far absent, if the four months of summer were 'extreamly disagreeable, excessive hott, much thunder and lightening and muskatoes and sand flies in abundance',[17] none of this diminished the overwhelming sense of arrival which coloured the teenage Eliza Lucas's world. The Atlantic-bordering low country of South Carolina in the 1730s was the place in which the gentry was liberated into the world it had always desired. The original constitution for the colony, drawn up in part by John Locke, had envisaged a dominating, hugely rich and vastly propertied aristocracy. 'We ayme not att the profit of merchants', the Lords Proprietors of Carolina had said in 1674, but 'the incouragement of landlords.'[18] Antony Ashley-Cooper, the colony's great promoter, after whom the two rivers of Charles Town were named, like to call it 'my darling'.[19] That attitude was not going to last in the new century and by 1720, the small-time Carolina planter-gentry were in charge of their own destinies, dominating the House of Assembly and experimenting with new crops for the Atlantic trade.

Wappoo was a pretty and gentle place, mild and sheltered, with huge oaks and bays, and woods filled with magnolias and in the springtime 'the scent of the young mirtle and the yellow Jesamin with wch the woods abound.'[20] From the very first day that her father left her there, Eliza was both at home and in command. The letters she immediately began to dispatch across this Atlantic world brim with an amazing authority:

> Wrote to my father on business of various sorts desiring he will not insist on puting my sister to school. I will undertake to teach her French. Also gave him an account of my poor Cousen Fanny Fayweather's melancholy.[21]

In part, this was because she was not alone. Her father had left her in the lap of a deeply effective and protective gentry network, which maintained a manner of life which would not have been out of place in southern England. Little three-cornered invitations have survived in the Lucas-Pinckney archive: 'Governor Lyttelton will wait on the ladies at Belmont'; 'Mrs. Drayton begs the pleasure of your company to spend a few days'; 'Lord and Lady Charles Montagu's Compts to Mrs and Miss Pinckney, and if it is agreable to them shall be glad of their Company at the Lodge'[22] – no sense here that the Atlantic had done anything to alter, let alone destroy, the ligatures of sociability on which the gentry had always relied.

The teenage Eliza was immediately running a big and productive enterprise. At Wappoo she relied on the slave Mulatto Quash as her factor and mainstay but there is no question she was closely involved in the practicalities herself. 'I have the business of 3 plantations to transact', she wrote to her old friend Mrs Boddicott in London,

> wch requires much writing and more business and fatigue of other sorts than you can imagine, but least you should imagine it too burthensom to a girl at my early time of life, give mee leave to assure you I think myself happy that I can be useful to so good a father. By rising very early I find I can go through with much business.[23]

She usually got up at five in the morning, read until seven, walked through the plantation, saw that the 'Servants', as she called them, were at their work, and then had breakfast. The first hour after breakfast was spent at her harpsichord, the following 'in recolecting something I have learned, least for want of practise it should be quite lost, such as french and short hand'. The rest of the morning was spent teaching her younger sister 'and two black girls who I teach to read, and if I have my papas approbation (my mamas I have got) I intend for school mistress's for the rest of the Negroe children'. More music in the afternoon, and then needlework until the candles were lit. 'Thursday the whole day except what the necessary affairs of the family take up, is spent in writing, either on the business of the plantations or on letters to my friends ... I hate to undertake anything and not go thro' with it.'[24]

Her energy and commitment to self-improvement were relentless: she planted a fig orchard 'with design to dry them, and export them', as well as an oak grove for timber staves, established a nursery of tender plants for export to English greenhouses, grew rice for the English market, beef for the Caribbean, supervised the collection and storage of pitch and tar from the Garden Hill plantation, experimented with cotton, maize, ginger, indigo, cucumbers, peach trees and potatoes.[25]

This was the new version of an old story. English gentry families had always used their landscapes to demonstrate who they were. Order, antiquity, rootedness, coherence, their own prominent place within their surroundings: this was the governing image of the class. But Eliza Pinckney's version of this ancient marking of the territory had taken on a specific Enlightenment colouring. Her approach to her father's lands was, above all, inventive. Improvement had long been part of the gentry enterprise but with Eliza Lucas improvement of the land and improvement of herself became two parts of a single enterprise.

Education – the Lockean idea that education and experience made a person what they were – dominated her consciousness. In his famous *Essay Concerning Human Understanding*, published in 1690, Locke had maintained that the human understanding at the beginning of life was like 'white Paper, void of all Characters'.[26] Any aspect of your identity only came from later experience, from what life did to you, and the way in which your mind then processed and combined those experiences. This was a revolutionary idea, the first erosion of the ancient principle of heritability, the idea that what you were was largely a product of what your parents had been. After Locke, there was nothing essential in a person, nothing unchangeable. You were what you became. In this way, every mind and every person was an America. There was nothing metaphysical about it; the only duty for every thinking being was to make themselves good. Locke saw the true philosopher as a simple gardener, 'an Under-Labourer ... clearing Ground a little, and removing some of the Rubbish, that lies in the way to Knowledge'.[27] The soil of America and the receptive folds of the young mind were the same thing. Inheritance and material things were not enough; bringing to fruition the potential in the soil was the definition of a useful life. That is what cultivation meant and that was the goal to which she dedicated her life.

In many ways Eliza, under her father's encouragement and love, was a self-made person. Her letters are full of extraordinary moments of self-recognition in which she understands her own place in this cultural framework. Looking into the pages of Virgil, lent to her by Mr Pinckney from Charles Town, she suddenly found herself confronting the cultural origins of what she had imagined until then were her own ideas:

> I have got no further than the first vol of Virgil, but was most agreably disapointed to find myself instructed in agriculture as well as entertained by his charming penn, for I am persuaded 'tho he wrote for Italy it will in many Instances suit Carolina. I had never perused those books before, and imagined I should immediately enter upon battles, storms and tempests, that put mee in a maze, and make mee shudder while I read. But the calm and pleasing diction of pastoral and gardening agreably presented themselves not unsuitably to this charming season of the year, with wch I am so much delighted that had I butt the fine soft Language of our Poet to paint it properly, I should give you but little respite 'till you came into the country, and attended to the beauties of pure Nature unassisted by Art.[28]

With however much irony this was expressed, the English-Antiguan-Carolinan teenage girl suddenly recognized herself as a classically inspired English squire, if one who presided over an elegant American landscape maintained by African slaves.

It is, overall, a beautiful and charming picture but the fact of slavery in the centre of it cannot be glossed over. That fact confronts, in a particularly polarized way, one of the central questions about the gentry: was this deeply attractive kind of civilization, which nurtured and developed many virtues and graces, reliant, in the end, on the exploitation of people weaker and poorer than the few beneficiaries on whom this book has dwelt?

It can certainly look that way. If invited to dinner in Charles Town, Eliza and her mother, as her great-granddaughter Harriott Horry Ravenel described in the 1890s, wore their 'brocade, taffety [and] lutestring dresses' tightly stayed.

> Their slippers, to match their dresses, had heels even higher and more unnatural than our own. Their cloaks, expansive to cover their enormous hoops, were much like the Mother Hubbard cloaks worn a few years since. They were made of silk, satin, or cloth, lined and quilted, very full and set into small yokes.[29]

In these voluminous and brilliant clothes, they set out from Wappoo for Charles Town in a

> low boat, probably a long canoe, hollowed out of a mighty cypress thirty or forty feet long, with sitting room for half a dozen in bow and stern, and rowed by six or eight negroes, all singing in faultless time and cadence as they swung their paddles.[30]

These singing, paddling Africans were her father's slaves. The eighteenth-century gentry always accepted slavery as a normal part of life. In Eliza's letters that level of acceptance deepened into a kind of domesticity indistinguishable from English gentry attitudes to the servants and employees on an English farm. 'June comes for thread, for the negroes are in want of their Cloaths', Mr Murray, Eliza's manager on the Waccamaw plantation, wrote to her:

> Please send a Cooper's broad ax for Sogo. it must be turned for the left hand, Smith Dick knows how to doe it, and a Cross Iron. Pompey has been very bad Twise with the Plurisy & I could not get the new barn finished being obleeged to take Sogo to make barrells.[31]

Sogo was the plantation cooper, Dick and Pompey blacksmith and carpenter, June the captain of the boat, all slaves.

Much later Eliza described to her daughter the domestic economy of her household, and the intimate connections she had with her slaves.

> Mary-Ann understands roasting poultry in the greatest perfection you ever saw, and old Ebba the fattening them to as great a nicety. Daphne makes me a loaf of very nice bread. You know I am no epicure, but I am pleased they can do things so well, when they are put to it, and as to the eating part I don't think I shall miss Onia at all. I shall keep young Ebba to do the drudgery part, fetch wood, and water, and scour, and learn as much as she is capable of Cooking and Washing. Mary-Ann Cooks, makes my bed, and makes my punch, Daphne works and makes the bread, old Ebba boils the cow's victuals, raises and fattens the poultry, Moses is imployed from breakfast until 12 o'clock without doors, after that in the house, Pegg washes and milks.
>
> Thus I have formed my household, nobody eats the bread of idleness when I am here, nor are any overworked. Mary-Ann has pickled me some oysters very good, so I have sent you a little pott by the boat. Moses gets them at low water without a boat.[32]

Why was there no difficulty in accommodating slavery to a gentry frame of mind? Partly because the class-income-status gap between gentry and their servants was so extreme anyway. If, as was clear from John Oglander's accounts, a member of a gentry family could expect to live on an income at least sixty times the average income of the people who were working for him (see page 111), they were living in different conceptual universes. A man paid next to nothing, with no resources to fall back on, was only in a conceptual sense a free man. In reality, he had little room for manoeuvre. Besides, the system of indentured servants, by which white people travelled to the Americas as bound employees throughout the seventeenth and eighteenth centuries, was a form of temporary and inefficient slavery – white people working hard in tropical heat tended to die too easily – but the gap between servants who were paid next to nothing and slavery was not difficult to cross.

If slavery was psychologically near to hand, it was also economically efficient. The cost of a slave for life was no more than eighteen months' wages for a free man.[33] It was prudent and rational to buy slaves as a necessary part of the household economy. Slaves, like cheap petrol, made possible the expensive civilization, with its imported accoutrements, which the planter-gentry required.

It must also, in part, have been legitimated by the eighteenth-century's classical ideals. 'The calm and pleasing diction of pastoral and gardening', which Eliza found in the *Georgics*, had also relied for its elegance on slave labour. This is surely one reason that slaves were so often given Roman names – even if the repeated occurrence of 'Philander' as a name is clearly a dirty joke about black men's sexuality. When Eliza's son-in-law died, an inventory and valuation was made of his possessions. Among them were:

Dorinda £20 Caesar £90 Caeser £80 Caesar £40 Caesar £20 Hector £40 Trajan £70 Roxana (no value given) Percilla £100 Cupid £40 Philander £150 Philander £100 Philander £40 Pompy £70 Corydon £5 Cupid £5 Daphne £90 Roxana £5 Pompy £90 Carolus £30 Hanibal £35 Othello £50 Tamerlane £25 Cato £90 Pliny £60 Amorintha £70 Hercules £50 Jupiter £25 Paris £30 Chloe £40[34]

All this was part of the Virgilian vision. Slaves were an unremarkable, rational and elegant part of the gentry world. They were an apparently natural feature of the landscape of contentment. Mysterious as this now is, they must have seemed essential to the goodness these people were cultivating.

When Colonel Lucas left his teenage daughter in charge of his American possessions, he cannot have been entirely at ease. From Antigua, clearly worried that he had left this girl unprotected in the wilds of America, he had proposed to her two possible, rich but anti-quated husbands. Initially buried in the extreme formality with which she usually wrote to her father, her reply finally emerged into the full light of day:

> As you propose Mr L. to me I am sorry I can't have Sentiments favour-able enough to him to take time to think on the Subject, as your Indul-gence to me will ever add weight to the duty that obliges me to consult what best pleases you, for so much Generosity on your part claims all my Obedience, but as I know 'tis my Happiness you consult, [I] must beg the favour of you to pay my thanks to the old Gentleman for his Generosity and favourable sentiments of me and let him know my thoughts on the affair in such civil terms as you know much better than any I can dictate; and beg leave to say to you that the riches of Peru and Chili if he had them put together could not purchase a suffi-cient Esteem for him to make him my husband.[35]

The other candidate did no better. Eliza asked her father to put 'aside the thoughts of my marrying yet these 2 or 3 years at least' and assured him that she knew he would never make her 'a Sacrifice to Wealth'. Although earlier fathers had often consulted their daughters over their prospective husbands and given them the power of veto over a choice, and some sons had gone ahead with marrying girls their parents knew nothing of, the teasing, friendly jokiness of Eliza in this letter to her father, on what was conventionally the most important decision in a girl's life, is nothing short of revolutionary. Liberty, self-sufficiency and self-determination were all running in her veins.

She maintained this busy pitch of life, taking her mother to dinners and parties in Charles Town, looking after her sister and pursuing in particular the cultivation of indigo, the valued blue vegetable dye, whose trade was dominated by the French. Her correspondence with her father on the subject was as constant as the war would allow. He, now the deputy Governor of Antigua, had been involved in two futile raids on the Venezuelan shore, but, when he could, he sent her advice and even experts in the cultivation of the plants and the complex processing of the seeds; she sent him news of her experiments and those of her neighbours to whom she distributed the seeds.

> We please ourselves with the prospect of exporting in a few years a good quantity from hence, and supplying our Mother Country with a manifacture for wch she has so great a demand, and which she is now supplyd with from the French Collonys, and many thousand pounds per annum thereby lost to the nation, when she might as well be supplyd here, if the matter was applyd to in earnest.[36]

The cultivation did not go easily from the start and her father suggested that the brick vats in which they were steeping the indigo plants might have been the cause of trouble; timber might have been better. Frost ruined entire crops; the germination rates of the seed sent from the Caribbean were often poor. The man sent by Colonel Lucas from Montserrat in the Caribbean was failing, either deliberately or not, to produce a rich and deep enough colour in the cakes of dye. Another was sent. There was a valuable prize at stake, as the British had been buying £200,000 worth of indigo from the French islands every year. In 1744 the seed was largely saved and as an act of communal and neighbourly solidarity distributed free by Eliza to her gentry neighbours, 'in small quantities to a great number of people'.[37] Nothing about this enterprise, her engagement with experimental agriculture, with the Atlantic markets or with trade itself, seemed in any way contradictory to the gentry culture she was embracing with such fervour at the same time. One was a means of delivering and sustaining the other. The Horatian tension between *otium* and *negotium*, ease and business, elegance and struggle, had been swept away.

By 1747, 135,000 pounds of indigo dye cakes were made in South Carolina and exported to England for sale. Within the decade production had reached a million pounds of finished indigo a year. The British government immediately offered a premium of sixpence a pound on the dye, a protectionist measure which excluded French indigo from British markets. Eliza had added another commodity to the rice which South Carolina had been exporting to Britain for decades and South Carolina entered a long mid-century war-economy boom, during which the planters were doubling their capital every three or four years, all part of 'the transformation of a semi-tropical swamp into the most profitable colony in mainland America'.[38]

Ever since the Lucases' arrival in South Carolina, the gentry neighbours had attended to the fatherless family's wellbeing, none more carefully than the cultivated planter-lawyer Charles Pinckney. He had been born in Carolina but had been educated and trained in the law in London. He lent Eliza his books, to supplement the library her father had left for her, and introduced her to the string of elegant Virgilian plantations distributed around the Ashley and Cooper rivers that met at Charles Town. In early 1744, Charles Pinckney's wife, who had been ill for months, sickened and died. It was later said in the Pinckney family that the first Mrs Pinckney was so attached to Eliza that 'she had more than once declared, that rather than have her lost to Carolina, she would herself "be willing to step down and let her take her place"'.[39]

Pinckney followed his dead wife's suggestion to the letter. Within a month or two of the first Mrs Pinckney's death, Eliza became the second. Her dowry was paltry and she wrote to her father to thank and forgive him:

I have had too many instances of your paternal affection and tenderness to doubt your doing all in your power to make me happy, and I beg leave here to acknowledge particularly my obligation to you for the pains and money you laid out in my Education, which I esteem a more valuable fortune than any you could now have given me.[40]

This was more than filial courtesy. Eliza Lucas Pinckney's understanding of herself was not as an heiress but as an educated and self-educating operator in the real world. Allied now to the Pinckneys, she was established as a 'person of Character and Distinction'.

This is how her life continued. Solid silver sauce boats and candlesticks were ordered from London workshops, emblazoned with the impaled arms of Pinckney and Lucas. Eliza experimented with the cultivation of silkworms and planted the mulberry trees whose descendants still grow wild in the lands bordering the ancient Carolina plantations. The Pinckneys built themselves a large, beautiful columned house on the shorefront in Charles Town itself, looking across the waters of the harbour where it reached out towards the Atlantic. It was made of small, dark, English bricks, with stone copings, and a tall slate roof. A wide flagged hall stretched from front to back of the house, and two drawing rooms on the first floor, with high coved ceilings and heavy cornices, looked over the water.

> The whole house was wainscoted in the heaviest panelling, the windows and doors with deep projecting pediments and mouldings …
> The mantel-pieces were very high and narrow, with fronts carved in processions of shepherds and shepherdesses, cupids, etc., and had square frames in the panelling above, to be filled with pictures.[41]

In a life with no hint of provincialism, Eliza and Charles administered the Pinckney properties that were scattered along the rivers leading in towards the South Carolina hinterland. Charles became rich, children emerged, beautiful and adored, with 'fine black Eyes'[42] and parties were held. The Pinckneys rode a happy boom and Eliza loved and revered her husband: 'I can indeed tell you I have the greatest esteem and affection imaginable for you; that next to Him that form'd it, my heart is intirely at your disposal, but this you knew the day I gave you my hand.'[43]

The presence of this contented rich family and the new and intimate father figure in her life meant that when it was announced in *The Gentleman's Magazine* for 11 January 1747 that '*Geo. Lucas*, Lieut.

Col. of *Dalzel's Reg.* and Lieut. Governor of *Antigua*' had not only been 'taken in an *Antigua* ship' and was now a prisoner at the great French naval port of Brest, but had then died in captivity, Eliza's life – she was now twenty-four – did not capsize.[44] For a culture which put such vivid emphasis on the beauty and importance of human affections, the demands of the Atlantic world were particularly harsh. Not only was the separation by distance very long – ten weeks to Carolina from England, three weeks from Carolina to Antigua – but there was also the threat of illness and death; and other hazards of war.

In 1753, Charles was appointed interim Chief Justice of South Carolina, but within a couple of months, against all expectations, the appointment was not confirmed, and he was replaced by a venal English politician, who was being conveniently shuffled off to the colonies so that he would be absent from Westminster. The disappointment for the Pinckneys was enormous and early that summer they decided to sail for England – Pinckney did not want to be in Charles Town as his replacement arrived. England would be where they would educate their sons and set themselves up as English gentry.

Soon after arriving, they moved into a rented house in Richmond-upon-Thames – not poky: they had two spare beds for visitors[45] – just down the road from Henry Lascelles. The Pinckneys did not operate on anything like the scale which Lascelles had engineered for himself but they were, as one of their new Richmond neighbours said, 'persons of Character and Distinction in the Country from whence they came'.[46] They had their two sons with them, Charles and Thomas, both in London to be educated, and their daughter Harriott, still only seven. She had brought with her some beautiful American birds: an Indigo Bunting in the mineral, lapis blue of his summer plumage; a red-breasted and blue-headed Painted Bunting, or the Bruant Nonpareil; and an American Goldfinch, whose flickering, dancing *su-weet, su-weet* filled the air like a canary's. The presence and song of these exotic birds sets this family apart from anything you might have found in the Lascelles house. Here was the eighteenth-century gentry domesticated, civilized, familial, cultivated, in love with nature and at ease with themselves.

On Eliza's arrival in Richmond, chat poured from her pen. 'We visit 10 or a dozen agreeable familys', she told a Charleston matron[47] and recounted at length the 700-mile tour they were to take around the south of England. All was fine except that the English played cards too much. The Americans were already working harder. There were plans for a tour of the north. Charles was being difficult and 'has many [y]earnings after his native land'[48] but Eliza had her mind on something else. She was set on paying a visit to the Princess of Wales, who lived a mile away from their Richmond house in Kew. Eliza's long, discursive letter about this meeting describes an emblematic eighteenth-century gentry moment, an encounter with inherited authority between people who – in some ways – had ceased to believe in it.

That year, Augusta, 'The Princess Dowager of Wales', as she was known, was in her early thirties, only three years older than Eliza.[49] She had begun life as an obscure princess in the principality of Saxe-Gotha, deep in the agricultural heart of Germany, and had arrived in England in 1736, aged sixteen, homesick for her governess and unable to speak a word of English, destined for the hand of the difficult, sophisticated and argumentative Frederick, Prince of Wales. But Augusta was a subtle and instinctive politician and was soon loved in England for her air of innocence and simplicity, which she cultivated carefully as the foundations of influence on court and English life. The Waleses had many children and she had herself painted with them clustered around her, a model of refined, domestic sensibility, wearing only simple English fabrics, unlike the court of George II, her father-in-law, which was stiff with mistresses in lace and French silks. Augusta became the patron and promoter of the new botanical garden at Kew and a paradoxical heroine for those who loathed the King. When the Prince of Wales died suddenly in 1751, Augusta acquired the unique and powerful role of Mother to the Future King, George III, and became for a while (her reputation would sink later) the guar-antor of national virtue, a mother-governor of the nation, living with her large young family in their elegant and simple William Kent villa at Kew. This was the woman Eliza Pinckney wanted to meet.

Her interest was not, in the light of this history, mere royalty gawping. The two women were of a generation. Both of them put a high and public priority on the needs of their children, both combined family management with a commitment to British commercial enterprise, both were deeply interested in experimental botany, and both as young women had engaged with an alarmingly powerful masculine world and triumphed within it. It is perfectly possible to suggest that Eliza Pinckney was visiting her hero.

The Americans had some contacts in England but, as Eliza wrote to a friend in Charles Town, actually getting in to see the Princess

> was attended with great difficulty as the attendance about the Princess are extreamly causious who they admit to her presence. We mentioned our desire to see the Royal family and to have our little girl present the birds to a gentleman here [Richmond] who we know to be well acquainted with some about the Princess, he very readily undertook it, and next day went to Kew where the Princess of Wales and all her family reside during the Summer Season; they gave the Princess a Prodigious Character, and said they would mention it to her Royal Highness; but let him know at the same time how great a favour they did him, by saying it was a thing very rarely permitted, especially to those they were not acquainted with.[50]

This is Eliza's manner: proper but direct, her gossiping energies constrained by a corset of dignified, classical language. From her tone there is no doubting the scepticism she felt about these flunkies, puffed up as usual, and it might be tempting to see that impatience as American; but it is indistinguishable, for example, from John Oglander's 1630s distaste for the degenerate courtiers around Charles I. The gentry tradition had never been obsequious. But the Pinckneys were given an appointment, 'at Eleven o'clock any day the next week'. They duly turned up, if a little late, and we found the Princess gone a airing with the Princess Augusta [her eldest daughter, then sixteen], and it was uncertain when she would return. We carried the birds in the Coach with us, and wrote a card to give the child in her hand, in case we should not go in with her. The card was this.

Miss Harriott Pinckney, daughter of Charles Pinckney Esqr, one of His Majesty's Council of South Carolina, pays her duty to her Highness and humbly begs leave to present her with an Indigo bird, a Nonpareil, and a yellow bird, wch she has brought from Carolina for her Highness.[51]

They left the birds, with the card, and went home, 'lamenting as we went the uneasy situation of those who had favours to ask or are dependance on a Court!'[52]

That night they had a message that the birds had done their work and the Princess 'would be glad to see Miss Pinckney at one o'clock the next day'. It was another mark of the nature of this hybrid eighteenth-century civilization: the formal invitation was issued to the seven-year-old Harriott. They went to Kew the following day 'in full dress' and, after a delay talking to an old German lady, were taken through a suite of grand, public rooms until they arrived at the Princess's dressing room, where the Princess

came forward and received us at the door herself, with Princess Augusta, Princess Elizabeth, Prince William, and Prince Henry. She mett us with all the chearfulness and pleasure of a friend who was extreamly glad to see us; she gave us no time to consider how to introduce ourselves or to be at a loss what to say, for she with an air of benignity told us as soon as we entered she was very glad to see us, took Harriott by the hand and kissed her, asked her how she liked England, to wch she answered, not so well as Carolina, at wch the Princess laughd a good deal, and said it was very natural for such a little woman as she to love her own Country best. She thanked her for the birds, and said she was afraid one of them might be a favourite of hers; spoke very kindly sometimes to Mr Pinckney, sometimes to me, and then to the Child.[53]

The attendants and courtiers withdrew and the Princess went through the conventionalities, all of them standing talking in the room, which was decorated with 'a great deal of China upon two Cabinets' and presumably with the bright American birds singing in their cages.

But Harriott was a little overwrought and her distress broke through the crust. The Princess suggested that she should sit down in a chair, which alarmed Eliza's sense of propriety:

> I told her I could not suffer her to sit in her presence. Puh-Puh, says the Princess, she knows nothing of all that; and sat her down and told her she had no pretty things here for her, but when she went to London she would get something that was pretty and send to her.[54]

Puh-Puh: the culture of sensibility addresses the rigidities of the past. The younger Wales children then went to have dinner and the Pinckneys were left with the princess and her eldest daughter for more intimate conversation.

> She asked me many little domestick questions as did Princess Augusta among wch if I suckled my children. I told her I had attempted it but my constitution would not bear it. She said she did not know but 'twas as well let alone, as the anxiety a mother was often in, on a child's acct, might do hurt. I told her we had Nurses *in* our houses, that it appeard very strange to me to hear of people putting their children out to nurse, we had no such practises in Carolina, at which she seemed vastly pleased; she thought it was a very good thing, the other was unnatural. Princess Augusta was surprized at the suckling blacks; the Princess stroakd Harriott's cheek, said it made no alteration in the complexion and paid her the compliment of being very fair and pretty.[55]

Their talk ranged beyond the domestic, to political affairs in Carolina, the relationship of the colonists with the Indians and the French, earthquakes and hurricanes (waters the year before had surged four feet deep into the Pinckneys' Charles Town house), the growing of silk there (in which Eliza was experimenting) and how far South Carolina 'extended back' – away from the Atlantic coast into the great unknown interior of America. This chat, the world of Puh-Puh, breastfeeding, the psychological benefits of calm in motherhood: Eliza was undeniably modern.

After a couple of years, their time in England turned from delight and pleasure in their country house at Ripley in Surrey, their visiting of neighbours, their hobnobbing with the minor aristocracy, 'to gloomy anxiety'.[56] Once the Seven Years War against the French had started in 1756, the Pinckneys received 'continual alarms from abroad' and they decided to sever all connections with America. But to do so they had to go back there. 'Mr. Pinckney came to a resolution to return to Carolina for two years, and wait an opportunity to dispose of the greatest part of what he has there, and fix it in a more secure tho' less improvable part of the world'.[57]

The instinct in mid-eighteenth-century Americans, when conditions looked bad, was to cut and run for 'Home', 'the Mother Country'. In 1758, with deep reluctance at leaving their sons behind at school in England, Charles and Eliza decided to sail back to Carolina, preparing to wind up their operations there.

> How uncertain are human dependancies! four years ago we left a fine and flourishing Collony in profound peace; a Collony so valuable to this nation that it would have been lookd upon as absurd to have the least doubt of its being protected and taken care of in case of a Warr, tho' a Warr then seemed a very distant contingency, and indeed I lookd upon an Estate there as secure as in England, and upon some acct more Valuable, especially to those who have a young family; but how much reason we have had to change our sentiments since the beginning of this Warr, is too plain to every one ever so little acquainted with American Affairs.[58]

It was another turn in the long gentry dance of uncertainty and establishment.

They let their house in Surrey 'with the furniture standing till our return',[59] and in March 1758 sailed for America on a ship of the Royal Navy. But now the central catastrophe of Eliza's life occurred: three weeks after landing in South Carolina, Charles Pinckney, who had been to her 'that dear, that worthy, that valuable man, whose life was one continued course of active Virtue',[60] sickened of malaria, which he had caught when touring his plantations, and died.

For many years her spirit was broken. Her letters, which had been so bright and funny when she had been happy, now became long, sad and serious, for year after year turning back to the loss she had suffered, instructing her sons in England (they were going to Westminster School) on how to follow their dead father's example. Her life stiffened, no longer an adventure, more a case of keeping going, holding a candle to the ideal of virtue which the memory of Charles Pinckney represented for her. To think of him, she wrote,

> pleases while it pains, and may be called the Luxury of grief. O! Had Heaven added but one blessing more and spared him to see his dear children brought up and let us have gone to the grave hand in hand together, what a heaven had I enjoyed upon Earth![61]

She continued to send pet turtles, 'Non-parriels' and American Summer Ducks to her friends in England. She couldn't find any wild Turkeys for them and got hold of some Turkey chicks, which she raised herself, but behind all that, as she wrote in May 1759, she was 'wholly taken up with my own moloncholy concerns'.[62] She longed to go back to England to see her sons, but as she explained to a correspondent in February 1761, she was caught in a desperate bind:

> You obligingly enquire when we return to England. I wish I could with any certainty fix a time for, though all countrys are now to me alike nor would I take the pains to cross again the Ocean for the best fortune in England. I have such inducements for coming that when I can

prudently leave this Country and have fixt a sume in England to soport my self and the children in a retired, comfortable, and decent way – not in a ostentatious or vain one, for I have no ambitious views of any sort – nither fatigue, or suffering any thing in my own person, shall detain me longer from them for my heart bleeds at our separation. 'Tis no paradox to say nothing but the greatness of my affection keeps me from them, as it appears to me and my friends here that it will (with Divine blessing) be much to their advantage for me to continue here a couple of year longer; and when the question is whether I shall please my self or do them real service I should be inexcuseable to hesitate a moment.[63]

This extraordinary paragraph not only dramatizes the emotional reality of the eighteenth-century Atlantic family; it is the testament of a mother whose life was entirely and consciously given to the service of her children, an attendance to her posterity which is unequalled in these stories. It is the heroism of love, but love that was founded on entirely real and material concerns. The development of an American estate in the boom conditions of the mid-eighteenth century was the greatest act of love she could perform for her distant children. And the combined Pinckney–Lucas estate was both huge and scattered, spread across the full range of river basins, coastlands and coastal islands on the Atlantic side of South Carolina.

Eliza threw herself into work. So much

care, attention and activity [is needed] to attend properly to a Carolina Estate … to do ones duty and make it turn to account, that I find I have as much business as I can go through of one sort or other. Perhaps 'tis better for me, and I believe it is. Had there not been a necessity for it, I might have sunk to the grave by this time … A variety of imployment gives my thoughts a relief from melloncholy subjects.[64]

Not a drip of self-pity in that; but clarity and seriousness regarding the sombre and important truths about herself.

She was growing pomegranates and overseeing the inoculation of her slaves against smallpox, supervising the small hospital in which they were confined when ill, opening a magnolia nursery, from which two- and three-year-old seedlings would be shipped to England, denying the gossip that she was to be married again, arranging for her husband's clothes to be altered for her sons, making enquiries over the suitability of Westminster School, feeling exhausted and falling ill for seven months in 1762, gently toying with the 'Romantick' idea that she might live in Geneva after the boys had finished at Oxford.

With all this, her roots were slowly penetrating the South Carolina earth. At Belmont, the Pinckney plantation five miles from Charles Town, she re-created the garden:

> I am myself head gardener and I believe work much harder than most principal ones. We found it in ruins when we arrived from England, so that we have had a wood to clear, and indeed it was laid out in the old taste, so that I have been modernizing it wch has afforded me much imployment.[65]

She began to treasure the ancient trees, looking 'upon an old oak with the reverencial Esteem of a Druid' and raging against their destroyers 'as sacriligious Enemies to posterity'.[66]

When Eliza's youngest child Harriott was nineteen, she married a rich South Carolina planter, Daniel Horry, whose plantation at Hampton about forty miles from Charles Town sat among the slave-worked rice fields on which his fortune rested. The elder son, Charles Pinckney, came back to South Carolina in 1769, a qualified lawyer, radicalized against the British government by the Stamp Act of 1765, which had required all American public documents to carry an embossed stamp which could only be produced – and paid for – in London. Deeply ingrained English gentry instincts against arbitrary and unrepresentative acts of government fuelled the rage. Charles immediately became a member of the South Carolina Commons House of Assembly and on into the 1770s moved swiftly towards American independence. Five years after Charles, his brother Tom returned from England. Both fought in the war against the British, both became generals, both were captured, both were released in prisoner exchanges and both were seriously wounded.

A passionate American patriotism, a sense that honour and America were one substance, was now running in their veins. 'I entered into this cause after reflection and through principle', Charles Pinckney wrote during his captivity. 'My heart is altogether American, and neither severity, nor favour, nor poverty, nor affluence can ever induce me to swerve from it.'[67]

To his friend and brother-in-law Edward Rutledge, he was even more unequivocal: 'If I had a vein that did not beat with love for my country, I myself would open it. If I had a drop of blood that could flow dishonourably, I myself would let it out.'[68]

The war in South Carolina was bitter and vicious, the British armies laying waste the whole country, plundering and burning plantation houses including the Pinckney plantations at Ashepoo and Belmont. Tom reported the depredations to his mother on 17 May 1779. The British

> took with them nineteen Negroes, among whom were Betty, Prince, Chance, and all the hardy Boys – They left the sick women, and the young children, and about five fellows who are now perfectly free and live on the best produce of the plantation. They took with them all the best Horses they could find, burnt the dwelling House and books, destroyed all the furniture, china, etc, killed the sheep and poultry and drank the liquors.[69]

'Independence is all I want', Eliza wrote consolingly. It is an intriguing use of the word – financial independence for themselves, but also political independence for their country. As she went on, 'a little will make us that. Don't grieve for me my child as I asure you I do not for myself. While I have such children dare I think my lot hard? God forbid!'[70]

South Carolina was tyrannized by the British Legion troops led by Lieutenant-Colonel Banastre Tarleton, a daring and cynical cavalry commander, son of a sugar- and slave-trading mayor of Liverpool, who soon after the outrages became the subject of one of Joshua Reynolds's most glamourizing images of the romantic warrior.

Eliza spent much of the war at her daughter Harriott's Hampton plantation, about fifty miles north-east of Charleston on a creek of the Santee River.

Remote and protected, Hampton looked like a refuge from the troubles of the war. But one night Harriott was alone in the house, with her children, asleep upstairs, when she heard horse hoofs outside, 'and then a man's voice begging admission at the door'.[71] It was Francis Marion, an unprincipled slave-owning Indian-hunter, now guerrilla leader of the resistance to Tarleton's occupation of South Carolina. He was on his own and needed food. He asked for supper and while it was cooking, fell asleep in a chair. But as he slept, the British arrived outside. Harriott woke Marion, showed him the back door, 'pointed down the long garden walk to the creek at its foot, and told him to swim to the island opposite, and lie there in the rushes until the English left'.[72]

'He was off like a wild duck', swam the stream and lay hidden in the reeds until morning, when he made his way up the river to rejoin his men. Delaying while she could, Harriott opened the front door to see Tarleton in front of her. His troopers searched the house and found nothing. Tarleton sat down to eat the supper that had been cooked for Marion, requiring Harriott to sit there with him and to be his hostess. When he left, he took with him 'a fine volume of Milton, of a beautiful Baskerville edition, bound in crimson and gold'.[73] The second volume, and the chair in which Marion slept, are still in the house. There was no shortage of courage in this world.

Hampton was subject to another night-time visitation the following year. Eliza herself was there this time, along with Daniel Horry and Tom Pinckney and others. They were all asleep when suddenly the entire household was woken by screams. As Eliza's great-granddaughter, Harriott Horry Ravenel, described it, a beautiful girl rushed into Eliza's bedroom, shouting,

'Oh, Mrs. Pinckney, save me, save me! The British are coming after me.' The old lady [she was fifty-nine] stepped from the bed (one can fancy her majestic in bed-gown and kerchief!), and, pushing the girl under her own bed-clothes, said, 'Lie there and no man will dare to trouble you,' and such was the power of her presence … that those ruffians shrank abashed before her and offered no further insult.[74]

The war ended in American victory in 1782 and Eliza luxuriated in the pride she felt at the dignity of her sons:

when I contemplate with what philosophick firmness and calmness they both of them supported pain sickness, and evils of various sorts, and withstood the utmost efforts of the enemies malice, and see with what greatness of mind they now generously conduct themselves to all; my heart overflows with gratitude to their great preserver, for continuing to me such children!

When I take a retrospective view of our past sufferings, so recent too, and compare them with our present prospects, the change is so great and sudden! it appears like a dream, and I can hardly believe the pleasing reallity, that peace with all its train of blessings are return'd, and that every one may find Shelter under his own Vine, and his own Fig tree, and be happy. Blessed be god the Effussion of human blood is stop'd![75]

In 1791 Washington himself came to Hampton to meet Eliza and Harriott, now a widow as her husband, Daniel Horry, had died of liver failure in 1785.

Together the two ladies greeted Washington in the portico Harriott and Daniel had added to the house a few years before. They were 'arrayed in sashes and bandeaux painted with the general's portrait and mottoes of welcome' and 'after a stately reception he was led to the large ball-room, just built, where an elaborate breakfast awaited him, the gentlemen of his suite, and many of the neighbors, who had gathered to greet him'.[76]

Before leaving, Washington observed 'a handsome young oak growing rather too near the house, which Mrs. Horry proposed to cut down, as it interfered with the view. The general advised that it should be kept, as an oak was a thing no man could make.'[77] It is still there, obscuring the portico but sanctified by the great man's casual remark, with which undoubtedly Eliza would have agreed. When she died in Philadelphia of cancer in May 1793, Washington, at his own request, was one of her pall bearers, there to honour the mother of patriots.

One could end the story there, with that dignity, but maybe it is better to return to the material and actual foundations on which this self-consciously noble superstructure was built. After Daniel Horry's death in 1785 – he had turned an intense yellow as his liver failed – an inventory was made of his possessions at Hampton.[78] In the Long Room, the Blue Parlour, the Hall, Study and Dining Parlour, there were plenty of mahogany tables, some sofas and eight French armchairs, several hundred books but no pictures beyond some prints, a harpsichord and a guitar, several card tables, Turkey rugs and rolls of Wilton carpet, a cased clock, some silver, a few gilt mirrors and eight mahogany beds in the seven bedrooms, all curtained. Outside there were forty-four oxen at £4 each, as well as a dozen horses, and many stock cattle, sheep and hogs. The most valuable single thing the Horrys owned was their schooner, worth £500, their connection with the outside world.

Without fuss, attached to this list of possessions in which every piece was valued, was the inventory of 326 slaves, of which every one was valued too. As well as names of the classical figures, there were some from the Bible:

Solomon £70 Susannah £1 Isaac £100 Jacob £80 Rachel £60 Nimrod £80 Isaac £40 Daniel £100

And some named in a way that looks as if no one could be troubled to give these people any kind of human identity:

York £1 Cork £60 Glasgow £90 Belfast £100 Belfast £5 Cambridge £40 Oxford £100 Wapping £80 Lisbon £100 Tower-hill £1 Glasswindow (£20), Lazy (£20), Muddy (£80), Bounce (£70), Fork (£45), Safe (£20), and Monday (£40).

The old were practically valueless, twenty of them valued at a nominal £1 each.

The reality can be seen only in the full cumulative list, arranged like bricks, the basement for nobility:

Ned £80 Toney £80 Sally £80 Lye £40 Lizzy £40 Jule £150 Roxana, Percilla £100 Old Percilla £1 Thomas £90 Baran £100 Jemmy £50 Wambaw Philander £150 Jennet £80 Lucretia £1 Oxford £100 Muddy £80 Samuel £20 July £5 Sabina £5 Bella £30 Monday £40 Darcas £50 Wapping £80 Frank £20 Amey £30 Moll £5 Jassamin £80 Penelope £30 Sebell £80 Savey £60 Binah £25 Margery £20 Sukey £5 Pliny £60 Clement £60 Old Chloe £1 Lisbon £100 Matilda £40 Kent £70 Cato £90 Camilla £40 Mingo £90 Susanna £50 Cynthia £50 Glasgow £90 Strah £90 Sylvia £60 Lady £30 Moses £15 Paul £5 Cambridge £40 Cupid £40 Charlo £70 Nick £80 Hector £40 Trajan £70 Cudjo £15 Tom £30 Deborah £80 Pompy £70 Charles £150 Hagar £70 Corydon £5 Billy £90 Bella £70 Perry £40 Affy £20 Charles £15 Nelly £5 Andrew £1 Debo £40 Sharper £90 Lexette £80 Belfast £5 Old Guy £1 Robin £90 Grace £30 Lucy £80 Diana £50 Primus £100 Sam £60 Solomon £70 Myrah £30 Saul £70 Patty £40 January £90 Mary £70 Bob £80 Nick £30 Phillis £10 Old Bess £1 Big Sharper £20 Prince £30 Baker £80 Bounce £70 Mark £50 Affy £40 Cinda £5 Susannah £1 Sharp £70 Jonathan Bella £500 Peter Hannah £80 Big Patty £120 Juliet £50 Flora £25 Isaac £100 Old Frank £150 Sarah £20 Mathews £100 Little Frank £90 Fanny £40 Dick £25 Peggy £5 Sam £120 Rose £1 Hannah £70 Abba £5 Natt £100 Minda £50 Charlotte £80 Tenang £30 Limos £90 Katey £60 Dick £5 Old Amorintha £1 Venture £30 Caeser £80 Jacob £80 Bess £80 Safe £20 Potena £20 Minte £15 Old Statira £1 Daphne £80 Harry £100 Old Mary £1 Nimrod £80 Rosetta £40 Old Mount £1 Little Mount £80 Jacky £150 Maria £25 Seipis £40 Phebe £5 Quash £100 Sarah £70 Josey

£15 Little Phebe £5 Johnny £10 Amelia £5 Nancy £60 Thomas £90 Old Benbo £1 Miley £80 Cotto £80 Little Benbo £20 Jemmy £15 Cupid £5 Caesar £90 Johnny £120 Philander £40 Nanny £5 Betty £80 Jack £100 Morris £90 Tower-hill £1 Caroline £50 Elsey £5 Ralph £50 Cook £20 Jacky £90 Mark £50 Lyddia £25 Marianne £80 Barne £80 York £1 Isaac £40 Anthony £100 Old Dick £40 Nelly £40 Rachel £60 Eboe John £90 Juliett £50 Billy £120 Hammond £90 Jenny £90 Cuffy £40 Susey £40 Flora £30 Bevis £30 Tamerlane £25 Caesar £20 Hope £1 Closs £1 Maria £1 Peter £50 Chance £30 Little Peter £5 Musa £1 Old Chloe £1 Melia £20 Dorinda £20 Caesar £40 Capers £40 Cumberland £50 Corporal £50 Collin £50 Cork £60 Prosper £30 Paris £30 Roger £30 Sophia £20 Glasswindow £20 Calipso £1 Lazy £20 Phidella £20 Balaam £30 Sarah £20 Daniel £100 Philander £100 Saby £80 Violet £50 Archer £60 Chloe £40 Amorintha £70 Hercules £50 Babbette £30 Big Joney £25 Jupiter £25 Othello £50 Kitt £35 Ripley £30 Fork £45 Benson £50 Barber £50 Jack £40 Davy £100 Mimbo £60 Onia £80 Abba £70 Sogo £40 Celia £60 Catherina £20 Peter £15 Lin £80 Benebo £70 Metto £25 Hannah £15 Jemmy £10 Billy £80 Rose £50 Betty £5 Doll £5 Tom £80 Hanibal £35 Ossea £35 June £45 Daphne £80 Hellen £20 Cudjo £10 Big Sarah £50 Bess £10 Douglass £40 Little Sarah £50 George £10 Sansons £35 Old Bella £1 Cyrus £5 Beck £50 Carolus £30 Betty £1 Dye £70 Myrtilla £70 Mary £30 Pompy £90 Flora £80 Doll £80 Celia £50 Molly £15 Mary £10 Sue £50 Nelly £70 Roxana £5 Die £100 Daphne £90 Patty £90 Richard £40 William £40 Johnson £5 Libby £70 May £60 Sandy £25 Jenny £25 Archer £10 Cuffy £5 Hannah £1 Boat Negroes: Ormsby £100 Tom £100 Abram £100 Belfast £100 Bob £100 Will £90 Bluff Bob £40.

PART V

The Failing Vision
1790–1910

Every gentry man and woman was strung between past and future. Every new portrait joined a rank of others – the predecessors staring down, painted parenthood receding though the generations – and yet fragility hung in the gentry air. William Butler Yeats, the father of a son and daughter and the articulate voice of the class into which he was born, proudly if a little absurdly descended from the Norman Irish magnates who gave him his middle name, expressed the ancient conundrum.

> From my old fathers I must nourish dreams,
> And leave a woman and a man behind
> As vigorous of mind, and yet it seems
> Life scarce can cast a fragrance on the wind.[1]

The family stories in this book are all lingerings of that ancient scent, easily blown away by the turns of life and chance: the natural declension of the soul, too much business with the passing hour, too much play, or marriage with a fool. Those are all Yeats's phrases and any one could bring the curtain down.

The paired gentry stories here embracing the nineteenth century come from opposite ends of the spectrum. The Capels were a family that plummeted into the gentry from the disintegrating aristocracy above them; the Hugheses came bursting up into it from the realm of huge, stumbled-on industrial wealth. The Capels were victims of feck-lessness; the Hugheses drove in the opposite direction, on untold quantities of money, towards an overblown and self-important fantasy.

It was not difficult in the early years of the nineteenth century for a junior branch of an aristocratic or upper gentry family to slip down and out of the world into which it had been born. Strict settlement of estates, by which the vast bulk of a family's fortune remained in the hands of a single heir, condemned many younger brothers to an unenviable condition.

That predicament lies behind the history of the Capels. If the gentry can be defined as the class that absorbed its members from the social layers that surrounded it, this is a story of a family bursting chaotically through the upper membrane. It was not an easy landing and a sense of desperation colours the whole process. Everything the Victorians would find alien in the age that preceded them is here: luxury, a gambling attitude to life and other people, nothing earnest, an openly sexualized world.

Victorian novelists made hay with the squires who failed to move on from that Regency world into the stricter, more highly moralized environment of mid-nineteenth-century England. None was more ludicrous or disgusting than Thackeray's filthy Sir Pitt Crawley in *Vanity Fair* (1848), MP for the rotten borough of Queen's Crawley, 'an old, stumpy, short, vulgar, and very dirty man, who smokes a horrid pipe and cooks his own horrid supper in a saucepan'.[2] This was the rump of the gentry, absurd, degenerate, mendacious, self-indulgent, occasionally endearing but a class that had lost touch with the nation and with its political purpose, made irrelevant by the power of the aristocracy above them, a pod of beached whales on a dropping tide. They remained a constant feature of English life through the eight-eenth and nineteenth centuries. Sir Tatton Sykes, 4th Bt, was their late embodiment, arriving booted and spurred at his London house in the 1850s, 'hating the smart world but impressed in spite of himself that his son "knoa's oo t'hond leadies in curriage"'.[3]

As part of their love affair with the Middle Ages, and contempt for the self-indulgence of the age that preceded them, the Victorians re-summoned a vision of the squire as the generous, religious, community-minded father of his people. More often than not, this fantasy of the old was dependent on money made in the great industrial cities of the Midlands and the north. Thackeray had described the squire of thirty years earlier but R. S. Surtees's bouffant Squire Jawleyford of Jawleyford Hall became the magnificent, full-blown Victorian embodiment of community-conscious Gentry-as-Fraud. Hundreds of newly gothicized manor houses take flight in his appalling rhetorical displays. Jawleyford's

communications with his tenantry were chiefly confined to dining with them twice a year in the great entrance-hall, after Mr. Screwemtight had eased them of their cash in the steward's-room. Then Mr. Jawleyford would shine forth the very impersonification of what a landlord ought to be. Dressed in the height of the fashion, as if by his clothes to give the lie to his words, he would expatiate on the delights of such meetings of equality; declare that, next to those spent with his family, the only really happy moments of his life were those when he was surrounded by his tenantry; he doated on the manly character of the English farmer. Then he would advert to the great antiquity of the Jawleyford family, many generations of whom looked down upon them from the walls of the old hall; some on their war-steeds, some armed cap-à-pie, some in court-dresses, some in Spanish ones, one in a white dress with gold brocade breeches and a hat with an enormous plume, old Jawleyford (father of the present one) in the Windsor uniform, and our friend himself, the very prototype of what then stood before them.[4]

The story of the Hugheses, awash with mineral and banking money, describes an attempt to recreate that style. They enjoyed the Indian summer of the 1860s, but life became difficult in the 1880s and '90s as the effects of newly globalized markets in grain and meat destroyed British agriculture for a generation. A deep and long-lasting agricultural depression had struck in 1879, as corn imports from Australia and the USA, combined with the new highly efficient production of bacon in Denmark and the new refrigerated ships that could bring frozen beef from South America, all began to cut holes in the British food market. Rents dropped by an average of 22.6 per cent between 1878 and 1893.[5] The capital value of land crashed. When death duties were added to the burdens, the gentry's long love affair with the land came to an end. As Lady Bracknell put it in 1895,

> What between the duties expected of one during one's lifetime, and the duties exacted from one after one's death, land has ceased to be either a profit or a pleasure. It gives one position, and prevents one from keeping it up. That's all that can be said about land.[6]

By the end of the nineteenth century, the gentry were no longer central to the social, political, economic, philosophical, aesthetic or entrepreneurial aspects of national life. For all but the most superbly well funded, gentrydom was over.

Fecklessness

The Capels

London, Brussels and Lausanne

The Capel family began deeply embedded in the aristocracy. John was born in 1770, a younger son of the Earl of Essex by his second marriage, one of the richest men in England, with lands generously distributed across ten English counties from Hertfordshire to Herefordshire and Hampshire. At the time this story begins in 1814 John was forty-three, known to everyone as Capel and already on the slide. His much older half-brother (born in 1757) was the new Earl. Capel was married to the ethereally beautiful Lady Caroline Paget, four years younger than him, the sister of the great beau and cavalry commander Henry Paget, Earl of Uxbridge. Capel's sister was Lady Monson, Caroline's sisters Lady Galloway, Lady Erskine, Lady Enniskillen and Lady Graves. They belonged to the class which most people in this book spent their lives aspiring to join.[1]

Capel was 'un bel homme', as his daughter Harriet described him in 1815, 'tall & large – a bald head – with dark eyebrows *meeting* in the Middle'.[2] The one image of him that survives shows him a few years earlier, in 1803, in his mid-thirties, as a pugnacious blade wearing the uniform of the Light Company of the Sussex Militia, with a martial air, big sideburns, a sabre in his hand and a huge fur-crested 'round hat' emboldened with a dark green cockade. This was a glamorous uniform, worn by no run-of-the-mill infantry officer but a captain of skirmishers and sharpshooters.[3] He was undeniably attractive, a ne'er-do-well, loved by women and his friends, despised by more serious members of society. He had run through what small legacy his father had left him. There was no sign that his half-brother the Earl would distribute any more. He was essentially propertyless but living in a culture which did not encourage a life of work or enterprise. The army might have been a source of glamour and prestige but it did not pay. His social milieu would not allow him to enter business. He was caught like a piece of porcelain in a cabinet: elegant, unused, irrelevant. The gambling boom, which overtook such men in the closing decades of the eighteenth century, might be seen as a rational response to this younger son predicament. If you had no money and could not bring yourself to work, the green baize table might well have looked like an oasis in the desert: money for free, money for daring.

Caroline's father, the old Earl of Uxbridge, who was richly possessed of lands and mines in Staffordshire and Anglesey, had been appalled when she fell in love with him; and still more when Capel asked to marry her. As Lady Uxbridge had reported to her son, old Lord Uxbridge had told Capel 'he must give up all thoughts of Caroline, for no *persuasion* or *any* thing *else could or would* make him consent to his marrying her – nothing could be more violent or determined'.[4] Uxbridge told his wife that 'he had rather see Car dead than married to Capel'.[5]

Despite this, they got married and had eleven children. Now, in early June 1814, with the new peace after the defeat of Napoleon, Capel and Caroline were going abroad with their many sons and daughters. Four maids and Thorpe, the housekeeper-cum-nanny, were with them. The eldest son, Arthur, who was eleven, was already at Eton, where his fees were paid by an annuity from the will of his grandfather, the Earl of Uxbridge.[6]

This was no holiday outing. The Capels had long been in trouble. Ten years before, Caroline's mother, Lady Uxbridge, wrote to her son Arthur, recently appointed British Ambassador in Vienna:

My heart is almost broke upon a subject that you are no Stranger to, tho' you are to the Extent and dreadful Consequences that must ensue. You had not left this Country many days before I was acquainted by lady Essex [Capel's mother] and her Lawyer of the Magnitude of [Capel's] debt, amounting (I tremble to name it) to £20,000. Neither Ways nor Means to be found to discharge craving Creditors &c.[7]

Using average earnings as the multiplier, that is equivalent to about £15 million today. His brother-in-law Uxbridge found him a couple of sinecures – as Tax Collector in Staffordshire and the equivalent in British Guiana – neither of which places he had any need to go anywhere near. But the £2,000 income these offices produced was halved by the interest on the debt Capel owed, never mind any repayment of the capital. His own half-brother Lord Essex refused to help, except on the impossible terms that the Capel children should be removed from their parents' care, a plan which 'at present Caroline won't listen to'.[8]

Life abroad was cheaper (and further from any creditors) but any earlier plans to escape the country – Naples and Dresden had been suggested – had come to nothing[9] and they had staggered on, living either with Caroline's mother at Surbiton or in a rented house at Horton in the Thames valley. Now, though, they were heading for Brussels, where there was the chance of cheap lodgings,[10] cheap provisions and some distance from the debts.

Soon they were afloat on the gaiety of the foreign capital, increasingly filled with other versions of 'Lord and Lady Bare-acres'[11] – Thackeray's name for England's self-indulgent aristocracy. Thomas Creevey, the politician and memoirist, 'the only man … in society who possesses nothing',[12] registered their arrival: 'There is at present a kind of *click* of your Capels, Grevilles and a few more stupid shattered grandees, who would willingly keep the young frogs and everything else entirely to themselves.'

The exchange rate was marvellous, silk and satin shoes for 4s. 6d. a pair, walking shoes for a shilling less. Caroline wrote to her mother:

> It is wonderful how cheap every thing is here and the exchange is improving every day – two pounds of bread for three half pence – Mutton 3 pence, beef 4 pence per pound … Oh Mama, you would *die* of the Lace here, & the comparative cheapness of it.[13]

Orders were taken and goods shipped back to England.

An inveterate and reptilian gossip, the Duchess of Richmond, presided over the little local society, alongside the Austrian-Belgian Duchess of Beaufort, 'a very amiable Ugly little woman',[14] as Caroline called her. Gossip burbled across the city. The governing classes of Europe had been militarized in the preceding quarter-century of war and the salons and drawing rooms were awash with officers. Lieutenant-General Sir Ronald Craufurd Ferguson,[15] the second-in-command of the British forces in Belgium, was a constant presence in the Capel household. 'My dearest little darling grand Mama,' the 21-year-old Harriet Capel wrote on 23 June,

> We are all *in love* with General Ferguson. He is just the age when people (that is to say *Men*) *begin to grow moving* – he is two or three and forty – very handsome, very pale and lame from a wound he received – & his manners perfect – & to crown all a *widower*.[16]

In the heat of that summer, the émigrés partied, able to forget the debts back home, alive to a kind of extraordinary, febrile gaiety. 'It is impossible to move till quite the Evening – or to bear anything but a loose Gown',[17] Caroline wrote. The temperature 'exceeded West India hear [sic], we were all dying with it tho' it did not prevent our dancing with real success'.[18] Ball followed ball, in their own rented house, then at Lady Mountnorris's and then at Lady Waterpark's. Georgy, who was 19, was ecstatic. 'We have been very gay lately', dancing 'without cessation for three nights. I think people appear to like us, at least a hundred times better than they do in England.'[19]

Brussels had melted the frost of impoverishment. Life itself felt like a holiday. There was a breakfast in the Bois Forêt: 'I never saw a more animated scene or a more Motley Group, consisting of Ladies, brilliant Uniforms of various Colors, Hussars attendant upon general officers, Peasants and "Sprigs of gentility" from the Village of Soigny.'[20]

The Prince of Orange was 'like a Boy just out of school'.[21] Girls like Charlotte Greville 'adopted all the Foreign Fashions & you cannot distinguish her from one of the most *outré* of the Natives'.[22] Parades were held and *feux de joie*. Wellington arrived and then left. Lord Clancarty gave a ball for 500 people. On the Duke of York's birthday the Guards 'gave a Ball & Supper in the handsomest way possible', an evening in which 'the Supper Room was fitted up with Scenes to represent a Wood & hung with Flowers & lights'.[23]

The girls were living in a kind of love soup, an affection web, in which the most prominent aspects of reality were the emotional attachments they felt, for each other, for their mother, their father, their grandmother in England, the babies in the family, the gauche old men, the young officers, the other girls from other families swimming beside them. It was a culture of extraordinary openness. 'My dearest Grand Mama I must now take leave of you', Georgy wrote to her. 'With all my Heart I love you. God bless you and make you as happy as I am sure you deserve to be.'[24] The dull old commandant of the Brussels garrison could not be kept from the Capel house:

He is one of those odd beings that are seldom liked. *A Perfect down-right Honest Creature* who tells us of our faults & of any thing he thinks wrong, with an openness and an interest in us that has gained all our hearts from Papa to Menii [the three-year-old Amelia]. It is quite amazing how we have *unstiffened* the German Formality of our two Foreign Friends, the Duchess of Beaufort and the Marquise D'Assche. The Ladies have learnt how to receive one without 5000 Curtseys.[25]

By the autumn Caroline had put up with enough. 'My unfortunate Feet are in a state of Mortification.' Having passed 'a week of complete *Racket* & terminated with a most brilliant ball, Illuminations & Fireworks — I wish I could get into the Country for a little while — I sigh for perfect quiet & green Fields, If it was only for a Fortnight'.[26] It was not to be. In September, another young general in his mid-forties arrived from England, Sir Edward Barnes,[27] a veteran of the Peninsular War, where he had been on Wellington's staff, and an old friend of the deeply admired General Ferguson. 'He is likely to be a gt. favorite of ours',[28] Muzzy told her grandmother. Caroline adored him, as

> one of the most amiable & best creatures I ever met with & doubly devoted to every individual of the Family from Capel to Adolphus [aged one] – he is very rich & most liberal minded … there is nothing handsome that Lord Wellington does not say of him in a Military point of view.[29]

His governing virtues, like Ferguson's, were honesty, simplicity, integrity, all bound up in the one word 'amiability'. It was a lovability which came from a truth of character. In the novel which Jane Austen was writing that summer, Emma claimed that her charming new friend Frank Churchill was amiable. 'No Emma', Mr Knightley said, 'your amiable young man can be amiable only in French not in English. He may be very *aimable*, have very good manners, and be very agreeable; but he can have no English delicacy towards the feelings of other people: nothing really amiable about him.'[30] Mr Knightley's keen understanding of that difference was the measure of his worth, the sign that his character deserved his name.

The presence in the Capel household of these two amiable, beautiful, marriageable generals, replete with the noble understanding of emotional truth, created havoc. General Barnes fell in love with seventeen-year-old Muzzy, but Muzzy was already flat in love with General Ferguson. Nothing could be resolved. 'The amusements [went] on with unabated ardor – Mr. Greville declares every body has been *bit* by a *Tarantula*.'[31] Other marriage crises bubbled up and erupted. Lord John Somerset was to marry Lady Catherine Annesley even though 'they cannot have above 1000 a year between them & without any Prospect of more and he used to Quiz & abuse her at all rates'.[32] Miss Arden would not now marry Mr Warrender because her father, Lord Alvanley, had lost her £10,000 dowry at cards, 'which is the preventative'.[33] The Duchess of Richmond was trying to matchmake her daughter Georgiana with Lord Hotham, who was 'quite young, in the Guards, hideously ugly, very stingy and has £20,000 a year'.[34] Georgiana was not keen. Her sister Sarah told Harriet Capel that everything was off between herself and Lord Apsley 'for want of that odious necessary thing called Money'.[35]

Meanwhile, in secret, another deeper and more desperate affair began.

Ernst Trip was glamour itself, a forty-year-old Dutch nobleman, a patriot, not the most conventionally handsome man, but dangerously attractive and captivating, 'the most attaching, the most engaging person I know', as one of the Capels' acquaintances described him. 'I can't conceive his shewing the *slightest degree* of preference for any Girl, without her feeling a most *lively* one in return.'[36] He was a reader of Oliver Goldsmith and had become deeply anglicized ever since the French invasion of the Netherlands in 1795, when he had escaped to England. In 1800 he bought himself a commission in the Prince's Regiment, 10th Light Dragoons, the smartest in the British army, and in 1808 served as ADC first to Arthur Wellesley, not yet Duke of Wellington, and then to Caroline Capel's brother, Henry Paget, the most inspiring cavalry commander in the Peninsular War. He did well and by 1814 when he was a lieutenant-colonel, he was appointed ADC to the Prince of Orange and came over to Brussels to join him.

Trip was 'an agreeable boaster, swearing like a hussar, and speaking a sort of *baragouin*, half German, half French-English, which was very entertaining'.[37] Walter Scott remembered him as 'a dandy of the first water, and yet with an energy in his dandyism which made it respectable. He was one of the best-dressed men, and his horse was in equally fine condition as if he had had a dozen grooms.'[38] His magnificent tailors' and outfitters' bills, often unpaid for a year or more, portray a beautifully appointed, sweet-smelling man. He was welcomed into London society above all as a waltzer, introducing that disturbingly intimate dance to an older generation filled with apprehensions and with it conquering English society. He and his dance were now in Brussels. 'The Duke of Richmond', Muzzy wrote to her grandmother, 'will not let His daughters Waltz. But as hardly anything else is danced here he must soon give up the Point.'[39] On 20 October Caroline wrote to her mother:

> One of the People we see most of here, & like the best is – Guess who? Baron Trip himself, who I ever used to think the most self-sufficient odious man that ever breathed; he must be very much altered, or I was very much deceived, for now I find him most agreeable, amiable, & delightfull.[40]

A fascinating change of attitude becomes clear in these words of Caroline. Self-sufficiency is no virtue for her; only connectedness and openness to others can contribute to a man's goodness. But she was surely wrong about one thing. Trip was not amiable, he was *aimable*. He understood the central point made by Lord Chesterfield, the great eighteenth-century apostle of deceit, that a man must 'have a real reserve with almost everybody; and have a seeming reserve with almost nobody; for it is very disagreeable to seem reserved, and very dangerous not to be so'. 'Whoever is not *Aimable*', Chesterfield had written, 'is in truth no body at all.'[41] Of these difficult, subtle and cynical dance steps, Trip was a master.

The serious and passionate Harriet Capel, almost twenty-two, a reader of Byron's most uncompromising hymns to love, 'remarkable for a sort of Paget face', as the diarist Thomas Moore later remembered her, 'and very black piercing eyes',[42] could not take those eyes off the Dutchman. Soon Harriet and her favourite sister Muzzy were meeting the Baron away from the parental circle. A roughly written pencil note survives among his papers: 'Nous nous rendrons a 5½ heure a la place sur le rempart ou Vous etiés hier au soir quand je vous ai rencontre avec Charles [?] & la D'ième inconnue.' (At 5.30 we will be at the square on the ramparts where you were yesterday evening when I met you with Charles and the second woman, unknown to me.)[43]

She didn't know what drew her to this glamour capsule, but was powerless in front of it. Much later, and alone, she wrote to him:

I will tell you what it is, Ernest, or rather I *cannot* tell you what it is, that is so *dangerously* attractive in you. I very often ask myself questions upon the subject but never can I answer them. I say 'is it personal beauty – is it his manners – his conversation – his sentiments?' No, all these of course *help*, but still, the *danger* does not lie in *any* of these, but in a sort of *nameless indescribable something*, that winds *round* and *round* & *round* one, as silk round a silk worm and entangles, irretrievably entangles one, before one is aware where one is – is it *something* which like [Byron's] *Lara* 'seems to *dare* you to *forget*' –[44]

She was caught in a surging vision of romantic freedom with him: 'Then above all that *expression* of mind, that liberality of feeling, that *indulgence pour les faiblesses*, that freedom from prejudice & that independence of principle & action, which *amalgamates* so completely with me.'[45]

It seems as if he was exercising some kind of self-control in front of this adoration, because on Christmas Eve 1814 Harriet wrote a letter to him and put it in an envelope on which she wrote 'To be opened Christmas Eve 1815':

I without hesitation commit to paper my sentiments and glory in them, – I am in full & perfect conviction that time will only add strength & fervancy to them – & that every Christmas day I may live to see, will find me equally devoted to the only Being I ever have or ever shall adore – faithful, unalterable, unchangeable devotion I feel & ever shall feel – I exult in being *at the feet of one* who has told me he can never be to me more than friend – Friend! What a cold word for what I feel – no let me be his slave – & I ask from him but pity & compassion –[46]

She knew what she was doing, that she was stepping out of the orderly, mother-governed realm of amiability into something more perilous, swapping the world of Jane Austen for something much more like that of the Brontës. Most of this remained below the surface, but not all. In the New Year, Caroline began to refer in her letters to 'the Wretch' on whom her beloved Harriet was throwing herself.

Nevertheless, Caroline ensured that the Capel household continued on its way. Still more generals joined the party. 'General Maitland is another of our friends – very handsome – a Widower & therefore *very moving*, full of Accomplishments, & so *good* that of course some people call him a Methodist.'[47]

By the time she had written that, another disaster had already occurred: Muzzy had turned General Barnes down. 'What you heard relative to a Certain Person', Muzzy wrote sweetly to her grandmother,

is true, and though I am well aware that it would, in a *Worldly Point of view*, have been a desirable thing, yet with all his agremens [or grace notes] that I hear *so much* of, he is not indeed the Sort of Person, that would ever have made me happy. And I am too happy in my present situation to wish to change it unless to be still more so; I know *my* extraordinary *taste*, or rather want of taste, has caused, does now, Much astonishment to every body & more particularly to my own Family, which I am very very sorry for. – On this subject I am not I think very Romantic, for I do not think *violent Love* necessary to one's happyness, but I think you will agree with me that a *decided preference* is absolutely so, and that, that preference even, I never could feel. Therefore there was but one way of acting.

I must acknowledge to you that, General F—son suited my taste and feelings *much much* more, but there was one very decided obstacle, in that way, & indeed the *only* one, (which was, *want of that horrid Money*.)[48]

Caroline wrote sagely to her own mother:

I assure you that it is no objection of Capel's or mine that has prevented it, but her own decision – I think a *Veto* we have a right to, If Unfortunately it ever becomes necessary, but I am afraid of *persuasion* because if the thing did not turn out happily I could never forgive myself – She knows how much Capel & I love & value him. Her sisters quite doat on him & and rowe her from Morning till Night for her want of taste, &

He, after keeping away for a few days after the *sad reverse*, has lived here as much as ever. – & People now ask me 'which of your Daughters is Gnl. B to marry? Or is he to marry *them all*?'[49]

Capel himself seems to have been scarcely involved in these gyrations, half absent, shooting in the country outside Brussels, going to parties, or hunting for wolves in the Belgian forest. Caroline had found she was pregnant, again, for the thirteenth time, but she was left alone holding the family fort. The other girls continued with their flirtations but at some time early in 1815, Harriet's love affair with Baron Trip plunged into new and wildly dangerous territory. Much later, in one of her letters to him, she remembered the moment when he stepped beyond friendship:

I am writing this, Ernest, *from* the room *on* the couch where you *once* promised to be *Mine* for ever –

This dear couch where I passed three *such* hours! Where I clasped on a throat whiter than snow the chain which you promised should *never* leave it.

I have been here above half an hour – recollecting every circumstance of those moments of bliss – de cet heure de Bonheur, *too exquisite* to last – I was determined to take one last view of this dear, dear room, – don't be angry with me –

I have touched nothing except a little Vicar of Wakefield & a few old poems. Your dressing table drawer was open & I looked in hopes of finding a comb or brush which had touched that dear *picturesque* brown head – but only found two old combs of my *own*, one which fell out one night on the Ramparts, the other I left in your room myself on that never to be forgotten night![50]

It is difficult to tell, but these words surely mean that they slept together.

In Trip's beautiful rosewood dispatch box, now preserved among Lord Anglesey's papers, tiny objects remain which hint at the realities of the love affair. First, there is the case itself, stuffed to the brim with the letters he had received. Among them is the twist of paper on which Trip wrote 'De celle qui chantait d'être aimé' (From the one who used to sing of being loved). Inside its folds are two tiny fragments of jewellery, a broken gold ring and a jewelled cinquefoil in pink and white, with the words, in Harriet's hand: '1814 The First proof of Ernest's Love'.

In another, on which Trip has written 'de celle qui j'ai la plus de raisons d'aimer Janvier 1815' (from the one whom I have the most reason to love January 1815), Harriet has sent him a lock of her light brown hair, held with a mulberry-coloured thread. What could be more touching or more beautiful than this? But sadly the box reveals more than Trip himself ever could or would. There are four beautifully embroidered little pochettes, each with love letters from a different girl.

All of them sent Trip either locks of their hair or in one case her self-portrait. Harriet Capel was only the latest in a long string of conquests made by this beautiful, alluring and treacherous man.[51]

Then the whole world changed around them. In early March, news reached London and Brussels 'of the Tyger having broke loose'.[52] Napoleon had escaped from Elba and was on his way to Paris, the people and armies of France flocking to support him. War would begin again. Trip had to go Paris himself and before he left he said something disturbing but maybe wonderful to Harriet. She wrote to him, excited, anxious:

Thursday

Je suis si peu d'accord avec moimême – & am half distracted. – What you said last night made me so happy. Confirm it I beseech you – but be frank – You can perhaps call again before you go – If impossible, write. This uncertainty will kill me.[53]

He was to visit the Capel house before he left and she waited for him. Then, as the hours passed, on the bottom of the same piece of paper, she wrote again:

Thursday night

I had written the above, intending to give it to you when you called.

Why did you not come? It was not kind to disappoint me – I cannot now mention a time when you could find me alone; but I never go out till about 5, & would not go out at all if there was any chance of your coming – One decisive conversation à coeur ouvert is necessary for my repose; and after all that has passed, have I not a right to ask it?[54]

After all that has passed. He had left without a word to her. Nor did any letter come. The couriers to Brussels were arriving daily from Paris but they brought nothing for her. She was in a constant state of wretchedness and agitation. When they heard at the beginning of April that Napoleon had reached Fontainebleau outside Paris, she took it to mean that Trip would soon be back with her in Brussels.

But surely you *will* come back here? I do not know what I am doing or writing – Ernest, Ernest, have pity upon the most miserable wretch that ever breathed. Have you got a large packet I sent two days ago? In mercy write to me and tell me something! Will you see me privately when you do come back – you must indeed, you must I am quite, quite distracted – Oh Ernest.[55]

As the prospect of a renewed war became more likely, the life of the English in Brussels took on a more hectic air. It seems that Capel had taken a certain marquise as his mistress, or at least so Harriet thought. The French royal family passed through, seeming dowdy and defeatist, to general disparagement. Wellington arrived with Caroline's brother and the rest of his staff. An exhausted Caroline wrote to her mother, 'The balls are going on here as if we had had none for a year. Paget gave a Most magnificent Dinner to above 100 People, & Lord Hill a Breakfast.'[56]

Only the ever-loyal Sir Edward Barnes, with whom Caroline herself was half in love (he was only three years younger than her), acted the man of constancy. He would in time become the great road-building, system-building colonial administrator in Ceylon and India. In this flushed and feverish Regency world, he seems like a monument of calm, the proto-Victorian. Caroline wrote to her mother:

I know to a certainty that *Harriet* might marry at this moment, if she chose it, that bravest, most amiable, most excellent of Men. Who has already met with a disappointment from *Muz*; & what will perhaps make you laugh thro' your annoyance, I am *sure* that if the latter were to give him any encouragement he is ready to renew the business again with *her* – But no such luck! He is infatuated with the Family & H, tho' she made him her Confidant & that he is aware of all her errors he still thinks [her] the finest & most Superior of Creatures! … & yet would throw herself away upon a Wretch![57]

Eventually, in April, the Wretch returned to Brussels and resumed with Harriet. The gossiping diarist Thomas Moore heard the stories:

Their private walks together at last became the talk of the place, and her father expostulated with the Baron, who gave his word these assi-duities should be discontinued – He however was seen with her in the same way again, & the father wrote him an angry letter, which Tripp considered so insulting as to authorize his calling Capell out.[58]

Even the suggestion of sex with an unmarried woman, even in this loose and desperate atmosphere, remained enough in 1815 for a duel to become a possibility. Capel may well have discovered that the Trip affair had involved more than mere letter writing or the reading of Byron on moonlit ramparts, and said as much in his letter to Trip.

Whatever happened, there is no doubt that the whole of Brussels had been talking for months. The middle-aged Isabella Seymour had already told Harriet that 'never were two people so *completely cut out* for each other, & that she was quite sure it would be the *happiest ménage*, that ever existed … then she said that it was *much too late in the day to talk of friendship!* Too late indeed!'[59]

Those are Harriet's words to Trip. On 13 April, the challenge was issued and 16 Sunday was appointed as the day for the duel. 'You may suppose what the blame must have been to have induced so peaceable a Nature as Capel's, the Father of a Family, to have taken such a Step,'[60] Caroline wrote to her mother. Capel said not a word to any member of his family about what he was doing, but arranged for the Duke of Richmond to be his second and a Dr Hyde to attend them. Trip found his own colonel and a surgeon in support.

On the Sunday morning, Capel said he was going to call on General Barnes and left the house for the duel. It is not clear where they met but Caroline gave an account to her mother:

> They *both* fired (Capel within a hair's breadth of his Antagonist's Ear) and the astonishment of the Duke as well as even the Baron's Second at his having fired at Capel is not to be described. I have suffered a great deal but God has given me Strength to go thro' it all & will enable me I hope to bear with patience the reports & illnatured Stories that an Affair of this kind too often gives rise to.[61]

Rumours of the moral decline of the entire Capel family were now circulating in London and Brussels. Harriet had slept with a notorious seducer, Capel had taken a mistress, there had been the duel, Muzzy would not accept the general who loved her, nor would Harriet to whom his attentions were now transferred. Muzzy was in love instead with a hopelessly impoverished officer. It was said that all the Capel girls had embarked on a 'Correspondence with Men'.[62] Their financial situation was dire. And now twenty-year-old Georgy was also in an amorous '*scrape*' and had been having 'what is called a *flirtation*' with a man who 'has *every thing* to recommend him but that detestable article *Money*, A little of which, at least, one cannot do without'.[63]

Caroline had to write urgent denials to her mother, insisting that Georgy had behaved 'with a degree of feeling & good sense that does her credit', and had said to Caroline, 'Mama may I die if I ever conceal a thought, word or look from you For I fully see the wretchedness it entails.' It was Harriet's 'System of Concealment which so deeply wounded' her. The grandmother was to have no fear: 'I early saw the sort of Place this was & that certain restrictions were necessary; These have always been in force & I will *defy* any body to bring forward an Instance to the Contrary.'[64]

For all Caroline Capel's anger, dignity and strength in these trials, there can be no doubt that the loucheness of Brussels in 1815, its temporary and war-heightened atmosphere, acted as a kind of solvent on manners and sexual mores. Caroline was outraged.

> What would you say if you heard of your Grand-daughters riding out without Father, brother or Chaperone of any kind with 5 or six young Men? & this repeatedly – or if you heard of one of them siting [sic] in a public Ball room which had been a Theatre & where the Boxes remained, in one of these Boxes with *a Captain* Somebody who she was flirting with, for half the Evening! Or if you heard of them walking in the Public walks arm in arm with men & without any Chaperon with them?

Harriet, of course, had done all this and more. From the turmoil, Caroline looked back to her own mother as a kind of haven: 'When I write to *you*, I feel so secure that I can almost say anything, So, dearest Mama, I can tell you the extent of my feelings of provocation.'[65]

Her love for Capel was undiminished – 'had I wanted any thing to increase My attachment to My dear Capel his Conduct now would have done it'[66] – but still he seems curiously absent. And Harriet's obsession with Trip, even after he had tried to kill her father in the duel, was if anything on the rise.

In early June, Napoleon was beginning to mass his armies on the Belgian border and Wellington and the Prussians were making their own dispositions between those invaders and Brussels. The speed of life in this strange, capsule city did not diminish. On the night of 15 June, Georgy, Muzzy and Capel went to the 'sort of farewell ball' given by the Duchess of Richmond at their rented house in the rue de la Blanchisserie. The heavily pregnant Caroline, Harriet and the younger girls stayed at home in the Château de Walcheuse.

At this most famous ball,

in the midst of the dancing an express arrived to the Duke with an account of the Prussians having been beat and the French having advanced within 14 miles of Bruxelles – You may imagine the Electrical Shocks of such intelligence – Most of the Women in floods of tears and all the Military in an instant collected round their respective leaders and in less than 20 minutes the room was cleared.[67]

War had come, it was an 'Awful moment' and 'to have one's friends walk out of one's Drawing Room into Action, which has literally been the case on this occasion, is a sensation far beyond description'.[68] Napoleon's brilliantly covert manoeuvring and concentration of his forces, and the failure of the British intelligence service, had humbugged the Duke. 'This has indeed come upon us like a Thief in the Night', Caroline wrote to her mother. 'I am afraid our Great hero must have been deceived for he has certainly been taken by surprise.'[69]

Over the next three days, the Capel women were tormented with the thoughts of what was happening to the men they loved. Caroline's brother, Lord Uxbridge, all the clustering generals, the handsome young men and Baron Trip, who was with the Dutch forces, were all now to be exposed to the intense and murderous form of battle which the Napoleonic wars had devised.

There was a pause the next day, as the British and Prussian armies pulled back towards Brussels, agreeing to join up and meet the French at Waterloo. The city was rife with rumour and panic. Capel tried to hire horses, a carriage or even a barge to take his family away in case the French won the coming battle. But there wasn't a horse to be found and they waited in mounting anxiety:

The Horrors of that night [17–18 June] are not to be forgot – the very elements conspired to make it gloomy – For the rain and darkness and wind were frightfull and our courtyard was filled the night with poor wounded drenched soldiers and horses seeking refuge and assistance which you may imagine we administered as well as we were able.[70]

301

The following day, Sunday 18 June, the noise of battle rolled across the city all afternoon and deep into the evening. 'To an English ear unaccustomed to such things', Caroline wrote that day, 'the Cannonading of a real Battle is Awful beyond description. Let us hope the best, my blessed mama – in the mean time *We* are all packed up and ready for a Start if necessary.'[71] She waited to hear the worst, as about 48,000 people were being killed and wounded twelve miles to the south of her.

Harriet had no idea where Trip was or what he was doing. On the day after the battle she went into the city from the chateau and must have encountered him, perhaps in the street, perhaps at Lord Uxbridge's headquarters, to which he was attached. In a letter, 'scrawled in an enormous hand and much stained by tears',[72] as Henry Anglesey has described it, she then wrote to him:

Oh Ernest, Ernest – *hearing the cannonading* feeling that every shot had perhaps deprived me of all I love – of every prospect of future happiness, not daring to ask a question – never hearing your name mentioned – Oh God Oh God, every wrong thing I ever have done has been sufficiently punished! These are the first tears I have been able to shed – every vein has been burning my head – my heart, all, all – oh Ernest, am I never to be happy? Then in this dreadful state to come here to the scene of all my happiness, of all my miseries – to see all the rest of the staff – to know that you are close to me – and to be unable to throw myself into yr. arms, & at *your* feet to thank God for having preserved you![73]

Every day she was taking a hundred drops of laudanum. Her eyes were swollen with tears and she continued to write to him, now in a small notebook:

Oh God, whatever my errors have been surely they are too severely punished! I must go – God, God bless you – may all the *pains* of Life be *mine* – all the *pleasures yours, this* is my only prayer – & if the moment ever comes when you no longer enjoy them, – *then* call on *me* to *love* you – give up the best days of yr life to others, *I* will be satisfied if you will let me stay with you when you are tired of the world. Oh Ernest, God bless you.[74]

Waterloo had cut traumatic holes of many kinds in their lives. Edward Barnes had survived, even though two horses were shot from under him. Tens of thousands of others did not. Caroline's brother Lord Uxbridge, who had led one cavalry charge after another, had his leg destroyed by grape shot in the last moments of the battle. Baron Trip was unscathed. It was a victory, 'But what horror was it accompanied with!' Caroline wrote. It was 'the most glorious, but without exception the most bloody victory that was ever gained'.[75] Wellington 'never was known to be in such low spirits as he was in consequence of the blood shed at Waterloo'.[76]

Trip was soon in Paris, with the conquering armies camped in the Bois de Boulogne like a *fête gallante*, cruising the expatriate society. On 4 August 1815, another Harriet, this one the mondaine Countess Granville, wrote to her sister Lady Georgiana Morpeth in England about a dinner party she had just held in Paris: 'Baron Tripp and Henry Pierrepoint dined with us today, and the former was very agreeable, giving details, some of which I hope were true, of the battle.'[77] You can imagine that scene, his modestly self-promoting account, his beautiful uniform, his 'air *pittoresque*'. Later that month, Lady Granville told her sister that 'The dandies are broken in hearts and fortunes,'[78] and listed Baron Trip among them. The cause of his despair would not have been Harriet Capel.

I wish I could give this story a happy ending, but it doesn't have one. On 16 July 1815, Caroline Capel gave birth to another baby girl in Brussels, Priscilla Elizabeth. The family doted on her but by 25 September the baby had died. Capel himself and the ten-year-old Janey were both seriously ill in bed and they heard that the chateau they had rented was cheap because it had the reputation of making its inhabitants ill. Harriet went to stay with some friends in The Hague while the rest of the family took a sad holiday travelling up the Rhine. Harriet was no better than she had been in the summer. Caroline wrote to Lady Uxbridge: 'It is a melancholy sight to see a young & fine Creature losing her best days in misery & regret; she speaks with the warmest gratitude of My kindness to her, but says it is daggers to her, & that she wishes I would hate her.'[79]

By early November Caroline was back with the children in Brussels. At some time during that month she discovered what she must long have dreaded: Capel had been gambling heavily in Brussels and had lost. Once again, she wrote to her own mother:

Never apologize to me, My dearest Mama, for anything you say – all that comes from you I must take kindly – But you are in error on a certain very painfull subject; Can you for one moment believe that I was aware of what was going on without interfering?[80]

Capel had been pestered to join what was called the Literary Club by Lord Waterpark, 'a steady Family Man ... It was not considered at that time as a place where there was any gaming, but merely where the Newspapers were read.'[81] Caroline had not the slightest inkling of what was going on. 'No creature ever hinted it to me, & the only time I felt any alarm was during the time of the Races when a great deal of betting was going forward & I spoke to him in a warning voice, which he took very kindly & said I should have no cause for uneasiness.'[82]

By December, Caroline was contemplating the possibility of moving further on into Europe. Much as Brussels was 'cheaper than England there are certainly parts of the Continent infinitely cheaper than this'.[83] Their lease would run out in June and the landlord would let them renew it only at an inflated rent which they could not now afford.

Harriet was also returning in desperation to the source of all her sorrows. In The Hague on New Year's Day 1816 she wrote again to Trip, now in London.

Do not think that I am going to attempt entering into a correspondence with you – No Ernest – I neither require nor expect an answer nor will I ever again take a step like the present – Not a Human being on earth knows of it, & nothing but peculiar circumstances should have tempted me to do it.[84]

She would come with him not as a wife but as a sister, a friend.

Sell your commission, Ernest, & let us depend but on each other, – in a *middling* situation our being together might cause you additional expence, but in a state of absolute poverty we should mutually assist each other. I have hands – strength, & some talents; all – all should be devoted to you, & the proudest as well as the happiest moment of my life would be that in which I laid at your feet, my little earnings.

Ernest – bear in my mind that my existence hangs upon you – Only be open – tell Papa your situation – I will tell him my determination, et nous irons où le destin nous ménera – Remember, Ernst, what we have been to each other – Oh my beloved friend, there are moments the recollection of which almost distract me – Le premier – le dernier baiser qu j'ai reçu de vous, brûle encore sur mes lèvres.[85]

The first *and last* kiss that he had given her? Was all this about no more than a single kiss? Harriet Capel, and perhaps her mother, was contemplating the possibility of a descent straight through all the layers of a carefully graded society to the point where she had nothing but love. Baron Trip responded to this passionate and almost metaphysical hymn of adoration and self-abasement with silence.

In June the family left for Switzerland, where they lodged in a cramped villa on the shores of Lake Geneva. In October, they moved into an apartment in Lausanne. And at the end of that month Baron Trip shot himself dead with a pistol when in Florence.

Lady Granville described the *on dit* to her sister:

There are various reports. One of pecuniary distress; one that he was in love with that pretty little Mrs. Fitzherbert, who was a Miss Chichester, and that he sent to her husband to borrow the pistols with which he destroyed himself; and another that upon Mr Capel sending to tell him he no longer would oppose his marrying his daughter, he avowed a secret marriage and said he had a wife and five children, and then, unable to reconcile the difficulties of his situation, shot himself. It was on returning from a party.[86]

Within a few days the news reached Lausanne. Capel came as close as he ever had to Harriet and, as Caroline wrote to her mother, for 'the first two nights he slept in her room because he could not bear she should be without one of us'.[87]

Caroline heard the news with relief. She imagined 'this fine creature … being one day restored to herself'.[88] Trip had left a letter for Lord Uxbridge, Caroline's brother, elevated since the Battle of Waterloo as the Marquess of Anglesey, but neither Caroline nor Harriet knew its contents. It may well be that Trip's letter entrusted Harriet's letters to Anglesey, which is the reason they have survived, as they are now in the muniment room of Lord Anglesey in Plas Newydd.

Harriet was experiencing a strange calm:

After two years of agitation and anxiety, of alternate hopes and fears, there is a kind of comfort even in such tranquility as *this* – my mind feels so stunned, so worn out, that at least it can never again suffer much of any sort, – its best – its warmest affections, have been torn to pieces, & all that resembles enthusiasm is annihilated for ever.[89]

It was as if the crisis was over. The following March, Lady Uxbridge died, and on Boxing Day 1817, Harriet married a 43-year-old Welshman called David Okeden Parry-Okeden of Moor Crichel in Dorset; he had previously been called David Okeden Parry, but had changed his name to qualify for an inheritance from his mother's father. He was distantly connected to this world of the dissolute aristocracy, but clearly provided for Harriet a destination that felt safe, good and secure. He was a member of the gentry, everything Trip and his kind were not. His first wife had died seven years before and he was the same age as Harriet's mother. She had joined the '*middling sort*'. The next year, in October 1818, the cynical Thomas Moore dined at Bowood with his friend the Marquess of Lansdowne. Harriet and her husband were at dinner. There was music in the evening and she played the Ranz des Vaches, a Swiss cowherd's tune, and some melancholy Italian variations on the piano. To his diary, not to the assembled company, Moore retold the story of the Baron's suicide:

Miss Capell upon hearing the catastrophe, put on mourning for him & has worn it ever since, notwithstanding a grave elderly gentleman has been kind enough to convert her into Mrs Oakden – they are *both* in mourning at this moment, *le Mari* being obliged, I suppose, to put it on in self-defence.[90]

When Moore himself stood up to entertain the company with his singing,

the most trumpery person of the company (as will always happen) Mrs Oakden, took her station in the remotest corner of the room, where she could not hear a note, and employed her wise self in writing letters – yet this creature likes her own bad playing amazingly.[91]

Harriet was pregnant at the time and the following June 1819, in giving birth to a son, George Fitz-Maurice Parry-Okeden, she died. She was twenty-six. Her father, Capel, had died two months before 'in Convulsions or in a state of Insensibility'.[92] He was forty-six and his debts died with him.

Harriet's sisters, with no dowry to boast of, married either English and Irish squires or into the minor French and Swiss nobility. As a whole, they stepped down from the high-octane and destructive world in which their father had lived, and which their mother had suffered, into something more settled and secure. In that way, the story of this Capel family is of the gentry becoming the harbour and refuge for children brought up surrounded by the risk and rootlessness of aristocracy. Every one of the Capel children transmuted, in effect, into Victorians. One of the sisters married a doctor. One of the brothers became a captain in the navy. Another became the 6th Earl of Essex in succession to his uncle and lived a blameless and uneventful life as a Victorian grandee. Harriet's son, George Fitz-Maurice Parry-Okeden, changed his name to the more down-to-earth William Parry-Okeden and built himself a severely handsome Jacobethan manor house at Turnworth in Dorset. In the light of these outcomes, what does Victorian England look like but a return to gentry virtues, even among the aristocracy, after the moral anarchy and pain of their parents' generation?

After Capel's death, Caroline herself entered a long and relatively burdenless widowhood. She never married again and lived in Rutland Gate on the edge of Hyde Park in London. In her drawing room, to entertain her many grandchildren, she kept tame canaries in cages and from time to time let them out to fly around the room so that for a moment or two they could enjoy the experience of freedom.[93]

Fantasy

The Hugheses

Kinmel, Denbighshire and Grosvenor Square, London

This story of a slow Victorian dance between money and dignity – the dynamo of all gentry lives – begins long before on a hill just inland from the little port of Amlwch on the north coast of Anglesey. Parys Mountain is the most poisonous place in Britain. The rust-red streams that run down from it to the coast are the most polluted waters in the country; 40 per cent of all the heavy metals in the Irish Sea come from here. Any attempt to channel that water in metal pipes has led only to the pipes dissolving in the acidity. There is nothing artificial about this: Mynydd Parys is an acid mountain, thick with sulphur, made poisonous when its rocks were formed 440 million years ago. Almost nothing will grow there beyond sprigs of black heather, strange, acid-tolerant lichens, a few mosses and the beautiful, beaded fronds of Black Melick. Where buildings have collapsed and the lime in the mortar has neutralized the soil, there is a patch of odd bright green grass. Otherwise, even on a sunny day, Parys Mountain is dark, Martian, metamorphic, orange and ochre, a mineral anti-world, made alien by the metals and chemicals it contains.

It looks as it does because it has been robbed. Everything valuable it once contained, even 1,000 feet down, far below sea level, has been dug out, so that now it sits in the middle of Anglesey's green pastures like a vast rotten tooth, more cavity than hill. More than five million tons of sterile spoil have been raised from its depths. Just as the story of the Throckmortons floated on grass and the Lascelles on sugar, the rise and fall of the Hughes of Kinmel begins in the money that Parys Mountain once contained.[1]

In 1765, the 26-year-old Reverend Edward Hughes arrived in Anglesey to become curate to Robert Lewis, a vicar there. Hughes was an educated man. He had been to Jesus College, Oxford, as all the anglicized Welsh gentry did, where he had received his MA three years before, but he was no grandee. The origins of the family 'had it seems given rise to considerable speculation, much of it patently malicious among the Anglesey and Caernarvonshire squirearchy. There were rumours that Edward's father Hugh had been, variously, a cowman at Penrhos, Holyhead, a stable boy at Lleweni, a servant and a tailor.'[2] That was jealous talk. Although there is some muddle over the genealogy, they were probably ancient, small-time, English-speaking Flintshire squires. Hugh had spent most of his life in England, as secretary to the Chancellor of the diocese of Hereford, and had finally bought himself a small estate in Anglesey near Beaumaris.[3]

In the months after Edward arrived in Anglesey in 1765, he became engaged to his vicar's third daughter, Mary Lewis – she was twenty-five – and that August they were married. She had as her inheritance a small farm called Llysdulas near Amlwch, which included on its margins the most unpromising of assets: half of half of a small 'barren hill' named after a man called Parys who had owned it in the fifteenth century. The grazing there was poor and its annual rental was £25. Her half of the mountain was shared with a man who owned the whole of the other half, Sir Nicholas Bayly, a rich and powerful baronet from the other end of the island.

It is not quite true that when Edward Hughes married his blue-eyed, pale-skinned girl,[4] nobody knew what Parys Mountain contained. There had been ancient workings here. In the early 1760s, Bayly had opened various 'ventures' on the hill. The poisoned streams and the very barrenness of the earth pointed towards the possibility that the hill might contain something worth having. But none of the workings seemed that productive[5] and all were on the point of being abandoned when, on 2 March 1768, the world changed. A local miner,

Roland Puw, stumbled on an unimaginably vast mass of ore coming to the surface at a spot on the barren hill called 'The Golden Venture'.[6] Quite suddenly, all parties realized that Parys Mountain was their future. Puw was given a bottle of brandy and rent-free accommodation for the rest of his life. The two families that owned the hill could gaze into the future with equanimity.

A long, angry and complex court case followed in which Sir Nicholas Bayly struggled with the Hugheses to establish their respective rights to what the hill contained, but by 1775 they had reached a conclusion.[7] Bayly had wanted to keep all the ores that were raised himself but Hughes, no retiring vicar, required 'assurance that he would get half the ores, not half the proceeds of the sale, for he intended to erect his own smelting works, and his profit would be reduced if he did not receive the ores themselves'.[8] There was no question of exaggeratedly gentlemanly behaviour on either side: instead, a straightforward, bullet-nosed and appallingly expensive legal battle for an enormous fortune.

Within three years, according to commercial imperatives, all differences had been buried. Edward Hughes had gone into partnership with a brilliant and entrepreneurial Anglesey lawyer, Thomas Williams, who had been acting for him in the case, and with a London banker, John Dawes. Together they formed the Parys Mine Company and in 1778, Sir Nicholas Bayly leased his half of the hill to the company. From then on, under Thomas Williams's guidance, the company would work the whole of the hill, paying a royalty to both the lucky families who owned it.

This was no small-scale enterprise. Even in the 1770s, 3,000 tons of lead ore and 4,500 tons of copper ore were being raised in a year, the ore worth £27,000 at the quayside, with annual expenses of some £4,500, giving a profit even in these early days of £22,500 a year.[9]

About 220 people were working in the mine at the time but the business soon exploded into life. The hulls of the Royal Navy, policing the seaways of the Atlantic and the route to India, were exposed as never before to the teredo shipworms which could destroy the oak in a matter of years. Sheathing the hulls in copper plates (fixed with copper nails) could not only save an expensive hull; the copper itself was a form of antifouling which kept the underwater profiles of the ships clean and fast, a critical element in victory at sea. This huge new market for copper (in which all European navies soon joined), combined with Thomas Williams's comprehensive manipulation of the market and the setting up of large smelting works at Swansea, at Ravenhill in Lancashire and at Temple Mills in Buckinghamshire, meant that the Parys Mine Company soon straddled the world copper business.

Within a dozen years the company was dominant. Some of the rock was 40 per cent pure metal[10] and by 1784 a hole had been opened in the hill 40 yards wide, 100 long and almost 80 feet deep. Further workings drove deep into the hill, 'supported by vast pillars and magnificent arches, all metallic; and these caverns meander far underground',[11] as the excited Thomas Pennant wrote in 1783.

The mine was the talk of the kingdom and romantic tourists dropped by. The Reverend Edward Bingley stood aghast in the summer of 1798:

The shagged arches and overhanging rocks, which seemed to threaten annhilation to any one daring enough to approach them, when super-added to the sulphureous smell arising from the kilns in which the ore is roasted, made it seem to me like the vestibule to Tartarus.[12]

Thomas Pennant witnessed a saturnine and diabolical world:

Suffocating fumes of the burning heaps of copper arise in all parts and extend their baleful influence for miles around. In the adjacent parts vegetation is nearly destroyed; even the mosses and the lichens of the rocks have perished: and nothing seems capable of resisting the fumes but the purple Melic grass, which flourishes in abundance.[13]

By the 1780s 1,500 people were working in and around the mine, the men underground, or with gunpowder in the open pits, blowing up the walls of the ever-enlarging chasm and then nibbling away at the loosened rock with picks. Boulders were lifted in baskets to the old ground surface, where women sat with hammers, all year, all their lives, breaking the boulders of ore into pebbles which could be more easily smelted. The fires that burned in the kilns used peat from the hill. In the blocks of peat, chemical reactions had sometimes occurred between the buried plant material and the copper-thick water, so that mysteriously perfect branches, plant stems, leaves and nuts of pure copper could be picked out of the dirt.

The number employed at the mountain went up by a factor of six or seven and the production with it, bringing an annual profit for the Hugheses in the very best years of the 1790s of more than £150,000 a year.[14] Sir Nicholas Bayly's son, by now the Earl of Uxbridge and the father of Lady Caroline Capel, enjoyed the same kind of revenues.

As the Hugheses grew rich, those working for them were living in penury: the masons building the giant docksides and the bins for the 'roasted ore' were paid 1s. and 3d. a day; miners 1s. and 4d.; the carriers of the ore from the mine to the docks, a single shilling; the carters of the turf for the kilns 3d. a cartload.[15] These were the mathematics of ownership and dispossession: £150,000 a year for the Reverend Edward Hughes; £19 11s. a year for one of his miners – a multiplier of 7,692:1.

From the early 1780s onwards, and for the next twenty-seven years, the Reverend Edward Hughes started to pour his mineral money into land, first buying Greenfield Hall, on the North Wales coast near Flint, where the Parys Mine Company had a works making rolled copper sheets for naval hulls. Then in 1786, he bought the Kinmel estate, for £42,000, a beautiful slab of country lying across the borders of Denbighshire and Flintshire, on a range of limestone hills overlooking the coastal flats, conveniently halfway between Greenfield and Anglesey.

Large tracts of Anglesey itself were bought for £113,000, further pieces around Kinmel and in 1813 as the culmination of the whole story, the Lleweni and Cotton Hall estate, just outside Denbigh, for £209,000. By 1815, when he died, Edward Hughes had spent a total of £496,000 on land in North Wales and had bought something approaching 85,000 acres.[16]

The Hughes land holding was a province of money made flesh. At Kinmel Hughes built an elegant neo-classical villa, with Samuel Wyatt as the architect, on a beautiful shelf of land looking east towards the Clwyd Hills, the wide vale of north Denbighshire and Flintshire laid out below it and the sea in the distance stretching away to the Lancashire coast.[17] By the time he died in 1815, Hughes must have thought, and with some justification, that he had established a dynasty. His youngest son had become a colonel in the 18th Hussars, his second son a partner in the Chester and North Wales Bank, which the family had founded in 1792, and his eldest son, William, was pushing his way into politics. The constituency of Wallingford in Oxfordshire had been acquired for William in 1802. After his father's death, he remained a liberal and entirely undistinguished Whig Member of Parliament for twenty-nine years until, at the coronation honours in 1831, he was raised to the peerage as Lord Dinorben, a title derived from an ancient hillfort just above Kinmel.[18]

This may look like an accelerated form of the life stories in this book – a happy sequence of luck, enterprise, money, politics, grandeur and establishment – but all was not well. By his first marriage, Dinorben had two sons and eight daughters; but only four daughters and a single son survived, and that son an 'Epileptic idiot',[19] 'incapacitated, by imbecility of mind, from the exercise of the privileges of his rank'.[20] Everybody understood that he could never be Dinorben's heir. Two of the surviving daughters were weak and, although married successfully to a baronet and a peer, also looked unlikely to survive. Lord Dinorben was faced with the prospect of his nephew, Hugh Robert Hughes, born in 1827, inheriting everything he had.

Dinorben didn't like him. They were opposed politically, the older man more liberal, favouring the abolition of the slave trade, the emancipation of Catholics, Jews and dissenters, the abolition of the Corn Laws and parliamentary reform.[21] The nephew, who would come to revel in his initials HRH, was by instinct a deep Tory, increasingly interested in genealogy and heraldry, three generations away from the raw money-making phase at Parys Mountain and coming to conceive of himself as a member of an ancient family of high standing. The vast estates were strictly entailed: only the male heir to the Hughes line could inherit them but to the end of his life, despite a sequence of disasters, Dinorben manfully struggled to keep Kinmel out of HRH's hands.

Dinorben's first wife had died in 1835 but five years later, in February 1840, when he was seventy-two, he married again, a young Irishwoman, forty years younger than him, whose connections, vim and breedability looked promising: her sister Penelope had run off with Carlo Ferdinando di Borbone-Due Sicilie, Principe di Capua, married him at Gretna Green and soon given birth to the spankingly healthy half-Irish, half-Neapolitan Francesco and Vittoria.

This was clearly suitable stock for a man in Dinorben's position, the mild air of scandal was acceptable in the circumstances and he now fathered two more children on Gertrude, the Princess's sister. The first, a girl, died in infancy. The second, born in 1845 when Dinorben was seventy-eight, was no good either: another girl. It looked as if HRH would come into his inheritance.

This was not a good end to a life. Dinorben's precious eldest daughter had died in 1829; the Irish mother of his putative heirs had failed to deliver; his elegant Wyatt house at Kinmel had burnt down in 1841 after a fire had started in her dressing-room;[22] nothing was insured and the cost was estimated at £35,000.[23] The house was rebuilt as 'a Grecian villa', with Thomas Hopper as the architect, but by the time it was completed, another disaster had struck. Dinorben's fourth daughter, Frances, Lady Gardner, had died in December 1847 and the old man was sunk into an embittered gloom.

At precisely this moment, the young HRH, aged twenty-one and beginning to spread his wings, poked his head up into the Kinmel air. In January 1848, a month after his cousin Lady Gardner had died, he went to stay with Dinorben's neighbours, Sir John Hay Williams and his young family, who lived at Bodelwyddan Castle, a neo-Gothic fantasia even then under construction. It is about a mile away from Kinmel across the park and when staying there, the young HRH committed two cardinal sins: he did not leave his card at Kinmel, announcing his presence to his uncle and implicitly asking if he might come to visit him; and he went dancing at the Denbigh Ball, the annual winter gathering of the North Wales gentry.

Dinorben was disgusted. 'His conduct towards myself has been anything but respectful,' he wrote to Philip Humberston, a Chester solicitor who was HRH's brother-in-law.

> There was no reason why in his first visit to Boddelwyddan he should not at ye least have offer'd his card at Kinmel and none then on my part why he should not have been kindly received. But his conduct on a recent occasion, the indecency of which drew general observations, has greatly offended me & I must forget the unfeeling act of disrespect, the going to a public ball in my immediate neighbourhood ere the remains of my dearest child was cold in the grave, before I can consent to see him.[24]

This is how old people behave when exhausted by grief and disappointment, when the succession of a family-in-a-place looks insecure, but the resentment did not disappear. The following January, 1849, Humberston wrote to Dinorben. HRH ('Hugh') was going to stay at Bodelwyddan again over 'a few days for some gaieties' – surely the wrong word in the circumstances –

> that are going on in the Neighbourhood. And as he will be so near to Kinmell we are Wishful if it would be quite agreable to your Lordship that he should call at Kinmell during his Visit at Boddelwyddan and make himself known to your Lordship.[25]

The language was symptomatically and painfully status aware: Humberston could not allow himself any form of assertion. He could not even 'wish' but merely 'be Wishful'. He never said 'you' to Dinorben, always only 'Your Lordship', as if unable to look the greatness of the man in the eye.

Dinorben replied coldly, explaining how HRH's behaviour the previous year had been so grievous to him, and Humberston was forced to make the excuses. This mid-Victorian thickening of the arteries is a sad decline. Property, status difference, the corset of financial expectation, the loathing of an heir, particularly a brother's son, the implicit bullying of moneyed power: material things had taken over from human relations. It is certainly possible to see in this Victorian tableau a descendant of all the human relationships this book has described; but mid- and late nineteenth-century Kinmel feels like a bleak place to arrive at.

On 13 January, Sir John Hay Williams, HRH's cheerful host at Bodelwyddan, wrote to Humberston:

My dear Sir,

I am sorry to say that no relenting has taken place in Lord Dinorben & consequently we have not called, but Lady Sarah [his wife] has had a communication from Lady Dinorben, & she is very kind in the matter & her advice is that Mr Hughes should write a kind letter to his uncle when he gets to Chester, and that he should express how grieved *he* is that his uncle is somehow alienated from him, who never intentionally gave him any cause of pain.[26]

Back in Chester, HRH duly wrote the crawling letter, of which an anxious, much doodled-on, pencil draft survives:

Chester Monday

My dr Uncle,

On my return to Chester on Sat. evening I read with much concern your letter to my Brother-in-law and am grieved to find that my going to the Denbigh Ball last year should have occasioned you so much pain and displeasure. Had there been the ordinary intercourse of relationship between my poor Cousin and myself I should have known at once what course to pursue, but I was in fact personally a stranger to her, wh. I will hope may exonerate me from the charge of want of feeling toward her memory. And that you will attribute my inconsiderateness on that occasion to youth & inexperience, rather than to any desire to show disrespect or to give you any pain to yr Lordship which I may truly say has ever been far from my intention – With regard to the calumnious reports about me which I know have reached you from time to time, I am confident you will find them either entirely fabulous or gross exaggerations –

Trusting that this explanation may in some degree remove the unfavourable opinion ~~your Lordship has~~ you have formed of me, I hope you will allow myself to subscribe myself

Yr affect. nephew[27]

The letter had no effect and on 10 February 1852, Dinorben died without mending the breach. Five days later, the Kinmel steward, Thomas Williams, wrote to Humberston in Chester:

My dear Sir

I received a note from Mr. H R Hughes this morning stating that he intended coming here on *Tuesday* and I was requested to inform him that the House would be quite full on Tuesday & that it would not be convenient to receive him. Lest he may leave London without receiving my note I shall be obliged by your communicating the substance of it to him as he states he shall be in Chester tomorrow.[28]

The young Dowager Lady Dinorben relented from this angry exclusion and both HRH and Philip Humberston were in the end invited to the funeral. Old Dinorben was interred in the churchyard at St George just outside the park gates and next to his first wife in the stone mausoleum he had built for her, a squat, crocketed, gothic chapel decorated with the Dinorben arms supported by a Welsh dragon and a half-naked Ancient Briton.[29] On each side, there is an elaborate traceried window, stone filled, glassless and blind.

The unmarried idiot son was dead within eight months. The title died with him but his death meant that in 1852 HRH came into his material inheritance. The anger still comes reeking out of the papers. He immediately began a prosecution of the Dowager Lady Dinorben, for £12,000, the residue of a £20,000 mortgage which her dead husband had taken out against the Kinmel estate after the fire in

1841. It is a measure of HRH's bitterness that he did not allow her to keep a penny of it. She had been left lands at Llysdulas by her husband, but Kinmel was entailed to a male heir and the law stipulated that it should come to HRH whole. That is what he insisted on, even though the lands he now owned had an annual income of £27,000 and Dinorben's personal estate was valued at £300,000.[30] It is one of the mysteries of upper gentry life that vast wealth generates meanness.

The story of the following sixty years at Kinmel is of a man relentlessly denying the memory of an uncle who had wanted to exclude him; of a vastly rich Victorian squire who spent the bulk of his life enraged; and of a desire to expunge the memory of having once been the grasping nephew and the anxious inheritor. He had money but he wanted dignity.

In August 1853, less than a year after coming into his inheritance, HRH married Florentia Liddell, the daughter of the vastly coal-rich Lord Ravensworth, and brought her back to Kinmel for what was, in effect, a coronation. Thousands 'of people, comprising large numbers of the élite of the county', came to welcome them at the house, before proceeding 'to the refreshment booths erected in the park'.[31] The newly married couple received gilded tributes from the 306 farm tenants of the estate and their families, a medieval-level gathering of what would have been called 'the affinity'.

To Hugh Robert Hughes Esquire.
Sir,
We your Tenantry residing on the Kinmel Anglesey and Carnarvonshire Estates beg leave with sentiments of profound respect most cordially to welcome you and your amiable and accomplished Bride to Wales, and to offer you our warmest congratulations on your arrival at Kinmel the Hall of your Ancestors to take up for the first time your residence among us. We beg to assure you that we hail the event with feelings of not ordinary satisfaction and pleasure attended as it is with the most auspicious hopes arising from your high and benevolent character and it is our

earnest prayer that the Almighty may be pleased to spare you and yours through a long course of years in the full enjoyment of the choicest blessings of this life and of all the honours connected with your high and influential position in Society.[32]

They were keen that he should have children and somehow get himself a title, that the rupture caused by the difficulty with the Dinorbens should be seamlessly mended.

It was a pair of goals he shared and he soon started on the task, fathering two sons and five daughters on Florentia and ensuring by a deep engagement in the London Season that the family would begin to find its way back into the national élite. Each year from April to early July, when Parliament was sitting, the governing class of Britain gathered in rented houses in Mayfair and Belgravia. There were public events – the Derby at Epsom, balls – but the heart of the Season was the ferocious round of dinners, breakfasts and lunches to which the great of imperial Britain invited each other, a mass bout of concentrated networking, not only to introduce girls to husbands but to establish the social ligatures on which the government of the country relied. Boiled down to its essence, the Season was the meeting of money, lunch and power. Anyone with a hope of acquiring a title would need to thrive there.

The Hugheses' London visitors' book for the 1850s and '60s, a monument to social ambition, has survived.[33] For the three months of the Season they rented 39 Grosvenor Square for about £960.[34] It was a spacious, high-glamour house, first built in 1727, but heavily adapted for the use of its many elite clients.[35] In 1857, the Hugheses arrived in mid-April from the country, spending £92 13s. 6d.[36] on bringing family and staff from Denbighshire. Within a day or two the social life began and it lasted from 23 April until the Season tailed out at the beginning of July, seventy-eight days in all. HRH and Florentia held parties, or at least tried to, on sixty of them, a relentless round of entertainment, gathering in the great and rich of England from the surrounding streets and squares of Mayfair and Belgravia.

The social ambitions were enormous. Among the invitees were 4 dukes and duchesses, 4 marquises and marchionesses, 23 earls and countesses, dowager and otherwise, 12 viscounts and their wives, 40 lords or ladies and 30 knights or baronets and theirs. Very nearly 4 in 10 of the Hughes's intended guests were titled. Along with a scattering of admirals, colonels and politicians – Mrs Gladstone and Mrs Disraeli both came, on separate occasions – the family from Kinmel managed to land 48 members of the titled élite as their guests in Grosvenor Square.

They asked a total of 292 people to these parties but a faint air of unsuccess hangs over the whole business. There were 11 days on which no one accepted their invitations and 15 when they had to make do with a single guest at dinner (33 per cent of dinners with one acceptance or none). Dining with the Hugheses was not, apparently, a hot ticket and it got worse as the weeks went on: a 59 per cent acceptance rate in April, 49 per cent in May and 39 per cent in a catastrophic June. The worst day was 13 June: 7 invitations issued (Mrs Walpole, Mrs Liddell, Dowager the Lady Hinton, Lord and Lady Bloomfield, Lady Charlotte Portal, Mr Beaumont and le Comte Alfred de Choiseul), only 1 of whom, Lady Charlotte, accepted. This was part of a disastrous run between 12 and 18 June when the Hugheses asked 19 people to dinner and only 5 came. It was a house of immense wealth; it was not one brimming with delight. Like old Lady Macleod in Anthony Trollope's *Can You Forgive Her?*, published in 1864, who was 'a devout believer in the high rank of her noble relatives',[37] HRH and Florentia 'could almost worship a youthful marquis, though he lived a life that would disgrace a heathen among heathens'. It doesn't seem as if they were worshipped back.

But there was a political dimension to this. HRH's ambitions to go up in the world would certainly be helped by a seat in Parliament and in 1861 his chance came. In May, Thomas Lloyd-Mostyn, the sitting Conservative member for Flintshire, died suddenly aged only thirty-one and HRH put himself forward. But there was to be a sharp contest for the vacant seat, as the 24-year-old Lord Richard Grosvenor, popular and grand, a younger brother of the 1st Duke of Westminster, was standing as a Liberal against HRH, the Conservative. In a fatal and early error, HRH had split his party by printing an address to the electors in which he ran down the virtues of the budget proposed the year before by Gladstone, Chancellor in Lord Palmerston's government. Gladstone had not only raised income tax to the scandalous level of 10 pence in the pound, or just over 4 per cent; he had begun to canvass the idea that votes should be extended to the skilled working class. Many Conservatives felt great loyalty to Gladstone and would not have him criticized; HRH felt deep antipathy towards him.[38]

The only answer was money and HRH started out on a stupendously expensive election campaign.[39] His election cash book survives, a meticulous account of breathtaking corruption. His first action was to draw out £3,410 in cash from the family bank, which he began distributing to the electorate. Over £1,550 was paid out in varying amounts for 'professional services' to strings of Flintshire gents in all the districts of the county, esquires and reverends happily mopping up the money. Printing and advertising came to a mere £178, but another £1,500-odd in smaller amounts was given to people for 'canvassing', for hire of committee rooms, for refreshments or for service as 'messengers'. Everyone in this class of recipient was described simply as 'Mr'.

These are enormous amounts of money, the equivalent in 2010 of £238,000, using the retail price index as a multiplier, or £2,200,000, using average earnings. The money was distributed to a small electorate over the course of a campaign that lasted just over two weeks. It was a style of electioneering which had long allowed the gentry to buy their way into Parliament and which was only eradicated with the 1883 Corrupt Practices Act.

Setting up election committee rooms in pubs, 'treating', or giving dinner and drinks as a means of persuasion, or even simply handing out cash: all this was part of mid-nineteenth-century electioneering, as it had been since the seventeenth century. HRH's election bill undoubtedly meant he did it all. But to no avail. The Grosvenors had purses just as long and HRH was short on another commodity: charm.

The election was held on Saturday 25 May.

The rival candidates, Lord Richard Grosvenor and Mr. Hughes, were stoutly upheld by their partisans, the former winning the show of hands, the latter demanding a poll. The struggle turned on the question whether Flint approved of the Budget and the Government of Lord Palmerston. Mr. Hughes's seconder, Mr. Roper, openly challenged Mr. Gladstone with using his influence in the county to defeat the Conservatives.[40]

Wales was about to embark on its long and powerful Liberal career, fuelled by the energies of the nonconformist churches. Hughes could probably depend on the votes of his tenants – voting was entirely in public before Gladstone's Secret Ballot Act of 1872 and tenants could not afford to alienate their landlord – even though at least half of them would have been Welsh monoglot speakers and almost certainly nonconformist. This combination ensured that a large landowner would have a head start in any vote but the slightly stuffy, established-church, English-speaking and self-important Conservatism of HRH was not the style of the future.[41] Almost inevitably, 'The Liberal candidate has carried the day,' *The Spectator* reported the following week. 'Lord Richard Grosvenor took the lead at the poll and steadily kept it, ending a winner by a majority of 322. The numbers were: Grosvenor, 1254; Hughes, 932.'[42]

Grosvenor went on to a distinguished ministerial career and a peerage in his own right; HRH never tried politics again and never rose above plain H. R. Hughes, Esquire.

This defeat by a younger, smarter and more brilliant man cannot have been easy and after it, HRH's ambitions and energies went inward and downward. The incomes from the Anglesey mine had for many years been in decline as the orebody was worked out and from now on, Kinmel itself would become the focus of his life. HRH began building there and over the next fifteen years created one of the most extraordinary agglomerations of gentry fantasy grandeur this country has ever seen. In doing so, he spent most of what his grandfather had made for him.

Even before the election defeat, he had done some significant building. Between 1852 and 1855, the Mayfair-based Scotsman William Burn designed a huge neo-baroque set of stables and carriage houses next to Lord Dinorben's 'Grecian villa': manly, rusticated, symmetrical, it could be a mansion in itself.[43]

For the time being, HRH left his uncle's Hopper house as it was and began to attend to the estate, building cottages in the village of St George just outside the park gates, and a little neo-classical lodge there in which a woodman was housed. Just down the road, at another entrance to the park, Burn designed another lodge with thickly mustachioed bargeboarding on the gables and HRH's monogram over another woodman's door.[44]

But in 1866, Hughes met the architect who would transform Kinmel. William Eden Nesfield was thirty-one, at the height of the most inventive and energetic phase of his career. He was comfortable in the company of the rich and grand. There was none of HRH's tense awkwardness about him. He had been to Eton, where his father, William Andrews Nesfield, was the drawing master. The father had become the most sought-after landscape designer in mid-Victorian England, living in comfort in one of the Nash terraces off Regent's Park, and designing elegant gardens among many others for the Dukes of Norfolk and Northumberland (among the Hugheses' guests at 39 Grosvenor Square – the Northumberlands actually came). By the mid-1860s, the son had already designed model farms or dairies for the Earl of Sefton at Croxteth Hall in Lancashire and for the coal millionaire Alfred Miller Mundy at Shipley Hall in Derbyshire.

The young Nesfield was rich, a drinker, a charmer of both men and women, a large-spirited, gifted Bohemian, previously a pupil of William Burn's. Now, with his friend Norman Shaw, he was taking mid-Victorian architecture away from the strict seriousness of Gothic antiquarianism towards a wholly new and more delightful approach, striving for eclectic, witty buildings, filled with light and air. It is not difficult to imagine Hugh and Florentia Hughes falling for this shimmering Nesfield double act.[45]

HRH commissioned a model farm from the son and an accompanying garden from the father, at Llwyni, down on the flat land below Kinmel where he and Florentia could feel happy. They might have been surrounded by, and were certainly drawing their rents from, hundreds of small, under-capitalized and impoverished Welsh farmers, for almost none of whom the great agricultural revolution of the previous hundred years had meant much, and most of whom were living in damp hovels, but that did not prevent the Hugheses from having Nesfield create for them an exquisite, Welsh, half-gothicized, towered Petit Trianon, with carefully drawn and beautifully made ironwork on doors and windows, and a yard with cowsheds and pig pens outside.

By 1866 it was ready, with a dairy, a shaded verandah and a tall dovecot, the buildings scattered all over with flowery 'h' monograms – lower case; the atmosphere too sweet for any 'H's – and coats of arms surrounded by sunflowers in pots.

The father laid out an orchard and 'croquet panel', with a hexagonal rustic hut, a little stream dammed to make a duck pond, with 'strawberry slopes', a 'natural bank for wildflowers', standard currants, raspberries and gooseberries, dwarf apple and cherry standards, a mulberry or spiral pear, a dahlia bed and some cages for 'fancy fowls'.[46]

Inside, there were panels of flowery, stained glass and an atmosphere designed for happiness and delight. The whole place, by intention, was miles away from the angry nonconformists who had failed to elect HRH to Parliament, from the disdain of the dead uncle and from the grandees of the London Season who had refused their invitations to dinner. This was the gentry in wonderfully expensive retreat.

Hughes had now got the taste for building and constructed a new nonconformist chapel and some cottages down on the marshy flats between Llwyni and the coast, largely, it was said, to get the sound of their singing out of the village of St George so that when he and Florentia were at church they could pray undisturbed.

In 1868, more adventurously, and clearly taken with the cheerful and elegant game playing of Nesfield's architecture, Hughes now commissioned from him the beautiful Golden Lodge at another of the park gates. This is a palace in miniature, covered in carved flowers in pots, with disproportionately huge coats of arms, both 'H's and 'h's. Giant dormer windows are bursting with yet more sunflowers under the curved pediments, and a frieze around the whole building is spotted with what Nesfield called 'pies' – the inspiration was from patterns on Japanese porcelain – but which in fact look more like hybrids of sunflowers with *tartes tatins*.

Golden Lodge had left the play-farm architecture of Llwyni behind and looks like what it was: a trial run for HRH's grandest project of all and by far the grandest construction in this book – the rebuilding and quintupling in size of the 1840s house he had inherited from his uncle.

On 25 May 1868, Nesfield made a note in his sketchbook: 'Went to Hampton Court. Mr. Hughes, Mrs. Hughes and children. Mr. Hughes drove his drag – very pleasant – hot.'[47] It seems clear that on that hot May afternoon, HRH asked Nesfield to remake a version of Christopher Wren's great brick and stone façades, to build a new Hughes version of Hampton Court Palace in Denbighshire.

It was, needless to say, no slavish imitation. Nesfield added a set of cavernous, slated mansard roofs above the level stone parapets, but the ambition was palatial. The huge building, after an uncertain start and with some interruptions, was not complete until 1874.

Kinmel Park in photographs tends to look a little stolid and pompous, overblown, a giant French chateau adrift in North Wales. But that isn't the impression when you arrive. It is, first, in a beautiful position, gazing eastwards from its entrance front across the park and the wide expanses of the vale of Clwyd. To the south there is a wooded hill; northwards the view is to the coast and a pale strip of sea. Nesfield's sense of delight is apparent everywhere. As the architect and critic H. S. Goodhart-Rendel described it, Kinmel Park was 'a Gothic game played with classical counters'.[48]

The symmetries of the building are slightly disturbed; the centre of one façade is not opposite the other. Chimneystacks vary in height.

The slightly cooked salmon pink of the perfectly laid brick is set against creamy limestone dressings under green-grey slate roofs. It looks like a house designed more for a party than for power or dominance. Exaggeratedly tall, eighteen-pane sash windows surround the front door and an enormous Queen Anne-ish hood announces the main entrance. A carved keystone above each window hints at the function of the room inside: an owl and a globe outside the library; a tambourine, a violin and a comic mask outside the ballroom; fish, fruit and fowl outside the dining room.

Nesfield's pies are scattered all over the building, inside and out, up in the cornices of the servants' wing, scattered like frisbees on staircases and panelling inside, an attempt to stay playful in the face of the overwhelming bulk of a building which stretches over 500 feet, through various hidden subsidiary courts, from ballroom to stable.

Inside, seven giant reception rooms are laid out in front of you: a hall on the entrance front, a rackets-court-size dining room on the garden front, a saloon beside them, and beyond that an L-shaped drawing room and an L-shaped ballroom, each larger than the dining room. A beautiful breakfast room, with morning sun, is on one side of the entrance hall, a library on the other. You could fit four or five perfectly good manor houses inside this suite of rooms.

Next is a little nest of masculine offices: Mr Hughes's own study and muniment room, where the deeds were kept; a business room for meeting tenants and senior employees; a top-lit, green-glazed billiard room; and a small smoking room or 'retreat'. A giant chapel sticks out of the building towards the garden and beyond that is a maze of service rooms: the knife room, the safe room, the under butler's room, the shoe room, the brushing room, the lamp room, the butler's room, the groom of chamber's room, the china room, the kitchen, the pantry, the meat larder, the cook's kitchen, the scullery, the servants' hall, the bakehouse, the wood room and the WCs. Then you move on to the luggage court, the carriage houses and the stables.

Lieutenant-Colonel Carstairs Jones-Mortimer was taken round the new Kinmel by HRH soon after it had been completed in 1874:

A footman accompanied them to open and close the doors. On entering a small room on the ground floor [the Colonel] asked Mr. Hughes for what purpose it was used. He confessed that he did not know, and enquired of the footman, who, with due gravity, supplied the answer. 'It is used for ironing the newspapers, Sir.'[49]

On the floors above, in a labyrinthine tangle of rooms, stairs and corridors, it is impossible not to get lost. There were thirty principal bedrooms up there and enough further rooms to accommodate sixty-two servants, visiting and resident.

The Hughes filled this vast container with oceans of stuff. When the fortunes of the family finally reached the point when the great house had to be abandoned, it took nine days in June 1929 to auction off the contents.[50] Even then, the greatest of the paintings had been sent up to Sotheby's in London, to a higher-class sale: a Renaissance gentleman by Lorenzo Lotto; a beautiful seventeenth-century *Portrait of a Boy with a Falcon*, thought by Hughes to be by Albert Cuyp, now in the Metropolitan Museum of Art in New York; an early sixteenth-century *Adoration of the Magi* by the Dutch painter Quentin Massys, also now in the Metropolitan; a Calvary by Cornelis Engebrechtsz now in the Rijksmuseum; strings of other Renaissance portraits, including one by Bartolomeo Veneto, several Canalettos and many others.[51]

These masterpieces hung in an atmosphere of overwhelming materiality. When it came to furnishing the Hugheses' gargantuan house, the influence of Nesfield's light aestheticism did not penetrate far. The interior of Kinmel was a world of thickness and substance, of gilt and crimson velvet settees, ebonized torchères, Buhl chests, 'a heavy crimson velvet table cover, with fringe', 'fine feather cushions in magenta silk', eighteenth-century gilt mirrors, 'heavy crimson plush curtains', 'a black and gold lacquer cabinet' and so on almost ad infinitum. A 'small rounded settee in crimson and yellow silk damask', now in the V&A, had been commissioned from Gillows by Lord Dinorben and some of these furnishings were probably inherited from him by HRH. Giant Axminster carpets filled the rooms. The mahogany dining table had seven spare leaves and thirty linen damask banqueting cloths, each 24 x 24 feet, plus another four that were a more modest 20 x 20. There were silver claret jugs and cream jugs, a pair of superb Adam mahogany urns and the most beautiful Paul de Lamerie coffee pot decorated in silver with exquisitely modelled leaves of the coffee plant.

Dead animals played their part: in the Grand Corridor, beside the gong and beater on a mahogany frame and the Queen Anne grand-father clock, two stuffed eagles under glass shades joined a stuffed figure of a pheasant and another of a sparrow hawk, a stuffed figure of an angora rabbit and a 'dessert service of the finest quality'. Further stuffed golden eagles and a selection of stag heads could be found in the Lounge Hall.

The billiard room had its obligatory red leather settees and engrav-ings by Spy. The library contained a valuable first edition of the New Testament in Welsh, tales by la Fontaine in fine eighteenth-century bindings, shelf on shelf of archaeology and antiquarianism, 200 volumes of *The Gentleman's Magazine*, the Waverley novels and untold yardages of genealogy, among them Burke's gloomily entitled 1866 volume on *Dormant, Abeyant, Forfeited and Extinct Peerages*, material for the long sad evenings in which H. R. Hughes Esq. fingered its mournful pages.

Don't weary of this tour: the accumulation of stuff is the purpose of this building. It is a monument to standing and taste, a display of HRH's self-conception as a prince of Wales, a piling up of the rich and old to demonstrate that the mind of the Hugheses was nothing new or vulgar. The chapel had a combined lectern and pulpit in oak and many rush-seated pews. The altar was adorned with brass candle-sticks and 'a very fine altar frontal worked in gold and silver thread and many different coloured silks with the Annunciation on a magenta silk ground'.

Upstairs, great lumps of furniture fill the cavernous spaces of the corridors: mahogany cupboards, lacquered cupboards, a choice Italian cupboard, a Charles I chest in walnut, a massive carved seven-teenth-century oak court cupboard. There were thirty bedrooms suit-able for visiting gentry, all fitted with beautiful antique beds, Japanese screens, hip baths, large enamel hot water cans, japanned coal boxes and writing tables. Every bed had a hair bed and then a feather bed, a white honeycomb quilt, a feather bolster and a down pillow. Some had 'a quantity of specimen shells under a glass shade'. One had a mahogany bidet. Several had engravings of country mansions by John Nash.

Penetrate into the twenty-six furnished bedrooms of the servants' wing – the maids' separate from the men servants' – and the beds were much narrower here, 3 foot 6, with wool mattresses, but all rooms with fireplaces, the furniture mostly painted but some 'grained'. Downstairs, the upper servants enjoyed well-appointed fragments of privacy, with a ruby-red Axminster carpet on the floor of the cook's room, and some repro-Chippendale and ebonized chairs in the house steward's room.

HRH's fiercely exact style means that the existence of his family and household at Kinmel remains carefully accounted for in book after book of figures. Kinmel was, in many ways, life as a list, every book signed off on every page, usually by Florentia but often by HRH himself, either with those initials, or more often as 'H of K', Hughes of Kinmel.

Through the middle part of the century, up until the early 1880s, there were always about twenty-eight indoor servants here and a further fourteen in the stables, serving HRH, Florentia, their two sons and their five surviving daughters (one had died young). The indoor servants and stablemen were liveried when on display, part of the decorative scheme of the house, footmen matched for height and appearance, their wigs powdered. The twenty-five men and boys working in the kitchen garden did not have to wear livery. But the head coachman wore a gold-braided cream jacket and red waistcoat, with silver-plated buttons bearing the Hughes crest – 'Out of a baron's coronet, a demi-lion rampant, holding a rose', supplied by Sherlock & Co. of King Street, Covent Garden – with breeches of thick red velvet, black shoes with large buckles, white cotton socks and a powdered wig.[52]

The extraordinary subdivision of rooms and functions in the plan of the house – a map of human hierarchy from the plushed-up grandeur of ballroom and library at the north end to the steward room boy's WC far to the south – extends into a taxonomy of human beings. It was as if Kinmel had its own system of genera, species and subspecies, an organo-gram of the ideal gentry establishment, descending from the stupendous heights of HRH himself, with his monogrammed linen and the man who came from London to cut his hair, to the menials in the washyard, the underpaid casual labour called 'helpers' in the accounts and those few poor of the parish, usually no more than three or four a week, who received a bowl of soup at the back door.

Leaving aside the head coachman, Edward Bradley (on £45 a year), and the second coachman, Charles Ogden (£30), the world of the servants had two monarchs: the butler, George Nash, paid £80 a year, and the housekeeper-cook, Mrs Selina Moore (on £70). Under the butler were two footmen, William Hambrook and Edward Jarraway (£41 10s. a year each), and a steward's room boy, Ernest Wooding (£20), plus the head lady's maid, Mrs Mee (£32), the second lady's maid, Marie Charlton (£32), and the third lady's maid, Jessie Goode (£25). The needlewoman, Janette Faure (£29), was part of Mrs Mee's department.

Mrs Moore, the housekeeper, managed the head housemaid, Laura Evans (£30), who in turn controlled the second housemaid, Clara Moore (£26), and the third housemaid, Annie Randall (£30). In the kitchen, Bessie Jones was the first kitchenmaid (£25) and she had under her the scullery maid, Ellen Wood (£21). The first laundry maid was Kate Bell, operating in another part of Mrs Moore's empire, on £28 a year, with Amelia Clarke as second laundry maid (£24) and Elizabeth Davies as third laundry maid (£10).[53]

Impressive as this list from 1896 might be, it had shrunk a little from the complement twenty-five years earlier, when there had been a cook separate to the housekeeper, a postillion in addition to the second coachman, two dairymaids, a valet and an under-butler as well as a nurse and under-nurse.[54]

Careful accounts were kept, and signed off, of precisely who was eating what in the servants' end of the house. The weight of meat in the larder was calculated daily (on 1 January 1858 it was 250 lbs)[55] and the strangers dining that day were '5 stable people, 4 gardeners, 1 bailiff, a forester and his daughter, the land steward's clerk, 3 dairy people, the head keeper and 3 of his family'. The postman was also given lunch in the servants' hall. That day 46 people were having lunch in the building: 18 'family' – in the medieval sense of members of the household – and 21 strangers in the servants' hall, plus 3 family in the kitchen, 3 nurses in the nursery and a governess in the parlour. No member of the Hughes family was present.

This was an establishment consuming itself. The money pouring out was enormous and the tradesmen who had to be paid for their wares formed the basis of yet another giant ledger:

Butcher, Butterman, Poulterer, Fishmonger, Milkman, Baker, Fruiterer, Greengrocer, Iceman, Brewer, Earthenware supplier, Glazier, Confectioner, Coalmerchant, Ironmonger, Brushmaker, Bookseller, Cutler, Tailor, Bootmaker, Hatter, Wigmaker, Farrier, Harnessmaker, Sadler, Blackingmaker, Cheesemonger (Paxton and Whitfield), Tallow chandler, China dealer, Upholsterer, Clock cleaner, Newsagent, Auctioneer, Spirit merchant, the supplier of an ice refrigerator (October 1854), Cooper, Timber merchant and Wine merchant.[56]

In this way the accumulated money from the mine, the rents from the hundreds of Welsh farms and the proceeds from the family bank were being distributed around the economy.

There was not much stinting on the wine cellar. On 1 January 1857, it held 2,558 gallons of ale and 1,080 gallons of small beer, as well as 76 bottles of delicious Johanisberg Hock, plenty of Moselle, sherry and Madeira, 244 bottles of 1844 Lafitte, some magnums of 1834 Latour, plenty of 1848 Margot, 251 bottles of sparkling champagne and 130 of still.[57]

Attempts were made to impose some economies. HRH took to questioning entries in the servants' lunch book. 'Carman', the housekeeper entered one day. 'From where?' HRH wrote. In the week beginning 21 February 1858, he placed a big fat question mark against

'Carpenter? Shoemaker? 2 carpenters? Tailer? 2 servants, Mr Edwards Mr Jenkins?'[58] all of whom had been happily enjoying a spot of Kinmel lunch.

The cook was not ordering particularly elaborate ingredients: occasionally some fondu cases but usually 'old ale for ham', potatoes, two pairs of chickens, oranges and lemons, duck and fowls, lamb, tongue, veal, mushrooms, eggs, an occasional salmon, fish from Liverpool and sweetbreads. It was not luxury but the sheer scale of the establishment that was draining the resources.

Everything was ranked, but even so, totals were massive:

Summary of House accounts for 1863

Wages, board and liveries	£1319 5 2¼
Groceries	£529 9 2½
Oil, candles, coal, charcoal and faggots	£447 13 5½
Butcher's meat	£784 10 9½
Milk, cream, butter, eggs, poultry and fish	£474 4 8
Malt, hops and flour	£383 18 11
London house rent and expenses	£1148 3 6
Sundries inc cheese and potatoes, the chaplain and the doctor	£695 5 8½
Coach and stables	£708 1 9½
Wine consumed, 1188 bottles	£297
Total expenditure for the year 1863 after one or two small adjustments	£6770 11 2¾[59]

The emotional lives of HRH and Florentia and their children lie buried within the confines of this vast exoskeleton they had constructed and bought for themselves. At this distance they seem like beetles scuttling around the body an abandoned lobster. The hints that can be found are not happy. HRH used to go shooting and his game book has survived. He was often busy with it, shooting on eighteen days in September 1859, fourteen days in October, but often on his own, or with a single neighbour or Liddell relation of Florentia's. To begin with, the quarry was mostly partridges and hares, but over the years they went downhill and were replaced by pheasants and rabbits. A full-time warrener and keeper were employed but anger and discontent come seeping out through the pages of the game book.

1877–8

Another bad season. Barely a stock of Partridge left on the estate. Hares much diminished in number. And as for pheasants we are entirely dependent upon those reared by hand and many of these were destroyed by wet in July. Discharged 'James Bushnell' who is utterly incompetent. He obtained a place with the shooting tenants at Lleweni.[60]

Bleaker than the atmosphere revealed in the game book is the story told by the Kinmel visitors' book which runs from July 1865 until August 1881.[61] It is a sad and curiously thin document. As the years went by, a decreasing number of people came to stay. In 1865, the Hugheses had 62 people to stay, and the following year 53. But by 1874, when the new house was at least nearing completion, there was no great surge of sociability. For February, March and April that year, over which the Hugheses could have had 2,670 individuals to stay for one night each, in strings of richly furnished bedrooms, with tens of servants to look after them, they had precisely 29 guests, 13 of them vicars or their wives.

In the high visiting season of August and September that year, during which 1,830 people might have come to stay, they managed to invite only 39 guests, nearly all of them for a day or two at a time, including 13 vicars and their wives and a single titled lady, the Dowager Lady Willoughby de Broke (a neighbour), who came for the night of 9 September.

By 1880, when you might have imagined Kinmel would be powering ahead into its full flood of social delight, there were only 28 guests in the whole of August, September and October, the number of reverends remaining high at over 50 per cent (a bishop, a canon, nine vicars and their wives). Of a possible 2,760 bed-nights, some 84 were slept in (guessing at an average three nights a guest), an occupancy rate of 3 per cent. Even for the great celebrations of the Hugheses' golden wedding in 1903, only 13 people came to stay, including HRH's unmarried younger son, his daughters and his wife's relations.

Here is the fact at the heart of this gentry story. For all the money, comfort, the extraordinary inventiveness of Nesfield, all the acres, the flowering lawns, all the servants, the pot plants and grapes brought in from the greenhouses, the mushroom house, the gravelled ways, the palms and cut flowers, the mountains of meat and vegetables in the larder, for all the contacts created by the London Season, the expense, strain and effort of life at Grosvenor Square, nobody wanted to come and stay at Kinmel. HRH was not a loveable or perhaps even a likeable man. The enormous house was never anything like full. The only life it had, the only vitality, deceit, lust and delight, was in the servant's wing. Its grander bedrooms and corridors remained empty for years at a time. Two of HRH's daughters, Frances and Horatia, remained single for the rest of their lives, their parents unable to attract any young man into marriage with them. Kinmel, for all its show, was an echoing sham.

There is a photograph of a tea party, taken in about 1908 outside the huge Palladian mansion of Baron Hill in Anglesey, at which an alert and bearded Edward VII looks at the photographer from among a bouquet of fragrant Edwardian ladies. In the foreground, a slightly louche figure, Sir Richard Williams Bulkeley, the owner of Baron Hill, half-lounges in an upholstered bamboo chair. Behind them all stands the tense and recessive figure of HRH, not princely but disengaged, unachieved, unrecognized by the world in which he had wanted to shine.

Hughes took refuge in the consolations of snobbery. He became the leading expert on the genealogies of the Welsh gentry. He was particularly keen that his own coat of arms, impaled with his wife's, should look splendid on buildings and writing paper. In 1863 he wrote to Sir Bernard Burke, the great entrepreneur of Victorian genealogy, at the College of Arms:

My dear Sir Bernard

The older heralds were frequently in the habit of marshalling the Arms and quarterings of the wife, even when not an heiress, alongside of those of her husband. Will you kindly tell me under what circumstances this is allowable. The effect is to materially enrich the appearance of a large Escutcheon which otherwise looks one-sided and ill-balanced, when the quarterings of the 'Baron' are impaled with the simple paternal shield of the 'Femme' …

Yours very truly,

H.R. Hughes of Kinmel[62]

The nearly medieval language, the split infinitive, 'alongside of', the pretension, the implication he was somehow a 'Baron' by default: none of this can have struck HRH as ridiculous and he steamed ahead establishing the ancient importance of his ancestry. The Hugheses were 'derived by uninterrupted male succession from Cadwaladr, 2nd son of Gruffyd ap Cynan, King of North Wales, and his second wife Dyddgu, dau. of Meredith ap Bleddyn ap Cynfyn, Prince of Powys', while the Lewises, through whom the money had come, were descended from a twelfth-century figure, '*Hwfa ap Cynndelw*, founder of the first of the fifteen noble tribes of North Wales'.[63] For all that, and despite doing his time as High Sheriff of Anglesey and Flintshire, as a colonel in the Denbighshire Yeomanry and Lord Lieutenant of Flintshire, despite his daughter Mary becoming a maid of honour to Queen Victoria, no hint of a title ever came his way.

Over the fireplace in the hall at Kinmel, HRH had Nesfield erect a giant faux-Jacobean overmantle, covered with little Nesfield touches, random pies, sunflowers scattered among the pilasters, but dedicated to a tabular display of HRH's Welsh ancestors and their coats of arms back to the kings of North Wales whose status he longed to match.[64] Fellow genealogists wrote teasingly to him about the low social status of his ancestors, particularly Hugh Hughes in the eighteenth century. 'The various occupations assigned to him are vastly amusing,' he replied.

Such anecdotes die hard. In fact they are imperishable. Even the most amiable people love to minimize a neighbour whose social position is better than their own. You and I do it freely! Not ill-naturedly I am sure, but only to our genealogical proclivities. But I need not tell you that. In Wales more especially, when properties were being perpetually subdivided and 20 years ago the humblest employment was quite consistent with gentle birth and ancient descent. For example you mention Sir Robert Williams. His father in early life was a servant in the employ of the Hollands of Plas Ilsa, Conway. His mother being the daughter of a publican in that town. When it became evident that he would inherit the family baronetcy a subscription was made to pay for his education.[65]

Status was not about money, but deep, inherited grandeur. The family was obsessed with titles as he was. In the photograph album belonging to Mary Florentia Hughes, his daughter, there is a group photograph of a small shooting party at Kinmel in November 1900, surrounded by the signatures of those who had been there:

Lady Frances Gresley
Katherine *Duchess of* Wellington
Honble Alice Douglas Pennant
General the Hon Sam Mostyn
Sir Robert Hurley
Lord Penrhyn
Lord Powerscourt

Each of the guests had signed their names. The words in italic were added by Miss Hughes.[66]

To all the forms of failure to which the Hugheses fell victim – social, political and aesthetic – can be added, finally, the most unlikely: economic. In the great Victorian survey of landownership in Britain, officially called the *Return of Owners of Land, 1873*, but known then and ever since as the 'New Domesday Book', Hugh Robert Hughes, of Kinmel Park, Denbighshire, was listed as owning 15,177 acres, with an annual rental of £19,626. This survey did not include either wood-land or waste and so the figures are an under-estimate. Even so, they suggest that his landholding was already well down on what he had inherited from his cousin twenty years before.

There was also trouble ahead. Already, by 1885, HRH had a mort-gage debt of £52,000 secured on his land. On into the 1890s, Hughes was selling off more of his assets, including the Glan y Wern estate, the Bee Hotel in Abergele, and many farms and cottages, and building land in the new railway-accessible holiday resort of Rhyl on the north Welsh coast.[67] The picture was unravelling; the impetus provided by the now-long-exhausted Parys Mountain was losing its force. HRH had replaced a perfectly reasonable house at Kinmel with his gargan-tuan palace. It was, in retrospect, a ridiculous mistake, a crime against the first gentry principle of survival: take no risks. He was caught in the pincer of a changing world and his own destructive fantasies.

On a personal level, the family was also falling apart. HRH had disinherited his eldest son, Hugh Seymour Bulkeley Lewis Hughes, known as Seymour Hughes. In 1885, he had married Mary Caroline Stewart Hodgson, the daughter of James Stewart Hodgson, a partner in Baring's Bank, and a close friend and patron, among many other artists, of Frederic Lord Leighton. Leighton painted Mary Caroline and her sister Agatha soon after they were both married, in a portrait of adult sisterhood which their father treasured. But then a disaster. Seymour fell in love with a show girl, Florence Treseder, from Newington in south-east London, whose father was stage manager at the Lyceum and whose stage name was 'Lily Maud'.[68] HRH would have none of that and he cut Seymour out of his will. Fred Bradley, the eleven-year-old son of the head coachman at Kinmel, 'well remembered the day [Mr Seymour] came to say Goodbye to them all. He kissed Mrs Bradley and said he would never see them again.'[69] Seymour got a divorce from his first wife, married the show girl and went to live with her in a little cottage on Jersey, where he died in 1918, aged fifty-six.[70]

Florentia died in 1909 and HRH sixteen months later, in April 1911, aged eighty-three. The estate went to a second son, Henry, a bachelor captain in the 14th Hussars and then a lieutenant-colonel in the Royal Engineers. After the 1914–18 war, Colonel Hughes struggled to maintain his inheritance but the legacy of HRH's overpowering need for self-aggrandizement had made it impossible. Much of the park was let out as a military camp. Another 1,000 acres were sold off to the Kinmel Bay Land Company in 1925. In 1929 Colonel Hughes left the great house and sold its contents. The house itself was sold in 1934 and over the rest of the century it became a school, a spa, a military hospital, a school again and a religious conference centre. Colonel Hughes died in 1940, making his sister's daughter, Mrs Fetherstonhaugh, his heir. Her great-grandson Dickon Fetherstonhaugh now owns and manages the 4,000 remaining acres of the Kinmel Estate and lives in Nesfield's wonderful model farm at Llwyni.

As for the great house, a fire in 1975 burned through large parts of it; a property company bought it, failed to sell it and went bust; now (April 2011), largely watertight but empty, it is in the hands of receivers and is for sale at £3.5 million, needing several million more spent on it. It may become a hotel, the destiny it failed to achieve under its creator.

Yeats understood the phenomenon: 'a rich man's flowering lawns' and his 'escutcheoned doors', 'The pacing to and fro on polished floors/Amid great chambers and long galleries', even in their beauty and gentleness, are all monuments to pain:

> Some violent bitter man, some powerful man
> Called architect and artist in, that they,
> Bitter and violent men, might rear in stone
> The sweetness that all longed for night and day,
> The gentleness none there had ever known;[71]

PART VI

The After-Life
1910–2010

Ambivalence hung over the gentry after their social and political decline at the end of the nineteenth century. The democratization of political power, nationally and locally, their accumulated debts, higher inheritance taxes and the decimation of the English officer class in the First World War all combined to erode them. They did far worse than the better-insulated aristocracy, which had stronger links to the world of business and finance, and survived the twentieth century, diminished but surprisingly intact. In the late nineteenth century, the Marquess of Bristol and the Duke of Marlborough had both married railways, the Earl of Carnarvon and the Marquess of Cholmondeley banks and Lord Curzon and the Earl of Suffolk a Chicago department store.[1] Titles were always welcome on company boards, and by 1896 167 peers were being paid as company directors.[2] As a result of this deep penetration of the modern world, 70 per cent of the grandee families that had owned great estates upwards of 10,000 acres in 1880 were still landowners in 1980; 33 per cent still owned between 3,000 and 10,000 acres; and 24 per cent still owned over 10,000.[3] Despite the widespread mourning for the death of the English country house, five out of six that existed in 1900 were still upright and occupied in 2000.[4] The twenty-first-century Dukes of Beaufort, Bedford, Devonshire, Grafton, Marlborough, Norfolk, Northumberland, Richmond and Rutland still live in their enormous art-encrusted palaces and castles at Badminton, Woburn, Chatsworth, Euston, Blenheim, Arundel, Alnwick, Goodwood and Belvoir. The twentieth century turned out to be a perfectly good time to be immensely grand.[5]

It wasn't like that for the gentry. Half of the families in the 1863 *Burke's Landed Gentry* did not appear in the 1914 edition.[6] By the 1920s, so many of the old gentry families had lost their lands that the ownership of land was no longer a requirement for a family to appear in the book at all. Between 1880 and 1980, over half of those who had owned between 3,000 and 10,000 acres went out of land entirely. For those with less than 3,000 acres, the rate of attrition was more like 80 per cent.[7] Although the question of definition is as difficult as ever, at the end of the twentieth century less than 1 per cent of England belonged to the gentry, perhaps 500 families owning 1,000 acres each.

The triple shock of the agricultural depression, death duties and the ebbing of self-confidence had all dealt them a blow far worse than anything they had experienced before. Death duties were first raised on land in 1894 at a rate equivalent to two years' net income. This was about the same as the fines imposed on the Royalist estates by the Parliamentary committees in the 1640s, but the atrocious returns from agriculture and the much better income available from industrial investments or government bonds made the burden more difficult to bear. The Finance Act of 1919 raised that tax from 12 per cent to 20 per cent, a level which encouraged many families to leave land entirely. Between 1918 and 1927, six to eight million acres, including at least 25 per cent of Britain's farmland, changed hands.[8]

Land was no longer the ultimate valuable. In 1880, it was estimated that the estate of the Marquess of Camden, which yielded £1,700 after all expenses had been paid, would sell for £190,000. If that capital sum were invested in government bonds it would yield £5,700 a year. The case was put in court:

One man would say 'I would rather have the £5,700 p.a than £1,700 p.a. – I would rather have the money than the land; and another would say 'If I have enough to live on, as long as I can make ends meet, I would rather have the land, and no amount of money can compensate me for the loss of an ancient estate on which my ancestors have resided and in which many may have been buried.'[9]

If the aristocracy were thinking that, the gentry thought it in spades. Their history in the twentieth century was one of shrinkage, nostalgia and fragmentation. Their lower margins were more indistinct than ever. The land they were unable to hold on to was usually bought by its tenants, so that where 10 per cent of land was owned by the man who farmed it in 1914, that figure rose inexorably to 21 per cent in 1921, 37 per cent in 1927 and 49 per cent in 1960.[10] Approaching two-thirds of all farmland is owner-occupied today.

The effect was that the distinction between the great lords and the gentry widened; and that between yeomen and gentry disappeared. Many gentry families started to till their own land. Many became culturally illiterate. When in 1944 the aesthete James Lees-Milne, Secretary to the Historic Buildings Committee of the National Trust, visited an ageing Colonel Freddy Wingfield Digby at Sherborne Castle in Dorset (Digby headquarters since 1617, the year in which they took it over from a disgraced Sir Walter Raleigh), he found a man and a consciousness which had survived the centuries but had now sunk towards the condition of the unlettered squire:

> The Colonel is a stooping M.F.H. with the manner of one. Very autocratic, very conscious of his not inconsiderable dignity. He took us through the very beautiful wooded walks round the lake. Here we came upon Pope's seat, where the poet wrote letters to Martha Blount. The Colonel showed little interest in these fascinating associations. When I responded excitedly, the Colonel snorted, 'Pope indeed. I've no idea which pope it could have been.'[11]

On cold winter days, the Colonel used to climb one of Sherborne's many towers with his rifle and from there shoot the ice on the lake so that the people of Yeovil, who liked to skate on it, would sink.

The *nouveaux pauvres* clung on in their damp cold manor houses. Many sold up or demolished, incapable of maintaining what the modern world could not sustain. A *Punch* cartoon from the late 1940s showed an old gentry squire dressing down his playboy son: 'Unless you behave yourself, I won't leave the place to the National Trust.' Sherborne remained in the hands of the Wingfield Digbys and their website describes the modern situation:

> In changing times we now act as host to wedding ceremonies and receptions, a country fair, classic car rallies, film crews, sporting events and a variety of other corporate and private events. Our Tea Room serves morning coffees, light lunches and delicious afternoon teas. The Gift Shop has a selection of gifts, souvenirs and our very own Sherborne Castle wines.[12]

The most pitiable word in that list is 'host'. According to Simon Jenkins, Marilyn Monteith, hanging on in Cochwillan Old Hall at Tal y Bont, near Bangor, keeps warm by jumping up and down on a trampoline, because she can't afford the heating.

The two twentieth-century families in this book dance in and out of that mainstream. Both their stories are bound tightly to the question of land and inheritance, not only material but moral and psychological; the first as a theatrical and paradoxical renunciation which in fact carried within it many continuities from its own family culture; the second as a dogged and determined persistence in the face of the deep structural difficulties to which most of the gentry have succumbed and whose threat will not go away.

Renunciation

The Aclands

Killerton, Devon and Holnicote, Somerset

In the eighteenth century the Aclands could walk from the shores of the Bristol Channel in Somerset to the shores of the English Channel in Devon without setting foot on another man's land. That, anyway, was the emblem of the family,[1] an estate that spread from sea to sea. It was almost true. A series of brilliant marriages, with Blackford, Dyke, Arundell, Wroth and Fox-Strangway girls, had funnelled estates into their hands, so that by 1800 Aclandshire stretched to about 45,000 acres spread across the fifty-odd miles from the beach at Porlock, over Exmoor, down the steep, moss-cushioned valley of the Exe, to Exeter and Exmouth, with large outliers to the west in north Devon, around Bude and Trerice in Cornwall and eastwards in Somerset.

The estate shrank a little in the 1800s, but some 35,000 Acland acres survived into the twentieth century. This chapter describes how, in the middle of that century, under no compulsion but with a mixture of high idealism and fierce political ambition, the last Acland squire got rid of every last stick. It was a moment in which the gentry's belief in itself did not exactly die but was turned on its head.

If you sit down outside the limewashed church at Selworthy in the middle of what was once the Aclands' Holnicote estate, you are given an image of what people in this book dreamed of and fought for: a blessed valley, rising to the dark, stag-rich heights of Exmoor to the south, with deep sessile oak and beech woods clinging to the lower moorsides and a skirt of pastures and hedges, coppiced and laid, below them.

Yews stand in the churchyard and there's an orchard of old cider apple trees. In 1828, around the sloping green to the west of the church, Sir Thomas Acland built a perfect little run of thatched, bow-windowed cottages coming down the hill beside a leat, now with wobbly box hedges around their gardens and lichened apple trees inside them. There are wrens in the hedges, toadflax and polypody ferns by the pathway.

It is a little vision of completeness. Inside the church, under a beautiful wagon roof spangled with angels, are memorials to nine-teenth-century Aclands: two young men who died in the 1820s and '30s, victims of the diseased conditions on ships of the Royal Navy's West Africa Squadron, stationed off the gulf of Benin to suppress the Atlantic slave trade; and a brass to their father and brother, succes-sive squires of Holnicote and Killerton, both called Sir Thomas Acland:

> The father and son were in succession owners of Holnicote for more than 100 years.
> They were deeply attached to this valley and devoted to the welfare of its inhabitants. Animated by a strong affection for their hill country home, they constantly strove to render the natural beauty of its surroundings more available to their neighbours and to visitors from afar.
> Let us who come after them gratefully rejoice in their benevolence and follow their good example.

This brass plaque, set up in 1898 by the son of the second Sir Thomas, concentrated every element of the old gentry gospel: land, beauty, neighbours, charity, godliness and leadership. Here, sanctified by the late Victorians, were the founding principles of gentrydom. Only in 'visitors from afar', a phrase from the railway age, can one detect the faintly self-conscious, revivalist tone.

The twentieth-century Acland story is only intelligible in the light of these nineteenth-century roots. The first Victorian Sir Thomas (1784–1871) had been a liberal Tory, doling out welfare to the poor on the estates, building a school just outside the park fence at Killerton, another in Broadclyst just down the road and another in Selworthy. As MP for Devon, he advocated religious liberty for both Catholics and dissenters as early as 1813, fulminating against the extravagance of the royal family, deprecating the conditions in the cotton mills, excoriating the 'horrible and infamous slave trade',[2] calling the game laws savage and the Corn Laws, which kept grain prices high for the benefit of farmers and punished the poor, iniquitous. But he was no burning radical. At the Great Reform Bill in 1832, he finally voted against any extension of the suffrage.

On his estates, Acland was the benevolent despot. Along with his indecipherable handwriting and impulsiveness – 'a walk in London with Acland is like walking with a grasshopper'[3] – he was a man of reckless generosity. One of his friends told him he was guilty of 'benevolent careless self-indulgence' – a finely aimed phrase – 'but not sufficiently considering that the day of self-denial must come, when, in more justice to yourself and your family, present and future, you must restrain yourself'.[4] It was never quite possible to tell in Sir Thomas whether great altruistic gestures were acts of generosity, of egotism or both.

In 1841, he built a new chapel at Killerton. The historian of the family, Anne Acland, described its theatre:

Its whole style reflected the views of its patron. The seats were arranged along the walls, in rows facing each other, so that he could see the entire congregation of family, servants, estate workers and tenants, all sitting in their appointed places. Sir Thomas himself was the presiding figure. Here in miniature, was society as he wished it to be: a paternalistic hierarchy, held together by the cohesive element of Christianity and expressed in corporate worship. Here he could believe in Church and State as one.[5]

These were some of the ingredients in the immensely powerful Acland family tradition, a phrase always abbreviated among them to 'the A.T.':[6] great riches, energy, seriousness, generosity, religiosity and an unquestioned sense of command. There was no doubt the Aclands were members of the governing class.

The second Victorian Sir Thomas was more radical than his father, a friend and contemporary of Gladstone and of F. D. Maurice, the high-minded founder of Christian socialism. This younger Sir Thomas became a Liberal in 1867, and was instrumental in setting up new education policies, but even he was not interested in giving the vote to the unpropertied classes until 'education, thrift and sobriety'[7] had done their work.

In the election of 1885 this Sir Thomas became Liberal Member of Parliament for Wellington in Somerset, his eldest son, Charlie, for Launceston in Cornwall and his second son, Arthur, for Rotherham in Yorkshire. 'Aclands are trumps!'[8] Gladstone wrote to the father excitedly. But the A.T. amalgam of grand humanitarian gentry government, a form of progressive patriarchy, began to break down in this third Victorian generation. Charlie and Arthur came to loathe each other, Charlie taking on the mantle of the rural squire, turning more conservative, his interests local, while Arthur became increasingly important and radical as education minister in Gladstone's 1892 Cabinet. He was the new Labour party's particular ally within the Liberal establishment.

Aclandshire was scarcely part of this democratic ideal: 'The place is full of my former self,' Arthur wrote of Killerton in 1883, 'whom I look at as if a different creature. The huge trees, the big garden, the mass of servants, how grand I once thought all this and seem to dislike it now.'[9] Rather than the smartness of the Charlie-dominated Acland estate, Arthur took his family to Clynnog on the Welsh coast for sailing and sandcastles, where Elsie, Arthur's wife, in her loose Liberty clothes, could indulge the 'high-thinking and plain living' she loved.[10]

When Sir Thomas died in 1898, Charlie inherited the estates: 16,000 acres in Somerset, 15,000 in Devon, 5,000 in Cornwall. He was, according to his brother, 'quite the monarch,'[11] his mind increasingly feudal. It was Charlie who set up the medieval-nostalgic brass plaque in Selworthy church to the gentry virtues of his father and grandfather. The house at Killerton was enlarged with a new drawing room and billiard room. Portraits of Charlie and his wife, Gertie, were added in plaster to the dining room walls, developments at which other Acland noses wrinkled. The whole place 'smelled of beeswax, woodsmoke and freesias',[12] delicious things, thought to be too much by the severer members of the clan.

Under Charlie's and Gertie's guidance, Killerton saw no diminution of the lord-of-the-manor style. Farm tenants came to chapel every Sunday to hear their landlord read the lesson and shake hands with him after the service. If they did not turn up, a Killerton groom was sent the following morning with a summons to the house, where the farmer would be required to account for his absence. The interviews were held in Charlie's study, always followed by a glass of whisky.

A young girl, invited to Killerton, found herself overwhelmed by the experience of this other kingdom:

I remember the excitement of arriving by train at Exeter, where a footman would be waiting for us on the platform looking very smart with a cockade at the side of his top-hat. There was a carriage and pair outside and we were driven out to Killerton with two large Dalmatians running beside the carriage. As we got near Killerton everyone recognized the carriage and the village men and boys all touched their hats, while the women and girls made little curtsies. The footman blew a whistle as the carriage approached the lodge at the bottom of the drive and an old lady, who lived there rent-free for this purpose, came out to open the gate.[13]

There was nothing unique about this. Estate after estate imposed these daily dramatics. As Walter Bagehot had written in 1867, the English were a 'deferential community' in which the 'rude classes at the bottom … defer to what we may call the *theatrical show* of society'.[14] Other Aclands noticed the steep social differences. As Anne, the

355

wife of Charlie's grandson, later wrote, a gamekeeper came to the house every morning to brush the dog, 'but next to the keeper's cottage where the pheasants were raised, there was a family of children so hungry that they came out early to eat the boiled rice and chopped hard boiled egg put out for the birds'.[15]

The world was changing. In 1906, fifty Labour members were returned in the Liberal landslide, the portent of the ending of Liberal England at the moment of its greatest triumph. Charlie had no children, but his younger brother Arthur had a son, Francis, who was therefore heir to the Acland fortunes. Inheritance by the nephew of a childless man has always been fraught. In this case ideological difference exacerbated the problem. Francis and his gifted wife, Eleanor Cropper, the daughter of a rich Lake District paper-making family, were well on the radical side of the braided Acland inheritance. She was a brilliant woman, had got a first in history at Somerville College, Oxford, in 1900, and was a strong feminist and pacifist, a writer and pamphleteer on the Labour end of Liberal. In 1906, Francis was elected Liberal MP for Richmond in Yorkshire, after a campaign in which both he and Eleanor covered the entire, hilly constituency on bicycles, only hiring a car on polling day. 'Where his bicycle won't carry him, he carries his bicycle',[16] his supporters said.

Francis and Eleanor inevitably looked on their future inheritance in the West Country with some trepidation. As she wrote to her sister in 1911, when staying at Killerton, she was

> wondering more and more how we shall tackle the job when it is ours. It's all so alien to us, & I don't see how one can be a good land-lord when one's heart & head are not in the system. We shall probably be horrid betwixt & between, offending our neighbours and puzzling our dependents.
>
> However I think Dick [her eldest son, Richard, then five] shapes for a good old Tory so perhaps he will restore the name of Acland to its ancient prestige. I very much wish he could spend his childhood here & really get soaked in the place as we were in Westmoreland. I keep thinking of Father's happy Christian name sort of terms with 'John' &

James & Anthony. But I don't know if that is possible on an enormous estate – I fancy the land-lord would always be more hedged about with state. Luckily we have three sons & we need not leave all to one.

Dick and Arthur [then three] are enjoying themselves here. It is jolly to be able to turn them loose in a big garden. They play at being polar bears and lambs alternately. You have to be careful if you go too near them when they are polar bears – you generally know which it is by the various noises.[17]

For all that room and space, and the growling games at Killerton, Eleanor was 'not happy at heart about it all'. Francis did not care for the self-importance of the landowning life. His father, Arthur, had refused a peerage, as his father and grandfather, the two Sir Thomases, had both done. He remained in London until his death in 1926. Francis inherited the Acland estates on his uncle's death in 1919, but remained a peripatetic Liberal MP in various constituencies. His career was not a happy one, coinciding with the decline of Liberalism from a great governing movement to a party which split and which, especially in the south-west, was becoming a regional, anti-metropolitan protest group.[18] This was scarcely Aclandish. Large-scale, national, principled government had been their stock-in-trade for generations. After a zigzag career, partly as a minister in Asquith's government, Francis ended up in the 1930s as the Liberal MP for North Cornwall, which he remained until his sudden death aged sixty-five in 1939. The estates were an adjunct not a fulfilment of his life. The idea that landowning and government were two aspects of one vision had now pulled apart. What would become of the great A.T.?

There is one footnote to this Acland pre-history. In 1917, two years before Charlie's death, he had given a lease for 500 years to the National Trust on what the Earl of Plymouth, Chairman of the Trust, a little airily called 'seven or eight thousand acres'[19] of Exmoor. The Aclands would continue to enjoy 'the rents and profits and all the ordinary rights and powers of an owner' but not the ability to develop the land. The acres were not being given away but this was a covenant and the Aclands were thinking of 'visitors from afar'. It was, above all, a public signalling of benevolent intent. Charlie's heir, Francis, thought it 'Jolly to think it'll all be national!'[20]

This was the shape of the inheritance – material, moral and political – which confronted the Acland who became central to their 20th century story. Richard had not been, as his mother had said in 1911, 'at all huggly' when a boy, 'much less than his two brothers'.[21] Bone thin and bird-like (his wife's nickname for him was 'Buzzard', shortened to 'Buckie'[22]), he was a taut, gawky, excitable and intelligent man. He was later described as 'the kind of prefect who is not very good at games but makes up with it by force of character'.[23]

At first, Richard slid straightforwardly into the role the A.T. had prepared for him. He was to be the 15th Acland baronet; immediately after leaving Oxford in 1927, he therefore became a Liberal candidate. 'I just regarded it as my job to put over the Liberal policy,' he wrote later. 'It was just an assumption that I was there to present the Liberal case.'[24]

Even with all the traditional Devon deference to Aclands, Richard lost at Torquay in 1929 and again two years later in Barnstaple. In 1935, he decided to approach the election with rather more vim. 'Acland is the Man', his election fliers said, and there was no doubting which side of the Acland dualism he had come down on. He was up against the squarest of Tories for the seat. 'I've found out I do want to win the election,' he wrote to Anne Alford, the young Architectural Association student he had fallen in love with,

> just because I loath my opponent with an almost uncontainable loathing. A man who is 'very agreeable to meet in conversation' he has no character, no brains, no inspiration, no real concern in bettering the life of his country, plenty of money, & his wife has more, never had a job and never tried to have one, so bone stupid that he has decided the only thing he can do is go into Parliament … I do want to wipe the floor with him.[25]

Anne, an exceptionally strong-minded woman from a prosperous family – her parents lived in Cheyne Walk in Chelsea – was up to this trashing of the Tory enemy. 'I do hope he loathes you back,' she replied. 'It's so much more satisfactory.' In a disastrous election for the Liberals, who were returned with only twenty-one members – there were over 100 Labour gains – Richard nevertheless won Barnstaple – by a squeak; no floorwiping – and became the ninth successive head of his family to take his seat in the House of Commons.

He had kissed Anne for the first time on 16 June 1935 and in April the next year they were married. She had contracted polio as a girl and perhaps in response to that crippling disease had developed a toughness and resolution that were perfectly capable of meeting the Acland strength of mind head on.

The early years of their marriage remain opaque. Before her death in 1994, Anne deposited their correspondence in the Devon Record Office, but she had weeded it heavily. Few letters survive from the late 1930s. Only later hints suggest that relations between her and Richard were not easy. 'It's an added marital suffering', Richard wrote to her in September 1939, 'that we may have to suffer a good deal for each other.'[26] In April 1941, he could look back to a time 'when it seemed quite possible it wouldn't work' as a difficulty they had overcome.[27] His own combination of excitability, self-fascination, sense of destiny and a desire to make a splash cannot have been easy to live with; while her rather dogged need to control the lives of those around her would have made it difficult for her to follow where he led. He also had 'a trademark snort-sniff'[28] to which she became hyper-sensitized.

Certainties were not to hand. Liberalism was dying, the ground taken away from it by the polarized politics of the 1930s. As soon as Acland was elected, he started to drift left, visiting Spain and Czechoslovakia, meeting the intellectuals and activists of Victor Gollancz's Left Book Club and then at Easter 1938, while on holiday at Killerton, experiencing a moment of revelation, what he called an 'imperative suggestion' from an unknown source: 'Politicians are wholly mistaken. People don't need your pandering promises. They have to be told that if they want peace and better times they have to be better people.'[29]

Morality and politics were now fused in his mind. Political leadership looked to him like a kind of prophecy and the following year, as his first son, John, was born, Richard came to realize that the foundation for all he would do in his life would be the radical heart of Christianity. A version of Christian Socialism had been alive in the Acland family for almost a century and so Richard's leftward move was no struggle, no rejection of what his family had long thought. Anne's own radicalism had already been leading him this way. 'There was a time when you were rather dissatisfied with my politics', he would write to her early in 1940, 'because you *felt* Socialism to be right and thought I was content with the policy of the Liberal Party, – so that may be what did it.'[30]

Just at this moment of conversion and radicalization, Richard's father died and he inherited the vast lands and the title that went with them. The 33-year-old politician and his architect wife were now Sir Richard and Lady Acland. 'Do you remember how depressed we were at the prospect of having titles?'[31] Anne wrote to him two years afterwards, and their eldest son, John, later recalled that 'they didn't want the title, they didn't want anything grand, it was just awful for them'.[32]

At the end of 1939, with this new predicament thrust upon him, Richard started writing his great testament, the book which would be published in February the following year as *Unser Kampf: Our Struggle* – one of the Penguin Specials which marked the beginning of the war and became part of the great national debate over the future of Britain and the world.

'What, after all, are we fighting and sacrificing *for*?' Acland asked.[33] He plunged into the debate, feeling doubly qualified: not merely with his newly minted vision of a Christian commonwealth, but with the assumption, given him by the generations of Aclands standing behind him, that he would be heard. 'It is the right and duty of the progressive', he announced in the first pages of *Unser Kampf*, 'not merely to give the people what they do desire, but to teach them what they should desire.'[34] Britain was a wickedly unfair society, in which '1½ per cent of our population are drawing one quarter of the national income'.[35] It was a world built on selfishness, riddled with inequality, envy, malice, greed and strife. There was one thing which lay at the root of all this pain: the private ownership of property. 'Every fifty years, at the year of the Jubilee, which Jesus upheld, the land was re-apportioned to the families, no matter who might have acquired it in the meantime.'[36] That was the model which Britain now had to follow: 'There is no ultimate reconciliation except in a system of common ownership.'[37]

The language of the grandee sometimes crept into the Jeremiads of the visionary. The inequality in modern Britain was 'perfectly hideous'.[38] Few sights were more nauseating than the petite-bourgeoisie:

Snug little men and women with comfortable little jobs or fortunate little investments which bring them in three or four hundred pounds a year deceive themselves, and, what is worse, disqualify themselves from taking a proper part in the councils of the nation, if they form a mental picture of a world mainly made up of snug little people living on three or four hundred a year.[39]

Coming from the owner of 22,000 acres of the West Country, with an annual rental income of over £30,000 a year,[40] that doesn't read comfortably. Nor does the wafting airiness of some of his propositions: 'Would it not be rather wonderful to live in a world in which we did not all have to think about ourselves all the time?'[41]

His plan for world peace was little better:

To banish all risk of war for ever, let there be no more armies and navies and air forces 'owned' by individual countries. In this way, and this way only, shall we be saved from the fear of war. Here surely is an idea sufficiently majestic to stand on its own feet against all the maelstrom of world forces now unleashed.[42]

'Ten thousand little know-alls will rush in to say it is not practical,'[43] he wrote pre-emptively and in places the book was dismissed as an 'uprush of warm-heartedness',[44] but Acland's seriousness and conviction struck a chord. This was not a plea for economic equality, nor a Marxist vision of an essentially material world, but one in which it now seemed right that the dignity of self-possession, the mainstay of the gentry for centuries, should be extended to humanity as a whole. Property was a cheat, a denial of that dignity to others and, according to Acland, it was 'the larger properties [which contained] the larger element of inheritance and swindling'.[45] Only in common ownership could that institutionalized theft be eliminated and true neighbourliness re-created.

One of the ironies of this position, which sent shudders of anxiety through the more conventional West Country gentry, was its profoundly traditional nature, its vision of completeness derived from a golden age, when

> No Fences parted Fields, nor Marks nor Bounds
> Distinguish'd Acres of litigious Grounds:
> But all was common, and the fruitful Earth
> Was free to give her unexacted Birth:[46]

Richard Acland, whether he knew it or not, was as much of a Virgilian as any squire in this book.

Devon nevertheless was agog at the cuckoo of Killerton. As Richard wrote to Anne, he was getting reports of

> intense discussion of 'this man Acland' in the county, *but*, you are not the humble little thing bobbing at the lodge gates. On the contrary, you are the villain of the piece, – … in fact it is strenuously argued that 'if only he'd married someone in the county he would probably have developed quite normally.'[47]

This, he hoped, would make her 'howl with something but I'm not sure what'.[48]

Unser Kampf was a massive and immediate success, selling through printing after printing. More than eight hundred letters came through his letterbox.

Having once made this public commitment to a grand theoretical vision of a new society, Acland could no longer be accommodated within the old political structures. The book's proposals marked a break with anything the Liberal party could sponsor and it slowly became clear that Acland's only possible political future lay in the foundation of a separate movement which would turn in time into a new political party, with Acland as its leader.

Enormous courage was needed for him to stick to his guns. In November 1940, at the opening of a new session of the House of Commons, as German bombers were deep into their campaign to destroy British cities and the morale of their inhabitants, and as the whole of Parliament was surging with emotional support for Churchill in the face of the German invasion fleet then gathered in the Channel ports, Acland had the temerity to stand up in Parliament and say:

> We are in the hands of remote, well-satisfied mandarins far removed from our will. The people of Britain are being asked to make an immense sacrifice for the war. That sacrifice will not be forthcoming unless those who hold personal power over the economic life of the country are prepared to give it up. [49]

Privately, he considered Churchill 'a monster'.[50]

His life continued to polarize. In December, as bombs were falling on London, destroying Euston station and Sloane Square, Anne wrote to him from Devon, asking: 'Have you fixed a shoot? Because you *must*. I think it had better be the Sat. before Xmas & have Audrey and Hedesman as well as the farmers. Tell me what you arrange.'[51] At the same time, his followers and admirers were telling him that he was the natural leader of the 'inarticulate' mass of young people who needed 'a Voice crying in the wilderness, where indeed they are. You are the Voice.'[52]

In January 1941 Richard received his call-up papers and joined the Royal North Devon Yeomanry not as an officer but as a soldier in the ranks, relishing the escape from his class identity. As he wrote to Anne, he couldn't 'get over being an ordinary person,' disparaging 'the fools who think its worth struggling to preserve all the things which prevent them being ordinary people ...'[53]

I've never enjoyed any new suit as much as the uniform … It really is rather fun to go in to a country pub without knowing that everyone there will notice one's smart clothes with resulting 50 per cent drop in the general matey-ness of the atmosphere.[54]

It is difficult to think that Acland could ever pass for anything he was not. In a piece for the *Partisan Review*, George Orwell skewered him on his unsheddable class mannerisms. Acland was

not in any way a man of the people. Although of aristocratic and agricultural background (he is a fifteenth baronet) he has the manners and appearance of a civil servant, with a typical upper-class accent. For a popular leader in England it is a serious disability to be a gentleman, which Churchill, for instance, is not. [Sir Stafford] Cripps [then leader of the House of Commons] is a gentleman, but to offset this he has his notorious 'austerity', the Gandhi touch, which Acland just misses in spite of his ethical and religious slant.[55]

From a more private and forgiving perspective, Anne encouraged him:

The village is divided into those who think it's wonderful of you to have gone into the ranks, those who think it's Mad Acland, & those who think it's frankly indecent. "T'isn't right for Sir Richard to be sitting down at the same table as my Tom might be' as Marjory said. Proportions are about 4:2:1.[56]

How does one look at this man seventy years later? Was this posturing, a game played by the profoundly privileged, toying with the sensations of a virtuous simplicity, a Petit Trianon of the self, thinking property irrelevant because he had so much, doing what his ancestor Sir Thomas four generations back had done, tossing off acts of 'benevolent careless self-indulgence'? Or was this a claim on deep principle, an engagement with the possibilities of a good society by a man whose entire family culture had led him to this point? Was it vision or self-regard? Was Richard Acland's career a monument to love or self-love?

The war forced Richard and Anne Acland to lead largely separate lives. Their correspondence is full of regret, of each missing the other. Sometimes she felt 'how utterly tasteless life is without you';[57] sometimes she told him to 'try & wash all over as much as you can & not sleep in all your clothes.'[58] He re-iterated his love for and devotion to her: 'As time goes on I want you more & more & feel more angry with the whole war for robbing us of each other.'[59]

But there was also the feeling that each of them was pursuing their natural bent, on separate and parallel paths: he increasingly busy with the often febrile creation of the new movement; she with the running of the Devon and Somerset estates and their own family. It was a role that started to grow on her. 'I hate being Lady Acland when I am not in Devonshire,' she wrote to him in April 1941, after visiting her brother. This was an extraordinary and inadvertent confession. In Devon the socialist architecture student had become Lady Acland. 'It seems natural there & I don't think about it but it's horrid being my-ladied by Billy's maid.'[60]

She got pregnant again on one of his visits home, but the management work continued. Tom Jeffrey, the Killerton agent, told her that the estate masons were being 'lazy': '(He would.) I have had a nice long morning in the office & have things in hand.'[61] 'Mrs Glen has left Dr Glen after a frightful midnight row involving jug throwing and the village policeman',[62] but for all that Devon

really does feel like home to me now. Today Waifs and Strays Committee, tomorrow rent audit & I am more and more glad that you are not home this week. We will have a heavenly time when you do come with peaceful pregnant picnics in the bluebells.[63]

He often told her of his triumphs at meetings and rallies and she replied, a little lonely:

How I wish that I could just invent some story of overhearing some-body saying I was absolutely marvellous but I can't. However I am very glad *you* did darling & I happen to think you are too, so there. I feel quite extra fond of you tonight.[64]

They were playing their traditional gentry roles. Richard was promoting his great idea, persuading business to back it, gathering supporters, travelling the country, canvassing cities in the north of England and in Wales – 'What an amazing thing to be living and bringing up children at a time like this,'[65] he wrote to her – while she was 'spending every morning in the estate office, & every afternoon going round the estate men and round the farms'.[66] There were 30 estate staff, 30 farm tenants and 120 cottage tenants to see to. 'Wages were paid every fortnight from a Gladstone bag fetched by myself from the bank.'[67] But she was also falling in love with the 'red Devon cattle and the cream cob walls'[68] of these damp and fertile valleys.

She suspected the Holnicote manager wasn't telling her everything he should, worried about the estate saw mill, bought seventy-six presents at Christmas for the estate children, thought of handing over the private Acland schools at Holnicote to the County Council and was always looking to the bottom line. In 1941–2, after all costs had been deducted, Holnicote and Killerton ended up making a profit of £1,300. Richard had paid no attention and apologized to her:

I'm wondering if you are feeling pretty peaved about anything because quite honestly I think you have every right to be if you aren't, because although it was something that we mentioned on the telephone, I didn't write a word about the £1300 profit on the estate. I do think it incredibly good …[69]

'Someday,' the innumerate Acland told his wife, 'I must get someone to explain the whole business from the start in words of two syllables …'[70]

In the summer of 1942, Richard merged his new movement, called 'Forward March', with the '1941 Committee', a similar group around

J.B. Priestley, to form Common Wealth, a political party in all but name, committed to common ownership and a moral vision of politics which embraced the idea that individual ambition and desire should come second to the needs and requirements of the community. The three large parties in the wartime coalition had entered a pact not to compete against each other in by-elections. Common Wealth was not bound by that truce and the prospect opened up of their winning by-election seats as they arose. 'I've never known a more tense or exciting situation,' Richard wrote to Anne in April. 'I am wonderfully hopeful.'[71] The old loathed political establishment might now begin to suffer:

> It is rather beastly of me, but after all these years of looking at the smug confident faces of those men who can't think of the possibility of their not being the ruling class, I do wish I'd seen them when the first shadow of impending defeat spread across their path.[72]

It was a form of visceral hatred more appropriate to the 1640s than the 1940s, but moderate accommodation was scarcely Acland's style.

The two realms of their lives, the West Country estates and Richard's national political ambitions, now began to converge. Money was the motivating factor. If Common Wealth was to fight a series of by-elections, it needed funds to set up an organization in the constituencies. At the same time, the Acland family advisers were worrying about the impact of death duties on the estates. The tax on death had been introduced in 1894 and raised to 10 per cent in 1910 by the Liberal chancellor, David Lloyd George, one of Arthur Acland's protégés. Since then it had risen to 20 per cent and was now in danger of eroding the great inheritance. It was only sane to do something about it.

Through 1942, the Aclands slowly picked their way through this double problem. 'Unless we do put by for death duties we shall certainly have to sell Killerton or Holnicote next time,' Anne wrote to Richard in February.[73] Should he insure his life to create a death duty fund? The question was asked against the rather awkward background of Richard's campaign to rid the country of all private property. Anne had her answer:

If the system changes, well & good & the whole thing will be forfeited anyway but if this system should go on, the two estates might just as well be owned by us as by some horrible absentee speculator ... I found a celandine in bud yesterday.[74]

Her attachment to the estates, and perhaps to the standing that came with them, was deepening even as his vision of a new world was opening before him. But they could at least be united, from their divergent points of view, against the unspeakable vulgarity of the 'horrible absentee speculator'. The deep Christian socialist and the increasingly gentrified estate manager could hold hands over that particular form of snobbery.

Anne was certainly under strain that summer. Exeter had been blitzed in May and all the estate records destroyed in the solicitor's office where they were kept. She was having to copy them all out again from the tenants' own agreements. A bombed-out family of six was living with them at Sprydon, their house on the Killerton estate, and sniping at her for the way she looked after her own children. Her hay fever and migraines were getting worse. Ethel, the nanny who looked after the young boys, was called up and Anne was left with no help.

By the end of June 1942, the Aclands had managed to agree on a plan. They would sell five farms, the beautiful quintet of Hindon, Wydon, Wilmersham, Buckethole and Stoke Pero, all on the borders of the Holnicote estate in Somerset, as well as the Falcon Hotel at Bude in Cornwall and two further farms near it. Marginal properties were to be cashed in so that the ancient core could be preserved. The money generated would pay for death duties, investment in the estate and what was rather grandly called 'education policy' – school fees for their sons. 'I feel fairly sure myself that the money will be more use to us than the farms,' Richard wrote to Anne. 'The real body of the estate proper will not suffer by their loss.'[75] Not much evidence in those words of the gospel of common ownership. 'I *think* the policy which I suggest will be so much more fun – and much more satisfying – for you, and, if politics turn bad on me, for me, than the death duty insurance plan.'[76]

And yet, alongside all this, in this crucial letter from Richard to Anne written on 30 June 1942, there are signs of his sensing a divergence between them.

> I think we have, now, a fairly high determination to make a good show of the estate. At the moment this determination is in you, rather than in me; and if politics go in such a way as to take up most of my life, I think this will perhaps always be so.[77]

'Changes in the war and in politics are affecting my feelings about the estate too,' he wrote a little ominously, 'and a lot of things are tied up together ... Taking the much longer term view of the potential developments does mean to me that the long term problems of the estate become very much more real and alive to me.'[78]

Despite these inner rumblings, the future must have looked pretty settled to Anne and the advisers. The Acland inheritance was to be secured. But there was a problem: this solution could provide no money with which to further the fortunes of Common Wealth, which was then, as it would be for the rest of its life, desperate for cash. Besides, it was inherently and philosophically unstable for Richard Acland to be feathering his ancestral nest while saying the sort of things he was saying in public. In *The Forward March*, a sequel to *Unser Kampf*, he had written this:

> Whatever there is of hardship before us, that we will share; whatever there is of toil, that we will share; whatever there is of gaiety in our struggle – and there will be much – that, too, we will share; and in the years to come, years after all not so far distant that we may not ourselves hope to see them, years when we shall have rebuilt this land fairer and nobler than it was before, why then all that there is in it of wellbeing, that too we will share.[79]

There was not much room in that for 'avoid the taxes', 'secure the estates' or 'plan for the school fees'. He was in a muddle.

Here, though, at the critical juncture, the record fails. Between mid-summer 1942 and January 1943, next to nothing has been preserved in the Acland archive. Anne destroyed it all. All that remains is a single-page document written by John Acland, Richard's and Anne's eldest son, in the 1970s and annotated by Anne in 1981. It is now in the Devon Record Office, and known to the Aclands as Anne's 'Final Testament'. It consists of little more than hints and suggestions but it is the best evidence for what happened at the great crisis of their lives. Like the tradition from which it emerged, the story is a complex, woven and plaited thing.

Until the beginning of October, 'there was no idea of getting rid of the estate in anybody's mind'.[80] Richard then came home to Sprydon for the weekend of 8–11 October 1942. Common Wealth was in dire financial straits. 'It is suggested that estates are sold & money given to C.W.' Acland was removing the muddle at a single blow. His life from now on would be one of singular integrity. 'A[nne] resists very strongly. Period of wrangling till Xmas. The estates are important not only as property: they are communities of people for whom she feels responsible. It can be assumed that letters about this have been destroyed.'[81]

The arguments between them were undoubtedly bitter and brutal. The evidence is a letter written by Richard to Anne in January 1943, after the Sturm und Drang was over and they had come to some kind of reconciliation. He was waiting for the train that would take him back to Westminster:

Taunton waiting room
  5 January 1943
  I can't tell you how much I'm glad to hear you say so firmly that we *won't* live our lives apart. I'm sure for us and the children this is more important than any other decision we could possibly make.[82]

She had threatened to leave him over this, playing as her stake the family's happiness and the survival of their marriage against his drive for political significance.

What exactly had happened is not clear but it is likely that through the autumn and early winter they had been at war. All year, politically, Acland had been driving ever further from the Churchill-loving consensus, saying at the London conference of Common Wealth that 'the war was being conducted by men who regarded it as an unfortunate interruption to business life'. Others at the conference described Churchill as 'the leader of the party of privilege and stupidity'. Only they understood the necessary place of goodness in national life. 'Political and economic decisions must be governed by morality instead of expediency.'[83] It is possible that for Lady Acland, confronting the daily management decisions of the estates, this grandstanding was exasperating.

After Christmas, Richard and Anne went for five days together to Mevagissey on the Cornish coast to work things out. Anne's 1981 final testament says as much:

> During this period I am sure that we hit upon the idea of giving the estates to the NT, reserving some cash to buy a London house for after the war *and* give a considerable sum to CW. This compromise satisfied R's scruples about private property and my own concern for the long-term well-being of the estates. Having come to this decision we presented a united front to everybody without pretence & have always maintained it.[84]

But it wasn't quite as neat as that. Papers in the National Trust archive reveal that as early as October 1942, the Trust opened negotiations with the Aclands to buy the freehold on the 6,000 acres of Holnicote land which Charlie had leased to them in 1917.[85] Richard Acland sent the Trust a valuation for this land in the course of November and in December the Trust decided to buy it, even if at a price lower than Acland had offered.[86]

The critical point is that the National Trust was already in the frame before the Cornish holiday, not as the possible recipient of a gift but as a buyer of land at commercial values. In February the following year, in widespread publicity from which the National Trust and the

Aclands both emerged glowing with virtue, the entire transaction was portrayed as a gift. Richard's own statement, reported in the *Guardian* on 27 February 1943, was explicit:

> What we are doing is ... the only thing which can keep the estates together as they are now and prevent them from being spoiled at any time. I do hope that nobody will think that giving them away is any very terrific thing. It is an extraordinarily small thing in comparison with thousands and thousands of people all over the world who are at this moment willing to give their lives.[87]

A leader in the same paper made the convenient political point:

> Sir Richard, who comes of a public-spirited and Liberal line, has chosen to give all while it is still unspoiled to the nation, to let it enter – to play on the name of the new party he leads – into the 'common wealth' of his fellow-countryman.[88]

The *Observer* the following Sunday said it was 'thanks to the generosity' of Sir Richard Acland that 'a great expanse of fertile and beautiful soil' was now 'a piece of common wealth'.[89] 'I do think this whole business comes at a *very* good moment politically,' Anne wrote to him that week.[90]

But it was not entirely a gift; it was a mixed bag, part gift and part sale. A rough outline of the deal had been agreed in January 1943 before the announcement, but its details continued to be worked out through the year that followed. There were one or two obstacles to overcome. First, the debts: £21,000 of death duties still owing on Richard's father's estate, plus £11,000 accumulated debt. (For corresponding 2011 sums, multiply these figures by 100 – a total debt equivalent to £3 million.) Acland also needed between £7,000 and £10,000 for a London house suitable for a party leader (2011: £700,000 to £1 million). Common Wealth, which won its first by-election in April, needed large amounts of money and the boys had to be educated. Various sums were in play but by the autumn the arrangements had come clear. The National Trust would have to commit £178,000 to the acquisition of the Acland lands, a total it could reduce to £134,000 (2011 equivalent c.£13.5 million), by then selling off the Bude estates for £44,000.[91]

Richard Acland's champions in public could inadvertently find themselves coming near the bone. 'It is particularly satisfactory that there have been so many gifts to the Trust during the war' – Beatrix Potter had just left the organization 4,000 acres in the Lake District – the *Guardian* leader writer said in February 1944,

for this is a time when speculation in land is apt to be dangerously active and may be particularly mischievous in its results. Sir Richard Acland, who has been most unfairly attacked for his public-spirited action in transferring his estates to the Trust, could, for instance, have sold them for £150,000.[92]

That was no more than 10 per cent wide of the figure he actually received. In private with the National Trust Acland was forthright:

I am not giving you all my property. I am keeping some of it to live on, some of it to buy a house, and some of it I am giving to Common Wealth. With what is left I pay off as much of the debts as possible, and then hand over the rest to you, leaving you, I regret to say, to look after what is left of the debts.[93]

One of the greatest ironies of this story is the source of money which allowed the Trust to buy Acland out. In September 1942, Mrs Ronnie Greville had died in her suite in the Dorchester Hotel in London.[94] She left Marie Antoinette's necklace to the Queen of England, £25,000 to the Queen of Spain, £20,000 to Princess Margaret and £10,000 to Osbert Sitwell. Much of the rest (a total estate worth £1.6 million, equivalent to £170 million today) went to the National Trust. She was the stepdaughter and heir of the Edinburgh beer king William McEwan, inheriting two-thirds of the brewery, and had lived a luxuriant and opulent life at the heart of the Edwardian establishment, afloat on oceans of bitter, fawning on the court and feeding the ancient aristocracy. 'One uses up *so* many red carpets in a season,' she said famously.[95] She found Hitler charming and Americans acceptable only if they were plutocrats recognizably equal to herself. Cecil Beaton saw her as 'a galumphing, greedy, snobbish old toad who watered at her chops at the sight of royalty … and did nothing for anybody except the rich'.[96]

The Aclands would not have liked Mrs Ronnie Greville but it was her money that the Trust drew on for Holnicote and Killerton and which allowed Richard to make the greatest philanthropic gesture of his life. This is not to suggest it was an act of hypocrisy on his part. The Aclands held on to some beautiful things, eighteenth-century family silver plates and dishes, portraits and landscapes, a group of family miniatures, an early nineteenth-century piano, which they kept at Sprydon; they were able to buy a nice house in Hampstead at 66 Frognal Street; there was to be an education fund for the boys; and Common Wealth received about £65,000, allowing it to win two more by-elections. Apart from that, the Aclands were left essentially propertyless. They kept the right to a flat in Killerton rent free (later transferred to the tenancy of Sprydon) and one of the pretty thatched cottages at Selworthy, but otherwise the inheritance had gone and they entered a strangely weightless, post-gentry world in which murmurings of their past hung on like ghosts in the landscape.

The 'Memorandum of Wishes' which Richard presented to the National Trust enshrined that gentry world.[97] On both estates, 'the tenants, many of whom have been in occupation for a great number of years, are to be sympathetically treated … In case of any doubt [over the employment, dismissal and pensions of the staff] the National Trust will consult me or Lady Acland.' The foremen at Killerton and at Holnicote, the forester, gardeners and gamekeeper, Mr Cornell, were all to be carefully looked after. 'Mr Cornell had an extremely bad time in the last war, and generous treatment is called for.' The Trust was to continue with annual payments to local charities and the traditional fortnightly dole to the old and widowed. Richard asked that the family should retain some rights over Selworthy, including the gift of the living at the parish church.

The leader of Common Wealth was also to remain a country gent. 'I desire to have permission to shoot game limited to 30 pheasants off each estate in any year, such shooting to be arranged as to suit the convenience of the shooting tenants.' He was to be allowed to fish with one rod on the reservoir at Nutscale.

The public vision was there: 'I hope all the mansions will be made available for public or semi-public purposes including agriculture, horticulture or forestry or as holiday centres,' but the Aclands were to be consulted on any tenancy agreement or any new building. In many ways, the world would notice no change:

> I have already arranged that Stag Hunting and Fox Hunting is to be permitted on the Holnicote Estate so long as the sport is carried on over a substantial part of the adjoining lands and I hope that every effort will be made for the opening meet of the Stag Hounds to be held at Cloutsham as heretofore.[98]

It was to be change with no change, a perpetuation of the great A.T. under a new form of common ownership whose nature and style the Aclands would oversee. 'My goodness I do feel jolly about the National Trust,'[99] Richard wrote to Anne from his campaign hotel in Midlothian in January 1943, and you can see why.

Their sons were not consulted; they were too young. The political impetuosities of Acland's life meant he could not wait until they were old enough. The family's own employees and advisers restricted themselves to saying that what Sir Richard had done was 'a high-minded gesture'.[100] Anne's conservative family was appalled. She wanted an education fund set up, as she wrote to Richard, explicitly because of

> people like my brother Dick who will be a perfect nuisance in any case I dare say & who will certainly suspect you of plunging us all heedlessly into destitution. But if we can say oh no it's all settled & we shall have

so much a year, about, & the education business is so & so, they will be stymied. People will think us pretty improvident & sudden in any case you see so we'd better not appear madder than we need.[101]

The West Country gentry disapproved, but with more of a sense of pity than contempt. Richard's and Anne's second son, Robert, asked a cousin 'how my father was perceived in the neighbourhood and she said "They thought he was fool, a sincere fool."'[102]

In September 1943, Anne had to give up running Killerton. The Trust installed its own manager, 'a fully qualified man of about 55 called Senior',[103] and at the end of January 1944, the public handover was made at two ceremonies, one in Broadclyst near Killerton and another in Allerford near Holnicote, at which Richard explained that the ownership of such an extensive property had been 'an increasingly heavy burden on my conscience'. Unless he had made 'gifts of this kind' death duties would have picked away at the estates. 'This would mean that farms were sold over the heads of tenants, desirable building sites would be sold to builders.' At the end of the ceremony, 'Sir Richard and Lady Acland were presented by the tenantry with a painting by Mr. A.J. Munnings, R.A.'[104]

The Aclands no longer owned Aclandshire but the nature of the 'gift', as it was always called, remained deeply ambivalent. The gentry were 'giving away' their property so that in future it could continue to be as it had been before, under long gentry guidance. Giving it away was a means of keeping it. As the tenantry had been, so it would be. But this act was also portrayed as a moment of heroic selflessness. 'Transferring this property to the people', Richard said at the ceremony, was 'the only right and proper course' he could think of.[105] It was a grand political gesture on a national stage and it put him in a powerful position within Common Wealth. Through 1943 and 1944, he built a large following in the country, as a man of integrity, a politician who had done what he urged others to do. He might have been laughed at in the House of Commons for describing ICI and Standard Oil as 'creatures [that] bear all the hallmarks of a dead-end', for urging that 'private ownership of all substantial resources must now be supplanted by common ownership' and because 'he often intoned his speech' with 'a seer-like earnestness',[106] but beyond Westminster those failings were an advantage. His millenarian habit of mind and phrase found a response in a country which wanted no return to the compromises and social and economic failures of the 1920s and '30s. Acland the politician was the man who had denied himself everything his inheritance had given him. The fact that he had also denied that inheritance to his children, and that he would spend its proceeds on supporting the marginal and eventually futile political party he had founded, was never raised in public.

A deep, hidden swing to the left had gathered pace during the war but in the electoral truce between the big parties, only Common Wealth could capitalize on it. The party's 10,000 members were middle class and excited by the transformative visions Acland spun for them. 'It is essential to us to resolve that all the banks, all the land, all the railways, all the harbours and all the factories, except small one-man concerns, are going to be owned in common and worked by all,' he repeatedly told them.[107] In April 1944 he said that the Duke of Westminster should have his lands nationalized and His Grace should be compensated with '£1,000 a year for life and after that to his son nothing'.[108]

On these egalitarian promises, Common Wealth won in West Derbyshire in February 1944, and again in Chelmsford in April the following year, but as soon as the Labour party put up candidates in the general election of 1945, Common Wealth's support collapsed and the party folded. Despite Acland's enormous donations, it had run out of money. He lost his deposit fighting Putney for the party, where he came a devastating third to Labour and Conservative. He then joined the Labour party and was elected Labour MP for Gravesend in 1947, finally resigning in 1955 over the development of the H-bomb. But his political career had effectively ended in 1945. The war had seen the crisis and the climax of his life. The family recognized it. Soon after the election in 1945, they sold the Hampstead house which was to have been his base as party leader in London.

In Devon, the vision of happiness had not materialized either. In the spring of 1945, William, a fourth son, to join John, Robert and Henry, had died shortly after he was born. The relationship with the National Trust and its manager, Mr Senior, soured. The Aclands and the Trust fought over the minor ingredients of the place: should a favourite tree be felled if it had dropped a single limb; should Anne's ideas for rebuilding the village hall be followed; how should the garden be divided outside their flat in Killerton?

The lack of complete control was painful and Anne wrote to Richard in March 1951:

> The Tomkins [farm tenants] near reduced me to tears with more tales about Senior and the Trust. I do feel so terribly our continuing responsibility to the estate & that when I go away things will be even worse. I wonder if we could make out that they are not carrying out the memorandum of wishes? They're not, in the spirit.[109]

All this came with the territory. Right up until the end of his life, Richard was niggling at the Trust over the direction of the estate, even in 1984 wanting to clear up 'one of the main points which has caused difficulty and misunderstanding between us in the last year or so' and suggesting to the Trust's Regional Director that he insert a new clause into their agreement:

> It is agreed that, unless there be some strong reason against it, the traditional practice of the Killerton estate (in so far as it can be ascertained) and not the judgment of the Trust's officers shall normally be the decisive factor.[110]

Needless to say, the keepers of the flame and the arbiters of what was or was not the Killerton tradition – the new morph of the ancient A.T. – were always going to be Richard and Anne. The Regional Director, P.W. Broomhead, saw this as something that gave 'the Aclands the final veto on what does and does not happen at Killerton rather than the Trust'.[111]

The Trust's solicitor recognized the realities, replying to Broomhead: 'I believe you should accept that Sir Richard and Lady Acland have the last word for as long as they live as they have always had in the past.'[112]

The ambivalence of the twentieth-century Aclands penetrated far into their lives. Henry Acland, their youngest son, who taught sociology and social policy at the University of Southern California, remembers the atmosphere in the 1950s:

> It was confusing because we were still the emblematic, the symbolic and yet the quite real family on the estate but our power had now gone, our real basis for authority and position had departed. We were special but not.
>
> You know that the estate workers were expected to attend church in the old days. We kept up a version of that, sitting in our special pew, in Killerton chapel, quite near the main house, with a sense of looking round and seeing who was there and who wasn't. That went on well into the 50s and 60s.
>
> It was all about the residue of this culture. My mother even re-instigated the tenants' dinner, an annual event when the tenants would gather, full of bonhomie and camaraderie. She expected my eldest brother John to go along. But the Acland business at Killerton was over. I know John hated it.[113]

In Henry Acland's memory, his mother was the source of this form of social antiquarianism, as a kind of theatre of nostalgia. She was quite at ease with it, as she was with the visits 'to have cups of tea in tenants' houses', always agonizing for the boys. His father was the opposite,

> a person wrapped up in his books. He had a saying: 'I love humanity but I don't like people', and he was very awkward socially, he didn't have an easy touch with people. I remember him describing the experience of arriving at a dinner party and the person to each side of him turning to the person on the other side ...

He loved to entertain and be jolly, but the more I have thought about it, they were always set pieces. He didn't improvise. So he would carry around a piece of bright blue string, and he would do some string figures, his party piece. That is how he related to children. He wasn't genial. At some profound level he was not at ease.

In the Fifties, Anne seems to have become an increasingly severe and controlling presence in their lives, the holder-together of a family which had disappointment at its heart.

She wasn't a natural mother. She was so gobbled up with her own emotional landscape she didn't have a lot of room for other people's. And her view about upbringing was Spartan.

I wondered how the sons had taken the story of 'the Gift', when they realized what had happened?

John was furious. It was never a focused fury but he did go up against our parents. He did say, 'You have made a mess of my life. If only I had inherited, particularly the Holnicote estate, or what was left of it, everything would have been fine. That was my birthright, you took it away.' Just bedrock resentment that this opportunity had been denied him.

After a career as a teacher, first in East Africa and the Karoo, and then in Cambridge and Bristol, John came with his family to live on the Killerton estate at Sprydon, inheriting the baronetcy on his father's death in 1990. His younger brothers, Robert, who lives in Kentucky where he is professor in micro-surgery at the University of Louisville, and Henry, who between 1970 and 2010 was at Harvard and then in California, made their lives away from this troubled and knotted piece of landscape. 'My solution to the situation would have been for us to have left completely,' Henry says.

This strangely complicated, mixed experience of being there and not being a real part of it … If I could rewrite history I would say 'OK we are giving it to the National Trust, good bye, we are leaving, we don't have a role to play here any more.'

Only recently does Henry Acland feel that he has got his relationship straight to the place and to his family structure. Richard and Anne had decided that his elder brother, John, should inherit all the ancient possessions of the family which they had held on to. The other sons found it difficult when Richard and Anne and then John himself sold off most of that silver and the pictures. 'I did raise objections,' Henry says. '"This ain't fair. If you are going to liquidate stuff, it should be shared." And they did for a year or so but not for long.'

More than the questions of money and material objects, the longest-lasting residue of the decision made in the winter of 1942–3 is the painful combination of attachment and rejection which Anne and Richard's children have felt for the rest of their lives. I spoke to Henry Acland in January 2011. He was then sixty-seven, a tall, bony, handsome, clever, unmistakably Aclandish man, now back in England after spending his working life in Los Angeles.

HENRY: So long as I played along and was agreeable and signed up to the family story about the Gift and Richard's role and the subsequent history and primogeniture being used as a way of handling this problem, I felt that perhaps by remaining a player in this situation there might be a redemption somewhere, there might be a resolution, something might happen. I finally realized not long ago that it's not going to happen. It is time to let it go, to walk away.

AN: Sixty years later. Wasn't that an appalling burden for your father to have imposed on his children?

HENRY: Yuh, he didn't have much of an idea of that …

AN: A wise dog might have waited until you were twenty, say. And then sat down with you and explained that this was his ideal, this was his beautiful idea, what do you think, are you signing up to that, or how else might we arrange things? That would have been the generous and humane thing to have done, wouldn't it? And mightn't the hostile view be that it was an act of vanity not to have done that, an act of ego promotion?

HENRY: That's right.

AN: Could that be true of him?

HENRY: I do think so.[114]

In the Devon Record Office, John Acland (who died suddenly as the result of a car crash in September 2009) left a note written in March 1994 for anyone who might come to read the papers. In it he described how he had made many requests that his mother 'should explain to me why the Killerton and Holnicote estates had been given to the National Trust in the 1940s'.[115] In response, she arranged for him to look at the letters between her and Richard but John found on reading them that she had destroyed all the documents from the critical period at the end of 1942. Her explanation to him was that 'she had never kept any contentious letters'. His note continued: 'Anne only talked to me once, in 1989, about the gift of the estates. The talk lasted for several afternoons. Her principal contention was that she and Richard had been in complete agreement at every stage.' Perhaps all this secrecy, the denial of the story, was an attempt by Anne and Richard to protect themselves from the rage of their children.

After Richard had resigned his seat in the House of Commons over the H-bomb in 1955, and after his failure to be re-elected as an independent, he became a teacher at a comprehensive school in Wandsworth and then at St Luke's College in Exeter, one of his Victorian ancestors' great educational foundations. But like many ex-politicians he was a little adrift.

For all of Henry Acland's youth, his father was 'trying to recapture the moment when *Unser Kampf* was written, when he had really touched a nerve'. Occasionally he would come out to play, build boats or go canoeing on the Exe. But, like the old scholar Casaubon in *Middlemarch*, he wanted to write 'the book', the statement that would say everything. It was difficult for him as he was not a natural writer and one day Henry suggested he should simply 'write down the record of how this happened and then that happened. But he couldn't stop himself turning that into a polemic.' When Henry asked him what the title was going to be, he replied, 'I think I'll call it *A Story of Failure*.'[116]

For all that, Richard's radicalism, his belief in the possibilities of moral government, his reaching for nobility and his loathing of the capitalist conspiracy never diminished. When, in 1982, the National Trust allowed the Ministry of Defence to build a giant nuclear command bunker under its land at Bradenham in the Chilterns, Richard fired off a passionate letter to Lord Gibson, the Trust's Chairman, telling him that although he would always 'stand up for the National Trust because I so deeply believe in its basic purpose, ... on this issue I feel that I have been betrayed'.[117]

Richard died in 1990, Anne in November 1992. After the death of Sir John Acland in 2009, his son Dominic Acland (the 17th Baronet, but he doesn't use the title) went to live in Sprydon. He commutes to work in Torquay, where he runs the Torbay Coast and Countryside Trust, a wildlife and heritage charity, looking after 1,700 acres of beautiful South Devon landscape, all of it accessible to the general public. Dominic was still living at Sprydon when I spoke to him and I asked if he still had anything from his ancestors' possessions. 'Well, I have this,' he said, holding up the little finger of his left hand on which there was a signet ring bearing the Acland arms. He had been given it on his twenty-first birthday in 1983. 'And I have had to have it repaired. The gold had worn through.'[118] Apart from that was there anything? A collection of photographs and a pair of bellows, he said, also emblazoned with the family's chequered coat of arms and the one-word motto: *Inébranlable*, or 'Indestructible'.

Continuity

The Cliffords

Frampton on Severn, Gloucestershire

On one of the first shooting days of the winter of 2010 the party gathers, just before ten o'clock, in the yard of Manor Farm in Frampton on Severn. It has already been a beautiful morning, with the underside of the clouds over the Severn Vale pink and red in the sunrise. The frost has turned the yews grey in the garden and the whole of Gloucestershire is quietly smoking, as if just out of the freezer. The chickens are pecking on the edges of the yard, the Gloucester Old Spots' run is corrugated in the frost and breath hangs in puffs that come and go in front of the sows' nostrils. It could be any morning in the last 600 years.

About thirty men and their dogs, Labradors and spaniels, one or two quivering terriers on leads, are standing in the yard outside the old stone dovecote – a cider-making shed now – between a huge and beautiful Tudor barn and a row of stables, the blanketed horses hanging their heads out over the half-doors.

The men, as usual on these occasions, are all dressed in the same colour, a brownish dun green. 'We don't do us and them here,' Rollo Clifford says. He is the squire of Frampton and he and his family are the last of this gentry sequence. Rollo looks exactly as he should, his face the sort Gainsborough would have painted, a little careworn but tinged with an almost-boyishness, the ever-present possibility of a smile. He is sixty-six now and has the sloping shoulders and bowed legs of a man who has spent his life in the saddle, a snaggle tooth under his upper lip, and a slight, dropping tone at the end of everything he says. There is no doubting this man's strengths – he has dug his life into this place, supporting the people here and everything it means to him – but his convictions are coated in an extraordinary gentleness.

For nine years in his twenties Rollo Clifford was a cavalry officer in the 14th/20th Hussars, and then continued as a part-time soldier in the Royal Gloucestershire Hussars. He still has something of a softened military air, giving quiet commands to his wayward spaniels Pocket and Zephyr. He begins but often doesn't finish his sentences, as if circling before deciding to land and settle. 'He's not …' he says, describing a man he has had trouble with in the past. 'I don't think I am the only one …'; then a long pause as he looks at you sympathetically. 'He is not, I wouldn't say, very … He was never very *personable*. We certainly had some … I think they used to imagine that we would give in. Not that we would.' All this to describe a long, grumbling disagreement, which has now stretched over three generations, between the Cliffords and a family of neighbours, who are very definitely not here this morning.

But it is time to get things organized. There are seven guns – Rollo himself is not shooting – and twenty-odd beaters, men from Frampton and the surrounding villages. He knows them all well. 'Far too many,' Rollo says to me. 'They are only here because we'll give them all lunch afterwards.' Every one of them, carrying their ash and hazel sticks, calls him 'Rollo' and is wearing rough, bramble-scratched Barbours and waterproof trousers for the job in hand.

The guns wear ties and breeches and are a selection of the sort of people who have inhabited this book. Time has not passed: there is Colonel Ker, smart-looking in the neat, almost dandyish way of professional soldiers, who once commanded the Green Jackets, a man with a distinguished military record, mentioned in dispatches from Borneo in the 1960s, decorated for services in Northern Ireland, but now a little hesitant on his feet after a hunting accident. ('It was stupid,' Rollo says. 'They should never have told him to get back on.')

Talking to him is Shaun Parsons, a long-standing Gloucestershire County Councillor, like Rollo once an officer in the Royal Gloucestershire Hussars and the senior financial controller in Coutts Bank. He has endless stories for me about families in which the young men play fast and loose throughout their twenties 'but as soon as they turn thirty they all become boring as hell and the accountants can sigh with relief. It happens in every generation. It's all in the genes.'

Rollo introduces me to the writer Duff Hart-Davis, who has been discussing with Mark Cleaver, one of the beaters, the swap they are intending to make of some Hart-Davis partridges for a catch of grey mullet that Mark has made with his net in the Severn. Rollo's son Peter, a handsome, tousle-haired 25-year-old, who stands a foot taller than his father but has the same hesitant and gentle Clifford manner, has his great friend George James with him. They have been working together in George's fencing business. George's father Guy is here too, a local estate agent. He is worried that his shooting is going downhill and tells me how he is 'always going home nowadays with other people's Labradors. You can't really tell them apart, can you? But then you get home and you look down and you notice how there's something funny about your dog – the ears not quite right, a look in the eye, the wag going round the wrong way. And then you see it's not yours! Far, far too late!'

Finally, standing smiling at the side is a huge retired judge, Gabriel Hutton, 'twelve foot tall' as Rollo says, with big darned patches in the knees of his orange breeches, an army scarf knotted at the neck and perfectly dubbined size fourteen boots. I tell him he looks magnificent, he grins like a ten-year-old and I have the extraordinary feeling that the characters in this book have quite suddenly come back to life. The past has not passed. These are the friends of William Plumpton and George Throckmorton. Gentry consciousness knows no history.

Janie, Rollo's wife, comes out to see all is well. She is tall and gentle, a graceful 1960s beauty, with big grey eyes, her hair pulled back from her face, visibly Peter's mother. She is the daughter of a much-loved Appeal Court judge and Exmoor hunting man, and she too, like Rollo, has a relaxed familiarity with command, the at-homeness of someone who habitually decides and ordains. This is their place. There is no sense of imposed order but it is clear that these two are making this scene happen.

They complement each other. Just as Rollo has the habit of turning his sentences down towards the end, Janie has a way of lifting her words into slow and buoyant laughter. As she moves around the yard in her tweed plus fours and deerstalker, going from one knot of people to the next, saying hello and good morning to them, a bubble of that laughter follows her.

As in family after family in this book, authority in the Cliffords is subtly distributed between husband and wife. Largely, he fronts the performance and she supports it; but she is the better communicator and he the more reticent reservoir of knowledge. In public they very decorously refer to and engage with each other on any question. And, as he told me much later that evening, he knows that for any Clifford at Frampton, of any generation, by far the most important factor in his life is the woman who chooses to share it with him.

He pulls on his cap, gives his instructions to the assembled guns and beaters – no one is to shoot the foxes, people are to pick up their empty cartridges 'if you can' – and we leave for the first drive. Flocks of redwings and fieldfares fill the air between the little coverts and woods. We move out from the village, across its half-mile-long green which Rollo says was 'designed for long-bow practice', and on to the 1,500 acres of the Frampton estate. Its place in the Severn Vale becomes apparent. Over to the east are the dark blue wooded heights of the Cotswold Edge; to the west, beyond the Severn, the trees of the Forest of Dean; and between the two this long flat sliver of the Vale, low, wet country, criss-crossed by the ditches they call 'rhines' (rhymes with 'sheens') and with hedges lining those ditches. It is green and lush, born dairy country.

We come to the first drive and Rollo arranges his troops. 'Why don't you stand here?' he says to Shaun Parsons, the tall man in spectacles from Coutts, pointing to a spot under the high-tension wires that loop between pylons striding off to the south. 'Should I avoid the wires?' Parsons asks. 'Oh no,' Rollo, says, 'you can shoot them.' The atmosphere remains *League of Gentlemen* military. Rollo refers to the older men among his guests as 'the senior officers present' and disposes them at the near stands, the younger boys being sent off on the walk to the far end of the line. Colonel Ker is given a spot on the track at the corner and Duff Hart-Davis is placed next to him, in the fringes of a plantation of young walnuts which Peter Clifford planted last year. The others are spread out in a widely dispersed line to the north and Rollo and I walk off with Zephyr and Pocket to join the beaters who will push the pheasants on to the waiting guns.

It's not a highly organized shoot. There are no numbered pegs. The guns miss almost everything they aim at. The gamekeeper, Alan Franklin, is part time and unpaid. 'He wouldn't accept a tip if you tried to offer it to him,' Rollo says, 'so don't.' They only put down 250 young birds at the beginning of the season – one to every six acres of the estate – and they never sell a day's shooting here. 'I couldn't bear a commercial shoot,' Rollo says as he gives one long blast on his whistle to start the beaters off. One of the neighbours 'puts down a million pheasants on a small patch of land on our boundary and he is always moaning because we shoot their birds. They don't like that. They think I am creating a vacuum which their pheasants are going to flood into. But why should I have to put down birds which I don't think … which are against my better judgement? I know he thinks I am too mean …'

The beaters are making their chirruping way through the old, tired game crop and Zephyr and Pocket are huffing through the brambles in the ditch beside us. For about five minutes not a single bird appears and the guns stand silent. Then a cock gets up and flies, high and straight, towards Duff Hart-Davis. 'Ah,' says Rollo, 'there's the Frampton pheasant,' a joke which I imagine has been made by the Cliffords of Frampton since about 1420. Rollo follows its course steadily across the November sky. Hart-Davis sees it, raises his gun, tracks his muzzle towards it, squeezes the trigger, the *pock* of the detonation comes brightly over the field towards us and the pheasant flies on into the clear blue air towards Bristol and Somerset. 'Oh good,' Rollo says quietly. 'I am rather glad that one defeated Duff.'

The scene is a continuation of the past. Every figure in this book has been a hunter and shooter of one kind or another. For almost everyone a half-military air has hung around their lives. All have been taught to play the gracious host. Every one has used his piece of land as a theatre in which to display that courtesy, generosity and well-being. Every one would have seen himself, in one way or another, as a friend of the people who were his tenants, his community, his human surroundings, and at the same time would have been a little sceptical about their good intentions. Every one would have liked the idea that he was continuing the habits and practices of his father and grand-father, and to have seen his own son and his son's friends taking those habits on into the future. Except for an aberrational moment in late Victorian and Edwardian England, this way of going about a shoot, which is ad hoc, without any elaborate stocking or staffing, would have been the norm. Lunch was always an integral part of it. The whole day always revolved around little courtesies, between the guns, between the guns and the beaters, between host and guest. Men in these situations have always talked endlessly about dogs and horses. This is the world of Harry Oxinden and Oliver le Neve. These things, for all the vicissitudes of time, have been constant for hundreds of years. Of course there is modernity here, but the joint animation of these modern gentry is positively medieval. It is, extraordinarily, the inheritance of knightliness.

What is different? Everything: Rollo would never have been beating with me in the past. He would have been with his guns. The guns would not have been modern breech-loaders. I would not have been here. The farmed landscape itself is no more than half recognizable. Although the Cliffords have been careful to preserve as many as possible of the old hedges and greenways that cross their land, and there are still 117 separate fields on the Frampton estate, that is no more than half what was here until the 1950s. The fields are now drained. There are few cattle. The track we are on is made of planings scraped off the M5 when the surface was renewed a year or two ago. There is the noise of distant traffic. The pylons cross the land. A young crop of EU-subsidized oil seed rape extends in its usual hideous way across the field next to us. 'I rather … I really rather hate oil seed rape,' Rollo says as we walk along, 'but there seems to be an unending market for it.' All of the fields are surrounded by grassy headlands which are subsidized by EU agri-environment schemes. Just behind the trees to the west are two 100-acre lakes, the flooded gravel pits made when Frampton's most precious resource was dug out during the twentieth century. They are now rich with bird life, willow lined, much fished in and sailed on. To the north is the gently rising ground of what was until recently the site of a large and rather smelly landfill site, on whose five-figure annual fees the estate survived for thirty years until it too finally closed in 2008. The rubbish, first from foundries and then extending into food waste, was dumped in what had been yet another gravel pit. Nowadays the rubbish is sealed in, grass and maize grow on the surface and a tiny power station generates electricity from the methane given off by the slowly rotting remains of super-market dinners and pots of taramasalata lying far below.

The shot birds are now gathered up and strung in braces with baler twine. Their feathers are broken and ruffled by the shot that has gone through them, their coats torn in patches. They are joined in the trailer by the body of a myxy rabbit which Pocket had picked out of the hedge and Rollo had dispatched with the thick end of his hazel thumbstick. A beautiful big dog fox had slunk out between the guns, glossy on the pheasant dinners he had been enjoying, but no one raised a barrel to him. 'Good,' Rollo says when given the news. 'I like to hear the foxes are well.' He is a great hunting man – Senior Joint Master of the Berkeley Hunt – and is keen on the idea of preserving foxes so that one day the hounds can hunt them.

The Cliffords have been at Frampton at least since the Domesday Book was written in 1086.[1] Shaun Parsons told me as we sat on the bales in the back of the trailer that he had once at a dinner party said that the Cliffords had been at Frampton since 1110. '1110?' Rollo had said from the far end of the table with his eyes like saucers. 'What *are* you talking about? It's at least 1080.' A man called Pons, William the Conqueror's first cousin, came over in 1066 and ended up owning

Frampton among other places. He sounds important but he was the son of a younger son of a second marriage of the Conqueror's grandfather. The son of his younger brother, Walter Clifford, became the squire of Frampton. He probably lived in a house on the site of Manor Farm. From the beginning this place was always on the lower edges of gentry life.[2]

Apart from one flirtation with royalty in the twelfth century when the exquisitely beautiful Rosamund Clifford became the mistress of Henry II,[3] the Cliffords have maintained a superbly steady state ever since: often acting as local justices, very occasionally MPs, sometimes with a house in Gloucester, never one in London, never losing their place entirely, never reaching for the heights and never sinking into penury. One Elizabethan Clifford, James, nearly destroyed the enterprise by building a prodigy house at nearby Fretherne on the banks of the Severn, to which the Queen, although invited, never came.[4] Otherwise, the family has remained, in effect, Mr and Mrs Clifford for a millennium. Rollo is the 28th Frampton Clifford and Peter the 29th.

It has been the most braided of streams. Descent has often been through the female line. Husbands marrying Clifford girls have changed their names to match the inheritance. The Manor Farm has for long periods been in the hands of families other than theirs, but Cliffords have never been absent from Frampton. More often than not, they have lived on the other side of the green from the manor, on the site where the wonderful Frampton Court, a creamy chunky-Palladian villa in Bath Stone, was built in the 1730s.

Particular lines have come to an end and distant relatives have succeeded. Nephews have inherited, cousins have bought the estate. Marriages have been contracted with other gentry families of the vale and alliances made, above all with the lordly Berkeleys of Berkeley Castle nine miles to the south, but Frampton has never been immensely grand and never had its own castle. Manor Farm is a beautiful late medieval house, but Frampton Court was built with the money of a searcher in the Bristol Customs Office.[5] Money of that kind, derived from the moment when Bristol was a world-dominating city, afloat on sugar, slaves and the African trade, would never have emerged from here.

Go down to the little church in Frampton and the long story of what is essentially a lesser place becomes plain. St Mary's is old not rich. There is nothing here to match the church architecture you would find in the Cotswolds or East Anglia. It is the building of a rather poor and marginal parish. At the east end of the north aisle, the Cliffords have their chapel, but compared with other family chapels in other village churches around the country, this is simplicity itself.

There is a fourteenth-century Clifford warrior with his feet resting on his spaniel and his legs crossed in what was thought to be the Crusader way, with his lady next to him in her own niche, but neither is carved with any pomp or grandeur. There are some crudely lettered Clifford slabs from the 1500s on the floor of the vestry and one or two dignified marble plaques from the centuries that followed. They are all part of the Clifford inheritance but the names flicker and change as daughters inherit and men die childless. A Clutterbuck (the Bristol man) and then some Winchcombes appear and disappear again. The cumulative picture is of a relatively modest family continuing in its honourable but unflamboyant way. This is gentry normality, the tradition Rollo Clifford is heir to.

The memorials in the church make their slow approach to the twentieth century, finally reaching the point where the people on the walls are within touching distance. Rollo's grandfather, Henry Francis Clifford, is here, in gothic lettering on a brass plate, with his own coat of arms and motto on one side (*Dulcis Amor Patriae* – Sweet is the love of your country) and on the other those of the Royal Gloucestershire Hussars. He was a major in that yeomanry cavalry regiment and with it he died fighting the Turks on the borders of Palestine in January 1917. He was forty-five and his death left his widow, Hilda, pregnant with a daughter, Henriette, Rollo's mother, who never saw her father.

Fleurs de lys decorate Major Clifford's polished plaque. It aims to be a medieval thing, a reversion to the knightliness this family has embraced for a thousand years. The memorial carries a stanza from the *Epilogue to Asolando*, the last poem Robert Browning wrote, chosen by Hilda as an epitaph:

One who never turned his back but marched breast forward,
Never doubted clouds would break,
Never dreamed, though right were worsted, wrong would triumph,
Held we fall to rise, are baffled to fight better,
Sleep to wake.

Those lines identify a certain Clifford mentality: a sense of near-bafflement, of life not running quite with the grain, of difficulty all round you, but faced with a kind of principled obstinacy, a dogged insistence that things will come right in the end.

The Raid on Rafa in which Major Clifford died might have come out of a medievalist Edwardian illumination, a dream of gentry honour.[6] In the chill January of 1917, the Royal Gloucestershire Hussars were an element of a raiding party which attacked a Turkish force heavily dug in just south of Gaza on the southern borders of Palestine. The British cavalry rode to battle through a beautiful moonlit night for thirty miles across the desert and then on to the grassy plains of northern Sinai. The Warwickshire Yeomanry and the Worcestershire Hussars were with them, as well as the Imperial Camel Corps, some Australian and New Zealand cavalry and the Royal Horse Artillery. No infantry were there. All night they travelled past mud-brick villages and their gardens, the horses grazing now and then on the clover and young barley of the open plains. They bivouacked in the deep-shadowed orchards of pear, apricot and almond trees, only the almonds in blossom.

In the dawn of 9 January, 600 yards or so from the Turkish lines, the cavalrymen dismounted and began to attack on foot across an entirely coverless, shallow, sloping hillside. The Turks had set up their positions well and their machine guns effortlessly commanded wide fields of fire. Turkish snipers were buried up to their armpits behind small aloes. The Gloucestershire men were given the northern flank of the battle, where sand dunes spread in from the Mediterranean coast. Even here, though, the cover was minimal and under the machine-gun fire they could move only a few yards at a time. That is where a Turkish bullet killed Rollo's grandfather, instantaneously, 'with not a moment's pain, or knowledge he had even been hit', as his groom, Horton, wrote to Hilda in Frampton.[7]

Henry's body was taken 130 miles back to the military cemetery at Kantara on the east bank of the Suez Canal. At his funeral in the desert they sang 'The Lord is My Shepherd' and, according to his brother officer Frank Mitchell, he left 'a great blank in everyone's heart, and especially all the old yeomen'.[8] His dusty grave was marked with a wooden cross and outlined in a rough desert kerb.

The Raid on Rafa very nearly ended in defeat but the New Zealanders got round the back of the Turkish position and finally stormed it from behind, killing the defenders with their bayonets. After all was over, and the dead removed, the victors held 'The Desert Column First Spring Meeting' on the beautiful grassy downland of southern Palestine over which they had fought. Officers and other ranks raced for the Rafa Cup, the Promised Land Stakes, the Syrian Derby and the Jerusalem Scurry (for mules only, over five furlongs). Henry Clifford wasn't there but every Clifford in history would have loved it.[9]

As we walk towards the next drive on the shoot, across the fields still marked with the ridge-and-furrow of medieval farming, I talk to Rollo about what he believes in. What is it that is motivating him here? He is not the most voluble of men but first, or at least easiest, we talk about horses. 'That's an important element to register really,' he says, suddenly like a colonel in a novel. 'The old cavalry ethos of you look after your horse first, then your men, then yourself. Which I was certainly brought up with.'

He had loved the cavalry when he was in it and every summer at the Frampton Country Fair, a great celebration of the whole Clifford world of horses, dogs, hunting, shooting, river skills and rural crafts, to which 15,000 people come, Rollo and his fellow cavalrymen from the Royal Gloucestershire Hussars put on a stomping exhibition of horsemanship, riding at full gallop with lances extended, skewering burning tent pegs as they pass or amazingly re-enacting a scene from the battle of Waterloo. 'The idea', Rollo says, 'is to try to get your lance down the Frenchman's throat.' He must be one of the few men in the world who every summer gets to shout 'Charge' to 15,000 people at the top of his voice. It is like something out of the Mongol steppe. Janie is a little horrified by his performing like this on his strong horses, but his daughter Anna says 'It's nice to see my dad showing off.'

Since the Bronze Age, the hunt has been the continuation of a cavalry charge by other means, and hunting is in the Clifford blood. Rollo's mother, Henriette, 'lived and breathed horses. It was what lit her up more than anything else.'

Pictures in the Frampton archive both of her and of her own mother show strong, elegant and handsome women, taut with energy, almost always on or with a horse, hunting well into their seventies and even then coming back from a day's hunting 'saying I have never had such a thrill in my whole life'.

Alongside those pictures are letter after letter from all members of the family describing, like match reports, the breathless detail of hunt after hunt across the Frampton acres ...

... swinging right-handed before Parks, through Mincepie and along the edge of Withybed, Buster and Tim over the Tiger Trap south of Withy Bed but the rest over the ditch at Mince Pie & along Westward and into Marsh Lane where we met a very affable Coole [a farming neighbour]. Fox turned right in Coole's Cabbages by his house and across the rough diggings towards Park Corner Cottages. Everyone on & beaming faces ... on the Morse's [another farming neighbour] & fox to ground behind Whites Mill. Small place & he was bolted by a terrier. Fool of a fox could have gone straight to Johnny Teesdales [the portraitist, a Clifford neighbour] but turned *left* through the hedge & met the pack. They ran him one field and bowled him over in the open. Found again at once and ran the 'classic' line ...[10]

and so on for page after page, hunt after hunt, year after year. This is the language and thought pattern of the hunting gentry over the centuries. The Plumptons would have talked like this, the Oxindens, the Gawdys, the Aclands. It has always been a form of warfare in which no one dies, of *fun*, of bringing like-minded people together, of the storming use of rural England, but it is also more that, a form of enormously conspicuous consumption, a kind of displayed command of the country. Its florid indifference to usefulness – of time, horses, men, hounds, the environment, land – has always been, at least in part, its purpose.

Since the ban on hunting imposed in 2005 – or rather since the general antipathy to hunting began to take hold in the 1980s – things have not been quite the same. Rollo has put up a poster outside his kitchen window at the manor which says 'Vive la Chasse' in red and green and another on the road, but so high up a tree that no objector could reach it, which says 'Fight the Ban – Keep Hunting'. And Rollo is quietly reflective about his modern circumstances.

Development is the curse, Bristol coming up and Gloucester coming down. And the roads. Two motorways. The dreaded wire. It is very parochial now, even compared with my childhood, round and round in circles because of the motorways and the roads. Before the ban you could still have 5, 6, 7 miles points if you were lucky, up and down the vale, between the A38 and the river. And there is some very lovely wild country south of Berkeley which has only been intruded on by the two nuclear power stations. Two great lumps of concrete don't interfere in the way a road does.

But he has his visions of perfection:

What I always used to love was when the dog fox was out of his territory, on the lookout for a lady wife when you found him and then he made a wild run back home and the hounds hunted him all the way.

But do you know what I dream of? What I really long for? If you could orchestrate a railway strike, then we could hunt along the railway lines. You always have brambles and scrub there. If you could guarantee a railway strike … We have done it but it doesn't happen very often these days. Sadly. Mrs T is to blame for that.

So what was it about hunting? Why did people devote their lives to it? 'It was nothing to do with the demise of the quarry,' Rollo says, in language whose roots must surely stretch generations back into the nineteenth century, and then goes on in his usual, pausing, unfinishing, philosophical way:

The basic instinct, when you hear the hounds running … Nobody thought about the quarry being exhausted. The unpredictability of the chase, the glorious uncertainty … The fact that the hounds were doing the hunting for you. At the end of the day, a bit like after a day's skiing, that marvellous feeling of wellbeing.

'It is quite quiet sometimes,' he says.

You hear the birds singing. The uncertainty, that's important, the fusing of these things …

The best hunting moment is on a low winter afternoon just as snow is coming on … that was the best scenting moment, when the scent is just breast high on the hounds, the best moment of any possible year really, the hunt in the dark with snow coming in the cold air …

Love of the countryside, Adam, it's not produced with a camera and a note pad. The hunter-gatherer side forms a bond that is deeper and sounder than that. You slowly lose your blood lust as the years tick on. If you ever had a blood lust that is. But that connection to a place which you get by knowing it, as you do when you are hunting, that never goes.

This is not a very wordy culture and emotions rarely break surface; but it is, and perhaps always has been, a world of near-silent passion.

The shoot moves on from drive to drive. Through Blackthorn Covert, and then across Ploughed Piece and a small orchard of old perry pears, we drive the pheasants on to the guns who are standing in Sweet Meadow and one or two in Broad Croft. Rollo distributes lumps of dark chocolate at one pause. We push a few birds out of the game crop in Pear Tree Leaze and then through Old Withy Bed, the little covert between Pear Tree Leaze and Teazle Ground – where the teazles were once grown for the cloth industry. Finally, Rollo lines his guns up on the edge of the plantation called Pancake – so-called because it was first drawn by the Berkeley Hounds one Shrove Tuesday.

Rollo tells me to stay to one side 'in the 12/6s' while he arranges his friends in front of Pancake Covert. On the sound of the whistle, the beaters start to make their way through the maize. The old gentlemen wait for them patiently in front of the scrubby and brambly edge of the wood. A lemon-yellow sun shines down hazily on Gloucestershire. One or two pheasants come up out of the corn, fluttering to gain height, flustered at the trouble, like milkmaids disturbed from their work, and then soon enough sail high and straight through the winter sky towards the guns, their long tails quivering with each beat of the wing.

The men stand waiting as the birds come over. One after another the barrels rise hesitantly skywards, as if the men were manikins, puppet-like, the guns pulled up by strings attached to the flying birds. *Pock, pock, pock* – one after another shots are tossed into the winter air. None of them makes contact and the pheasants fly on, curving away to the cover in another wood. The low ones are allowed through. Occasionally a bird flutters in mid-air, a hesitation, almost a cough, as it is 'pricked' by the cloud of shot, and it drops into the wood behind. Dogs will retrieve them later. The old men miss nearly everything, pointing their firing sticks at the sky, looking to get on to a pheasant and then again and again losing the line.

It is a picture of the gentry, complete in all its archaic dignity. 'How can I live among this gentle/obsolescent breed of heroes, and not weep?' Keith Douglas asked of his fellow cavalry officers in the Western Desert in 1942. He saw them as 'unicorns, almost', beautiful, redundant, not part of this world, perfect but surely meaningless.

Those words come back to me on the drive over Pancake. But then, as I am watching, I see something else: Colonel Ker, who has not found it easy walking between the drives, raises his gun to a high and distant bird, flying fast and true towards him, perhaps ninety feet above, and as he tracks it, he fires and shoots the pheasant in full flight, the bird falling into the wood behind us as the Colonel breaks open his gun and replaces the cartridges for whatever might come next.

It was a long and friendly morning, the mild theatre of an English November. Alan Franklin, the keeper, said it had gone exactly to plan: lots of birds, most of them missed. 'All you want,' he said, 'is to show the guns something they can shoot at. You don't want them hitting everything.' There was a late lunch for beaters and guns in the big Wool Barn, everyone lined up at the long gingham-clothed table, gas heaters and red wine, rabbit stew and apples in trugs. Faces glowed like frost-caught pippins and we chatted on into the afternoon about elvers and the Environment Agency, Forest of Dean men and the ignorant millionaires now living in the Cotswolds, hunting and the National Trust, the techniques for netting fish in the waters of the Severn, the codling you could catch on a flood tide by the bridges, the tax status of inherited land, the end of dairying, the future of families, what 'gentry' means and whether it meant anything any more.

The shoot was one of the display days at Frampton. It dramatizes the place but it is not the whole story. Nor are hunting and shooting what Rollo and Janie Clifford's life is devoted to. The goal they have in mind is more straightforward than that. It is, simply put, the well-being of their community, driven by a sense of duty. Frampton, because of that, is what Rollo calls 'a glorious millstone', a borrowed phrase, which he first heard on his grandmother's lips.

'It's being friends with people,' he says. 'That is a vast part of it.' But being friends with people takes an enormous amount of time. Rose Hewlett, the Estate Secretary and a local historian, who is in love with Frampton and the Cliffords and who, unlike her boss, pours forth an unending and delighted cataract of talk, says 'Rollo is on the job 24/7.'

He is a parish councillor, as he has to be really, as the estate and village are so intertwined. He is chairman of the Frampton Wildlife and Sporting Association, which deals with all the possible conflicts between fishermen, sailors, wildfowlers, birders, their nets, walkers, paths, permissive paths, hunters. He is chairman of the Frampton Country Fair, which happens every summer and is an *enormous* amount of work. And the Cliffords give every single penny of what the fair makes to charity. He is chairman of the Trustees of the Royal Gloucestershire Hussars. He is chairman of the Point to Point. He does the shoot. He is joint Master of the Hunt and Field Master every other Wednesday. Thursday afternoons he does his historical research into the Hussars. He is a brilliant networker – and I don't like the word networker – but it gives him a buzz to bring people together. He copies half the world into something if he thinks they should know. It is all about stewarding the whole place, keeping it whole. It is not done on a whim. It is all done very, very, very carefully. Neither of them are getting any younger but there is no sign of them slowing down. He takes *so* long deciding. Every decision is important. You know exactly what he is going to say for ten minutes before he actually says it. He talks to the men for half an hour each morning. They all know exactly what they have to do anyway. But that is the point, going round and round the same tracks. When I first came to work here ten years ago, one of the files in the filing cabinet had been started in 1896 and was still going. Rollo doesn't do computers really. We have to do all that. But Frampton stays what it is because change has not been thrust on to it.

Everywhere there are signs of this deep, careful conservatism. A small noticeboard on the green announces that 'Only under 13-year-olds from Frampton families can fish in the ponds.' Rollo thought it was 'too gloomy to have too many old men stuck there day in day out'. The family owns about thirty cottages in the village, all of them let on affordable, non-commercial, short-term leases, with a heavy emphasis on providing housing for village families. There is an application list, but it is certainly not first come, first served. 'Londoners want to come here all the time but they haven't got a chance,' Rose says.

It is incredibly old fashioned here but that is why we love it. We are still quite feudal. If there is a lost dog, it gets brought to the estate office because that is the centre of the village. Frampton is the end of the road, a complete cul-de-sac, and arriving back in the village when you have been away is like going on holiday. Money doesn't interest Rollo. It is not about money. It's about being custodian of the estate. If you think what he owns, the Court, the Manor, the Orangery, the land, he would be a very rich man. But they don't behave or live like the rich, or want a life that the rich might lead.

No, they don't: they have battered cars, an ancient VW camper van in which they went on honeymoon – its roof leaks and in Scotland they drove for days catching drips in pans – and a smoky blue Morris Traveller. The heating in the manor is set well down, good thick jerseys are a winter necessity and the hot water is turned on only when a bath is required. Foreign holidays don't happen every year. The render on the timber face of the manor has come away in places, revealing the lathes beneath.

The story of the Clifford finances in the twentieth century is a salutary one. The death of Rollo's grandfather in Palestine in 1917 was a moment of reckoning. In the eighteenth century, the arrival of the Clutterbucks, who derived a good income from posts in the Customs Office in Bristol, and then the Winchcombes, who had connections with the cloth business in Stroud, had brought money to the Clifford enterprise. Through the nineteenth century, to support a huge number of Clifford brothers and sisters, very large mortgages were taken out against the value of the land, so that by 1917, when Major Clifford was killed, the 2,000-odd acres of Frampton Court Estate were encumbered with over £33,000 of debt, the equivalent of about £6.5 million today, involving annual charges of over £2,200, or in modern terms at least £400,000 a year. On top of that, the new level of estate duty at 10 per cent was charged on his death.[11]

These debts and tax bills forced Rollo's grandmother to sell three of the farms, a quarter of the estate, reducing the landholding to about 1,500 acres, a bitter moment which the Cliffords regret to this day. Through the course of the twentieth century, the essential un-viability of the reduced estate was for many years held at bay by income from gravel extraction, which ate away about 280 acres of farmland. Peter Scott, the great naturalist who set up the Wildfowl Centre at Slimbridge just down the road and was a great friend of the Cliffords, even encouraged them to claw away the whole of the park in front of the house, excited at the possibilities for even more wetland bird habitat that would open up. Thankfully he was resisted, and even now a single field remains in the midst of the gravel-pit lakes, the site of the very best gravel, not yet quarried and known to the Cliffords as the Field of the Cloth of Gold.

The gravel allowed the family to make of Frampton what they wanted. Rollo's father was one of the several men in Clifford history who changed his name after marrying the Clifford heiress. He was born Peter Haggie, became a flail tank commander on D-Day (where Janie's father, a gunner, was too) and after the war devoted his life to maintaining Frampton as a living organism.

'My father came out of the war seeing a great land of milk and honey,' Rollo says, 'and he did try to achieve that.' He believed in openness. As part of a social vision, he started the sailing club on the lake, encouraged the wildfowlers and the fishermen, and alongside Peter Scott pioneered wetland creation, planting willows around the lakes 'and in came these marvellous birds. There was an excitement about the whole thing and they were very generous about all that.'

Through the 1950s and '60s, the farm had gone slightly into abey-ance. Tenants had died or left and all the land was taken back in hand. There was a beautiful herd of Ayrshire dairy cows, whose milk went to the small factory opened by Cadbury's on the edge of the village, in which 'chocolate crumb' for Cadbury's Dairy Milk was made. But the gravel money meant the farm did not have to be driven too hard. By the time Roger Godwin, a new 24-year-old manager, arrived in 1973, the whole place was covered, as Godwin says, in 'permanent weeds'.

The gravel by then had come to an end, and for twenty-five years Godwin drove the land along a new high-intensity track, draining the wet fields, putting irrigation into the dry lands, taking out a lot of hedges, although fewer than most farmers because hedges were good for hunting, spraying off the precious weeds, growing cabbages, potatoes and Brussels sprouts, even wheat on the floodable washlands along the Severn, 'High Farming, as opposed to dog-and-stick farming'. Rollo's father loved having Roger there, introducing this surge of new energy to the place, and Roger thrived on the warmth Peter Clifford showed him. 'You are the same age as Rollo,' he told him when he first arrived, 'and I want you two to grow old together.' No sentence could have been more welcoming. 'It was his trust and confidence that locked me in,' Godwin says. He is still there, although now managing several other farms as well, spread across Gloucestershire, more than just the treasured Frampton fields.

The farm started to make a profit and that, combined with the revenues from the landfill fees, continued to keep Frampton afloat. But both of those income streams have now come to an end. The landfill was closed in 2008 and the fashion for high-intensity farming has also moved on. About 500 acres of Frampton are still ploughed and sown with wheat, rape and beans, but much of the rest of it, attracting more nature-friendly EU payments, has gone back to the permanent weeds Roger Godwin was so horrified by when he first arrived. 'We don't farm enough now to keep the estate,' he says quite straightforwardly.

Frampton Court is now open for delicious, deeply comfortable, upscale bed and breakfast but that does no more than contribute to the building's maintenance.[12] It cost £35,000 in the autumn of 2010 to mend a single chimney, far more than a year's profit on the B&B. The pretty Strawberry Hill Gothick Orangery, let out a week at a time for holiday-makers, does better.

Such things can scarcely match the income from high-productivity horticulture, landfill or gravel pits – or, looking further back, the bribes and fees derived from the customs business in the global entrepôt of eighteenth-century Bristol. The ending of this money sequence hangs over them all. How to maintain Frampton when all possible opportunities seem to have been tried and exhausted?

Rollo suggested to me one evening that 'farming people', making Frampton into a tourist business, might be the way out. They were already trying it in a small way: holiday lets in the Orangery, the bed and breakfast at the Court, to a small extent having these houses open, the odd wedding function. But could that really fill the gap left by the ending of the gravel and high farming which had sustained them through the twentieth century?

It is another version of the question which has confronted the gentry since the fifteenth century: how do you keep the enterprise going when the world changes? And without abandoning your ideals? There is no easy answer and the worry takes its toll on the Cliffords. Technical decisions over effective tax planning loom large and a certain sack-carrying weariness hangs behind these conversations, a sense of the glorious millstone dangling from their necks. At times it seems as if the whole community of Frampton on Severn, with all the niggles and discontents of any community, streams through the kitchen of the manor house, like a thousand needy children. Spend a day or two with the Cliffords in this beautiful and dignified place and you can have no doubt that the millstone has some weight in it.

The future is unresolved. Rollo's older brother David, a Bristol musician, knew since boyhood that the Frampton life was not for him. But a few years ago, there was a serious disagreement between Rollo and his younger brother, an environmentalist who now lives and works in America, over who should be involved in Frampton and its future. The family was pained by this confrontation and the younger generation does not want it to recur between them.

It is not certain who will take over. The Cliffords have three daughters, Jessie, Anna and Sarah, and a son, Peter, the 25-year-old who had come shooting in the morning. Jessie also lives in the village with her husband, Harry Spurr, a barrister and wine entrepreneur.

I talked to Rollo's and Janie's son, Peter, by the fire in the manor that evening, with the clock ringing the hours, the logs spitting beside us and the flames glimmering on the polished oak. Peter got Frampton in the blood as a boy, 'as a place where I felt totally free, total freedom, doing whatever I wanted'. He would only ever come inside to eat something and then get out again, on to the farm, to the woods, or the stacks of hay bales, or the shores of the great tidal river. And so, I asked him, did he want to do this, what his father had done, and his, and his great-grandfather and his and his?

Sometimes it terrifies me, and you want to run away. I didn't decide for a long time. My mother's dad asked me once a few years ago, 'Do you want to?' and I said – then – 'No way. Dad is so busy the whole time.' And so I went to Dad and asked him, 'Do you like living like you do?' And he said, 'Look at our lives. That is all you need look at. That is the life that comes with this place.'

This attachment to place is a strange addiction. Through their childhoods and their family culture the huge branding stamp of FRAMPTON has been imprinted on the Cliffords. And yet, because this is no superbly funded ducal estate, it is only partly a gift. It is, and will be, a struggle for the Cliffords merely to stay still, not to lose what they have had. That struggle to keep something precious is different from the struggle to gain something you have never known. It is the glorious burden to which Rollo repeatedly returns. I remembered suddenly the letters of Harry Oxinden in Kent in the 1660s as finally, at the end of all his travails, he was relieved of the weight of continued ownership which his estate had imposed on him, and the great inrush of freedom he felt even as he lost the thing that was more important to him than anything in the world.

It is nothing new for a gentry enterprise to feel under threat from the prevailing currents of modernity – every family in this book has struggled with that. Nor to wonder about the uncertainty that hangs over every heir, or set of heirs. But for now Peter Clifford is coming to feel his way to this succession, this continuity, this repeating of the pattern:

I'd love to keep it the same but improve it. To keep the buildings up, to keep farming, keep the timber going, keep the local guys in the cottages, not selling up to commuters. It's a beautiful place and it's a beautiful place for everyone to share. I'd like to improve the houses but not completely change them. I don't want to make them unaffordable. A nice balance, that's what we need.

A nice balance. Peter said it in the quietest of Clifford voices, murmuring beside the fire, the gentlest-possible statement of an ancient and almost never voiced philosophy. Perhaps this was the final landing of the gentry story. It had gone through such turmoil and struggle in its early years, had been so embroiled in self-assertion and self-dramatization in its middle years, but had now, by the twenty-first century, come down to a stoic search for calm and continuity in a noisy and troubled world.

CONCLUSION

Return of the Native

'To be gnaw'd out of our graves', Sir Thomas Browne wrote in *Urne-Buriall*, his long, slow meditation on loss and human vanity, published in 1658, 'to have our sculs made drinking-bowls, and our bones turned into Pipes ... are Tragicall abominations.'[1] The great Norwich doctor and antiquary may have disliked the idea but he was describing the point of this book: to scoop the life out of dead men's brains.

These stories are more a series of excavations into the skulls of the gentry than a comprehensive tour of their world and for that reason any general conclusions may be difficult. Nevertheless, it seems clear that the Gentry, as an institution, which might from a distance have seemed fixed and even decrepit, characterized by its overpowering sense of the past, its fading energies and crumbling fabric, turns out when looked at closely, in its own time frame and under its own microscope, to be turbulent and contingent, with uncertainty and struggle its dominant qualities.

It was never really characterized by what Edmund Burke called in the 1750s the 'unbought grace of uncontested ease'. If you set aside for a moment the gentry's graceful acts of self-display, the beautiful houses and landscapes, the clothes they wore, their consciously easy and courteous behaviour to strangers, what remains, above all in their private documents, is a profoundly restless state of mind, full of anxiety, in contest and conflict with neighbours and rivals, worriedly

411

looking to keep going in a world where heirs died young and marriages might be barren. The gentry's own account of themselves was never at ease.

Attendance to the realities of money was of foundational importance to them. None could afford to ignore the bottom line. Sir John Lowther, a seventeenth-century member of one of the great Cumbrian gentry families who would make their fortune from mining and trade, thought straightforwardly that 'without wealth, nobilitie or gentrie is a vaine and contemptible tytle hear in England'. Without money or property, a would-be gentleman 'will beare a bigger saile than he is able to maintaine'.[2] 'Nobility stript of means', the super-refined Geoffrey Hickes wrote in the early eighteenth century, 'makes no genteel Figure; it can't stand without golden supporters.'[3]

This close attention to the serious challenges of a competitive world, even among such overt elitists as Hickes, is a sign that the English gentry lived with an ever-present sense of social mobility and mutability around them. The world did not owe them a living. Every generation had to re-validate its place in the gentry universe. An ancestry and coat of arms may have provided a young man with a set of examples; it did not guarantee a continuation of them in him. This was the psychological power of the lineage: fathers and their fathers were not to be let down. The line should be kept going by a combination of honourable and entrepreneurial behaviour in the real world. Failure was the spur.

Only when the money – for which you can read 'land' over most of this history – had been sorted out could attention be paid to the qualities of gentlemanliness. And they, amid all this inconstancy, are curiously constant, a complex interplay of self-conception, social position, property, privilege, dress, education, the demands of honour, the constraints of obligation, the primacy of friendship, the concerns for beauty, 'stoutness' and justice. An anonymous writer in about 1500 identified the four central gentry virtues as 'Trauthe, pettee, fredome and hardynesse':[4] in modern English perhaps honesty, empathy, generosity and integrity. No translation can be exact and each of the medieval terms carries a different subtext. Truth then was to do

412

with piety, pity with social hierarchy, freedom with a sense of grace and hardiness with martial valour. This was the knightly inheritance that played out over the following centuries.

Compare that list with the requirements made in the early seventeenth century by the Carmarthenshire squire Sir William Vaughan:

> The means to discern a gentleman be these. First, he must be affable and courteous in speech and behaviour; Secondly, he must have an adventurous heart to fight and that but for very just quarrels. Thirdly he must be endowed with mercy to forgive the trespasses of his friends and servants. Fourthly, he must stretch his purse to give liberally unto soldiers and unto them that have need; for a niggard is not worthy to be called a gentleman. These be the properties of a gentleman, which whosoever lacketh deserveth but the title of clown or of a country boor.[5]

And this is Sir Gilbert Scott's description at the height of the Victorian re-creation of the squire ideal:

> The position of a landed propietor, be he squire or nobleman, is one of dignity. Wealth must always bring its responsibilities, but a landed proprietor is especially in a responsible position. He is the natural head of his parish or district – in which he should be looked up to as the bond of union between the classes. To him the poor man should look up for protection; those in doubt or difficulty for advice; the ill disposed for reproof or punishment; the deserving, of all classes, for consideration and hospitality; and *all* for honourable and Christian example.[6]

Scott may have imagined that he was speaking eternal verities in that paragraph. But there are symptomatic elements of change: by 1857 land was no longer the only wealth – this was now the most industrialized country on earth – and landownership, with its land power, had come to seem like a specialized subset of leadership. The insistence on the deference of others is also, subliminally, fragile – it had never needed such clumsy articulation before. A sort of sanctimonious and clammy piety has entered the room and Scott's words feel like an over-restored church.

Underlying the gracefulness of those moral qualities was a harsh reality. As Walter Benjamin, the great Jewish cultural critic in Nazi Germany, wrote in *Illuminations*, 'There is no document of civilization which is not at the same time a document of barbarism.'[7] Power, ownership, dominance and exploitation lie at the centre of these beautiful landscapes and elegant forms of behaviour. The relationship of the English gentry to those they employed, those they owned – as slaves in America and the Caribbean – and those who rented their land was not a love structure. None of the self-enhancing virtues apparent in these families would have been possible without an underpinning of money, derived from the gentry's enormous landholding and the rents it produced. Between the 1530s and the First World War, the gentry owned at least half the acreage of England.[8] Only rarely did individual families last that long but as one or other fell, through bad luck or bad management, another very similar took its place. That cloud-like economic constancy – rarely the same but always the same – was combined with a control of the political and judicial systems which placed them on little local summits all over the English counties. In those raw terms, this is a story of the political and economic dominance of a self-sustaining and cannily self-renewing class.

But the gentry's story is also about deep political, economic and social change, and the way in which they responded to it. Reduced to essentials, that gentry relationship to power pursued a simple arc: emergence in the late Middle Ages as supporters of the great feudal magnates; maturing into the natural governors of England under the shade of the increasingly potent state in the sixteenth and seventeenth centuries; outmanoeuvred by the aristocrats and merchants in England but thriving abroad in the eighteenth century; living a strange, half-real afterlife in the nineteenth century, when industrial and commercial money sustained a make-believe version of gentry style; poleaxed in the late nineteenth century by modern globalizing markets and a deep, democratizing shift in political culture; and finally in the twentieth century, carefully and at times desperately, attempting to manage decline. That is the whole story: the rise and fall of a ruling class. Gentry life became a quirky corner of England, not its soul. Of course the new rich, bankers and media stars, bought up estates and their houses, but they could make no claim on power as a result. That was the deepest of changes: gentrydom and government lost touch with each other.

It is difficult to tell who owns England now. The government's Land Registry is incomplete (40 per cent of land is unregistered) and no other source of information makes up the lack. Very roughly, though, it is possible to make out a picture of the revolutionary change that occurred in the pattern of English landholding in the twentieth century. The crown (now including large estates held by the Ministry of Defence, the Forestry Commission and other public bodies) has doubled its acreage from about 10 per cent to 20 per cent. The great landowners, now also taken to include large charitable bodies such as the National Trust, which play the socially prominent role of the ancient aristocracy, have also done well out of a century of cheap finance and plenty of land on the market, particularly in the unfarmed uplands. They now own about a quarter of England and Wales. The yeomen, now classified as owner-occupier farmers, have roared into prominence, buying up the land they used to rent. There are now 135,000 owner-occupiers, settled on about 35 per cent of the land. Urban land has increased a little and the church has effectively disappeared from the picture. The huge change is in the gentry, that is non-farming, non-noble, non-government landowners. Until 1914, they owned half of England. They now own less than 1 per cent of it.[9]

Through the twentieth century, the state, a cluster of ancient and well-funded aristocratic families and a few public bodies came to sit alongside the mass of farmers as owners of the country. The gentry, as any more than a few families hanging on to their plots, or some new men coming in from the City and buying up the plots which fading families have vacated, became a statistical irrelevance.

As a result, for much of the 1900s and because of the change in the relationship of government and society, the gent was a faintly ridiculous figure. In Bryan Forbes's script for *The League of Gentlemen*, written and filmed in 1959, the ex-officers who gather to rob a bank are all pitiable or absurd. Major Rupert Buckland Smith DSO 'wears only pyjama bottoms and still has a good figure, fleshy but still firm. The face is one we might see in *The Tatler*, smiling over a glass of bubbly at the Regimental Ball.' Captain Mycroft has been cashiered for gross indecency in a public place and is now masquerading as a vicar. All the others have failed and fallen on wrong or hard times. Their lives and values have become futile and irrelevant in a country dominated by the Welfare State and the needs of democracy. They are left over from a previous age and as a result Colonel Hyde, played by Jack Hawkins, is able to blackmail them into joining his gang. 'Where do I fit in?' he asks his new recruits rhetorically, dragging on a cigarette.

> Well, I'm afraid I have the advantage over you gentlemen. My criminal career is just beginning. You won't find anything on me – not a blemish. I served my country well and was suitably rewarded ... by being declared redundant.[10]

If the gentry were redundant in the statism of 1960s and '70s Britain, they were equally irrelevant to the Thatcherite experiment. For an enterprise culture whose heroes were the cutters and thrusters of an unregulated market and a booming, credit-based economy, the honour-conscious gentry were always going to look more out of date than ever. In the macho world of Thatcher's revisionist anti-socialism, those one-nation conservatives who were interested in the wellbeing of society were dismissed as 'wet'.[11] It looked for a while as if the species was dying out entirely.

In the early twenty-first century, though, the inadequacies of both the dirigiste and the free-market models created, quite unexpectedly, the appetite for a return to something that looked suspiciously like gentry-style government. The novelist Howard Jacobson reflected on the change in the summer of 2010, just as the new Conservative–Liberal coalition was being formed, led by gentry-style politicians of a style, ideology and manner which had not been seen in Britain for four or five decades.

> We are thinking about this in England at the moment, where class has returned to politics and the men of the hour are suddenly the men we supposed we had dispensed with. We had thought history had rendered them redundant, but it would seem that in our disillusionment with the self-made millionaires and bonus-driven bankers who have ruined us we have turned again to men of property and family and privileged education.[12]

True to their backgrounds, these politicians embraced the traditional gentry point of view. The whole of society was what mattered. They were prepared to lead it. The powerful and central state, of which they were now in control, was bad for the sense of general wellbeing. Power and authority should descend again to the localities, to the very county communities with which the stories in this book have been involved. The word 'gentry' was never mentioned – it still carried the baggage of its twentieth-century failure – but nothing that either David Cameron, the Conservative Prime Minister, or his deputy, the Liberal Nick Clegg, described in their first formative days of government was hostile to a longstanding gentry ideology.

'Frankly, for decades', Cameron told a meeting in the Cabinet Room at Downing Street on 18 May 2010, 'you've had politicians sitting round this table, making decisions, telling us all what to do, issuing orders and instructions and passing laws and regulations.' That had to go and 'step one is transferring power from the centre to the local'.[13]

> We want to give citizens, communities and local government the power and information they need to come together, solve the problems they face and build the Britain they want. We want society – the families, networks, neighbourhoods and communities that form the fabric

417

of so much of our everyday lives – to be bigger and stronger than ever before.[14]

Communities, localism, families, networks and neighbourhoods, all bound together in the metaphor of the fabric, one, single, woven social structure: what else had the gentry ever dedicated their existence to? But this modern version of the gentry vision has a flaw: it is sentimentalized. It doesn't grasp the fact, or perhaps even want to admit the fact, that competition, unkindness, rivalry and dominance always lay behind the beautiful sense of community which the gentry world embodied. The gentry owned their worlds, dispensed justice within them, punished wrongdoers, told people what to do and issued orders and instructions. They did, in fact, exactly what politicians do. Any idea that society could dispense with politics, at whatever level, is a futile dream, a soggy sock of wish-fulfilment. Life is a struggle and community is political.

If anyone wants to see a version of the gentry community in full and florid, modern action, they could do no better than tune in to Prime Minister's Question Time. The energy and anger of the chamber of the House of Commons have always been the truest model of who the gentry were: deeply competitive, hungry to gain advantage over the other, reliant on fierce, articulate and sometimes witty speech, ready to abandon allies in difficulty, but somehow out of that tussle and rage able to summon the warmth, charm, love, care and beauty which is evident in many of these pages.

NOTES

INTRODUCTION: Ungentle Gentles

1 See J. P. Cooper, 'Ideas of Gentility in Early Modern England', in *Land, Men and Beliefs*, ed. G. E. Aylmer and J. S. Morrill, London, 1983

2 G. E. Mingay, *The Gentry*, Longman, 1976, 77–8

3 James Harrington, *Oceana*, London, 1737, I, 243–4

4 Except, sadly, those in South Carolina, Antigua and Barbados

5 Felicity Heal and Clive Holmes, *The Gentry in England and Wales*, Basingstoke, 1994, 381

6 N. Upton, *De Studio Militari*, ed. F. P. Barnard, 48, quoted in Cooper, 'Ideas of Gentility in Early Modern England', in *Land, Men and Beliefs*, 48

7 Cooper, 'Ideas of Gentility in Early Modern England', in *Land, Men and Beliefs*

8 Thomas Fuller, *The Holy State and the Profane State*, 1841, 106

9 *The Pamphleteer*, vol. xxiii, 1824, 159–74

10 Sir James Lawrence, 'On the Nobility of the British Gentry compared with those on the Continent', *The Pamphleteer*, vol. xxiii, 1824, 160

11 E. A. Wasson, 'The Penetration of New Wealth into the English Governing Class from the Middle Ages to the First World War', *Economic History Review*, LI, 1, 1998, 25–48

12 E. A. Wasson, 'The Penetration of New Wealth into the English Governing Class from the Middle Ages to the First World War', *Economic History Review*, 40

13 Geoffrey Hickes, *A Gentleman Instructed in the Conduct of a Virtuous and Happy Life, Written for the Instruction of a Young Nobleman*, London, 1709, 29

14 Paul le Cacheuz, ed., *Actes de Chancellerie d'Henri VI, concernant la Normandie sous la domination anglaise* (1422–1435), vol. 2, Rouen, 1908, ccxxxvii

15 Anon., *Institucon of a Gentleman*, 1555, Sig. B, vii

16 Anon., *Institucon of a Gentleman*, 1555, Sig. D, ii

17 Lord Mahon, ed., *The Letters of Philip Dormer Stanhope, Earl of Chesterfield*, London, 1845, vol. I, xiv

18 Mahon, *Letters of Chesterfield*, 42

19 Mahon, *Letters of Chesterfield*, 74

20 Hickes, *A Gentleman*, 28

21 Hickes, *A Gentleman*, 14

22 Hickes, *A Gentleman*, 15

PART I The Inherited World 1410–1520

1 H. H. Lamb, *Climate, History and the Modern World*, London, 1995, 177–86

2 Polydore Vergil, *Anglica Historia*, Basel, 1534, 17

Survival

1 The Plumptons of Plumpton (or Plompton) near Knaresborough in the West Riding of Yorkshire – 'plump' was the word for a clump of trees in Yorkshire – are one of the few medieval families whose letter collections have survived. The originals have disappeared but a rather battered manuscript book of transcripts, made between 1612 and 1626, is now held by the West Yorkshire Archive Service. It is in the Leeds Record Office, where you can find it under 'Acc. 1731'. The letters were partly classified in social order – those from sovereigns first, then dukes, earls, barons and so on, sinking to ordinary gents and lawyers. The book and other Plumpton manuscripts were bought by a

Nottinghamshire antiquarian, J. E. F. Chambers, at a Sotheby's sale in 1883 and given to West Yorkshire Archive Service by one of his descendants in 1972. The letters were first published by the brilliant Victorian scholar Thomas Stapleton as *Plumpton Correspondence*, Camden Society, 4, 1839, from here on referred to in these notes as 'Stapleton'. Joan Kirby has also published a modern edition: *The Plumpton Letters and Papers*, Camden Society, 5th series, 8, 1996, referred to here as 'Kirby'. For Brafferton Ford, see Stapleton, Introduction, lx ff: 'The artikles of the Cardinall of Yorke of the offences and occasion done by Sir William of Plompton, Thomas Beckwith and other misdoers and rioters of the forest of Knaresboroughe', 1441.

2 Kirby, 2

3 Stapleton, xxiv

4 Stapleton, xlii, xlvi (note o), xlix

5 Stapleton, xlix

6 Ruth Wilcock, 'The Life and Career of Sir William Plumpton', *Northern History*, XLIV, September 2007, 36

7 Stapleton, lvii

8 Ruth Wilcock, 'Local Disorder in the Honour of Knaresborough, c.1438–1461 and the National Context', *Northern History*, XLI, March 2004, 47–51

9 Stapleton, lix

10 Stapleton, lix

11 Stapleton, lx

12 Stapleton, lx

13 Stapleton, lx–lxi

14 Stapleton, lxi–lxii

15 Wilcock, 'The Life and Career of Sir William Plumpton', *Northern History*, 37

16 Wilcock, 'The Life and Career of Sir William Plumpton', *Northern History*, 34

17 Family tree, Kirby, prelims

18 Stapleton, lxiv

19 Stapleton, lxiv

20 Stapleton, lxiv

21 Kirby, 322

22 Stapleton, xxxiv

23 Brian Rocliffe to Sir William Plumpton, December 1463; Kirby, 30; Stapleton, 155

24 Godfrey Grene to Sir William Plumpton, 5 December 1469, about various individuals stealing his fish; Kirby, 42–3; Stapleton, 172

25 Stapleton, lxxxvi

26 Henry VI to Sir William Plumpton, 13 March 1461; Kirby, 26; Stapleton, 151

27 A sailor's term, used of ships pitching up and down in a heavy sea; R. Holinshed, *Chronicles*, London, 1808, vol. III, 278

28 Holinshed, *Chronicles*, 278

29 V. Fiorato, A. Boylston and C. Knusel, *Blood Red Roses: The Archaeology of a Mass Grave from the Battle of Towton A.D. 1461*, Oxford, 2007

30 A. Boylston et al., www.brad.ac.uk/acad/archsci/depart/resgrp/towton/

31 G. Müldner and M. P. Richards, 'Fast or Feast: Reconstructing Diet in Later Medieval England by Stable Isotope Analysis', *Journal of Archaeological Science*, vol. 32, issue 1, January 2005, 39–48

32 Edward Hall, *Hall's Chonicle*, New York, 1965, 256

33 P. J. C. Field (ed.), Sir Thomas Malory, *Le Morte Darthur: The Seventh and Eighth Tales*, London, 2008, 80

34 Wilcock, 'The Life and Career of Sir William Plumpton', *Northern History*, 39; Stapleton, lxvii–lxx

35 William Shakespeare, *Henry VI, Part III*, Act III, Scene iii, line 157

36 M. Hicks, *Warwick the Kingmaker*, Oxford, 1998, 255–6

37 Stapleton, lxix

38 Stapleton, lxix

39 Stapleton, lxix

40 John Neville, Earl of Northumberland, to Sir John Mauleverer, 7 December 1464–9; Kirby, 44; Stapleton, 152

41 John Neville, Earl of Northumberland, to Sir John

Mauleverer, 7 December 1464–9; Kirby, 44; Stapleton, 152

42 Brian Rocliffe to Sir William Plumpton, 5 November 1461; Kirby, 27; Stapleton, 155

43 John Felton and John Warde to Sir William Plumpton, 14 September 1464–69; Kirby, 45; Stapleton, 165

44 Stapleton, lxxx

45 Brian Rocliffe to Sir William Plumpton, December 1463; Kirby, 30; Stapleton, 155

46 Indenture, 15 November 1463; Kirby, 258

47 Stapleton, lxxx

48 Stapleton, lxxvii

49 Stapleton, lxxvii

50 Stapleton, lxxvii

51 Stapleton, lxxvii

52 Wilcock, 'The Life and Career of Sir William Plumpton', *Northern History*, 49

53 Stapleton, lxxxix

54 Judgement, 16 September 1483; Stapleton, xci

55 Robert Grene to Sir Robert Plumpton, ?1486; Kirby, 68; Stapleton, 66

56 Sir Richard Tunstall to Sir Robert Plumpton, ?1487; Kirby, 73; Stapleton, 71

57 Edward Plumpton to Sir Robert Plumpton, 3 February 1597; Kirby, 116; Stapleton, 140

58 John Pullein to Sir Robert Plumpton, 18 May 1501; Kirby, 143; Stapleton, 95

59 Francis Bacon, *Works*, vol. 5, London, 1803, 166, 167

60 John Pullein to Sir Robert Plumpton, 18 May 1501; Kirby, 143; Stapleton, 95

61 Sir Robert Plumpton to Henry VIII, after April 1509; Kirby, 186

62 Stapleton, cvii

63 Sir Robert Plumpton to Henry VIII, after April 1509; Kirby, 186

64 Sir Robert Plumpton to Henry VIII, after April 1509; Kirby, 186

65 Sir Robert Plumpton to Agnes Plumpton, 9 September 1502; Kirby, 152; Stapleton, cxi

66 Sir Robert Plumpton to Agnes Plumpton, 9 September 1502; Kirby, 152; Stapleton, cx–cxi

67 15 January 1505; Kirby, 283

68 Stapleton, cviii

69 Stapleton, cxii

70 Kirby, 153, note 2

71 Sir John Towneley to Sir Robert Plumpton, 2 November 1502; Kirby, 152; Stapleton, 43

72 Henry Ardern to Sir Robert Plumpton, 1504; Kirby, 179; Stapleton, 83

73 Agnes Plumpton to Sir Robert Plumpton, 26 April 1504; Kirby, 174; Stapleton, 45

74 Stapleton, cxii

75 Thomas Savage, Archbishop of York, to William Plumpton, 24 Februrary 1503; Kirby, 161; Stapleton, 198

76 William Plumpton to Sir Robert Plumpton, 21 March 1503; Kirby, 162; Stapleton, 52

77 William Plumpton to Sir Robert Plumpton, 21 March 1503, Kirby, 162; Stapleton, 52

78 Sir Robert Plumpton to Agnes Plumpton, 13 February 1504; Kirby, 169–70

79 Agnes Plumpton to Sir Robert Plumpton, 19 March 1504; Kirby, 171; Stapleton, 47

80 Agnes Plumpton to Sir Robert Plumpton, 12 April 1504; Kirby, 172; Stapleton, 49

81 Agnes Plumpton to Sir Robert Plumpton, 12 April 1504; Kirby, 172; Stapleton, 49

82 Agnes Plumpton to Sir Robert Plumpton, 12 April 1504; Kirby, 172; Stapleton, 49

83 Agnes Plumpton to Sir Robert Plumpton, 12 April 1504; Kirby, 172–3; Stapleton, 49

84 Agnes Plumpton to Sir Robert Plumpton, 26 April 1504; Kirby, 174; Stapleton, 45

85 Robert Chaloner to Sir Robert Plumpton, no date; Kirby, 180–81; Stapleton, 79

86 Lady Neville to Isabel Plumpton, 28
     April ?1506; Kirby, 182; Stapleton, 82
87 Stapleton, cxix–cxxii
88 Indenture, 2 May 1515; Kirby, 291–2;
     Stapleton, cxxiii–cxxv
89 Stapleton, cxxvii
90 Stapleton, cxxxviii

PART II In the Renaissance State
1520–1610

1 R. A. Griffiths, 'Tudor, Owen (c.1400–
    1461)', *Oxford Dictionary of National
    Biography*, Oxford University Press,
    2004
2 Sir Robert Naunton, *Fragmenta
    Regalia* (1630), London, 1870, 25
3 Estienne Perlin, *Descriptions des
    Royaulmes d'Angleterre et d'Escosse*,
    Paris, 1558, 11. Perlin loved England
    but hated the English, who spat in his
    face.

Discretion

1 Thomas Fuller, 'The Good Yeoman',
    The Holy State & the Profane State
    (1642), London, 1840, XXXIII, 91
2 John Leland, *Itineraries* (1549), ed. T.
    Hearne, Oxford, 1770, vol. IV, 51
3 For a masterly exploration of the
    Throckmortons in the sixteenth
    century, see Peter Marshall, 'Crisis of
    Allegiance: George Throckmorton
    and Henry Tudor', in P. Marshall and
    G. Scott, eds, *Catholic Gentry in
    English Society*, Ashgate, Farnham,
    2009, 31–67; also for the rippling
    effects in later generations, see Peter
    Marshall, 'Faith and Identity in a
    Warwickshire Family: The
    Throckmortons and the Reformation',
    Dugdale Society Occasional Papers,
    No. 49, 2010
4 Marshall, 'Crisis', 33; Robert
    Throckmorton's Will, The National
    Archives (TNA) Prob 11/20
5 *Letters & Papers, Foreign & Domestic,
    Henry VIII*, ed. James Gairdner, R. H.
    Brodie and J. S. Brewer, Institute of
    Historical Research, 1864–1920,

available online at www.british-
history.ac.uk (henceforth L&P), 2 (ii):
3922
6 L&P, 4 (ii): 4543
7 L&P, 6: 119, 120
8 Much of the following is in George's
    full confession of October 1537,
    found among Cromwell's papers and
    now in the National Archives under
    SP 1/125 fols 247–56; summarized in
    L&P, 12 (ii): 951–2; transcribed and
    modernized in J. A. Guy, *The Public
    Career of Sir Thomas More*, Yale
    University Press, 1980, 207–12
9 Guy, *Public Career*, 210
10 SP 1/125 fol. 251
11 SP 1/125 fol. 251
12 SP 1/125 fol. 247
13 SP 1/125 fols 251–2
14 SP 1/125 fol. 247
15 L&P, 6: 1365
16 Marshall, 'Crisis', 37–8
17 R. Holinshed, *Chronicles*, London,
     1808, vol. IV, 52. These phrases were
     used by George's son Nicholas at his
     treason trial under Mary Tudor.
18 L&P, 8: 26
19 George's first, partial confession made
     in the Tower between December 1536
     and January 1537 was also among
     Cromwell's papers and is now in the
     National Archives under SP 1/113
     folios 60r–65r; summarized in L&P,
     11: 1406; this passage is under SP
     1/113 fols 62r–62v
20 William Roper, *The Lyfe of Sir Thomas
     More, Knyghte*, Kraus reprint, 1978, 72
21 *The Penguin Book of Renaissance Verse*,
     2005, ed. H. R. Woudhuysen and D.
     Norbrook, 84
22 L&P, 11: 1406; SP 1/113 fol. 60r
23 L&P, 11: 1406; SP 1/113 fol. 60r
24 L&P, 11: 1406; SP 1/113 fols 60r–60v
25 Proclamation by Robert Aske, 15
     October 1536
26 L&P, 11: 1406; SP 1/113 fol. 60v
27 L&P, 11: 1406; L&P, 11: 1406; SP 1/113
     fol. 65r
28 Marshall, 'Crisis', 47
29 L&P, 11: 1405; SP 1/125 fol. 199
30 SP 1/125 fol. 250

31 SP 1/125 fol. 249

32 SP 1/125 fol. 252

33 Guy, *Public Career*, 203

34 Marshall, 'Crisis', 54

35 Marshall, 'Faith and Identity', 10; TNA Prob 11/36

36 Marshall, 'Faith and Identity', 15

Control

1 Alison D. Wall's edition of *Two Elizabethan Women: Correspondence of Joan and Maria Thynne 1575–1611*, Wiltshire Record Society 38, Devizes, 1983, lies at the root of much of this chapter. The letters themselves belong to the Marquess of Bath and they are quoted here from the microfilm edition (microform R96703, 1950–) with his kind permission.

2 His mother said as much: Joan Thynne to John Thynne, 30 May 1595, Thynne Papers, v 73; Wall, *Eliz. Women*, 11–12

3 Philip Sidney and Mary, Countess of Pembroke, ed. and dedicatee, *The Countess of Pembroke's Arcadia*, 1593; Sir John Harington, translator, *Orlando Furioso*, 1591

4 A. Wall, *Eliz. Women*, and 'For Love, Money, or Politics? A Clandestine Marriage and the Elizabethan Court of Arches', *The Historical Journal*, 38, 3 (1995), 511

5 A. Feuillerat, ed., *The Countess of Pembroke's Arcadia*, Cambridge University Press, 1939, 143

6 Alison Wall, 'Faction in Local Politics 1580–1620, Struggles for Supremacy in Wiltshire', *Wiltshire Archaeological Magazine* 72/73 (1980), 121–9

7 A. Wall, 'Patterns of Politics in England 1558–1625', *The Historical Journal*, 31, 4 (1988), 947–63

8 Wall, 'Faction', 121

9 B. Botfield, *Stemmata Botevilliana*, London, 1858, pedigree of Thynnes descended from a man apparently called 'Thom at the Inne', 55

10 Mark Girouard, 'Thynne, Sir John (1512/13–1580)', *Oxford Dictionary of National Biography*, Oxford University Press, September 2004

11 Sir John Thynne to Christian Gresham, 5 February 1565; and to his son John at Oxford, December 1570, Thynne Papers (both on display at Longleat)

12 Ian Blanchard, 'Gresham, Sir Richard (c.1485–1549)', *Oxford Dictionary of National Biography*, Oxford University Press, 2004

13 D. A. Crowley (ed.) et al., *Victoria County History, Wiltshire*, vol. 13, 1987, 155–69

14 The Mervyns' Fonthill is long gone, replaced with one of the most beautiful eighteenth- and nineteenth-century landscapes in England, all paid for with the slave and sugar money of the Beckford family.

15 Barrett L. Beer, 'Seymour, Edward, Duke of Somerset (c.1500–1552)', *Oxford Dictionary of National Biography*, Oxford University Press, 2004

16 Wall, *Eliz. Women*, xviii

17 Wall, *Eliz. Women*, xviii

18 Wall, *Eliz. Women*, xviii

19 Wall, *Eliz. Women*, xix; Paul Slack, 'Hayward, Sir Rowland (c.1520–1593)', rev. *Oxford Dictionary of National Biography*, Oxford University Press, 2004

20 Richard Young to Sir John Thynne, 29 July 1575, Thynne Papers, iv, 79; Wall, *Eliz. Women*, 54

21 Richard Young to Sir John Thynne, 29 July 1575, Thynne Papers, iv, 79; Wall, *Eliz. Women*, 55

22 E. S. Cope, *Handmaid of the Holy Spirit: Dame Eleanor Davies, Never Soe Mad a Ladie*, Ann Arbor, 1992

23 C. Herrup, *A House in Gross Disorder: Sex, Law, and the 2nd Earl of Castlehaven*, Oxford University Press, 2001

24 Wall, 'Faction', 124–5

25 Wall, 'Clandestine', 511

26 Wall, 'Clandestine', 511

27 Wall, 'Clandestine', 511–12

28 Much of the story that follows comes from a many-paged manuscript among the Thynne Papers (Book 190, Box XCIII), not available on microfilm, a transcript of allegations, questions and depositions in a suit at the Court of Arches between 1597 and 1601. No page numbers. See Wall, 'Clandestine', 511, note 2

29 Book 190, Thomas Thynne's answer, 5 May 1601; Wall, 'Clandestine', 527

30 Book 190, Edmund Mervyn deposition, 29 April 1597

31 Book 190, Edmund Mervyn deposition, 29 April 1597

32 Book 190, Lucy Audley's deposition, 7 May 1597

33 Wall, 'Clandestine', 530

34 Book 190, Edmund Mervyn deposition, 29 April 1597

35 Book 190, Thomas Maudesley's deposition, undated, ?28 April 1597

36 Book 190, final hearing, 22 May 1601; Wall, 'Clandestine', 527

37 Searched online: http://www.lulu.com/product/ebook/orlando-furioso/579486

38 Wall, 'Faction', 123

39 Joan Thynne to Thomas Higgins, 15 April 1595, Thynne Papers, v 80; Wall, *Eliz. Women*, 8

40 Joan Thynne to Thomas Higgins, 15 April 1595, Thynne Papers, v 80; Wall, *Eliz. Women*, 8

41 Joan Thynne to John Thynne, 20 April 1595, Thynne Papers, v 82; Wall, *Eliz. Women*, 9

42 Joan Thynne to John Thynne, 20 April 1595, Thynne Papers, v 82; Wall, *Eliz. Women*, 9

43 Alison Wall interprets these words ('boteid and sporde' in the original) as 'butted and sported'; Wall, *Eliz. Women*, 9

44 Joan Thynne to John Thynne, 20 April 1595, Thynne Papers, v 82; Wall, *Eliz. Women*, 9

45 Joan Thynne to John Thynne, 8 May 1595, Thynne Papers, v 84; Wall, *Eliz. Women*, 10

46 Joan Thynne to John Thynne, 8 May 1595, Thynne Papers, v 84; Wall, *Eliz. Women*, 10

47 Joan Thynne to John Thynne, 8 May 1595, Thynne Papers, v 84; Wall, *Eliz. Women*, 10

48 Joan Thynne to John Thynne, 30 May 1595, Thynne Papers, v 73; Wall, *Eliz. Women*, 11

49 Joan Thynne to John Thynne, 30 May 1595, Thynne Papers, v 73; Wall, *Eliz. Women*, 11

50 Joan Hayward to John Thynne, soon after 10 October 1575, Thynne Papers, v 4; Wall, *Eliz. Women*, 1

51 Book 190, Thomas Thynne's evidence 5 May 1601; Wall, 'Clandestine', 527

52 Wall, 'Clandestine', 522–6

53 Elizabeth Knyvett to John Thynne, 16 March 1601, Thynne Papers, vii 200; Wall, 'Clandestine', 526

54 Book 190, Thomas Thynne's evidence, 5 May 1601; Wall, 'Clandestine', 527

55 Book 190, final hearing, 22 May 1601; Wall, 'Clandestine', 527

56 Wall, 'Clandestine', 527

57 Book 190, final hearing, 22 May 1601, Wall, 'Clandestine', 527

58 John Thynne to Joan Thynne, 26 July 1601, Thynne Papers, v 110; Wall, *Eliz. Women*, 20

59 John Thynne to Joan Thynne, 26 July 1601, Thynne Papers, v 110; Wall, *Eliz. Women*, 20

60 Sir James Mervyn to Maria Thynne, 19 August 1607, Thynne Papers, vii 335; Wall, *Eliz. Women*, 41

61 Maria Thynne to Joan Thynne, 15 September 1601, Thynne Papers, viii 12; Wall, *Eliz. Women*, 21

62 Lucy Audley to Joan Thynne, 10 June 1602, Thynne Papers, vii 232; Wall, *Eliz. Women*, 26

63 Lucy Audley to Joan Thynne, 10 June 1602, Thynne Papers, vii 232; Wall *Eliz. Women*, 26

64 Lucy Audley to Joan Thynne, 10 June 1602, Thynne Papers, vii 232; Wall *Eliz. Women*, 26

65 Maria Thynne to Joan Thynne, 13 June 1602, Thynne Papers, viii 16; Wall, *Eliz. Women*, 27

66 Maria Thynne to Joan Thynne, 27 July 1602, Thynne Papers, viii 18; Wall, *Eliz. Women*, 27–8

67 Joan Thynne to Lucy Audley, 8 August 1602, Thynne Papers, vii 237; Wall, *Eliz. Women*, 28–9

68 Joan Thynne to Lucy Audley, 8 August 1602, Thynne Papers, vii 237; Wall, *Eliz. Women*, 28

69 Then as now: Robbie Williams lives on the site of the Mervyns' Compton Bassett manor house; the site of Caus Castle is barely more than a lump of ruined wall and a scrubby wood in the middle of a sheep-dunged field.

70 Joan Thynne to John Thynne, 30 September 1600, Thynne Papers, v 97–8; Wall, *Eliz. Women*, 14

71 Joan Thynne to John Thynne, 30 September 1600, Thynne Papers, v 97–8; Wall, *Eliz. Women*, 14–15

72 Joan Thynne to John Thynne, 15 November 1600, Thynne Papers, v 101; Wall, *Eliz. Women*, 16

73 Joan Thynne to John Thynne, 18 June 1601, Thynne Papers, v 108; Wall, *Eliz. Women*, 19

74 Joan Thynne to John Thynne, 5 March 1603, Thynne Papers, v 122–3; Wall, *Eliz. Women*, 30

75 Maria Thynne to Thomas Thynne, *c.*1604–5, Thynne Papers, viii 1; Wall, *Eliz. Women*, 32

76 Maria Thynne to Thomas Thynne, *c.*1604–5, Thynne Papers, viii 1; Wall, *Eliz. Women*, 32

77 Maria Thynne to Thomas Thynne, *c.*1607, Thynne Papers, viii 6; Wall, *Eliz. Women*, 37

78 Maria Thynne to Thomas Thynne, *c.*1607, Thynne Papers, viii 6; Wall, *Eliz. Women*, 38

79 Maria Thynne to Joan Thynne, 1606, Thynne Papers, viii 10; Wall, *Eliz. Women*, 34

80 Maria Thynne to Joan Thynne, 1606, Thynne Papers, viii 10; Wall, *Eliz. Women*, 34. For an essay on Maria's rhetorical weaponry see Graham Williams, '"trobled *wth* a tedious discours": Sincerity, Sarcasm and Seriousness in the Letters of Maria Thynne, *c.*1601–1610', *Journal of Historical Pragmatics*, 11:2 (2010), 169–93

81 Maria Thynne to Joan Thynne, 1606, Thynne Papers, viii 10; Wall, *Eliz. Women*, 34

82 Maria Thynne to Joan Thynne, 1606, Thynne Papers, viii 10; Wall, *Eliz. Women*, 34

83 Joan Thynne to Thomas Thynne, 11 April 1607, Thynne Papers, viii 26; Wall, *Eliz. Women*, 38

84 Joan Thynne to Thomas Thynne, 11 April 1607, Thynne Papers, viii 26; Wall, *Eliz. Women*, 38

85 Joan Thynne to Thomas Thynne, 11 April 1607, Thynne Papers, viii 26; Wall, *Eliz. Women*, 39

86 Maria Thynne to Thomas Thynne, early 1610, Thynne Papers, viii 8; Wall, *Eliz. Women*, 49

87 Thomas Thynne to Maria Thynne, *c.*May 1610, Thynne Papers, xl 8; Wall, *Eliz. Women*, 50–1

88 Lucy Audley to Maria Thynne, early 1610, Thynne Papers, viii 59; Wall, *Eliz. Women*, 50

89 C. Herrup, *A House in Gross Disorder: Sex, Law, and the 2nd Earl of Castlehaven*, Oxford University Press, 2001

90 D. Burnett, *Longleat: The Story of an English Country House*, London, 1978

PART III The Great Century 1610–1710

1 Edward Hyde, Earl of Clarendon, *The History of the Rebellion and Civil Wars in England*, London, 1717, Book 1, 74

2 J. Addison, *The Spectator*, No. 411, 21 June 1712

3 Bassingbourne Gawdy to Oliver le Neve, 6 February 1697, BL Add. (see page 00[beg of ch6]) 27397

4 John Norden, *The Surveiors Dialogue*, 1618

Steadiness

1 Francis Bamford, ed., *A Royalist's Notebook*, London, 1936, 172

2 All Oglander's surviving Account Books remain the property of Ms Fanny Oglander but are kept in the Isle of Wight County Record Office (IWCRO) in Newport, Isle of Wight. They are quoted with her very welcome permission. All references in these notes are to the IWCRO 'OG' numberings. Clifford Webster, for many years the Isle of Wight County Archivist, has made an exceptionally valuable indexed transcript of the books in which the spelling of the text is modernized. Pages of his transcript are referred to in these notes simply as 'Webster'; my quotations are from the notebooks themselves.

3 Entries for December 1642–3; OG 90/6 fols ii–iii; Webster 807–9

4 OG 90/6 fol. v verso; Webster 816

5 OG 90/6 fol. iv; Webster 813

6 OG 90/6 fol. vi; Webster 817

7 OG 90/6 fols vi verso to xii; Webster 818–29

8 OG 90/6 page 96; Webster 888

9 OG 90/6 fol. vi; Webster 817

10 OG 90/4a fol. xi verso; Webster 614

11 Letter to Frances, 11 July 1643 OG/CC/52; Cecil Aspinall-Oglander, *Nunwell Symphony*, London, 1945, 99

12 OG 90/4a fol. iii verso; Webster 598; letter 26 July 1643; Aspinall-Oglander, *Nunwell Symphony*, 99

13 OG 90/6 page 61; Webster 889

14 OG 93/3a fol. 64; Webster 453

15 OG 90/4a fol. xxv; Webster 641

16 OG 90/4a fol. xxxiv; Webster 659

17 OG 17/10; Webster 963

18 OG 93/3b frontispiece 3 to fol. iv; Webster 482–9

19 OG 93/3b fol. i; Webster 483

20 OG 93/3b fol. iii; Webster 487

21 OG 93/3b fol. ii verso; Webster 486

22 OG 93/3b fol. i; Webster 483

23 OG 93/3b fol. i verso; Webster 484

24 OG 93/3b fol. i verso; Webster 484

25 OG 93/3b fol. iii; Webster 487

26 OG 93/3b fol. i verso; Webster 484

27 OG 93/3b fol. iii; Webster 487

28 OG 93/3b fol. iii verso; Webster 488

29 OG 90/4a fol. iii verso; Webster 598

30 OG 90/4a fol. xii; Webster 615

31 OG 93/3b fol. iv; Webster 489

32 OG 90/1 page 159; Webster 48

33 OG 90/1 page 157; Webster 46

34 OG/19/1

35 OG 90/6 page 95; Webster 887

36 OG 90/6 page 95; Webster 887

37 OG 90/6 page 95; Webster 887

38 Bamford, *A Royalist's Notebook*, 250; OG 90/6 page 97; Webster 889

39 OG 90/6 frontispiece; Webster 805

40 Bamford, *A Royalist's Notebook*, 250–1; OG 90/6 page 97; Webster 889

41 W. H. Long, *The Oglander Memoirs*, London, 1888, 7–9

42 Long, *Oglander Memoirs*, 6, 20–1

43 Long, *Oglander Memoirs*, 21

44 OG 90/4b fol. xv; Webster 711

45 OG 90/4b fol. xv verso; Webster 712

46 OG 93/3b fol. xvii; Webster 515

47 OG 93/3b fol. vii; Webster 495

48 OG 90/4b fol. 37; Webster 751; Aspinall-Oglander, *Nunwell Symphony*, 70

49 Aspinall-Oglander, *Nunwell Symphony*, 66

50 Bamford, *A Royalist's Notebook*, 72

51 Letter OG 0985/20; Aspinall-Oglander, *Nunwell Symphony*, 77

52 OG 90/4a fol. xx; Webster 631

53 OG 90/4a fol. xix verso; Webster 630

54 OG 90/4a fol. xx verso; Webster 632; Aspinall-Oglander, *Nunwell Symphony*, 81

55 OG 90/4a fol. vi; Webster 603

56 OG 90/4a fol. vi verso; Webster 604

57 OG 90/4a fol. vi verso; Webster 604

58 OG 90/4a fol. vi verso; Webster 604

59 OG 90/4a fol. vii verso; Webster 606

60 OG 90/4a fol. xxi; Webster 633

61 OG 90/4a fol. ix; Webster 609

62 OG 90/4b fol. xxvii verso; Webster 732

63 OG 90/4b fol. xxvii verso; Webster 732

64 OG 90/2 fol. 78; Webster 252 (on page of accounts 3 March 1627/8)

65 OG 90/4a fol. i; Webster 593

66 OG 90/4a fol. xi verso; Webster 614

67 Aspinall-Oglander, *Nunwell Symphony*, 90

68 Aspinall-Oglander, *Nunwell Symphony*, 93

69 OG 90/6 frontispiece; Webster 805

70 OG 90/6 frontispiece; Webster 805

71 OG 90/6 frontispiece; Webster 805

72 OG 90/6 frontispiece; Webster 805

73 OG 90/6 frontispiece 2; Webster 806

74 OG 90/6 fol. i; Webster 807

75 OG 90/6 page 8 verso; Webster 836; Aspinall-Oglander, *Nunwell Symphony*, 104

76 Aspinall-Oglander, *Nunwell Symphony*, 96

77 OG 90/6 fol. i; Webster 807

78 OG 90/6 fol. ix; Webster 823

79 Aspinall-Oglander, *Nunwell Symphony*, 97

80 OG/CC/51; Aspinall-Oglander, *Nunwell Symphony*, 98

81 OG/CC/52 11 July 1643; Aspinall-Oglander, *Nunwell Symphony*, 99

82 OG/CC/53

83 OG 90/6 fol. x; Webster 825

84 Now the super-salubrious Castle Lane in Victoria.

85 Aspinall-Oglander, *Nunwell Symphony*, 103

86 OG 90/6 fol. x; Webster 825

87 OG 90/6 fol. i verso; Webster 808; Aspinall-Oglander, *Nunwell Symphony*, 103

88 OG 90/6 fol. xi verso; Webster 828

89 Aspinall-Oglander, *Nunwell Symphony*, 108

90 OG 90/6 fol. xi verso; Webster 828 (1647)

91 Aspinall-Oglander, *Nunwell Symphony*, 110

92 OG 90/6 page 133; Webster 915

93 OG 90/6 page 46; Webster 864

94 OG 90/6 page 7; Webster 835

95 OG 90/6 page 16; Webster 844

96 OG 90/6 page 113; Webster 899

97 Or perhaps not. His father's is a much finer piece of sculpture than his own and this may be Crocker's work. Oglander had bought, at an earlier stage, 'a statue of a Turkish knight', which he kept in his cellar at Nunwell and which his will instructed his son

to put up in the church at Brading in his memory. So this image may be of a random Turk.

98 D. Wharton Lloyd, *The Isle of Wight: Buildings of England (Pevsner Architectural Guides: Buildings of England)*, Yale University Press, 2006, 94

99 Aspinall-Oglander, *Nunwell Symphony*, 174

Withdrawal

1 Cornelius Janssen arrived in Kent to paint many gentry portraits in about 1636 (Oxinden Letters I, 168)

2 The extraordinarily rich cache of Oxinden letters are all in the British Library in seven folio volumes running from 1589 to 1710, numbered Add. MSS 27999–28005. Harry's notebooks are there too under Add. 28010, 28012–3 and 54332–4. And there are still more Oxinden papers under MSS 28006–28012. The BL catalogue spells the name of the family 'Oxenden', which is an anachronism for the seventeenth century. The letters were bought by the British Museum in 1869 from Sir Henry Oxenden of Broome Park in Kent, a descendant of the people in this chapter, who spelled the name with two 'e's. Kent Archaeological Society in Maidstone has Harry Oxinden's Account Book. An outstanding edition of the letters was made by Dorothy Gardiner in two volumes: *The Oxinden Letters 1607–1642*, London, 1933, and *The Oxinden and Peyton Letters, 1642–1670*, London, 1937, from here on referred to in these notes as 'Letters I' and 'Letters II'.

3 Royal Commission on Historical Manuscripts, *The Manuscripts of His Grace the Duke of Portland: Preserved at Welbeck Abbey*, vol. 2, London, 1893, 280

4 Joan Thirsk, ed., *The Agrarian History of England and Wales*, vol. V.1, '1640–1750: Regional Farming Systems', 282

5 Letters I, xix–xx

6 Letters I, xx

7 Daniel Skynner to Harry Oxinden, 9 August 1648, MS 28002 fol. 55; Letters II, 139–40

8 Will of Richard Oxinden, of Barham, 1629, in Philpot's *Visitation of the County of Kent*, *Archaeologia Cantiana*, vi, 287

9 Harry Oxinden's Notebook for 21 December 1652; Letters II, 182

10 Elizabeth Dallison to Harry Oxinden, 18 November 1641; MS 28000 fol. 136; Letters I, 234

11 Painted *c*.1695–1705. Previously attributed to John Wootton (1682–1764) and before that to Jan Siberechts (1627–*c*.1703).

12 Henry Oxinden to Harry Oxinden, 21 April 1639; MS 27999 fol. 311; Letters I, 146

13 Henry Oxinden to Harry Oxinden, 30 May 1642; MS 28000 fol. 190; Letters I, 306

14 Sir James Oxinden to Harry Oxinden, 21 February 1635; MS 27999 fol. 223; Letters I, 111

15 Mary Prude to Harry Oxinden, 1636; MS 27999 fol. 101; Letters I, 120

16 Sir Peter Heyman to Harry Oxinden, 13 October 1635; MS 27999 fol. 213; Letters I, 107

17 Henry Oxinden to Harry Oxinden, 17 February 1635; MS 27999 fol. 221; Letters I, 110; and on the same subject from 'tui amantissimus' 8 January 1636; MS 27999 fol. 235; Letters I, 116

18 Robert Bargrave to Anne Oxinden, 1635; MS 27999 fol. 266; Letters I, 113

19 Harry Oxinden to Robert Bargrave, 23 September 1641; MS 28000 fol. 359; Letters I, 220

20 Letters I, 140

21 Harry Oxinden to Sir Basil Dixwell, 28 March 1635; MS 27999 fols. 201–2; Letters I, 98

22 Harry Oxinden to Sir Basil Dixwell, 28 March 1635; MS 27999 fols. 201–2; Letters I, 99

23 Sir Basil Dixwell to Harry Oxinden, 11 June 1638; MS 27999 fol. 288; Letters I, 139

24 Harry Oxinden to Anne Oxinden, 12 November 1637; MS 27999 fol. 268; Letters I, 129; her reply MS 27999 fol. 281, Letters I, 130

25 Anne Oxinden to Harry Oxinden, no date; MS 27999 fol. 281; Letters I, 131

26 Letters I, xxx

27 Henry Oxinden to Harry Oxinden, 29 December 1639; MS 27999 fol. 338; Letters I, 160

28 Lady Oxinden to Harry Oxinden, no date; MS 28000 fol. 47; Letters I, 179

29 Henry Oxinden to Harry Oxinden, December 1640; MS 28000 fol. 101; Letters I, 190

30 Sir Thomas Peyton to Harry Oxinden, September 1640; Letters I, 179

31 Sir Thomas Peyton to Harry Oxinden, September 1640; Letters I, 180

32 Sir Thomas Peyton to Harry Oxinden, September 1640; Letters I, 180

33 Sir James Oxinden to Harry Oxinden, 4 September 1640; MS 28000 fol. 27; Letters I, 180

34 Sir Thomas Peyton to Harry Oxinden, 5 November 1635; MS 27999 fol. 215; Letters I, 108

35 Henry Oxinden to Harry Oxinden, 18 November 1641; MS 28000 fol. 134; Letters I, 235

36 Sir Thomas Peyton to Harry Oxinden, 20 April 1640; MS 28000 fol. 2; Letters I, 163

37 Sir Thomas Peyton to Harry Oxinden, 6 May 1640; MS 28000 fol. 14; Letters I, 173

38 Sir Thomas Peyton to Harry Oxinden, 6 May 1640; MS 28000 fol. 14; Letters I, 172–4

39 Sir Thomas Peyton to Harry Oxinden, 14 May 1640; MS 28000 fol. 16; Letters I, 174

40 Henry Oxinden to Harry Oxinden, 18 November 1641; MS 28000 fol.134; Letters I, 235

41 Harry Oxinden to Sir Thomas Peyton, 21 June 1641; MS 28000 fol. 108; Letters I, 200

42 Harry Oxinden to Sir Thomas Peyton, 1 August 1641; MS 28000 fol. 110; Letters I, 206–7

43 Henry Oxinden to Harry Oxinden, 27 January 1642; MS 28000 fol. 148v; Letters I, 271

44 Henry Oxinden to Harry Oxinden, 27 January 1642; MS 28000 fol. 148v; Letters I, 272

45 Henry Oxinden to Harry Oxinden, 27 January 1642; MS 28000 fol. 148v; Letters I, 272

46 Letters I, 193

47 Henry Oxinden to Harry Oxinden, 27 January 1642; MS 28000 fol. 148v; Letters I, 272

48 Harry Oxinden to Elizabeth Dallison, 1 February 1642; MS 28000 fol. 153; Letters I, 277–8

49 Harry Oxinden to Elizabeth Dallison, no date; MS 28000 fol. 364v; Letters I, 236

50 Harry Oxinden to Elizabeth Dallison, 22 December 1641; MS 28000 fol. 370v; Letters I, 262–3

51 Harry Oxinden to Elizabeth Dallison, 1 February 1642; MS 28000 fol. 153; Letters I, 273–81

52 Harry Oxinden to Elizabeth Dallison, 1 February 1642; MS 28000 fol. 153; Letters I, 277

53 Harry Oxinden to Elizabeth Dallison, 1 February 1642; MS 28000 fol. 153; Letters I, 277

54 Harry Oxinden to Elizabeth Dallison, 1 February 1642; MS 28000 fol. 153; Letters I, 278–9

55 Harry Oxinden to Elizabeth Dallison, 1 February 1642; MS 28000 fol. 153; Letters I, 279

56 Harry Oxinden to Elizabeth Dallison, 1 February 1642; MS 28000 fol. 153; Letters I, 279

57 Harry Oxinden to Elizabeth Dallison, 1 February 1642; MS 28000 fol. 153; Letters I, 279

58 Harry Oxinden to Henry Oxinden, 1 February 1642; MS 28000 fol. 157; Letters I, 282

59 Harry Oxinden to Elizabeth Dallison, February 1641; MS 28000 fol. 381; Letters I, 289–90

60 Harry Oxinden to Elizabeth Dallison, no date; MS 28000 fol. 382v; Letters I, 299

61 Harry Oxinden to Sir Thomas Peyton, 14 November 1643; MS 28000 fols 283, 36

62 Harry Oxinden to Sir Thomas Peyton, 14 November 1643; MS 28000 fols 283, 37

63 MS 28000 fol. 281; Letters II, 33

64 MS 28000 fol. 278; Letters II, 34

65 MS 28000 fol. 279; Letters II, 34

66 MS 28000 fol. 284; Letters II, 35

67 MS 28000 fol. 284; Letters II, 34

68 MS 28000 fol. 284; Letters II, 34

69 MS 28000 fol. 284; Letters II, 34

70 Harry Oxinden to Sir Thomas Peyton, 6 February 1643; MS 28000 fol. 303; Letters II, 42

71 Sir Thomas Peyton to Harry Oxinden, 13 May 1644; MS 28000 fol. 327; Letters II, 48

72 Harry Oxinden to Sir Anthony Percivall, draft, no date; MS 28000 fol. 406v; Letters II, 21

73 See BL MSS Add. 44847 for their correspondence

74 Sir Thomas Peyton to Henry Oxinden, 20 October 1643; MS 28000 fol. 276; Letters II, 31, endorsed by Peyton 'From prison. Pray burne my letters.'

75 Edward Hasted, *The History and Topographical Survey of the County of Kent*, 1800, vol. 9, 231

76 Harry Oxinden to Thomas Denne the younger, November 1642; MS 28000 fol. 404; Letters II, 11–12

77 Harry Oxinden to Thomas Denne the younger, November 1642; MS 28000 fol. 404; Letters II, 12

78 Harry Oxinden to Katherine Oxinden, 4 May 1648; MS 28002 fol. 28; Letters II, 138

79 Harry Oxinden to Katherine Oxinden, September 1651; MS 28002 fol. 316; Letters II, 164

80 Harry Oxinden to Katherine Oxinden, September 1651; MS 28002 fol. 316; Letters II, 163

81 Harry Oxinden to Katherine Oxinden, 15 March 1654; Letters II, 190

82 Harry Oxinden to Katherine Oxinden, 7 March 1654; MS 28003 fol. 227; Letters II, 191

83 Sir Thomas Peyton to Harry Oxinden, 9 August 1653; MS 28003 fol. 163; Letters II, 186

84 Sir Thomas Peyton to Sir James Oxinden, 26 August 1653; MS 28003 fol. 175; Letters II, 186–7

85 Harry Oxinden to Katherine Oxinden, no date ?1651; MS 28000 fol. 307; Letters II, 174

86 Harry Oxinden to Katherine Oxinden, no date ?1651; MS 28000 fol. 307; Letters II, 175

87 Harry Oxinden to Katherine Oxinden, no date ?1651; MS 28000 fol. 307; Letters II, 175

88 Sir Henry Oxinden to Harry Oxinden, 26 July 1656; MS 28003 fol. 407; Letters, II, 220

89 Sir Richard Hardres to Harry Oxinden, no date; MS 28004 fol. 313; Letters II, 247

90 John Carpenter to Harry Oxinden, 3 June 1661, MS 28004 fol. 239; Letters II, 247

91 Letters II, 286

92 Letters II, 286

93 Harry Oxinden to Katherine Oxinden, September 1662; MS 28003 fol. 26; Letters II, 275

94 Harry Oxinden to Katherine Oxinden, 7 June 1647; MS 28001 fol. 252; Letters II, 114

95 Harry Oxinden to Katherine Oxinden, 16 April 1663; MS 28003 fol. 28; Letters II, 286–7

96 Harry Oxinden to Katherine Oxinden, 16 April 1663; MS 28003 fol. 28; Letters II, 287

97 Harry Oxinden to Katherine Oxinden, 16 April 1663; MS 28003 fol. 28; Letters II, 288–9

98 Harry Oxinden to Katherine Oxinden, 25 May 1663; MS 28004 fol. 372; Letters II, 292

99 Letters II, xxxviii

100 Harry Oxinden to Thomas Oxinden, October 1666; MS 28004 fol. 159; Letters II, 313

101 Harry Oxinden to Thomas Oxinden, October 1666; MS 28004 fol. 159; Letters II, 315

102 Letters II, 349

103 Letters, II, 348

104 BL MSS Add. Ch. 66191 Faculty to erect a tomb in Wingham church

Honour

1 Many of the late seventeenth-century letters written by the le Neve and Gawdy families and their friends and relations are in the British Library under Egerton MSS 2717–9, 2721 and Add. MSS 27396–7, 36989–90, 71573, 78698, 79491, 79532. Summaries and paraphrases of a large proportion of them were published in the late nineteenth century in Historical Manuscripts Commission, *Report on the Manuscripts of the Family of Gawdy*, London, 1885, from here on referred to in these notes as 'HMC *Gawdy*'; and Francis Rye and Amy Rye, eds, *Calendar of Correspondence and Documents relating to the Family of Oliver le Neve, of Witchingham Norfolk, 1675–1743*, Norwich, 1895, from here on referred to as 'Rye, *le Neve*'. Another large cache of le Neve papers is in the Norfolk Record Office under MC 1. Hobart accounts and some correspondence are also there as part of the Lothian of Blickling papers, MC 184, also calendared in Historical Manuscripts Commission, *Report on the Manuscripts of the Marquis of Lothian,* London, 1905 (from here on HMC *Lothian*).

2 For Hobart family culture see Stuart Handley, 'Hobart, Sir John, third baronet (bap. 1628, d. 1683)', *Oxford Dictionary of National Biography*, Oxford University Press, 2004

3 HMC *Lothian*, viii

4 For the Hobart estates earlier in the seventeenth century see Elizabeth Griffiths, 'Sir Henry Hobart: A New Hero of Norfolk Agriculture?', *Agricultural History Review*, 46, I, 15–34

5 HMC *Lothian*, 131

6 HMC *Lothian*, 121

7 HMC *Lothian*, List of a Gentleman's Wardrobe (Sir Henry Hobart), 1673, 117

8 HMC *Lothian* (Sir Henry Hobart), 1673, 118

9 Narcissus Luttrell, *A Brief Historical Relation of State Affairs: From September 1678 to April 1714*, Oxford, 1857, vol. 4, 422 (Saturday, 3 September 1698)

10 Bassingbourne Gawdy to Oliver le Neve, 17 April 1698, BL Add. 27397; Bassingbourne Gawdy to Oliver le Neve, 11 August 1700, BL Add. 27397

11 Robert Monsey to Oliver le Neve, 27 February 1694, Rye, *le Neve*, 22; Will Looker to Oliver le Neve, 10 May 1709, Rye, *le Neve*, 153

12 Robert Monsey to Oliver le Neve, 17 July 1698, Rye, *le Neve*, 54

13 Henry Rippingall to Oliver le Neve, 6 May 1697, Rye, *le Neve*, 49; Edward Earle to Oliver le Neve, 7 July 1694, Rye, *le Neve*, 25

14 John Ratey to Oliver le Neve, 28 March 1706, Rye, *le Neve*, 124

15 A. Halcott to Oliver le Neve, no date, Rye, *le Neve*, 187

16 Gerbriell Millicent to Oliver le Neve, 25 July 1705, Rye, *le Neve*, 118; Richard Ferrier to Oliver le Neve, 20 June 1700, Rye, *le Neve*, 66; and 16 July 1700, Rye, *le Neve*, 67

17 Will Reeves to Oliver le Neve, 25 March 1708, Rye, *le Neve*, 146; Robert Monsey to Oliver le Neve, 9 May 1694, Rye, *le Neve*, 23; and no date, Rye, *le Neve*, 179

18 Thomas Rose to Oliver le Neve, 3 June 1703, Rye, *le Neve*, 93

19 Peter le Neve to Oliver le Neve, June 1706, BL Add. 79491; Thomas Lubbock to Oliver le Neve, 19 February 1703, Rye, *le Neve*, 91

20 Christopher London to Oliver le Neve, 28 February, no year, Rye, *le Neve*, 177

21 Thomas Lubbock to Oliver le Neve, 2 May 1706, Rye, *le Neve*, 124

22 John Norris to Francis Neve, 26 July 1675, Rye, *le Neve*, 3; John Norris to Francis Neve, 24 February 1676, Rye, *le Neve*, 6; Edward Fuller to Oliver le Neve, 24 March 1695, Rye, *le Neve*, 38

23 Robert Fisher to Oliver le Neve, 29 December 1696, Rye, *le Neve*, 45

24 Will Looker to Oliver le Neve, 12 September 1706, Rye, *le Neve*, 127

25 Will Looker to Oliver le Neve, 15 July 1707, Rye, *le Neve*, 139

26 Jeremy Norris to Francis Neve, 15 June 1677, Rye, *le Neve*, 7, account for chintzes sold at 30*s*. 3*d*. a piece

27 Thomas Woodcock, 'Le Neve, Peter (1661–1729)', *Oxford Dictionary of National Biography*, Oxford University Press, 2004

28 John Millecent to Oliver le Neve, 1 June 1703, Rye, *le Neve*, 92

29 John Millecent to Oliver le Neve, 10 February 1706, Rye, *le Neve*, 122

30 Oliver le Neve to Thomas Browne, 5 March 1683, BL Add. 71573

31 Oliver le Neve to Thomas Browne, 5 March 1683, BL Add. 71573

32 Oliver le Neve to Thomas Browne, 5 March 1683, BL Add. 71573

33 Oliver le Neve to Peter le Neve, 5 January 1685, BL Add. 71573

34 Oliver le Neve to Peter le Neve, 5 January 1685, BL Add. 71573

35 Oliver le Neve to Peter le Neve, 25 January 1685, BL Add. 71573

36 HMC *Gawdy*, 198, 18 November 1663, letter from George Freeman, painter and tapestry designer, employed by their father as the deaf boys' London tutor, discussing Lely's opinion that Framlingham Gawdy 'should be perfect in his drawing, it being the chief ground of painting'.

37 George Freeman to Sir William Gawdy, 6 February 1665, HMC *Gawdy*, 200

38 HMC *Gawdy*, 191 (funeral bill 3 May 1661 for the two boys, including £3 8*s*. 6*d*. for two coffins, 1*s*. for rosemary and £4 10*s*. for wine at the Horn Tavern and the Pope's Head)

39 Oliver le Neve to Peter le Neve, 16 June 1686, BL Add. 71573

40 Agreement between Sir John Gawdy and James Young, ?1681, BL Add. 36990

41 Bassingbourne Gawdy to Oliver le Neve, 9 September 1695, BL Add. 27397

42 John Evelyn, *Diary,* 7 September 1677

43 Sir John Gawdy to Oliver le Neve, 4 October 1693, BL Add. 36989

44 Sir John Gawdy to Oliver le Neve, 7 July 1692, BL Add. 27397

45 Sir John Gawdy to Oliver le Neve, 25 November 1703, BL Add. 36989

46 Bassingbourne Gawdy to Oliver le Neve, 27 January 1697, BL Add. 27397

47 Bassingbourne Gawdy to Oliver le Neve, November 1692, BL Add. 27397

48 Giles Bladwell to Oliver le Neve, 30 December 1696, Rye, *le Neve*, 45

49 John Millecent to Oliver le Neve, 9 June 1700, Rye, *le Neve*, 66

50 Prudence le Neve to Oliver le Neve, 24 June 1704, BL Add. 79491 about Oliver's brother and her husband, Peter

51 Bassingbourne Gawdy to Oliver le Neve, 14 April 1692, BL Add. 27397

52 Bassingbourne Gawdy to Oliver le Neve, 14 April 1692, BL Add. 27397

53 Bassingbourne Gawdy to Oliver le Neve, 14 November 1692, BL Add. 27397

54 Bassingbourne Gawdy to Oliver le Neve, February 1693, BL Add. 27397

55 Bassingbourne Gawdy to Oliver le Neve, 11 August 1700, BL Add. 27397

56 A. Halcott to Oliver le Neve, no date, Rye, *le Neve*, 186

57 Bassingbourne Gawdy to Oliver le Neve, 14 February 1698, BL Add. 27397

58 John Millecent to Oliver le Neve, 15 October 1700, Rye, *le Neve*, 70

59 John Millecent to Oliver le Neve, 2 August 1701, Rye, *le Neve*, 80

60 John Millecent to Oliver le Neve, 7 March 1702, Rye, *le Neve*, 84

61 John Millecent to Oliver le Neve, 12 February 1695, Rye, *le Neve*, 29

62 John Millecent to Oliver le Neve, 3 December 1695, Rye, *le Neve*, 27

63 John Millecent to Oliver le Neve, 2 April 1695, Rye, *le Neve*, 30

64 John Millecent to Oliver le Neve, 25 August 1704, Rye, *le Neve*, 109

65 John Millecent to Oliver le Neve, 26 August ?1694, Rye, *le Neve*, 25–6

66 John Millecent to Oliver le Neve, 12 March 1696, Rye, *le Neve*, 38

67 John Millecent to Oliver le Neve, 7 December 1696, Rye, *le Neve*, 43

68 Bassingbourne Gawdy to Oliver le Neve, 11 August 1700, BL Add. 27397

69 John Millecent to Oliver le Neve, 7 January 1695, Rye, *le Neve*, 28

70 John Millecent to Oliver le Neve, 7 January 1695, Rye, *le Neve*, 28

71 Will Looker to Oliver le Neve, 8 August 1707, Rye, *le Neve*, 141

72 Bassingbourne Gawdy to Oliver le Neve, 15 March 1707, BL Add 27397; Erasmus Earle to Oliver le Neve, 10 April 1693, Rye, *le Neve* 30

73 Bassingbourne Gawdy to Oliver le Neve 25 January 1697, BL Add 27397

74 John Rous to Oliver le Neve, 3 September ?1700, Rye, *le Neve*, 68

75 Sir John Rous to Oliver le Neve, 4 July 1698, Rye, *le Neve*, 54

76 Oliver le Neve to Bassingbourne Gawdy, March 1704, BL Add 27397

77 Charles Middleton to Oliver le Neve, 24 February 1704, Rye, *le Neve*, 99–101

78 Thomas Rose to Oliver le Neve, 19 October 1706, Rye, *le Neve*, 128

79 Eliza Millner to Oliver le Neve, 12 August 1693, Rye, *le Neve,* 19

80 Charles Fisher to Oliver le Neve, 31 March 1694, Rye, *le Neve*, 23

81 Elizabeth Story to Oliver le Neve, 12 February 1695, BL Egerton 2718

82 Elizabeth Story to Oliver le Neve, 7 February 1696, BL Egerton 2718

83 John Millecent to Oliver le Neve, 28 April 1707, Rye, *le Neve*, 136

84 Bassingbourne Gawdy to Oliver le Neve, 3 February 1697, BL Add. 27397

85 Bassingbourne Gawdy to Oliver le Neve, 3 February 1697, BL Add. 27397

86 Bassingbourne Gawdy to Oliver le Neve, 10 November 1699, BL Add. 27397

87 Bassingbourne Gawdy to Oliver le Neve, 10 November 1699, BL Add. 27397

88 Bassingbourne Gawdy to Oliver le Neve, 10 November 1699, BL Add. 27397

89 Bassingbourne Gawdy to Oliver le Neve, 30 November 1696, BL Add. 27397

90 Bassingbourne Gawdy to Oliver le Neve, 24 October 1696, BL Add. 27397

91 Bassingbourne Gawdy to Oliver le Neve, 29 December 1696, BL Add. 27397

92 Bassingbourne Gawdy to Oliver le Neve, 25 February 1697, BL Add. 27397

93 Bassingbourne Gawdy to Oliver le Neve, 17 April 1698, BL Add. 27397

94 Bassingbourne Gawdy to Oliver le Neve, 29 June 1711, BL Add. 27397

95 For example, Thomas Rose in London to Oliver le Neve in Witchingham, 14 October 1701, Rye, *le Neve*, 81: 'I have sent you by the *Anne and Judith*, off Yarmouth, John Attwood, master, six cheeses, according to your order, as good as I could get, and as cheap; the bill is at the bottom.'

96 Bassingbourne Gawdy to Oliver le Neve, 3 February 1697, BL Add. 27397

97 Bassingbourne Gawdy to Oliver le Neve, 25 August 1692, BL Add. 27397

98 Bassingbourne Gawdy to Oliver le Neve, 10 December 1695, BL Add. 27397

99 Bassingbourne Gawdy to Oliver le Neve, 23 September 1696, BL Add. 27397

100 Bassingbourne Gawdy to Oliver le Neve, 24 October 1696, BL Add. 27397

101 Bassingbourne Gawdy to Oliver le Neve, 30 November 1696, BL Add. 27397

102 Bassingbourne Gawdy to Oliver le Neve, 17 April 1698, BL Add. 27397; Peter le Neve to Oliver le Neve, 17 March 1698, BL Add. 79491

103 Bassingbourne Gawdy to Oliver le Neve, 19 July 1692, BL Add. 27397

104 John Millecent to Oliver le Neve, 9 July 1697, Rye, *le Neve*, 49

105 Bassingbourne Gawdy to Oliver le Neve, 25 January 1697, BL Add. 27397

106 Robert Fisher to Oliver le Neve, 4 July 1698, Rye, *le Neve*, 54

107 Robert Monsey to Oliver le Neve, 17 July 1698, Rye, *le Neve*, 54

108 T. B. Macaulay, *The History of England: From the Accession of James I*, London, 1861, 96

109 T. B. Macaulay, *The History of England: From the Accession of James I*, London, 1861, 97

110 John Millecent to Oliver le Neve, 20 April 1706, Rye, *le Neve*, 124

111 *The Poll for Two Knights of the Shire for the Western Division of the County of Norfolk*, Norwich, 1837, 216–19

112 Sir Henry Hobart to Sir John Somers, 30 April 1696, Surrey History Centre, 371/14/L/18

113 R. W. Ketton-Cremer, *Norfolk Portraits*, London, 1944, 60

114 R. W. Ketton-Cremer, *Norfolk Portraits*, London, 1944, 61

115 Luttrell, *A Brief Historical Relation of State Affairs*, vol. 4, 422 (Thursday, 25 August 1698)

116 Oliver le Neve to Sir Henry Hobart, 20 August 1698, Norfolk Record Office FX 210/1

117 R. B. Manning, *Swordsmen: The Martial Ethos in the Three Kingdoms*, Oxford, 2003, 50, 198

118 Manning, *Swordsmen*, 61

119 For example, Sir William Hope, *The Sword-Man's Vade Mecum*, London, 1694

120 Samuel Butler, *Characters*, ed. C. W. Davis, Cleveland, 1970, 270, 304–5

121 Manning, *Swordsmen*, 228–31

122 Luttrell, *A Brief Historical Relation of State Affairs*, vol. 4, 422 (Thursday, 25 August 1698)

123 John Nichols, *Literary Anecdotes of the Eighteenth Century*, London, 1812, 416

124 Norfolk Record Office NRS 11129 25
E5; John Maddison et al., *Blickling
Hall*, 1987, 28

125 P. W. Jackson, *The Gawdy Manuscripts*,
Feltham, 2004, 83

126 Bassingbourne Gawdy to Oliver le
Neve, 13 March 1699, BL Add. 27397

127 Bassingbourne Gawdy to Oliver le
Neve, 31 January 1700, BL Add. 27397

128 John Millecent to Oliver le Neve, 23
March 1699, Rye, *le Neve*, 56

129 Bassingbourne Gawdy to Oliver le
Neve, 31 January 1700, BL Add. 27397

130 Giles Bladwell to Oliver le Neve, 10
October 1699, Rye, *le Neve*, 61

131 John Millecent to Oliver le Neve, 12
December 1706, Rye, *le Neve*, 129

132 Francis Blomefield, *An Essay Towards
a Topographical History of the County
of Norfolk*, vol. 1, 1805, 307

PART IV Atlantic Domains
1710–1790

1 Geoffrey Hickes, *A Gentleman
Instructed in the Conduct of a Virtuous
and Happy Life, Written for the
Instruction of a Young Nobleman*,
London, 1709, 26

2 *Spectator*, No. 383, 20 May 1711

3 The figures for *c*.1690 are derived
from J. P. Cooper, 'The Social
Distribution of Land and Men in
England 1436–1700', *Economic History
Review*, 2nd Series, xx (1967); those
for *c*.1790 from F. M. L. Thompson,
'The Social Distribution of Landed
Property in England since the
Sixteenth Century', *Economic History
Review*, xix (1966); and G. E. Mingay,
*English Landed Society in the
Eighteenth Century* (1963), Routledge,
2006. A version of the table is printed
in G. E. Mingay, *The Gentry*,
Longman, 1976, 59

4 S. D. Smith, *Slavery, Family, and
Gentry Capitalism in the British
Atlantic*, Cambridge University Press,
2006 (from here on referred to in
these notes as Smith, *Slavery*), 33

5 Smith, *Slavery*, 33

6 S. D. Smith, ed., *The Lascelles &
Maxwell Letterbooks (1739–1769)*,
microform 2003 (from here on
LMLB), 20 November 1747. A man
from Glasgow was applying for a
tutoring job but 'his chief defect will
probably be his accent'.

7 For an overview of Barbados in the
seventeenth and eighteenth centuries
see Jack P. Greene, 'Changing Identity
in the British Caribbean: Barbados as
a Case Study,' in N. Canny and A.
Pagden, *Colonial Identity in the
Atlantic World, 1500–1800*, Princeton
University Press, 1989

8 Quoted in Canny and Pagden,
Colonial Identity, 229

9 E. and W. Burke, *An Account of the
European Settlements in America*,
London, 1760, 91

10 William Beckford, *A Descriptive
Account of the Island of Jamaica: With
Remarks upon the Cultivation of the
Sugar-cane*, London, 1790, 48

11 Richard Ligon, *A True and Exact
History of the Island of Barbadoes*,
London, 1673

12 J. Thomson, *Timehri: The Journal of
the Royal Agricultural and Commercial
Society of British Guiana*, vol. 9
(1895), 63

13 LMLB, 28 March 1741; 16 February
1742

14 David Hume, *Essays and Treatises on
Several Subjects*, London, 1753, vol. 1
(Essay XVI: 'The Stoic'), 218

15 For Eliza's sense of her own standing
beyond gender or its restrictions, see
Darcy R. Fryer, 'The Mind of Eliza
Pinckney: An Eighteenth-Century
Woman's Construction of Herself',
*The South Carolina Historical
Magazine*, vol. 99, no. 3, Eliza Lucas
Pinckney (July 1998), 215–37

Dominance

1 For a richly detailed examination of
the eighteenth-century Lascelles
family, see S. D. Smith, *Slavery, Family,
and Gentry Capitalism in the British*

Atlantic, Cambridge University Press, 2006, from here on referred to in these notes as Smith, *Slavery*; for Henry Lascelles's wealth at death see Smith, *Slavery*, 87 and S. D. Smith, 'Lascelles, Henry', *Oxford Dictionary of National Biography*, Oxford University Press, 2004

2 See John Habbakuk, *Marriage, Debt and the Estates System*, Oxford University Press, 1994, 422. In 1756, for example, William Baker MP spent £21,000 on 3,911 acres at Bayfordbury in Hertfordshire.

3 S. D. Smith, ed., *The Lascelles & Maxwell Letterbooks (1739–1769)*, microform 2003 (from here on LMLB), 4 April 1744: a ship in the Barbados trade was sold for £800; in the 1730s a Bristol ship laden with goods worth £1,330 was planning to buy 240 slaves plus some ivory on the proceeds (E. Donnan, *Slave Trade*, Washington, 1930, vol. II, 327)

4 In 1737, 368 slaves were worth £8,391 in Barbados; 914 slaves were insured for £14,614 at Anomabu in 1742: The National Archives (TNA) C103/130 John Dunning's Commissions, 21 December 1737; George Hamilton to Thomas Hall, 19 September 1742; S. D. Smith, *Slavery*, 75; but slave prices could vary: in LMLB on 20 April 1741, slaves were selling at £18 each in Barbados but £31 each in Jamaica

5 Joan Thirsk, ed., *The Agrarian History of England and Wales,* vol V (i) 1640–1753 Regional Farming Systems, 73

6 William Page, ed., *Victoria County History, York: North Riding*, vol. I, 1914, 405

7 B. D. Henning, *The House of Commons, 1660–1690*, London, 1983, vol. II, 711

8 John Rushworth, *Historical Collections of Private Passages of State*, vol. 6, 1645–47, London, 1722, 118

9 For these first commercial Lascelles see Smith, *Slavery*, 43–53

10 D. Hayton, E. Cruickshanks and S. Handley, *The House of Commons,* *1690–1715*, vol. 1, Cambridge University Press, 2002, 589

11 K. G. Davies, *The North Atlantic World in the Seventeenth Century*, University of Minnesota Press, 1974, 74; R. S. Dunn, 'The Barbados Census of 1680: Profile of the Richest Colony in English America', in *William and Mary Quarterly*, 3rd Series, 26:3–30 (1969)

12 Hugh Thomas, *The Slave Trade* (1997), Phoenix, 2006, 386

13 Jack P. Greene, 'Changing Identity in the British Caribbean: Barbados as a Case Study', in N. Canny and A. Pagden, *Colonial Identity in the Atlantic World, 1500–1800*, Princeton University Press, 1989

14 Thomas, *The Slave Trade*, 432

15 For life expectations and conditions among slaves in the Caribbean see Smith, *Slavery*, 284ff.

16 TNA C 103/130 Thomas Hall, commercial papers and correspondence: George Hamilton to Hall from 'Annamaboo', 19 February 1738

17 LMLB 15 September 1741

18 LMLB 13 August 1740

19 LMLB 28 March 1740

20 LMLB 18 July 1745

21 LMLB 16 March 1745

22 LMLB 23 December 1740

23 LMLB 17 May 1740

24 LMLB 17 May 1740

25 LMLB 30 January 1741

26 LMLB May 1741 and throughout

27 LMLB 17 March 1740; LMLB 18 March 1740

28 LMLB 13 September 1740

29 LMLB 10 September 1744

30 LMLB 16 September 1743

31 LMLB December 1741

32 LMLB 16 September 1743

33 LMLB/Pares transcripts 3 November 1746

34 LMLB 20 October 1744

35 LMLB 16 September 1743

36 LMLB 29 September 1743

37 LMLB 16 September 1743

38 LMLB 7 November 1743

39 For example, LMLB/Pares transcripts 2 June 1756; LMLB George Maxwell to Brathwaite, November 1745

40 Speech to the House of Commons, 2 April 1792

41 TNA T 1/320/21 *Report of the Customs Commissioners on the case of Edward Lascelles, collector of the 4½ per cent duty at Bridge Town, Barbados*; for the whole story of the Lascelles brothers and the corruption charges against them see Smith, *Slavery*, 59–72

42 TNA T 1/320/21 *Report of the Customs Commissioners on the case of Edward Lascelles*

43 TNA T 1/320/21 *Report of the Customs Commissioners on the case of Edward Lascelles*

44 TNA T 1/320/21 *Report of the Customs Commissioners on the case of Edward Lascelles*

45 TNA T 1/320/21 *Report of the Customs Commissioners on the case of Edward Lascelles*

46 TNA T 1/320/22 *Memorial of Henry Lascelles on behalf of Edward, his brother, and Arthur Upton*

47 TNA T 1/320/24 *Copy of a 1744 letter from Robt. Dinwiddie, Inspector-General of the 4½ per cent duty*

48 Jack P. Greene, *Imperatives, Behaviors, and Identities: Essays in Early American Cultural History*, University of Virginia Press, 1992, 39

49 Jack P. Greene, 'Changing Identity in the British Caribbean: Barbados as a Case Study', in Canny and Pagden, *Colonial Identity*, 246

50 Greene, 'Changing Identity', 247

51 Daniel Defoe, *Curious and Diverting Journies, Thro' the Whole island of Great-Britain*, 1734, 126

52 This description of what Lascelles's interiors might have been like is based on John Wood, *Description of Bath*, 1749, vol. II, Preface, 2

53 Defoe, *Curious and Diverting Journies*, 102

54 Defoe, *Curious and Diverting Journies*, 102

55 Defoe, *Curious and Diverting Journies*, 126

56 Defoe, *Curious and Diverting Journies*, 103

57 J. Stow, *A Survey of London and Westminster*, revised by J. Strype, 1720, vol. iii, 63

58 This description is based on the account of the Great Tower Street office of Lascelles & Maxwell in *Royal Commission on Historical Monuments (England), London*, vol. iv (1929), 185. The building, along with the vast bulk of the precious Lascelles & Maxwell archive, was destroyed by German bombs on 29 December 1940. The Mincing Lane office has also disappeared, its site now occupied by a modern behemoth.

59 Edward Moore (Adam Fitz-Adam), *The World*, no. 125, 22 May 1755

60 Samuel Pepys, *Diary*, Friday, 8 August 1662

61 Defoe, *Tour*, 146

62 Defoe, *Curious and Diverting Journies*, 129

63 TNA C 103/130 George Hamilton to Thomas Hall, 19 April 1741

64 Smith, *Slavery*, 75

65 Smith, *Slavery*, 75; TNA C11/2189/18

66 TNA C 103/130 T. Hall to G. Hamilton at 'Annamaboo', 15 August 1740

67 Hugh Thomas, *The Slave Trade* (1997), Phoenix, 2006, 318, 328

68 All in TNA C 103/130 Thomas Hall to George Hamilton, 1 April 1740

69 TNA C 103/130 George Hamilton to Capts Rich and Pinnell, 13 August 1739

70 TNA C 103/130 George Hamilton to Richard Pinnell, January 1737

71 LMLB Henry Lascelles to Richard Crookenden, 22 February 1741

72 LMLB Henry Lascelles to Edward Lascelles, 6 December 1740

73 LMLB Henry Lascelles to Edward Lascelles, 27 October 1741

74 TNA C 103/130 Charles Benyon to Thomas Hall, no date

75 TNA C 103/130 George Clifford to Thomas Hall, 13 October 1741

76 TNA C 103/130 George Hamilton to Capts Rich and Pinnell, 13 August 1739

77 TNA C 103/130 John Dunning to Thomas Hall, 19 July 1747

78 TNA C 11/2189/18 for Lascelles's court case against George Hamilton

79 All in LMLB September 1743

80 LMLB 19 September 1743

81 LMLB November 1745

82 LMLB November 1745

83 LMLB 20 October 1744

84 LMLB 7 January 1745

85 LMLB November 1745

86 LMLB November 1745

87 LMLB November 1745

88 LMLB/Pares Transcripts 30 April 1757

89 LMLB Henry Lascelles to Thomas Stevenson, 27 October 1741; Smith, *Slavery*, 161, 163

90 'An Act to Dissolve the Marriage of Daniel Lascelles', Parliamentary Archives, HL/PO/PB/1/1751/25G2n79; Smith, *Slavery*, 185; Richard Pares, 'A London West-India Merchant House, 1740–1769', in *Essays Presented to Sir Lewis Namier*, 1956, 75

91 *London Gazette*, 9665, 26 February 1757

92 Smith, *Slavery*, 185

93 Smith, *Slavery*, 184

94 R. P. Butterfield, *Monastery and Manor: The History of Crondall*, Farnham, 1948, 99

95 K. Garlick and A. Macintyre, eds, *Diary of Joseph Farington*, Yale University Press, 1978, vol. II, 570

96 'The Diary of Thomas Gyll', 12 October 1753, *Six North Country Diaries*, Surtees Society, 1910, 118

97 LMLB/Pares Transcripts 20 November 1747; *Gentleman's Magazine*, 24 (1754), 325; Smith, *Slavery*, 88

98 Pat Rogers, *Johnson and Boswell: The Transit of Caledonia*, Clarendon Press, Oxford, 1995, 29

99 Isle of Wight Record Office, Oglander Account Books OG 90/6, 113

100 Revd J. L. Saywell, *History & Annals of Northallerton*, 1885

Courage

1 M. Mulcahy, *Hurricanes and Society in the British Greater Caribbean, 1624–1783*, Johns Hopkins University Press, 2006, 19

2 V. L. Oliver, *The History of the Island of Antigua*, London, 1894, i, xcv

3 Harriet Simons Williams, 'Eliza Lucas and her Family: Before the Letterbook', *The South Carolina Historical Magazine*, vol. 99, no. 3, Eliza Lucas Pinckney (July 1998), 264

4 Carol Walter Ramagosa, 'Eliza Lucas Pinckney's Family in Antigua', *The South Carolina Historical Magazine*, vol. 99, no. 3, Eliza Lucas Pinckney (July 1998), 242

5 For her Antigua background, see Ramagosa, 'Eliza Lucas Pinckney's Family in Antigua', 238–58

6 Ramagosa, 'Eliza Lucas Pinckney's Family in Antigua', 245

7 E. and W. Burke, *An Account of the European Settlements in America*, London, 1759, vol, 2, 114

8 Ramagosa, 'Eliza Lucas Pinckney's Family in Antigua', 248

9 Ramagosa, 'Eliza Lucas Pinckney's Family in Antigua', 248; in S. Max Edelson, *Plantation Enterprise in Colonial South Carolina*, Harvard University Press, 2006, 44

10 Harriet Simons Williams, 'Eliza Lucas and her Family: Before the Letterbook', *The South Carolina Historical Magazine*, vol. 99, no. 3, Eliza Lucas Pinckney (July 1998), 272

11 Williams, 'Eliza Lucas and her Family: Before the Letterbook', 264

12 Williams, 'Eliza Lucas and her Family: Before the Letterbook', 267

13 J. B. Martin, *The Grasshopper in Lombard Street*, London, 1892, 95

14 Williams, 'Eliza Lucas and her Family: Before the Letterbook', 266–7

15 Samuel Wilson, 1682, quoted in Edelson, *Plantation Enterprise*, 20

16 H.H. Ravenel, *Eliza Pinckney*, New York, 1896 (from here on referred to in these notes as Ravenel), 17–18

17 Ravenel, 18

18 Quoted in Edelson, *Plantation Enterprise*, 35

19 Edelson, *Plantation Enterprise*, 33

20 Ravenel, 19

21 Elise Pinckney, ed., *The Letterbook of Eliza Lucas Pinckney 1739–1762*, University of South Carolina Press (1972), 1997 (from here on referred to in these notes as *Pinckney Letterbook*), 5

22 Ravenel, 227

23 *Pinckney Letterbook*, 7

24 *Pinckney Letterbook*, 34

25 *Pinckney Letterbook*, 16

26 John Locke, *An Essay Concerning Human Understanding*, Book 2, Ch. 1, Section 2

27 John Locke, 'Epistle to the Reader', Drafts for the Essay, 10, quoted in J. R. Milton, 'Locke, John (1632–1704)', *Oxford Dictionary of National Biography*, Oxford University Press, 2004

28 *Pinckney Letterbook*, 35–6

29 Ravenel, 45

30 Ravenel, 43

31 Ravenel, 127

32 Ravenel, 245

33 Letter from Peter Fontaine, Westover, Virginia, 30 March 1757, in Ulrich B. Phillips, *Plantation and Frontier, vol. II 1649–1863* (1910), Cosimo Reprints, New York, 2008, 29–30

34 *Charleston District Inventories*, Book B (1787–1793), 38–42

35 *Pinckney Letterbook*, 5–6

36 Ravenel, 105

37 *Pinckney Letterbook*, xviii

38 David S. Shields, University of South Carolina, in Edelson, *Plantation Enterprise*

39 Ravenel, 68

40 Ravenel, 69

41 Ravenel, 111

42 Ravenel, 109

43 *Pinckney Letterbook*, xii; Eliza Lucas Pinckney to Charles Pinckney, no date, in Phoebe Caroline Pinckney Seabrook copybook, SCHS

44 *The Gentleman's Magazine*, vol. 47, 17. The same column announced the wedding of Edwin Lascelles Esq. to Elizabeth, the only daughter of the late Sir Darcy Dawes, Bart.

45 *Pinckney Letterbook*, 77

46 Ravenel, 145

47 *Pinckney Letterbook*, 80

48 *Pinckney Letterbook*, 80

49 John L. Bullion, 'Augusta, Princess of Wales (1719–1772)', *Oxford Dictionary of National Biography*, Oxford University Press, 2004

50 Ravenel, 144–5

51 Ravenel, 145–6

52 Ravenel, 146

53 Ravenel, 147

54 Ravenel, 150

55 Ravenel, 151–2

56 *Pinckney Letterbook*, 87

57 *Pinckney Letterbook*, 87

58 *Pinckney Letterbook*, 88

59 *Pinckney Letterbook*, 88

60 Ravenel, 175

61 *Pinckney Letterbook*, 101–2

62 *Pinckney Letterbook*, 114

63 *Pinckney Letterbook*, 133

64 *Pinckney Letterbook*, 144

65 *Pinckney Letterbook*, 185

66 *Pinckney Letterbook*, 185

67 Ravenel, 297

68 Ravenel, 297

69 Ravenel, 277

70 Ravenel, 276

71 Ravenel, 284

72 Ravenel, 285

73 Ravenel, 285

74 Ravenel, 286

75 Ravenel, 308–9

76 Ravenel, 311–12

77 Ravenel, 312

78 *Charleston District Inventories*, Book B (1787–1793), 38–42

PART V The Failing Vision 1790–1910

1 W.B. Yeats, 'My Descendants', Part IV of 'Meditations in Time of Civil War'

(1923), in *The Tower*, London, 1928, 2–5

2 W. M. Thackeray, *Vanity Fair* (1848), Harmondsworth, 2001, 82

3 C. Sykes, *Four Studies in Loyalty*, 1946, 18; quoted in F. M. L. Thompson, *English Landed Society in the Nineteenth Century*, London, 1963, 135–6

4 R. S. Surtees, *Mr Sponge's Sporting Tour*, London, 1853, 69

5 Mancur Olson, Jr., and Curtis C. Harris, Jr., 'Free Trade in "Corn": A Statistical Study of the Prices and Production of Wheat in Great Britain from 1873 to 1914', *The Quarterly Journal of Economics*, vol. 73, no. 1 (February 1959), 145–168

6 Oscar Wilde, *The Importance of Being Earnest*, 1895, Act I

Fecklessness

1 For these relationships see the Marquess of Anglesey, ed., *The Capel Letters*, London, 1955, from here on referred to in these notes as 'Anglesey'. A full family tree is tipped into the endpapers. The Capel letters themselves, many of them unpublished or only partly published in Lord Anglesey's book, remain in the muniment room in the basement of Plas Newydd, Llanfairpwllgwyngyllgogerychwyrndrobwllllantysiliogogogoch, Anglesey LL61 6DQ

2 Harriet Capel to Ernst Trip, undated, ?March 1815, Anglesey, 195

3 Portrait by Robert Dighton of Captain the Honourable John Thomas Capel, The Royal Collection

4 Lady Uxbridge to Arthur Paget, September 1791

5 The Earl of Uxbridge to Lady Uxbridge, September 1791

6 Note in Plas Newydd Papers, Anglesey, 227

7 Lady Uxbridge to Sir Arthur Paget, August 1801, Anglesey, 25–6

8 Lord Hylton, ed., *The Paget Brothers,*

1790–1840, London, 1918, 18; Anglesey, 26

9 Sir Arthur Paget to Lady Uxbridge in A. B. Paget, ed., *The Paget Papers: Diplomatic and Other Correspondence of the Right Hon. Sir Arthur Paget, G. C. B., 1794–1807*, London, 1896, vol. 1, 182–3; Anglesey, 27

10 Harriet Capel to Lady Uxbridge, 23 June 1814, Anglesey, 46. They rented rue Ducale 1056, au Parc, for £100 a year. The house no longer exists.

11 W. M. Thackeray, *Vanity Fair* (1848), Harmondsworth, 2001

12 C. C. F. Greville, *The Greville Memoirs: A Journal of the Reigns of King George IV and King William IV*, 1875, vol. I, 235

13 Harriet Capel to Lady Uxbridge, 23 June 1814, Anglesey, 46–7

14 Caroline Capel to Lady Uxbridge, 6 July 1814, Anglesey, 50

15 H. M. Stephens, 'Ferguson, Sir Ronald Craufurd (1773–1841)', revised by S. Kinross, *Oxford Dictionary of National Biography*, Oxford University Press, 2004

16 Harriet Capel to Lady Uxbridge, 23 June 1814, Anglesey, 47

17 Caroline Capel to Lady Uxbridge, July 1814, Anglesey, 59

18 Georgiana Capel to Lady Uxbridge, July 1814, Anglesey, 64

19 Georgiana Capel to Lady Uxbridge, July 1814, Anglesey, 60

20 Georgiana Capel to Lady Uxbridge, no date, ?July 1814, Anglesey, 61

21 Caroline Capel to Lady Uxbridge, August 1814, Anglesey, 66

22 Caroline Capel to Lady Uxbridge, September 1814, Anglesey, 71

23 Maria Capel to Lady Uxbridge, 19 August 1814, Anglesey, 67

24 Georgiana Capel to Lady Uxbridge, no date, ?July 1814, Anglesey, 64

25 Maria Capel to Lady Uxbridge, 19 August 1814, Anglesey, 68

26 Caroline Capel to Lady Uxbridge, 1 September 1814, Anglesey, 69–70

27 A. S. Bolton, 'Barnes, Sir Edward (1776–1838)', revised by James

Falkner, *Oxford Dictionary of National Biography*, Oxford University Press, 2004

28 Maria Capel to Lady Uxbridge, September 1814, Anglesey, 70

29 Caroline Capel to Lady Uxbridge, February 1815, Anglesey, 86

30 J. Austen, *Emma: A Novel*, London, 1816, vol. 1, 318

31 Caroline Capel to Lady Uxbridge, 26 December 1814, Anglesey, 81

32 Caroline Capel to Lady Uxbridge, 1 November 1814, Anglesey, 75

33 Georgiana Capel to Lady Uxbridge, 21 November 1814, Anglesey, 78

34 Georgiana Capel to Lady Uxbridge, 21 November 1814, Anglesey, 78

35 Georgiana Capel to Lady Uxbridge, 21 November 1814, Anglesey, 79

36 Lady George Seymour, quoted by Harriet Capel to Ernst Trip, no date, Anglesey, 191–2

37 *A Portion of the Journal Kept by Thomas Raikes, Esq., From 1831 to 1847*, London, 1856, 243

38 Sir Walter Scott, Journal, 4 October 1827, in John Gibson Lockhart, *Memoirs of the Life of Sir Walter Scott*, Paris, 1838, vol. 4, 139

39 Maria Capel to Lady Uxbridge, September 1814, Anglesey, 70

40 Caroline Capel to Lady Uxbridge, 19 October 1814

41 Lord Mahon, ed., *The Letters of Philip Dormer Stanhope, Earl of Chesterfield*, London, 1845, vol. I, 79, vol. II, 410

42 W. S. Dowden et al., *The Journal of Thomas Moore*, vol. 1, University of Delaware Press, 1983, 76 (27 October 1818)

43 No date, no author, Trip's dispatch box in the muniment room in Plas Newydd, Anglesey

44 Harriet Capel to Ernst Trip, no date, Anglesey, 192

45 Harriet Capel to Ernst Trip, no date, Anglesey, 192–3

46 Harriet Capel to Ernst Trip, 24 December 1814

47 Caroline Capel to Lady Uxbridge, February 1815, Anglesey, 85

48 Maria Capel to Lady Uxbridge, 1 March 1815, Anglesey, 87–8

49 Caroline Capel to Lady Uxbridge, March 1815, Anglesey, 88–9

50 Harriet Capel to Ernst Trip, 'Monday or Tuesday' 19/20 June 1815, Anglesey, 204–5

51 All these objects and small notes remain in Trip's dispatch box in the muniment room in Plas Newydd, Anglesey

52 Caroline Capel to Lady Uxbridge, 17 March 1815, Anglesey, 93

53 Harriet Capel to Ernst Trip, no date, ?23 February 1815, Anglesey, 189

54 Harriet Capel to Ernst Trip, no date, ?23 February 1815, Anglesey, 189–90

55 Harriet Capel to Ernst Trip, no date, ?March 1815, Anglesey, 196

56 Caroline Capel to Lady Uxbridge, June 1815, Anglesey, 102

57 Caroline Capel to Lady Uxbridge, April 1815, Anglesey, 199

58 Dowden, *The Journal of Thomas Moore*, 76 (27 October 1818)

59 Lady George Seymour, quoted by Harriet Capel to Ernst Trip, no date, Anglesey, 191

60 Caroline Capel to Lady Uxbridge, 19 April 1815, Anglesey, 197

61 Caroline Capel to Lady Uxbridge, 19 April 1815, Anglesey, 198

62 Caroline Capel to Lady Uxbridge, April 1815, Anglesey, 199

63 Caroline Capel to Lady Uxbridge, June 1815, Anglesey, 103

64 Caroline Capel to Lady Uxbridge, April 1815, Anglesey, 199

65 Caroline Capel to Lady Uxbridge, April 1815, Anglesey, 199

66 Caroline Capel to Lady Uxbridge, 19 April 1815, Anglesey, 197

67 Caroline Capel to Lady Uxbridge, 18 June 1815, Anglesey, 111–12

68 Caroline Capel to Lady Uxbridge, 18 June 1815, Anglesey, 111

69 Caroline Capel to Lady Uxbridge, 18 June 1815, Anglesey, 112

70 Caroline Capel to Lady Uxbridge, 19 June 1815, Anglesey, 114

71 Caroline Capel to Lady Uxbridge, 18 June 1815, Anglesey, 111

72 Anglesey, 202

73 Harriet Capel to Ernst Trip, June 1815, Anglesey, 202–3

74 Harriet Capel to Ernst Trip, 24 June 1815, Anglesey, 205

75 Caroline Capel to Lady Uxbridge, 19 June 1815, Anglesey, 115

76 Georgiana Capel to Lady Uxbridge, 26 June 1815, Anglesey, 120

77 F. Leveson-Gower, ed., *Letters of Harriet, Countess Granville (1810–1845)*, vol. 1, London, 1894, 70

78 F. Leveson-Gower, ed., *Letters of Harriet, Countess Granville (1810–1845)*, vol. 1, London, 1894, 73–4

79 Caroline Capel to Lady Uxbridge, October 1815, Anglesey, 149

80 Caroline Capel to Lady Uxbridge, November 1815, Anglesey, 152

81 Caroline Capel to Lady Uxbridge, November 1815, Anglesey, 152–3

82 Caroline Capel to Lady Uxbridge, November 1815, Anglesey, 153

83 Caroline Capel to Lady Uxbridge, December 1815, Anglesey, 154

84 Harriet Capel to Ernst Trip, 1 January 1816, Anglesey, 210

85 Harriet Capel to Ernst Trip, 1 January 1816, Anglesey, 211–12

86 F. Leveson-Gower, ed., *Letters of Harriet, Countess Granville (1810–1845)*, vol. 1, London, 1894, 89

87 Caroline Capel to Lady Uxbridge, 18 November 1816, Anglesey, 215

88 Caroline Capel to Lady Uxbridge, 18 November 1816, Anglesey, 215

89 Harriet Capel to Lady Uxbridge, December 1816, Anglesey, 217

90 Dowden, *The Journal of Thomas Moore*, 76 (27 October 1818)

91 Dowden, *The Journal of Thomas Moore*, 82 (27 October 1818)

92 Hylton, *The Paget Brothers*, 302

93 M. Strachan, ed., *The Diary of Lady Adela Capel of Cassiobury 1841–2*, Hertfordshire Record Society, 2006, 33 (24 September 1841)

Fantasy

1 For the story of the Hugheses of Kinmel, the two key archives (in fact two parts of a single archive which was split in 1953) are those held at Bangor University (reference code GB 0222 KIN), from here on referred to in these notes as 'Kinmel Papers', catalogued in E. Gwynne Jones, *A Schedule of the Kinmel Manuscripts and Documents*, 1955 (typescript), two vols, also published as *Transactions of the Denbighshire Historical Society*, vol. 4, 1955; and the residue of the collection, held at Plas Kinmel, St George, Abergele, Conwy LL22 9SF (uncatalogued) and from here on referred to in these notes as 'Kinmel Estate'. For a full account of Parys Mountain, see Bryan D. Hope, *A Curious Place: The Industrial History of Amlwch (1550–1950)*, Wrexham, 1994, and J. R. Harris, *The Copper King*, 2nd ed., Ashbourne, 2003

2 E. Gwynne Jones, *A Schedule of the Kinmel Manuscripts and Documents*, 1955 (typescript), Introduction, 7–8

3 Gwynne Jones, *A Schedule of the Kinmel Manuscripts*, Introduction, 7–8, 10

4 Portrait in Kinmel Estate Collection

5 Harris, *The Copper King*, 21–2

6 Kinmel Papers 1807–1809, Hughes-Bayly case papers, 1769–75

7 Kinmel Papers 1807, Affidavit of Edward Hughes, 15 December 1775

8 Harris, *The Copper King*, 34

9 Kinmel Papers 1807, Hughes-Bayly case papers

10 Hope, *A Curious Place*, 33

11 Thomas Pennant, *Tours in Wales*, 1784, 275

12 Hope, *A Curious Place*, 33

13 Pennant, *Tours in Wales*, 275

14 Kinmel Papers 1616, H. R. Hughes, draft of letter to Charles Mainwaring about Hugh Hughes, no date

15 Kinmel Papers 1807, Hughes-Bayly case papers

16 Gwynne Jones, *A Schedule of the Kinmel Manuscripts*, Introduction, 12–13

17 Elaine Boxhall, *Kinmel Characters*, Abergele, 1990, 35

18 *The Gentleman's Magazine and Historical Review*, vol. 191, 1852, 403

19 Kinmel Papers 1563, 18 February 1852, note by P. S. Humberston

20 *The Gentleman's Magazine and Historical Review*, vol. 191, 1852, 403

21 T. F. Henderson, 'Augustus Frederick, Prince, Duke of Sussex (1773–1843)', revised by John Van der Kiste, *Oxford Dictionary of National Biography*, Oxford University Press, 2004

22 J. G. and F. Rivington, *The Annual Register, or, A View of the History and Politics of the Year*, vol. 83, 1841, 97

23 *The Gentleman's Magazine*, vol. 16, 1842, 531

24 Kinmel Papers 1563, Lord Dinorben to P. S. Humberston, no date [January 1849]

25 Kinmel Papers 1563, P. S. Humberston to Lord Dinorben, no date [January 1849]

26 Kinmel Papers 1563, Sir John Hay Williams to P. S. Humberston, 13 January 1849

27 Kinmel Papers 1563, H. R. Hughes to Lord Dinorben, no date [January 1849]

28 Kinmel Papers 1563, Thomas Williams to P. S. Humberston, 15 February 1852

29 Kinmel Papers 1563, note by Humberston, 18 February 1852

30 Gwynne Jones, *A Schedule of the Kinmel Manuscripts*, Introduction, 13

31 Unsourced clipping, August 1853, Kinmel Estate

32 Tribute from 'your numerous Tenantry, Your People and Your Country', 30 August 1853, Kinmel Estate

33 Kinmel Papers 1693, 39 Grosvenor Square, W1, Visitors' Book

34 Kinmel Papers 1518, London house rent and travelling expenses

35 F. H. W. Sheppard, ed., *Survey of London*, vol. 40: The Grosvenor Estate in Mayfair, Pt 2, 1980

36 Kinmel Papers 1500, Cash Book, Travelling expenses of household from London to Kinmel July 1854

37 Anthony Trollope, *Can You Forgive Her?*, 1864, 4

38 *The Spectator*, 25 May 1861, 543

39 Kinmel Papers 1499, Flintshire Election Account, 1861

40 *The Spectator*, 1 June 1861, 572

41 By the 1851 census, 80 per cent of people in Wales who attended a religious service of any kind were nonconformist. See Dennis R. Mills, *Lord and Peasant in Nineteenth Century Britain*, London, 1980, 169

42 *The Spectator*, 1 June 1861, 572

43 It is not entirely certain that Burn was the architect. An isometric drawing by J. Crickmay of the house and stables, dated 1856, is preserved at Kinmel.

44 Kinmel Papers S1786b, drawings by William Burn of Dinorben Lodge

45 Thomas Seccombe, 'Nesfield, William Andrews', revised by Huon Mallalieu, *Oxford Dictionary of National Biography*, Oxford University Press, 2004; Nina James-Fowler, 'Nesfield, William Eden', *Oxford Dictionary of National Biography*, Oxford University Press, 2004; Mark Girouard, *The Victorian Country House*, London, 1979, 320

46 Kinmel Papers 1812, W. A. Nesfield, 'Plan of Details for Llwyni Dressed Ground', 11 June 1867. It is not certain whether all of Nesfield's garden plans were ever carried out.

47 Girouard, *The Victorian Country House*, 323. The sketchbook is in the RIBA.

48 Quoted in Girouard, *The Victorian Country House*, 325

49 Girouard, *The Victorian Country House*, 328

50 Sotheby's sale at Kinmel Park, 4–12 June 1929, 2,211 lots over nine days. 'A special through Char-a-banc' was laid on from Chester. This was Sotheby's first country house sale.

51 Sale at Sotheby's Bond Street, 3 July 1929

52 Boxhall, *Kinmel Characters*, 68

53 Kinmel Estate, Staff Accounts for 1896

54 Kinmel Estate, Staff Accounts for 1859

55 Kinmel Papers 1513, Kinmel Park Meat Book for 1858

56 Kinmel Papers 1500, Cash Book for 1854

57 Kinmel Papers 1501, Wine Cellar Book for 1857, W. H. Brophey's accounts

58 Kinmel Papers 1513, Kinmel Park Meat Book for 1858

59 Kinmel Papers 1518, Household Account Book for 1863

60 Kinmel Estate, Kinmel Game Book

61 Kinmel Estate, Visitors' Book

62 College of Arms files; Boxhall, *Kinmel Characters*, 55

63 B. Burke, *A Genealogical History of the Dormant, Abeyant, Forfeited, and Extinct Peerages of the British Empire*, London, 1866

64 The overmantle was moved in 1926 to Kinmel Manor, now a hotel, where it is still in the dining room.

65 Kinmel Papers 1616, draft of letter to Charles Mainwaring about Hugh Hughes, no date

66 Kinmel Estate, Florentia Hughes, Photograph Album, 1900

67 Boxhall, *Kinmel Characters*, 69

68 Information from Stephen Treseder

69 Mrs Bradley to Elaine Boxhall, *Kinmel Characters*, 71–2

70 Testament of Hugh Seymour Bulkeley Lewis Hughes, 8 October 1913, Jersey Archive D/Y/A/78/103

71 W. B. Yeats, 'Ancestral Houses', Part I of 'Meditations in Time of Civil War' (1922), in *The Tower*, London, 1928

PART VI The After-Life 1910–2010

1 John Habakkuk, *Marriage, Debt and the Estates System, English Landownership 1650–1950*, Oxford, 1994, 655

2 Habakkuk, *Marriage, Debt and the Estates System*, 654

3 Habakkuk, *Marriage, Debt and the Estates System*, 623

4 Trevor Rowley, *The English Landscape in the Twentieth Century*, London, 2006, 285, quoting Giles Worsley, *England's Lost Houses*, London, 2002

5 F. M. L. Thompson, *English Landed Society in the Nineteenth Century*, London, 1963, 343

6 Habakkuk, *Marriage, Debt and the Estates System*, 667

7 Heather Clemenson, *English Country Houses and Landed Estates*, London, 1982

8 Habakkuk, *Marriage, Debt and the Estates System*, 661

9 Habakkuk, *Marriage, Debt and the Estates System*, 658

10 Habakkuk, *Marriage, Debt and the Estates System*, 692, 704; Rowley, *The English Landscape in the Twentieth Century*, 256

11 James Lees-Milne, Diary, 28 January 1944, *Prophesying Peace*, London, 1977, 14–15

12 www.sherbornecastle.com

Renunciation

1 Anne Acland, *A Devon Family: The Story of the Aclands*, London, 1981, 21

2 Acland, *A Devon Family*, 54

3 Acland, *A Devon Family*, 67

4 Sir Robert Inglis (1845) in Acland, *A Devon Family*, 69

5 Acland, *A Devon Family*, 66

6 Acland, *A Devon Family*, 118

7 Acland, *A Devon Family*, 102–3

8 Acland, *A Devon Family*, 105

9 Acland, *A Devon Family*, 118

10 Acland, *A Devon Family*, 126

11 Acland, *A Devon Family*, 128

12 Acland, *A Devon Family*, 145

13 Acland, *A Devon Family*, 144

14 Walter Bagehot, *The English Constitution*, Oxford University Press, 1867, 48, 51, 54

15 Acland, *A Devon Family*, 144

16 Acland, *A Devon Family*, 143

17 Eleanor Acland to her sister Maisie Fletcher, no date (?1911), among the Acland Papers, Devon Record Office, 1148M add. 14 (unlisted)

18 For the developments in Aclandshire Liberalism between 1910 and 1929 see G. Tregidga, ed., *Killerton, Camborne and Westminster: The Political Correspondence of Sir Francis and Lady Acland, 1910–1919*, Devon & Cornwall Record Society, New Series, vol. 48, Exeter, 2006

19 *The Times*, letters to the Editor, 22 February 1917

20 Francis Acland to Eleanor Acland, in Acland, *A Devon Family*, 150

21 Eleanor Acland to her sister Maisie Fletcher, no date (?1911), among the Acland Papers, Devon Record Office, 1148M add. 14 (unlisted)

22 Richard Acland to Anne Acland, 12 February 1940, in the Acland Papers, Devon Record Office, 1148M add. 14 (unlisted), where all the surviving letters between them are to be found

23 *The Observer*, 23 May 1943

24 J. Melling interview with Richard Acland, 12 July 1990, in M. Hilson and J. Melling, 'Public Gifts and Political Identities: Sir Richard Acland, Common Wealth, and the Moral Politics of Land Ownership in the 1940s', *Twentieth Century British History,* vol. 11, no. 2, 2000, 163

25 Richard Acland to Anne Alford, August 1935

26 Richard to Anne, 2 September 1939

27 Richard to Anne, 11 April 1941

28 Interview with Henry Acland, 26 January 2011

29 Richard Acland, unpublished autobiography, MS, no date, in Acland Papers, University of Exeter library, 1.15; quoted in Hilson and Melling, 'Public Gifts and Political Identities', 162

30 Richard to Anne, 22 January 1940

31 Anne to Richard, 31 January 1941

32 Interview with Sir John Acland in Hilson and Melling, 'Public Gifts and Political Identities', 166

33 Richard Acland, *Unser Kampf: Our Struggle*, Harmondsworth, 1940, 25

34 Acland, *Unser Kampf,* vii

35 Acland, *Unser Kampf,* 26

36 Acland, *Unser Kampf,* 40

37 Acland, *Unser Kampf,* 39

38 Acland, *Unser Kampf,* 45

39 Acland, *Unser Kampf,* 45

40 National Trust Accounts at Heelis: Box 133.36

41 Acland, *Unser Kampf,* 94

42 Acland, *Unser Kampf,* 135

43 Acland, *Unser Kampf,* 135

44 *Manchester Guardian*, 1 April 1941, 6

45 Acland, *Unser Kampf,* 99

46 Dryden's translation of Virgil, *Georgics*, Book 1, lines 191–96

47 Richard to Anne, 22 January 1940

48 Richard to Anne, 22 January 1940

49 *Manchester Guardian*, 22 November 1940, 7

50 Richard to Anne, 10 July 1941

51 Anne to Richard, 5 December 1940

52 E. Pethick Lawrence to Richard Acland, 14 November 1941, Acland Papers, Devon Record Office, 1148M add. 14 (unlisted)

53 Richard to Anne, 15 February 1941

54 Richard to Anne, 20 January 1941

55 George Orwell, 'London Letter' to *Partisan Review,* reprinted in Sonia Orwell and Ian Angus, eds, *The Collected Essays, Journalism and Letters of George Orwell*, London, 1968, vol. ii, 289

56 Anne to Richard, 3 February 1941

57 Anne to Richard, 8 November 1941

58 Anne to Richard, 19 June 1941

59 Richard to Anne, 4 April 1941

60 Anne to Richard, 24 April 1941

61 Anne to Richard, 5 May 1941

62 Anne to Richard, 5 May 1941

63 Anne to Richard, 5 May 1941

64 Anne to Richard, 17 June 1941

65 Richard to Anne, 24 June 1941

66 Anne's 'Final Testament', 1981, in Acland Papers, Devon Record Office, 1148M add. 14 (unlisted)

67 Anne's 'Final Testament'

68 Anne Acland, talk on *Woman's Hour,* 27 August 1951

69 Richard to Anne, 20 April 1942

70 Richard to Anne, 4 November 1941

71 Richard to Anne, 29 April 1942

72 Richard to Anne, 30 April 1942

73 Anne to Richard, 20 February 1942

74 Anne to Richard, 20 February 1942

75 Richard to Anne, 30 June 1942

76 Richard to Anne, 30 June 1942

77 Richard to Anne, 30 June 1942

78 Richard to Anne, 30 June 1942

79 Richard Acland, *The Forward March*, London, 1941, 51

80 Acland Papers, Devon Record Office, 1148M add. 14 (unlisted), Anne's 'Final Testament'

81 Anne's 'Final Testament'

82 Richard to Anne, 5 January 1943

83 *Manchester Guardian*, 27 July 1942, 2

84 Anne's 'Final Testament'

85 National Trust Executive Committee minutes, 14 October 1942

86 National Trust Executive Committee minutes, 14 December 1942

87 *Manchester Guardian*, 27 February 1943, 6

88 *Manchester Guardian*, 27 February 1943, 4

89 *The Observer*, 28 February 1943, 4

90 Anne to Richard, 20 February 1943

91 For these figures, see National Trust file at Heelis, 1341: D. M. Matheson to Home & Birkett (Acland's solicitors), 15 June 1943; D. M. Matheson to Richard Acland, 17 August 1943; D. M. Matheson to Finance Committee, 13 September 1943; also analysed in Hilson and Melling, 'Public Gifts and Political Identities'

92 *Manchester Guardian*, 18 February 1944, 4

93 National Trust Papers, file 1341, Richard Acland to D. M. Matheson, 18 September 1943

94 Richard Davenport-Hines, 'Greville, Dame Margaret Helen (1863–1942)', *Oxford Dictionary of National Biography*, Oxford University Press, 2004

95 J. Pearson, *Façades: Edith, Osbert and Sacheverell Sitwell*, 1978, 134

96 R. Buckle, ed., *Selected Diaries of Cecil Beaton*, 1979, 215–16

97 Photocopy of original Memorandum, dated 10 January 1944, in National Trust files at Heelis: LMW/1 'Supplemental Memorandum of Wishes – Sir Richard Acland'

98 Photocopy of original Memorandum, dated 10 January 1944, in National Trust files at Heelis: LMW/1 'Supplemental Memorandum of Wishes – Sir Richard Acland'

99 Richard to Anne, 24 January 1943

100 Anne to Richard, 28 January 1943

101 Anne to Richard, 9 February 1943

102 Interview with Henry Acland, 26 January 2011

103 Richard Acland to his brother Cubby Acland, 19 September 1943

104 *The Observer*, 30 January 1944, 5

105 *North Devon Journal*, 3 February 1944

106 *Manchester Guardian*, 9 December 1943, 3, 6

107 *Manchester Guardian*, 1 February 1945, 6

108 *Manchester Guardian*, 10 April 1944, 2

109 Anne to Richard, 4 March 1951

110 R. Acland to P. W. Broomhead, 2 September 1984, National Trust file at Heelis: LMW/1

111 P. W. Broomhead to National Trust solicitor, 26 September 1984, National Trust file at Heelis: LMW/1

112 National Trust solicitor to P. W. Broomhead, 2 October 1984, National Trust file at Heelis: LMW/1

113 Interview with Henry Acland, 26 January 2011

114 Interview with Henry Acland, 26 January 2011

115 With Anne's 'Final Testament'

116 Richard Acland, unpublished autobiography, MS, no date, in Acland Papers, University of Exeter library

117 Richard Acland to Pat Gibson, 14 April 1982. A copy of Gibson's reply on 20 April 1982 is in National Trust file at Heelis: 2093/3

118 Interview, 25 January 2011

Continuity

1 C. R. Elrington et al., *Victoria County History, Gloucestershire*, vol. 10, 1972, 143–8

2 R. Hewlett and J. Speed, *Frampton on Severn*, Frampton, 2007, 29–30; Elrington, *Victoria County History*, 143

3 Hewlett and Speed, *Frampton on Severn*, 30–1

4 Elrington, *Victoria County History*, 160

5 Gloucestershire Archives, Clifford Papers D149/X7: Appointment of R. Clutterbuck as Searcher of the Port of Bristol, 1727

6 For the raid on Rafa see W. T. Massey, *The Desert Campaigns*, New York, 1918, esp. 103–15; Lt-Col C. G. Powles, *The New Zealanders in Sinai and Palestine*, Auckland, 1922, 64–81

7 Printed memorial notes in Frampton Archive

8 Printed memorial notes in Frampton Archive

9 For the Desert Column First Spring meeting see Massey, *The Desert Campaigns*, 122–9

10 Peter Clifford to Henriette Clifford, 'Frampy', 4 January 1970, Frampton Archive

11 'Summary of the Frampton Court Estate and of the Incumbrances thereon', late nineteenth century, no date, Frampton Archive

12 www.framptoncourtestate.co.uk/

CONCLUSION: Return of the Native

1 Sir Thomas Browne, *Hydriotaphia, Urne-Buriall; or a Discourse of the Sepulchral Urns lately found in Norfolk*, 1658, ch. v

2 Sir John Lowther, David Roger Hainsworth, *The Correspondence of Sir John Lowther of Whitehaven, 1693–1698: A Provincial Community in Wartime*, Oxford, 1983, xiv

3 Geoffrey Hickes, *A Gentleman Instructed in the Conduct of a Virtuous and Happy Life, Written for the Instruction of a Young Nobleman*, London, 1709, 29

4 Raluca Radulescu and Alison Truelove, *Gentry Culture in Late Medieval England*, Manchester, 2005, 29

5 In H. A. Lloyd, *The Gentry of South-West Wales 1540–1640*, Cardiff, 1968, 17

6 Sir Gilbert Scott, *Secular and Domestic Architecture*, London, 1857, 140

7 Walter Benjamin, *Illuminations*, London, 1970, 258

8 J. P. Cooper, 'The Social Distribution of Land and Men in England 1436–1700', *Economic History Review*, 2nd Series, xx (1967); those for 1790 and 1873 from F. M. L. Thompson, 'The Social Distributon of Landed Property in England since the Sixteenth Century', *Economic History Review*, xix (1966), and *English Landed Society in the Nineteenth Century*, London, 1963; and G. E. Mingay, *English Landed Society in the Eighteenth Century*, 1963, and *The Gentry*, 1976, 59

9 The nineteenth-century figures are from F. M. L. Thompson, 'The Social Distribution of Landed Property in England since the Sixteenth Century', *Economic History Review*, xix, 1966, drawing on J. Bateman, *The Return of Owners of Land*, London, 1873. Those for today are adapted from Kevin Cahill, *Who Owns Britain*, Edinburgh, 2001

10 Bryan Forbes, *The League of Gentlemen*, Final Shooting Script, Pinewood Studios, 1959, 28

11 'He's so wet you could shoot snipe off him,' from Anthony Powell's *A Question of Upbringing*, London, 1951, 14, was the accusation repeatedly thrown at non-Thatcherite Tories in the 1980s.

12 Howard Jacobson, *The New Republic*, 30 June 2010

13 http://www.cabinetoffice.gov.uk/news/government-launches-big-society-programme

14 'Building the Big Society', Cabinet Office, May 2010

ACKNOWLEDGEMENTS

I owe many thanks for the generous help of the following who have talked to me, guided me and corrected what I have written, as well as feeding and housing me, on my many enjoyable journeys around gentry England.

Joan Kirby; Ruth Wilcock; Peter Marshall; Kate Harris; Glenda Sluga; Steve Hobbs; Ms Fanny Oglander; Clifford Webster; Simon Dear; Colonel Aylmer; John Doyle; Matthew Rice and Emma Bridgewater; Karen Lynch; Simon D. Smith; Dr Roderic Vassie; David Sarsfield; Katherine Giles; Matthew Lockhart; Henry and Shirley Anglesey; Dickon Fetherstonhaugh; John Rushby; Einion Thomas; Jason Castledine; Janne White; Dominic Acland; Henry and Di Acland; Mary Hilson; Gemma Poulton; Denise Melhuish; Darren Beatson; Rollo and Janie Clifford; Peter Clifford; Jessie Clifford; Harry Spurr; George James; Guy James; Gabriel Hutton; Alan Franklin; Rose Hewlett; Jean Speed; Astrid Lever; Roger Godwin; Shaun Parsons; and Duff Hart-Davis.

My editors Susan Watt, Anne Askwith and Arabella Pike and my agent George Capel have all been irreplaceable.

Extracts from the letters, diaries and other manuscripts of the families described in this book are published here with grateful acknowledgement to the following people and institutions:

The West Yorkshire Archive Service for the Plumpton correspondence; the National Archives at Kew, for George Throckmorton's two confessions now in the State Papers; the Marquess of Bath, Longleat House, Warminster, Wiltshire for quotations from the Thynne Papers; Ms Fanny Oglander and the Isle of Wight County Record Office for quotations from the Oglander Account Books; the British Library for the Oxinden letters and the bulk of the le Neve and Gawdy letters; to the Norfolk Record Office for other le Neve, Gawdy and Hobart papers; Henry Robinson, Microform Academic Publishers and Wilkinson and Gaviller Ltd for extracts from the Lascelles & Maxwell Letterbooks;

South Carolina Historical Society and the University of South Carolina Press for quotations from the letterbook of Eliza Pinckney; the Marquess of Anglesey for quotations from the Capel papers; Bangor University and Dickon Fetherstonhaugh for extracts from the Hughes family papers and albums; Dominic and Henry Acland for quotations from the Acland papers held in the Devon Record Office (Exeter); the National Trust for papers held at their head office in Swindon; and Rollo Clifford for quotations from his family archive at Frampton.

Detailed references to these papers can be found in the Notes.

NOTE

Further details, links and images on the families in this book, their lands and history are to be found at www.thegentry.org.uk

INDEX

'Adam Nicolson's book is unobtrusively learned, rich in curious and purposeful detail, an ideal balance between fervent enthusiasm and elegantly witty detachment. The story of the translation's origins and production is a subject which, one always felt, would be nice to hear from a really sparkling and sharp guide. This volume strikes me as exactly that, a brilliantly entertaining, passionate, funny and instructive telling of an important and gripping story'

PHILIP HENSHER, *Spectator*

'Adam Nicolson has a nose for quirks, follies and ironies ... Nicolson fascinatingly demonstrates how these translators took the plain, sinewy prose of the fugitive martyr William Tyndale – written 80 years previously – and polished it to gem-like brightness, looking for words which would resonate with passion and ring sonorously amid the solemnity of worship ... He has written a marvellous book: there are few more stylish or sensitive introductions than this to the personalities, the sights and the smells, as well as to the words, of Jacobean England'
Sunday Telegraph

'Nicolson really deserves at least an 18-gun salute. This is a fine piece of history, ecclesiology and literature all rolled into one and, what's more, like the Authorised Version itself, it sings'
Guardian

'This is an easygoing, companionable exploration of Elizabethan and Jacobean England ... will delight the general reader, for whom it was written ... Nicolson takes one back to the Bible with a fresh eye and ear, which is not easily done these days'
New Statesman

'The story of the seven years between commissioning and printing fascinates from start to finish. It is told in a way which combines scholarship and entertainment'
Independent on Sunday

'Vivid, exhilarating, consistently intelligent, you can almost taste the air breathed by these Jacobean heroes, who gave English its most famous book. History at its best' SIMON JENKINS

'Nicolson vividly evokes many aspects of Jacobean England: the secret police, religious passions, a profligate court, an atmosphere of emotional extravagance, splendid architecture, stained glass ... Adam Nicolson has deepened my understanding of the greatest work of English prose, for which I am grateful' *Literary Review*

'A wonderfully engaging account … elegant and lyrical, this is a total delight'   *Good Housekeeping*

'A sense of determination, vision and optimism … dominates his wide-ranging biography of a beloved home'   *Scotland on Sunday*

'A close-focus (and very moving) family memoir, a richly textured history of a house … and a fervent blueprint for a progressive ideal of "heritage". *Sissinghurst* confirms … that Nicolson is one of his generation's most gifted, generous and persuasive writers about place'   *Independent*

'Unusual, impassioned and lucidly written … a gripping but serious history of Sissinghurst Castle'   *Sunday Telegraph*

'A wise, witty, enlightening, enchanting book'

ALAN GURNEY, Times Literary Supplement

'A passionate evocation of the Shiants which catches you up in its intelligence as well as its enthusiasm, and fills you with homesickness for a place you've never been to. Nicolson writes so well, with such modesty and deep feeling, that the book fairly sings in your hands'   WILL COHU, *Daily Telegraph*